PC Magazine®
Linux® Solutions

PC Magazine®
Linux® Solutions

Joe Merlino

WILEY

Wiley Publishing, Inc.

PC Magazine® Linux® Solutions
Published by
Wiley Publishing, Inc.
10475 Crosspoint Boulevard
Indianapolis, IN 46256
www.wiley.com

Copyright © 2006 by Wiley Publishing, Inc., Indianapolis, Indiana

Published simultaneously in Canada

ISBN-13: 978-0-471-77769-4
ISBN-10: 0-471-77769-2

Manufactured in the United States of America

10 9 8 7 6 5 4 3 2 1

1B/SY/QT/QW/IN

To Brad, who might find it useful, and to Rounders everywhere.

About the Authors

Joe Merlino is a freelance author and consultant in Boston. He has been running Linux since 1997 and writing about it since 1999. His books include *Mastering Unix, Introduction to Unix, Red Hat Linux 9 Visual QuickPro Guide*, and others.

William (Bill) von Hagen has been a Unix system administrator for over 20 years and a Linux fanatic since the early 1990s. He has worked as a systems programmer, system administrator, writer, application developer, programmer, drummer, and content manager. Bill has written books on such topics as Linux server hacks, Linux file systems, SUSE Linux, Red Hat Linux, GCC, SGML, Mac OS X, and hacking the TiVo. He has also written numerous articles on Linux, embedded computing, Unix, and open source topics. An avid computer collector specializing in workstations, he owns more than 200 computer systems. You can reach him at vonhagen@vonhagen.org.

Jaldhar Vyas is a 34-year-old Hindu priest and consultant specializing in Perl and Linux who lives in Jersey City, New Jersey with his wife Jyoti, daughter Shailaja, and son Nilagriva. Jaldhar has used Linux for ten years and has been one of the volunteer maintainers of the Debian GNU/Linux distribution for eight years.

Eric Foster-Johnson is a veteran software developer and the author or coauthor of over 18 books on programming, operating systems, and open source software.

Kenneth Hess has been using Linux and has been a member of the Linux Consultant's List since 1995. He began the Linux Users Group in Tulsa, Oklahoma in 1996. Ken has authored several articles using Linux in unique ways and is currently working on two different books featuring cross-platform solutions that include Linux. His experience over the past 20 years has included every version of DOS since 2.0, every version of Windows, the major distributions of Linux, most versions of the Apple and Mac OS and just about every flavor of Unix used in the Data Center Linux (DCL). Ken also founded and ran his own computer consulting and support firm for eight years. He now devotes his time to his family, technical writing, his day job, and his art. Ken can be reached via his website at www.kenhess.com.

Credits

ACQUISITIONS EDITOR
Katie Mohr

DEVELOPMENT EDITOR
Sara Shlaer

TECHNICAL EDITORS
Dee-Ann LeBlanc
Jason Luster

PRODUCTION EDITOR
Kathryn Duggan

COPY EDITOR
Maarten Reilingh

EDITORIAL MANAGER
Mary Beth Wakefield

PRODUCTION MANAGER
Tim Tate

VICE PRESIDENT AND EXECUTIVE GROUP PUBLISHER
Richard Swadley

VICE PRESIDENT AND EXECUTIVE PUBLISHER
Joseph B. Wikert

PROJECT COORDINATOR
Ryan Steffen

GRAPHICS AND PRODUCTION SPECIALISTS
Beth Brooks
Carrie A. Foster
Mary J. Gillot
Denny Hager
Joyce Haughey
Alicia B. South

QUALITY CONTROL TECHNICIANS
John Greenough
Jessica Kramer
Charles Spencer
Brian H. Walls

PROOFREADING AND INDEXING
Techbooks

Contents at a Glance

Part V   **Server Solutions**

Contents

Part IV   **Basic Administration**

Part V   **Server Solutions**

Acknowledgments

Many people assisted with this book, notably David Fugate at Launchbooks and Carole McLendon at Waterside, as well as Sara Shlaer, Katie Mohr, and all the fine folks at Wiley and *PC Magazine*. In addition, the following people contributed chapters: Bill von Hagen, Eric Foster-Johnson, Jaldhar Vyas, and Ken Hess. You all have my gratitude.

Introduction

Welcome to *PC Magazine Linux Solutions*. This book is a bit of departure for *PC Magazine*, as the normal focus hereabouts is on Microsoft's operating systems, but a growing number of PC users have become interested in Linux in recent years.

Linux was first released to the public in 1994. It was originally created by a Finnish college student named Linus Torvalds. He was looking for something he could run on his PC that would duplicate the functionality of his school's Unix mainframe. Finding nothing that met his needs, he decided to build it himself. Deciding that he needed help, he released it on the Internet, declaring that anybody who wanted a copy could have one, so long as they made any changes or improvements in it available to the public.

Apparently, there were quite a few people who were also looking for the same thing, because an army of developers took up the task, and within only a couple of years, Linux was a full-featured system.

I first discovered Linux in 1997, when I was working at Georgia Tech. I had met several computer science and engineering students who used Linux regularly. Encouraged by what they were doing, I installed Red Hat Linux 4.2 on an old 386 PC. It took hours, and when I was done, I had a machine with only a command-line interface. I was used to working on this type of machine, as I had worked on Unix machines in college, and with later employers. At the time, the current version of Windows was Windows 95. I had a Windows 95 machine at work, but at home, I was still using a 496 loaded with Windows 3.1. Both machines crashed often, and the Windows 3.1 machine was almost unusably slow. I remember how excited I was to have a machine that would let me get my e-mail and Usenet news quickly and without crashing.

As Linux matured and I accumulated better PC hardware, I was eventually able to run a graphical interface, and do things like surf the Web, play music and video, and manage documents. When broadband Internet access came to our town, I discovered the real power of Linux, running e-mail and Web servers, and using my old 386 as a router to share my Internet connection among several machines.

Around that time, I met my agent, David Fugate. He was looking for people to write about this new operating system that was beginning to get attention from a variety of quarters. The result of our meeting was a collaboration with other authors about the StarOffice suite of applications—a suite which eventually metamorphosed into the OpenOffice.org productivity suite, which can be found on just about every major Linux distribution.

Today, Linux is everywhere. What was once considered a "hacker's toy" is now a serious player in the server market and a legitimate presence on desktops. Linux distributions are produced by small groups of volunteers and by publicly traded corporations. After 11 years, Linux just keeps getting better. New features are added and refinements are made constantly. Great Linux-based software applications are being created all the time.

One of the best things about Linux, of course, is the price. Boxed sets of most major Linux distributions can be had for under $100, but, if you have access to high-speed Internet connection and a CD burner, you can also download at least the basic parts of most distributions for the cost of a few blank CDs. And what you get for this paltry investment is truly remarkable: an industrial strength operating system that runs on off-the-shelf hardware and can turn a modest PC into a small server or powerful workstation.

But the low cost is only part of the equation. Linux brings the power of a Unix machine to any-body with a PC and the time to learn the system. Computing functions that were once the sole provenance of governments, universities, and large corporations are now available to anyone.

Linux is as simple or as complex as you want to make it. If you want to use it for nothing more than e-mail and Web surfing, you can do that. But Linux doesn't limit you. If you can imagine something that can be done with your computer, there's probably a way to do it on Linux. Linux gives you direct control over your machine. You are not beholden to someone in Redmond or Cupertino to tell you what can or cannot be done with your computer. That's power, and that's what Linux gives you.

Who This Book Is For

If you've picked up this book, you're at least curious about Linux. You may be an experienced PC user, but you probably haven't used Linux much—or at all. In writing this book, we've tried not to assume any previous knowledge or experience about Linux or Unix. We recognize that certain concepts may be new to you, and we try to make your introduction to these concepts as easy as possible.

If you're a Windows user, this book will help you to add Linux to your environment without giv-ing up what you already know. We cover dual-boot systems (running Linux and Windows on the same computer) as well as live CD distributions. (Live CDs allow you to run Linux directly from a CD without having to install it on your computer.) If you find, after using Linux for a while, that you don't need Windows around any more, you can get rid of it. If you want to keep it, you can do that too. Linux is about giving you the power to choose how you use your computer.

We assume that you're interested in Linux either as a home or a business user. To the latter end, we do cover such business-related topics as managing multiple users; running e-mail, Web, and file servers; and the like; but we do not cover such heavy duty subjects as running an e-commerce server, as we feel that such topics are too complex to cover in a beginner-oriented book. There is a learning curve with Linux, and as with anything new, it's best to master the basics before you move on to the heavy stuff.

How This Book Is Organized

This book is divided into five parts. Each part is intended to help you conquer a particular aspect of the Linux experience.

Part I: Before Installation

This part is intended to help you understand the advantages and potential uses of Linux, and to help you gather the information that you will need in order to install it. Linux is not a monolithic entity. Anyone who wants to can create their own version of Linux, and many people, companies, and orga-nizations have done just that. There are many Linux *distributions* out there, and in this section, we tell you about a few of them, with an eye towards helping you pick the distribution that's right for you.

We also help you to gather all of the information that you'll need about your computer to help you install Linux.

Part II: During Installation

When you buy a computer these days, it almost always comes with an operating system installed. This has been the case long enough that most computer users have never installed an operating system. Because Linux doesn't have anywhere near the market penetration of Windows, however, odds are that very few people are buying computers with Linux installed. This means that you'll probably have to install Linux yourself.

Installing Linux is no more difficult than installing any other operating system, but of course, if the experience of installing an operating system is itself new to you, that's not much of a comfort. In this section, we walk you through the basics of a typical installation.

Part III: Running Linux

Now that you've got it installed, how do you use it? That's the question we answer for you in Part III. We show you how to log in and take stock of what you see when you do.

Linux has two major competing desktop environments: GNOME and KDE. Depending on the distribution that you install, you may have one or the other, or you may be given the choice of which you'd prefer. We show you the basics of both desktops and how to customize them so that you get an interface that fits you like a glove.

We also introduce you to the thing that truly sets Linux apart: the terminal. Unix, the system that Linux was modeled after, has been around since long before there were pretty graphical interfaces. From Unix, Linux has inherited a system of commands that is unrivaled in power and flexibility.

Part IV: Basic Administration

In this part, we go under the hood, and show you how to maintain and configure your Linux system. Linux systems typically serve multiple users, so you will learn how to make changes to the system that will affect and protect all users.

In addition, we show you how to back up data, add and remove software packages, manage your hardware, automate repetitive tasks, set up file sharing, manage your Internet connection(s), and keep your system secured.

Part V: Server Solutions

One of Linux's strengths is the ability to run servers. Whether you're looking for an e-mail server, a Web server, or something else, odds are there's an industrial-strength package that runs on Linux, and most of the time you can get it for free. In this section, we introduce you to three of the most popular servers on the Linux platform:

- **Apache:** The Apache Web server is not only the most popular Web server on the Linux platform; it's the most popular web server in the world.

- **Postfix:** The Postfix e-mail server is a simple but powerful mail server that can serve mail for a small domain or a large organization.

- **Squid:** The Squid proxy server allows you to cache frequently used Web objects to speed up performance. It also gives you the ability to analyze your network traffic and see who's going where. This is helpful in streamlining your network and improving your security.

What You Need to Use This Book

To use this book, all you really need, besides a healthy sense of curiosity, is a reliable PC with a CD-ROM drive. The CD-ROM provided with the book gives you a complete Linux distribution (more about this in the next section). If you prefer to use a Linux distribution other than the one provided, you'll need to have the installation CDs or DVDs for that.

What's on the Companion CD-ROM

The CD-ROM included with this book contains the Knoppix live CD Linux distribution. Knoppix is a distribution that can be used directly from the CD with no need to install it on your hard drive, so you don't have to worry about messing up your existing operating system. Chapter 9 helps you get started using Knoppix, and you can find more information at `http://knoppix.org`.

Where to Go from Here

By the time you finish this book, you should have all the skills necessary to install, run, and administer a Linux system. While this puts you well ahead of most people, it by no means makes you an expert. The flexibility and complexity of a Linux system is limited only by your imagination and the skills that you have to make that imagination a reality.

If you wish to become more expert with Linux, the first thing you'll want to do is to learn more details about your distribution. Each distribution has its own features, attributes, and idiosyncrasies. Fortunately, most distributions also have their own Web sites, and a great deal of documentation online. In addition, there are also many books written about the major distributions. For example, at the time of this writing, there are no fewer than seven books listed on Amazon.com *just about Fedora Core* 4!

If you're looking for a more general resource, `www.linux.org` is good portal to start with; or simply use your favorite Internet search engine to look up the topic of your choice. Linux was spawned on the Internet, and there are hundreds of Web sites devoted to it.

Part I

Before Installation

Chapter 1

Why Use Linux?

Welcome to the wide, wide world of Linux! The Linux operating system has gotten a tremendous amount of press over the past few years, and this book explains why you might want to see what all the fuss is about. In slightly over 10 years, Linux has blossomed from its roots in two free software projects to its adoption as the operating system of choice for most enterprise computing centers. It is also the default operating system used on inexpensive PCs sold at many consumer electronics stores. You can hardly open a computer magazine today without seeing articles about Linux, ads for companies selling Linux distributions, and ads for companies offering computers running different versions of Linux.

Linux is different and unique enough that anyone who is trying to learn about it has plenty of questions. Linux is free, so why are people selling it? It involves something called open source, but what the heck is that? What's this Unix thing I keep hearing about — is that the same thing? What do acronyms like GNU, GNOME, KDE, and X mean? How can there be so many different versions of one operating system? Can I actually do anything useful with Linux, or is it only for computer science students, geeks, nerds, and hackers?

This book answers those questions and more. This chapter provides all background information that you'll need to understand what Linux is, where it came from, and why it has become so popular. History lessons aren't usually a part of learning about a computer operating system, but Linux has strong social and philosophical components that make it more interesting than an off-the-shelf operating system that is just the product of some company. As you can see in this book, Linux is a powerful, dynamic operating system that is being worked on simultaneously by tens of thousands of developers all over the world. If you're just looking for a solution to your computing problems and aren't particularly interested in changing the world, that's fine — you don't have to wave the Linux flag just because you decide to use it. Plenty of other people are willing and eager to do that. For many people, Linux is just a powerful, inexpensive operating system that comes with tons of free, entertaining, and easy-to-use software that lets them do what they need to do.

Two points are worth clearing up right off the bat. First, what is Linux? Conversationally, Linux is the collective name for an operating system kernel and its associated applications, just like any other computer operating system. A *kernel* is the common name for the single program that is the actual operating system and runs directly on the hardware, managing your memory, disks, and peripherals, starting and stopping other programs, handling requests for resources from applications, and so on. As discussed in more detail later, *Linux* is technically just the name of the kernel — most of the applications that anyone uses with Linux come from other free software projects. However, a *Linux distribution* is the common term for a Linux kernel, a set of applications that can run on top of it (regardless of where they come from), and a tool to install everything and configure your system.

Secondly, how can Linux be free and sold at the same time? That's confusing, but easy enough to answer. The source code for Linux is indeed freely available from thousands of sites on the Internet. Anyone who wants it can get it, but building a complete system out of it that you can easily install on a computer is another thing entirely. When people sell Linux, they are selling a prepackaged and installable collection of free things — they're basically just charging you for the media that it comes on and the time and effort they invested in putting it all together; they're also "charging in advance" for any customer support that you might need if you encounter installation or initial configuration problems.

Now that those are out of the way, let's explore a bit of the history of Linux to give you an idea of where it comes from, why it is so powerful and popular, and how Linux distributions make it easy for you to install and get started with this exciting, powerful operating system.

The Evolution of Linux

The inspiration for Linux is an older operating system known as Unix, which was developed at Bell Labs in Murray Hill, New Jersey, beginning in 1969. The name Unix is a pun of sorts on Multics, which was an operating system research and development project being done at Bell Labs (then part of AT&T) in conjunction with the U.S. government, General Electric, MIT, and others. As the Multics program disintegrated from too much complexity and cost and time overruns, a number of ex-Multics developers and their associates continued their operating systems research, among them Ken Thompson, Dennis Ritchie, Doug McIlroy, Rudd Canaday, and J. F. Ossanna. They began developing a smaller, lighter-weight operating system on a much smaller system, a DEC PDP-7. Multics stood for *Multiplexed Information and Computing Service*, so UNICS was introduced as a humorous name that supposedly stood for *Uniplexed Information and Computing Service*, referring to the fact that Unix was developed and ran on much smaller systems than the mainframe on which Multics was to have run. Unix was eventually adopted as a sound-alike for UNICS, and the name that we now know was born.

The original motivation for developing the Unix operating system and file system on the PDP-7 was to facilitate running a game that Thompson had originally written for Multics, called Space Travel. As the capabilities of Unix grew, the operating system and associated utilities became much more interesting than the game, and the rest is history. The Unix team quickly outgrew the PDP-7, so the group eventually got a newer, more powerful machine, a DEC PDP-11. The purchase of the new machine was justified by using Unix as the foundation for a text processing system for the Bell Labs patent office, which was the first commercial, real-world use of Unix.

The C language

The process of moving any operating system and its applications to new hardware, known as *porting*, is typically extremely time-consuming. Unix was originally written in assembly language, which differs from machine to machine. To simplify porting, Thompson developed a language known as B, based on an older language from Xerox PARC known as BCPL, and attempted to write much of Unix in the higher-level B language, but his rewrite was hampered by shortcomings in the language.

Ritchie added concepts such as types and data structures to B, eventually ending up with a new language, which he called C. In 1973, Thompson rewrote as much of Unix as possible in C.

Minimizing the amount of machine-specific code required by Unix made porting it to new computer hardware much easier because only the machine-specific routines had to be rewritten for the new hardware. This portability was one of the big reasons for the initial popularity of Unix. The core portion of Unix remained written in machine-specific assembly language, but this was reduced to a few hundred lines. The portions of Unix written in C (which was most of it, at this point) could simply be recompiled for the new hardware once the compiler itself was ported to support the new machine's hardware instruction set.

Unix goes public

At the time that Unix development began, AT&T was operating under a government ruling that broke up its monopoly on the telephone system. To prevent AT&T from emerging as a monopoly in other areas, this ruling also prohibited the company from branching into other lines of business. Thus, it couldn't market its new operating system. For this reason, it was decided to freely license Unix to various academic and research institutions.

Once Unix hit the academic and research communities, its future was assured. Researchers and graduate students quickly adopted Unix as their platform of choice, using it as a daily platform as well as the reference platforms for many research efforts. Much of the reason for this quick acceptance was that the source code for Unix was freely available to licensees, which made it easy for developers to see how the operating system worked, fix problems that they discovered, and extend its capabilities. Later in this chapter, I come back to the notion of how having the source code for an operating system can help popularize it and facilitate its adoption — this same notion of freely available source code is one of the driving factors for the adoption and popularization of Linux.

Aside from the source-code issue, Unix was interesting to researchers and developers for several other reasons. I won't put you to sleep with all of the reasons (there are plenty of other books that can do that for you), but some of the most significant reasons are interesting. First, Unix was a true multi-user, multitasking operating system that ran on relatively small, relatively inexpensive machines. This meant that entire research groups could share access to and development time on the same machine. Secondly, Unix introduced a very interesting way of accessing and using devices. All devices attached to a Unix system, regardless of whether they are disk drives, printers, or network devices, can be accessed as streams of characters. This provides a single, consistent way of reading from or writing to any device, unlike the complex, specialized commands that other systems at the time required for accessing each different kind of device. (Some devices, such as disk drives, also offer block-oriented interfaces for performance reasons, but you always have access to the raw, character-oriented device.) Finally, Unix was the operating system chosen for development of the initial TCP/IP implementation, which means that Unix and the Internet (and before that, the ARPANET) have always gone hand in hand. The original TCP/IP implementation was done at the University of California at Berkeley (UCB), on Unix Version 7. UCB's collection of Unix enhancements eventually got to be large enough that they turned into the popular Berkeley Standard Distribution (BSD) of Unix, whose source code was freely available to any Unix licensee. (Conceptual derivatives of BSD are freely available today as FreeBSD, NetBSD, and OpenBSD.) All Unix systems since 1980 or so have supported TCP/IP networking.

Unix is traditionally associated with workstations, which are relatively high-powered desktop systems with sophisticated graphics capabilities. Today's workstation vendors, primarily Hewlett-Packard, IBM, Silicon Graphics, and Sun Microsystems, all purchased licenses for Unix from AT&T;

they have continued enhancing it and developing software that enables their version of Unix to take full advantage of the capabilities of their hardware.

Unix development is still taking place today, and almost all computer vendors now offer some version of Unix. However, Unix is rapidly being eclipsed by Linux for a variety of reasons, most notably lower cost, higher power, vendor-independence, and books like this one.

The GNU project

While the source code for Unix has always been available to licensees, the popularity of Unix has ensured that many other people wanted access to it. Originally owned by AT&T, some versions of the source code escaped into the wild thanks to its popularity in less controlled academic and research environments; but there were always legions of lawyers standing around, waiting to enforce AT&T's ownership and copyrights. AT&T's possessive attitude irritated some of the more progressive members of the software community, most notably Richard Stallman, who, in 1983, announced the GNU project, a project dedicated to developing software with source code that would always be freely available. Stallman is also well known as the founder of the Free Software Foundation (FSF, http://www.fsf.org), which was formed in 1985 as an institution to help raise funds for the GNU project, and to generally evangelize and popularize the concept of free software.

The GNU project (http://www.gnu.org) consists of a completely free operating system kernel and a huge collection of associated utilities. GNU is a recursive acronym that stands for *GNU's Not Unix*. Because the source code for every part of the GNU project is freely available, it is known as an *open source* project — the source code is always freely available from the FSF site and from anyone who uses it. Interestingly enough, though the source code is freely available, it is not unlicensed — the FSF owns the copyrights to all of the GNU source code and distributes it under the terms of open source licenses such as the GNU General Public License (GPL) and the Lesser GNU Public License (LGPL). These licenses largely stipulate that anyone who redistributes any GPL or LGPL software must also redistribute the source code for their version of that software, though the LGPL provides some exclusions for programs that simply link to libraries provided with GNU software.

The GNU project includes an operating system kernel known as Hurd and a better-known collection of enhanced versions of all of the standard Unix utilities, including an extremely popular collection of free compilers known as GNU Compiler Collection (commonly called GCC). Hurd is an acronym that stands for *Hird of Unix-Replacing Daemons*, whereas Hird stands for *Hurd of Interfaces Representing Depth* — those wacky computer scientists and their acronyms! GCC provides free and powerful compilers for the Ada, C, C++, Objective-C, Fortran, and Java languages. The GCC compilers are the most popular and widely used collection of compilers that have ever existed in the world of computer science.

Note

The C compiler in GCC is known as gcc, which is a frequent source of recursive confusion.

The development of GNU utilities occurred quickly, because they could easily be written, compiled, and tested on a variety of existing platforms, especially those on which the GCC compilers were already available. However, developing a new kernel is a somewhat more complex task. As of this writing, the GNU Hurd kernel is functional and usable, but is still not quite ready for prime time. Why? Largely because of a Finnish college student's project to develop a free, powerful kernel—and his friendly, open announcement on the Internet in 1991 asking for feedback.

Enter Linus

In 1991, Linus Torvalds was a college student at the University of Helsinki in Finland. Interested in computer operating systems and somewhat frustrated by the fact that the source code for the academic operating system that he was working with was not freely available and redistributable, Linus decided to write his own. His initial announcement was the following:

```
From: torvalds@klaava.Helsinki.FI (Linus Benedict Torvalds)
Newsgroups: comp.os.minix
Subject: What would you like to see most in minix?
Summary: small poll for my new operating system
Message-ID: <1991Aug25.205708.9541@klaava.Helsinki.FI>
Date: 25 Aug 91 20:57:08 GMT
Organization: University of Helsinki


Hello everybody out there using minix -
I'm doing a (free) operating system (just a hobby, won't be big and
professional like gnu) for 386(486) AT clones. This has been brewing
since april, and is starting to get ready. I'd like any feedback on
things people like/dislike in minix, as my OS resembles it somewhat
(same physical layout of the file-system (due to practical reasons)
among other things).
I've currently ported bash(1.08) and gcc(1.40), and things seem to work.
This implies that I'll get something practical within a few months, and
I'd like to know what features most people would want. Any suggestions
are welcome, but I won't promise I'll implement them :-)
Linus (torvalds@kruuna.helsinki.fi)
PS. Yes - it's free of any minix code, and it has a multi-threaded fs.
It is NOT protable (uses 386 task switching etc), and it probably never
will support anything other than AT-harddisks, as that's all I have :-(.
```

Linus's request for feedback sparked a few e-mail messages asking for copies and offering suggestions. The true communal development of Linux began a few months later, when he offered the source code to anyone who was interested and asked for people to contribute fixes and enhancements back to him. As you can see from the announcement, Linus was using the GNU utilities both for his kernel development and as the basic collection of things that ran on top of his new kernel. It's fair to say that Linux never would have happened without the GNU project, and for that reason many purists still refer to Linux as GNU/Linux to acknowledge the contributions of the GNU project to Linux distributions everywhere.

Free Software

Commercial software, produced by businesses with the goal of making a profit, is obviously important to anyone who uses an off-the-shelf computer system. There's a tremendous amount of great commercial software available, enabling real people to get real work done: writing documents, creating spreadsheets, sending and receiving e-mail, creating fantastic artwork, laying out complex books and advertisements, and much, much more. However, most commercial software is *closed source* software, meaning that users can't see the source code, fix problems, or extend its capabilities. Closed source software therefore has some attendant problems. It does what its author(s) wrote it to do — which is not necessarily the same thing that a user may want it to do. If a user discovers the software does not meet his or her needs, the only recourse is to contact the vendor's customer support personnel and hope that they care enough or have the resources to fix the problem and/or release a new version.

In comparison, free software, which is freely distributed in the first place, is written by people who either need a tool that does whatever the package does, or who are simply interested in that type of software and are savvy enough to write it. There are essentially two types of free software: software that makes available the executables but not the source code and software that makes available both the executables and the source code. When I refer to free software in this book, I'm referring to the latter, because that is the free software model that underlies Linux, the GNU project, and thousands of other great software packages that run on top of the Linux kernel.

Earlier I mentioned that Linux and related utilities had a strong conceptual and philosophical component. That component is free software, which is based on the philosophy that no one should control your access to the source code for a program that you depend upon, thus opening the possibility that you might find yourself in the position where you can't get your work done because of a bug that you quite literally can't do anything about (regardless of your sophistication as a programmer). The Free Software Foundation's Web page (`www.fsf.org`) expresses this better than anyone:

> Free software is a matter of liberty not price. You should think of "free" as in "free speech."

Of course, just because software is free doesn't mean that everyone has the skills necessary to fix or enhance it. Free software simply guarantees that this option is always available. Another great thing about free software is that because you can freely examine the source code for an application, you can understand the format in which it produces its output files. Even if you encounter a problem with a piece of free software, the fact that its output formats are easily determined makes it possible for you to reuse and recover data in ways that no commercial software could possibly provide.

The distributors

The processes of building a kernel, partitioning disks, creating file systems on them, filling those file systems with correctly compiled software, and configuring all of your system's hardware is not for the weak of heart. For software to succeed, especially an operating system, it has to be easy to install, relatively easy to configure, and at least provide good defaults for all configuration settings. This was certainly not the case for Linux in the early days. I can remember spending days downloading the bits and pieces of Linux from various Web sites, reassembling them on a disk partition that I'd formatted after booting off a floppy that I'd downloaded and written as an image, spending a day or two writing a configuration file so that I could run graphical applications on my Linux system, and so on. This is hardly a recipe for commercial success, though I do indeed have some geek nostalgia for the process.

Luckily, some people who had actually seen commercial software before recognized that Linux in its initial, primitive form was too difficult for mere mortals to install, and that no one was going to be able to see how good it was if you couldn't even install it without at least a master's in computer science or electrical engineering.

As discussed near the beginning of this chapter, a Linux distribution is the sum of a precompiled version of the Linux kernel, a set of applications that run on top of it, an installer that makes it easy to install and configure your system, and (if you're really, really lucky) some documentation and support for at least the configuration and installation process. Linux distributions began to appear shortly after use of the Linux kernel and GNU utilities spread outside of the initial Linux development team. The developers of the first Linux distributions were just as interested in popularizing the operating system as in working on kernel or application code. Developing Linux distributions and making them widely available has played a critical role in the adoption of Linux as an operating system because these distributions have made it possible for people to actually install and use Linux, the GNU utilities, and so on.

Early Linux distributions included Owen Le Blanc's Manchester Computing Centre (MCC) Interim Linux, introduced in 1992, Texas A&M University's TAMU, and Peter MacDonald's Softlanding Linux System (SLS). SLS was the first distribution to add things that Linux users take for granted today, such as graphics capabilities and the X Window System. 1992 also saw the release of Patrick Volkerding's Slackware Linux distribution, which is the longest-lived Linux distribution and is still available and updated today. Other Linux distributions that are still active today followed quickly, most notably SUSE (1992), Red Hat (1993), and Debian (1993).

The situation today

The Slackware, SUSE (now owned by Novell), Red Hat, and Debian Linux distributions are still going strong after more than a decade. However, many other Linux distributions are available — more than ever before — and the number keeps growing. Some very popular Linux distributions are specific to certain hardware — the best example of this is Yellow Dog Linux (`www.yellowdoglinux.com`), which has specialized in producing high-quality Linux distributions for Apple's Macintosh hardware since 1999. Many other Linux distributions are lovingly crafted by Linux fans with a special goal in mind: minimizing disk space requirements, creating distributions targeted towards playing multimedia, providing the ability to boot and run from a CD without requiring installation, and many more. There are over 300 Linux distributions available today. You can find information about most of these and their relative popularity at the Distribution Watch Web site, `www.distrowatch.com`. Some of the newer and most popular distributions for x86 desktop systems today, aside from those mentioned earlier, are Ubuntu (`www.ubuntulinux.com`), Mandriva (www.mandriva.com), Gentoo (www.gentoo.org), and TurboLinux (www.turbolinux.com). You can find more detail about most of these distributions, their focus and history, and their availability in Chapter 2.

Some Linux distributions have a specific geographic or international focus, even though most Linux distributions provide built-in support for internationalization and alternate character sets. There are Polish Linux distributions (`www.pld-linux.org`), Russian Linux distributions (`www.altlinux.com`), and Chinese Linux distributions (`www.redflag-linux.com`). Some of these are commercial, some are simply labors of love, but all share the desire of their authors to popular-ize Linux and help their audiences make the most of it.

Hundreds of special-purpose Linux distributions are also available that are rarely seen or recog-nized unless you are working in certain industries. The best example of this phenomenon is embed-ded computing, which refers to operating systems and applications that run on computers that are built into anything from factory assembly lines to telecommunications switches. Linux distributions are available for every processor architecture and family in the embedded computing market, each taking full advantage of the capabilities of the advanced single-board computers used in embedded computing today. Custom Linux distributions are also available and used in many popular consumer electronic devices, such as cell phones, home gateways, and the popular TiVo digital video recorder.

Today's Linux distributions provide better installers, sophisticated package management (to make it easy to install, update, and even remove applications and associated files), and easy-to-use system update capabilities, but the concept of a Linux distribution is still the same as it's always been. They're a bit larger now — the most widely used x86 Linux distributions now come on several CDs or a DVD — and they offer multiple configuration options (desktop, server, workstation, and so on) both to customize the type of software that is installed and to reduce the amount of space that an installation requires.

What Makes Linux Different?

With all the excitement about Linux and its penetration of almost every area of modern computing, it's natural to step back and think, "Why should I care? It's just another operating system." The fol-lowing is a list of the most significant advantages of Linux over other operating systems:

- **Multiprocessing, multiuser operating system:** Other desktop computer operating sys-tems, such as Microsoft Windows, started out as small operating systems that could only run one program at a time, and have been retrofitting the ability to run multiple programs at the same time ever since. Linux draws upon decades of computer science research in Unix, the effective use of hardware, how to run and service multiple programs at the same time, and general computer performance, and was created with these things in mind. No retrofitting necessary.

- **Always free and available source code:** This includes the Linux kernel and all of the components of a core Linux distribution. For many home computer users who just want an off-the-shelf operating system that "does the right thing," this doesn't matter directly. However, by making it possible for many different companies and groups to create, distribute, and maintain Linux distributions that are easy to install and use, freely available source code is the cornerstone of Linux availability. Linux distributions may include closed source applications, such as RealPlayer, that run on Linux, but the source code for the Linux kernel and the vast majority of Linux software is and will always be readily available.

- **No lock-in to a specific vendor:** Regardless of the operating system that you're currently using, you may have encountered problems with applications or the way things worked. However, if you're using an off-the-shelf operating system from Microsoft or Apple, you can get it only from Microsoft or Apple, it will work only the way that Microsoft and Apple think that it should, and it will always cost what Microsoft and Apple think that it should cost. On the other hand, Linux is open and free, so if you don't like the way that Red Hat's Linux works, how much it costs, or the type of customer support that's available, you can always switch to Novell's SUSE Linux. Or to Mandriva Linux. Or to Ubuntu Linux. Or to . . . I think you see where I'm going with this.

- **Thousands of free, powerful applications:** Need a word processor? Download and install OpenOffice Writer, AbiWord, Kwrite, or dozens of others. Need a database? Download and install MySQL, PostgreSQL, or many others. Need to create graphics or manipulate digital photographs? It doesn't get much better than the GNU Image Manipulation Program (GIMP). If anything, a problem with Linux can be that you have too many choices — which is a good thing for the people who write books like this one.

- **Interoperability with other operating systems:** Companies that write and sell an operating system (no names mentioned) are primarily interested in furthering that operating system and interoperating with other copies of itself. Windows networking and support for sharing disk drives over a network is a good example. Microsoft grudgingly added TCP/IP support after the Internet took off and added support for networked file sharing largely because other companies were already doing that (Artisoft, Banyan, Novell) and they were missing out on potential sales. Linux is written and supported by people who want to use it but can't ignore the fact that other operating systems exist. Linux has extensive built-in support for interoperating with networked drives on systems running Windows, Apple Mac OS and OS X, and Novell Netware. You can always get there from here on a Linux system.

- **Support for standards:** Linux and Linux applications are designed to support standards because these are the language of free intellectual commerce. Linux supports computing standards such as POSIX, FHS, and many more. Linux applications support modern application and data formats for audio, multimedia, document formatting, spreadsheet data, and many more. Because Linux is open and free, there can be no such thing as a proprietary Linux data or application format. This not only fosters data exchange between Linux applications but also guarantees that you'll always be able to get to your data.

- **Lower total cost of ownership:** If you want to use Linux on your desktop or throughout your business, it's free to obtain and there are legions of Linux wizards available who can help you do whatever you want with it. There are no licensing fees — if you need to pay for something, you can pay for updates and support from the vendor of your Linux distribution. I can have 50 Linux wizards at your doorstep faster than Microsoft can say "Please advertise for an MCP with MCTS, MCITP, MCSA, MCSE, and MCDBA certifications who actually understands enterprise computing requirements." Call me.

- **Stable, powerful, and virus-free:** Linux is a mature, multiuser system that is dependable, stable, and rarely needs to be rebooted (and then usually due to power failures or hardware moves). It is designed to support running hundreds of simultaneous processes and multiple users. It has built-in security and is immune to viruses except through system administration slip-ups. In comparison, Microsoft Windows is a petri dish for virus development and cultivation.

- **Wide range of hardware support:** Microsoft Windows runs on x86 boxes. Period. (Full stop for those of you in the U.K.) Apple's Mac OS and OS X run on PPC hardware (x86 hardware coming real soon now). Novell Netware runs on x86 boxes. Up-to-date Linux distributions are available for x86 hardware, PPC hardware, and on ARM, MIPS, Super-H, XScale, and other architectures in the embedded computing market. This may not matter much to you if you're just looking for a desktop operating system for home or business use, but if you're writing software or creating products with a built-in operating system, Linux gives you a wider range of modern hardware choices than any other operating system.

The discussion of some of the advantages of Linux may have wandered into evangelism, but they're all true. It's easy to get excited about an operating system that is as powerful, inexpensive, standards-conformant, and generally open as Linux is. The vendors of other operating system are not stupid — they're aware of the value and increasing popularity of Linux and other Unix-like operating systems. Apple's OS X operating system uses a version of Unix to provide its customers with the power and stability that it needs to run modern Internet services and do true multiprocessing on Macs. Microsoft has mailed me enough copies of its Unix Services CD (Unix commands for the Windows environment) that I now have coasters for up to 50 visitors who are having drinks at my home.

Summary

Linux is a stable, powerful, modern operating system with deep roots in computer science research. It is also eminently usable by anyone as a desktop operating system. Linux has significant advantages over other operating systems from a technical and conceptual point of view — and it is free. As I discuss in the next chapter, the many vendors who provide stable, supported, and up-to-date Linux distributions make it easy to install, configure, and use Linux. As you can see throughout the rest of this book, different vendors may do things differently, but the core concepts of Linux are the same in any Linux distribution — including ease of use, configuration, updating, and reconfiguration. The days when Linux came with a pocket protector are long gone. Today's Linux is the equal of any other operating system.

Chapter 2

Which Distribution Is Right for You?

Chapter 1 discussed the history of Linux and how the appearance of Linux distributions is the biggest key to the popularity of Linux and its growth as a challenger to off-the-shelf operating systems from companies such as Microsoft and Apple. This chapter discusses the most popular Linux distributions available today and provides information about the orientation and key features of each. The goal of this chapter is to help you select a Linux distribution to use or experiment with once this book has sufficiently inspired you.

As a quick refresher, a Linux distribution consists of a Linux kernel, software packages that make up a root file system containing applications and associated files, and an installer that probes your hardware and helps you configure that hardware so that it is suitable for use with Linux. *Live CDs,* which are preinstalled Linux distributions that you can run from a CD (or DVD), are quite popular today because they make it possible for you to experiment with Linux without actually installing anything. When you boot from a live CD, it does the same sort of hardware probing that installing a standard Linux distribution would do, but it stores all of its configuration information in a *RAM disk,* which is the file system that is created in a section of your computer's memory. Live CDs are great for experimentation, but they don't inherently provide any permanent storage; you usually have to either mount one of your computer's existing disk partitions and save data there or copy it to another machine over the network. Some of the most modern live CDs can be installed from CD-RW disks, which means that you can save incremental data to the same CD-RW that holds the bootable Linux distribution and access it later. For perhaps the best example, see the discussion of Puppy Linux later in this chapter.

This chapter is organized alphabetically to make it easier to find information about a specific distribution and to hide my own personal biases. Every Linux fan has his or her favorite Linux distribution, some of us motivated by philosophy and others by availability and support. The Distro Watch site (www.distrowatch.com) currently lists over 300 active Linux distributions. In a restaurant with 300 items on the menu, anyone can find a great meal.

Debian

Debian is one of the longest-lived Linux distributions available. Debian is pronounced "Deb'-ian," with a soft *e,* and is a contraction of the names of the founders of the Debian project, Debra and Ian

Murdock. The Debian project (`www.debian.org`) was founded in 1993 and has been delivering quality GNU/Linux distributions ever since. The Debian project is unique in terms of Linux distributions in that it produces versions of Debian that run on top of both the Linux kernel and other free, open source kernels, such as the GNU project's Hurd servers and associated microkernel. The rest of this discussion focuses on Debian's GNU/Linux distribution, but it's interesting to note that the project's focus is on providing a free, powerful operating environment for users rather than simply on GNU/Linux.

Debian is well known for stable releases based on thoroughly tested and completely integrated software packages. This focus on testing, integration, and stability has led to Debian's reputation among Linux aficionados as a slow-moving distribution that easily falls behind the cutting edge of Linux technologies. While that's true — there have literally been years between official Debian releases — there are always three versions of Debian available: stable (the released version), testing (the candidate for the next release), and unstable (the development version). The Debian project is also extremely picky about making sure that its distributions include only software that is completely open source and unencumbered by any licensing that might affect its distribution or taint its heredity. Debian has always been a socially aware distribution with a strong philosophical bent — see their Social Guidelines page (`www.us.debian.org/social_contract`) for more information.

One of the greatest contributions that the Debian project has made to the open source community is its pioneering effort to take the rocket science out of application and system updates. As you'll learn later in this book, many Linux software packages have dependencies on other software packages, most commonly shared libraries that are provided as separately installable software packages. This can lead to a nasty chain of dependencies between downloadable packages that can make it difficult, at best, to satisfy all of the requirements when you want to install or upgrade a given package. To facilitate tracking the identities of other packages that are required when installing or updating a given package, Debian introduced the DEB package format, which is an enhanced version of the standard Red Hat Package Manager (RPM). Debian also introduced its Advanced Packaging Tool (APT) and related utilities. Using the APT `apt-get` utility, you can issue command-line commands such as `apt-get install` *foo* to install the package *foo*, `apt-get update` *foo* to update the package *foo* that is already installed, or `apt-get dist-upgrade` to upgrade your entire distribution. You can also use `apt-get` to download, build, and install packages from source code, performing the same sort of dependency resolution in the process. Quite impressive.

Debian is a great distribution that provides a huge collection of stable software (over 15,000 available packages when this book was written) and pioneered much of the usability and administrative ease-of-use that has made Linux popular and successful. On the downside, installing and using Debian typically requires that you know a bit more about Linux systems and their organization than some other distributions. Other popular distributions, such as Xandros Linux and Ubuntu Linux, are based on Debian but have focused on further simplifying its administration and on being as up-to-date as possible.

Fedora Core

The Fedora project (`www.redhat.com/fedora`) is an open source Linux distribution that was founded and is hosted by Red Hat, Inc. (See the discussion of Red Hat Linux later in this chapter.)

The Fedora project develops and releases the Fedora Core Linux distribution, which is hosted by Red Hat but is supported by the open source community. Many Linux users still rankle at Red Hat's desertion of direct support for the home desktop market, but the Fedora Core distribution is an excellent replacement for Red Hat's old off-the-shelf desktop, workstation, and server distributions.

As an open source project, Fedora development moves quickly. CD-ROM images (ISOs) of the latest Fedora releases are available at many sites on the Web, as are a steady stream of updates that are delivered in RPM format, typically through the yum updater, which simplifies identifying, retrieving, and installing system updates much like Red Hat's up2date utility, except that it works from the Fedora command-line and can leverage many sources of installable packages, not just those from a single source such as Red Hat's. The yum software's name stands for Yellow Dog Updater, Modified, which was originally developed by Yellow Dog Linux (discussed later in this chapter) to simplify online updating. As open source software, the yum software was quickly picked up and included in many other Linux distributions. Graphical tools for using yum are also provided in current Fedora Core distributions.

Having spun off from the old Red Hat Linux distributions, Fedora has always been oriented towards the GNOME desktop environment, even though KDE can be installed and used instead. In general, Fedora is a popular distribution with official community-based releases and frequent updates.

Knoppix

Knoppix (www.knoppix.com) is a Debian-based distribution, the primary focus of which is in producing a live CD Linux distribution. A live CD distribution is one where the user boots an existing computer from the CD, and the CD starts Linux and standard Linux services, and enables the user to log in. Knoppix includes a full KDE implementation—booting from a Knoppix live CD therefore also starts the X Window system and the KDE desktop environment. A live DVD is also available, which provides even more software than the live CD. This book includes the Knoppix live CD so that you can experiment with Linux without having to modify your existing PC.

Knoppix is typically run from CD but can also be installed and executed from hard disk, flash, or any other bootable media that your system supports (though sometimes not without a bit of work). Knoppix is often used as a portable Linux toolkit because it provides all of the standard Linux applications that you can use to repair an existing Linux system that won't boot. You can even use Knoppix to recover data or repair Windows systems by mounting FAT32 or NTFS partitions and copying data from them. (Linux still does not have a great open source for writing to NTFS partitions.)

Knoppix is designed as a live CD and therefore isn't necessarily suitable for long-term use on systems that you must reboot often. Because Knoppix doesn't have a standard mechanism for storing its configuration information, you would have to remount partitions, reconfigure networking, and so on, each time you boot from a Knoppix CD. Also, because it is usually delivered on CD or as a CD ISO image, Knoppix is not updateable—you simply get the next release when it's available.

Knoppix is an amazing effort and a fantastic tool for showing people what Linux is like without requiring that they install software, repartition their disks, or anything at all. It is a great advertisement for the power and flexibility of Linux, as well as a great way of showing off Linux itself.

Mandriva

Mandriva (www.mandriva.com) is a French Linux distribution that was founded in 1998 and is perhaps best known under its former name, Mandrake. Unfortunately, a lawsuit by King Features, the owners of the *Mandrake the Magician* comic strip, led to Mandrake having to change its name. (How there could be any potential confusion between a Linux distribution and a comic strip, I'll never know, but such is the law.) Luckily, Mandrake purchased the Brazilian Connectiva Linux distribution around the same time, so the new name is an amalgam of the two.

Mandriva is a well-established Linux distribution that is extremely popular throughout Europe and South America (due to the Connectiva acquisition). Mandrake was always known for its impressive quality, hardware detection, and usability of its installer, which is still true today. Mandrake's installer was the first installer that enabled you to jump around in the installation sequence, which made it extremely easy to change your mind about certain aspects of the installation and configuration process. Most other Linux installers follow a strictly linear process, but Mandrake's sensitivity to how people actually install software made this an impressive feat. Mandriva uses the same installer today. Mandriva is also similarly sensitive to the needs of system administrators, grouping its system administration tools together into the Mandriva Control Center (MCC), which makes it easy for sysadmins to find the tools that they need to tweak and configure installed systems.

Mandriva is a KDE-based distribution, though the GNOME desktop is also available. Some of the best features of Mandriva are its urpmi command-line update tool and RPMdrake, the graphical front end to the urpm command suite. These tools make it easy to update or install selected packages, automatically resolving the chains of related package dependencies that typically plague RPM-based package updates and installations. The Connectiva acquisition provides Mandriva with more than just a new market; with some impressive Linux software for administrators, such as the Synaptic tool that provides a graphical front end for Debian package upgrades, the Connectiva team has demonstrated both technical excellence and user-sensitivity.

Puppy Linux

Puppy Linux (www.goosee.com/puppy) is a live CD distribution of Linux. It is relatively new but worth mentioning here because of the incredible amount of work that goes into it and its general excellence. A complete Puppy Linux CD image runs around 60MB, can be booted from CD or installed into bootable USB flash memory devices or permanently on systems. It is compact but also provides a generous amount of well-thought-out, well-integrated Linux software. Puppy comes complete with a graphical user interface, popular graphical tools for word processing (AbiWord), image editing (GIMP), instant messaging, CD and DVD playing, and much more.

Note

Though Puppy Linux itself provides an image that can boot from a USB device, you can use this image only if your computer system supports booting from USB devices.

As mentioned in the Knoppix discussion earlier in this chapter, one problem with most live CD distributions is that they do not provide a local way of storing persistent data — for example, configuration information that lives across reboots, files that you have created, and so on. Puppy has a great solution to this problem. One of the available Puppy distributions can be installed onto multisession, rewritable CD-RW disks. When you shut down this Puppy distribution and have a CD-RW drive in your system, Puppy automatically archives all of your personal files and configuration information to the CD so that it can reload it the next time you boot from that disk. Amazing! Puppy's USB flash memory distribution does the same sort of thing by creating a file on your USB memory device into which Puppy archives personal and configuration information when shutting down. Not only is this an impressive technical feat, it is the elusive *right thing* that software and operating system vendors are always searching for. Puppy's desktop environment and organization are very different from most other Linux distributions, but it provides exceptional utility and a great way to experiment with Linux.

Red Hat Enterprise Linux

Red Hat (`www.redhat.com`) is probably the best-known Linux distribution, though it has moved away from the home desktop market toward the greener and more lucrative pastures of enterprise computing. While this is a bad thing for the thousands of home users who faithfully purchased a long series of Red Hat releases, this is a good thing for Linux in general because it fosters the adoption of Linux in enterprise computing. Customer support, supported and tested releases, stable software, and a steady stream of software and security updates are core software requirements for enterprise, and Red Hat does an excellent job of delivering on those. Red Hat also provides a number of add-on technologies that are specifically targeted towards the enterprise computing market, such as clustering and its support for the Global File System (GFS), which Red Hat acquired through its purchase of Sistina Software.

Red Hat has pioneered many Linux innovations, most notable the Red Hat Package Manager (RPM, now officially renamed as the RPM Package Manager) and its associated file formats. The RPM package format and associated software make it easy for users and administrators to install software, see what software and versions of that software are installed on a given system, upgrade software, and remove software. RPM has been picked up by many Linux distributions other than Red Hat, including Fedora Core, Mandriva, SUSE, and Yellow Dog.

Hand in hand with its support for RPM are Red Hat's introduction of the Red Hat Network and its associated up2date software. The Red Hat Network is a subscription-based service that enables users and system administrators to download and install package and security updates from Red Hat's servers and also provides more advanced capabilities for system management. This makes it easy for licensed Red Hat Enterprise Linux users to keep their systems and software up-to-date (pardon the expression).

Red Hat's tip of the hat to the home desktop market and its existing home user base was its founding and support of the Fedora project, discussed earlier in this chapter.

Slackware

As discussed in Chapter 1, Slackware (`www.slackware.com`) was the Linux distribution that truly got the Linux ball rolling and was therefore the subject of most early Linux books. First released in

1992, the goal of the Slackware Linux project is to produce the most Unix-like Linux distribution available. The emergence of well-supported, commercially backed Linux distributions has largely eclipsed Slackware, but it is still well known and has a dedicated following of users who want a more hands-on Linux distribution. Slackware was founded by Patrick Volkerding, who still manages and maintains the distribution today.

Unlike most of the Linux distributions that are currently available, Slackware still uses a later 2.4 kernel by default, though various 2.6 kernels are delivered for testing purposes.

SUSE/Novell

SUSE (`www.novell.com/linux/suse`), originally a German Linux distribution but now owned by Novell, is probably the most popular Linux distribution in Europe. SUSE (pronounced "Soose") stands for *Gesellschaft für Software und Systementwicklung mbH*, which roughly translates into *Company for Software and System Development*. The SUSE distribution has its distant roots in Slackware but has added significant value by providing excellent installation and configuration utilities, as well as a large amount of software. SUSE Linux distributions deliver a wide selection of software packages in RPM format.

SUSE is a KDE-based distribution, though the GNOME desktop and related utilities are available and installable from the SUSE CDs or DVD. Aside from the handsome volume of tested, integrated software that a SUSE Linux distribution delivers, SUSE's best feature is its integrated system administration tool, YaST (Yet another System Tool). Many Linux distributions, most notably Red Hat and Fedora Core, provide a loose collection of standalone system administration tools from which it is often difficult to find the tools that you need to configure a specific aspect of your system. Though standalone tools follow the traditional Unix/Linux philosophy of do-one-thing-and-do-it-well, the result is confusion and irritation for system administrators. SUSE solves this problem nicely by implementing all of its system administration tools as modules that work within a single administrative framework. This makes it extremely easy to find and use sysadmin tools because they're all in one place and share the same user interface. In 2005, SUSE released its YaST framework to the open source community, and more distributions that follow this coherent and consistent approach to system administration are eagerly anticipated. SUSE has also funded some impressive open source projects, most notably Hans Reiser's ReiserFS, the first journaling file system to be integrated into the Linux kernel.

As a company with traditional roots in enterprise software, Novell's acquisition of SUSE led to the release and support of a number of different versions of SUSE targeted towards different markets. Novell's SUSE Enterprise Linux Server (SLES) and Open Enterprise Server (OES) products are targeted towards the enterprise market. The former is a pure Linux solution targeted towards enterprise computing, while the latter is more targeted towards businesses that are migrating from Novell's old line of NetWare products. Both offer substantial integration with existing NetWare services and software solutions. Similarly, the Novell Linux Desktop (NLD) product is targeted towards desktop users in enterprise computing environments and provides a powerful Linux desktop solution with various tools for existing Novell users. Unlike Red Hat, SUSE still actively distributes and supports a retail desktop Linux distribution targeted towards home users.

In 2005, SUSE opened its development to the open source community by announcing the OpenSUSE project, which is roughly equivalent to Red Hat's creation and sponsorship of the Fedora project. Though SUSE has always been a strong open source player, giving the community a stronger voice in the contents and direction of its Linux distribution is certainly a good idea and provides thousands of extra eyes to help inspect upcoming releases. SUSE 10 was the first SUSE release to benefit from the OpenSUSE project.

Ubuntu

Ubuntu Linux (`www.ubuntulinux.com`) is a relatively young Linux distribution that is rapidly growing in popularity. Ubuntu is a well-funded Debian-based Linux distribution with a strong commitment to the community and to internationalization. Ubuntu adheres to a strict six-month release schedule and guarantees support for its official releases for up to seven years. The combination of user-friendliness and commitment to its user community (as well as the excellence of its distributions) is a significant factor in Ubuntu's meteoric growth in popularity.

Several different Ubuntu distributions are available to satisfy the needs of different groups within the user community. Ubuntu itself is a GNOME-based distribution. A KDE-oriented Ubuntu desktop distribution, known as Kubuntu (`www.kubuntu.org`), is available through the related Kubuntu project. A Ubuntu distribution known as Edubuntu (`www.edubuntu.org`) is targeted towards younger users and the educational computing market and is being developed by the Edubuntu project. All of these projects are sponsored by Canonical, Ltd., a company founded by Mark Shuttleworth, a dot-com millionaire who has an impressive commitment to computing and the Linux community and literally puts his money where his mouth is. The world would be a better place if he was cloned a few times.

Ubuntu provides a good selection of easy-to-use system administration tools with their roots in Debian distributions, such as the traditional `apt-get` software, the Synaptic graphical update manager, and Ubuntu's own Ubuntu Update Manager. Ubuntu's installer is simpler than some (such as Fedora Core's or SUSE's) but is still quite useful. Ubuntu departs from other Linux distributions in its administrative model, which largely does away with the need to ever become the root user to perform administrative tasks. While this can be disconcerting to old-school Linux sysadmins (myself included), it works quite well and reflects the reality that desktop users need to do certain privileged tasks, so why not make it easy for people to do them as themselves.

Ubuntu has one of the strongest, friendliest user communities that has ever existed in the Linux space and offers support for its products through Canonical, Ltd., the Ubuntu community, and an impressive collection of Ubuntu experts and companies that you can find through the Ubuntu Marketplace and the Ubuntu Partner Program. Ubuntu also makes it easy for people to use — or simply experiment with — a live CD version of Ubuntu is freely downloadable (as are the Ubuntu distributions themselves). In addition, Ubuntu offers a free service that will ship you Ubuntu CDs (`shipit.ubuntu.com`), which is certainly a boon to people with slow or poor Internet connections. Ubuntu currently offers CDs for standard x86, 64-bit, and PPC versions of Ubuntu.

Xandros

Xandros Linux (`www.xandros.com`) is an impressively easy-to-use, friendly Linux distribution. Xandros has its roots in the old Corel Linux distribution, which was itself a Debian-based Linux distribution. Shortly after Corel exited the Linux market, Xandros purchased the rights to its Linux distribution and has been improving, extending, and updating it ever since.

Xandros offers Linux distributions targeted towards home users, enterprise users, and enterprise server environments. It also offers an impressive tool, the Xandros Desktop Management Server, which simplifies Xandros deployments in enterprise or other multidesktop environments, where you want to deploy exactly the same desktop on multiple systems. Providing enterprise-caliber software such as this shows an awareness of the needs of Linux system administrators and a commitment to Linux that goes far beyond simply providing and supporting a Linux distribution. Xandros also offers a custom distribution, the Xandros SurfSide Linux Edition, that is targeted towards Internet users and which provides out-of-the-box support for net-related tasks including Voice over Internet Protocol (VoIP). The Xandros SurfSide distribution even includes a USB headset in the box to make it easy for you to begin making calls from your computer.

Xandros has an impressive distribution network. Xandros Linux distribution is available online from CDW, Amazon, and many other e-tailers. It is even available at stop-and-shop locations such as Wal-Mart, both as a boxed product and preinstalled on PCs. Anyone who purchases Xandros Linux gets automatic access to the Xandros Network, an easy-to-use mechanism for online updates and for retrieving additional supported software that isn't delivered on the standard Xandros installation disks.

Yellow Dog

No discussion of Linux distribution would be complete without discussing Yellow Dog Linux, a Linux distribution targeted towards users of Macintosh computers. At the time that this book was written, modern Macintosh computers used different types of PowerPC chips from vendors such as IBM and Motorola, rather than the x86 processors from Intel and AMD that are used in most desktop computers today. PPC chips are therefore completely different internally from x86 chips and use a different instruction set. (Apple has announced that it is switching to Intel architecture chips in the near future.)

This departure into the hardware internals of modern desktop computers is necessary to make it clear that G3-, G4-, and G5-based Macintosh computers can't run the standard versions of Linux from the different vendors discussed in this chapter. While some of the other Linux distributions discussed in this chapter (Mandriva, Fedora Core, and SUSE) offer PPC versions of their Linux distributions, this isn't their primary focus. Yellow Dog, on the other hand, has always been exclusively focused on promoting Linux on PPC-based computers. Yellow Dog's distribution is a GNOME-oriented distribution that is based on Fedora Core but which offers a custom installer and extensive updates so that it can partition Macintosh drives, support the X Window system on Macintosh monitors, and so on. Yellow Dog is well known for the high level of quality in its distribution and its commitment to and expertise on the PPC platform. Yellow Dog also supports Linux on high-performance embedded computing hardware such as IBM's 970 reference boards and the newly released Cell processors from Motorola and IBM.

If you want to run Linux on Macintosh hardware, Yellow Dog Linux is simply the best Linux distribution available.

Special-Purpose Distributions

As mentioned in Chapter 1, there were over 300 active Linux distributions available at the time that this book was written. This chapter highlights the most popular desktop-oriented Linux distributions, but there are many more. See www.distrowatch.com for a complete list as well as some introductory information about each and pointers to where you can download or otherwise obtain these other distributions.

But why are there so many Linux distributions? There are only a handful of versions for Microsoft Windows and only one current version for Mac OS X. While the number of available Linux distributions can be bewildering, the reasons for their existence is not — that's the power of open source. Just as all of the Linux distributions discussed in this chapter got their start in someone's vision of what a Linux distribution should contain and how it could be managed, all of these other Linux distributions reflect someone else's notion of what's best in certain circumstances.

The explosive growth in the number of Linux distributions that are available has come about partly because of the relative ease with which anyone can download the Linux source code and build their own Linux distribution. The most significant reason why people want to do this is because they want to create custom Linux distributions targeted for specific purposes. Many people have created Linux-based rescue disks, which are bootable CD or floppy disk images that people can use to repair failed Linux (and Windows) systems. Many other people have wanted to create special-purpose Linux distributions tailored towards specific markets or groups of users. One common target for these other Linux distributions is laptop computer users or the users of older computer systems, whose systems typically have less available memory and disk space than today's desktop computers. Some other Linux distributions focus on providing alternate graphical environments, X Window system window managers, and so on. Some focus on portability, such as one of my favorites, the LNX-BBC distribution (www.lnx-bbc.org), which is a mini-Linux distribution that is small enough to fit on a CD-ROM that has been cut, pressed, or molded to the size and shape of a business card. Membership cards for the Free Software Foundation are actually bootable LNX-BBC CDs, which lets you show your fealty to the open source community and run Linux on just about anything at the same time. The BBC in its name stands for *bootable business card*.

Aside from Distro Watch, Ben Gross's Web site at http://bengross.com/smallunix.html is an excellent source of information about popular small-footprint Linux distributions. The Frozen Tech Web site (www.frozentech.com/content/livecd.php) is an excellent source for finding live Linux CDs, as well as the CD images for many Linux distributions.

Standalone, Dual Boot, or Live CD?

The question of how you want to boot Linux largely depends on how you plan to use it. *Standalone* refers to computers on which Linux is the only bootable operating system that is installed. Converting one of your systems into a standalone Linux system requires a certain level of commitment to Linux because you can't run other operating systems (though you can still run much Microsoft Windows software through open source projects such as WINE, www.winehq.com).

If you still need the ability to run Windows software natively (that is, by booting Windows), you can install Linux on one or more spare partitions and configure your system so that it gives you the choice of booting Linux or Windows when you turn it on. This is known as *dual booting,* and is discussed extensively in Chapter 8. Dual booting is a great alternative to standalone Linux systems if you have to depend on certain Windows applications but still want to explore the power and freedom that Linux systems provide. An alternative to dual booting is to run a package such as VMWare (www.vmware.com) that lets you run Windows within a virtual machine on your Linux system, but this costs money. Solutions such as Codeweavers CrossOver Office (www.codeweavers.com) and Win4Lin (www.win4lin.com) provide software for running Windows applications directly on Linux systems without requiring a complete Windows installation as VMWare does.

Live CDs are the best alternative if you simply want to experiment with Linux without reconfiguring your existing computer system. Live CDs are a great way of experimenting with different Linux distributions until you find the one that's right for you — and without spending a lot of time installing and configuring each test distribution along the way. Live CD versions of many Linux distributions are available, most notably Ubuntu and SUSE Linux.

Summary

Using Linux provides a much more powerful computing environment than any other desktop computing environment with the possible exception of Mac OS X. The bottom line for Linux is that it's about freedom — freedom from licensing costs, freedom to run any Linux distribution that interests you, and the freedom to make up your own mind about what the version of Linux that you run should include. This chapter highlights many of the most popular Linux distributions available for desktop computer users, explaining their strengths and focus areas. In the end, it's up to you. I'm quite happy with my Ubuntu and SUSE desktop systems, carry my FSF LNX-BBC distribution in my wallet, and use the Puppy Linux live CD to get the most out of a few older laptops that I can't bear to discard. As they say in Linux-land, YMMV — *your mileage may vary.*

Chapter 3

Preparing for Installation

Before you install Linux, you need to determine whether your system is compatible with Linux, as well as decide what type of Linux software you plan on installing. Most Linux distributions come with literally thousands of software packages, including everything from complex mathematical software, Web-server software, office applications, geographical information systems, grid computing infrastructure components, and more programming languages than you've probably ever heard mentioned.

Linux takes advantage of the collective work of thousands of computer-savvy professionals worldwide, leading to a huge base of available software. Installing every software package can lead to an unintelligible mush of packages. So, before installing, you should decide what type of packages, in general, you want to install. For example, you need to determine if you intend to use your Linux computer to perform software development, run business applications, or perhaps act as a server for data, files, Web pages, e-mail, and so on.

Furthermore, before you start installing Linux, you should make sure your computer is compatible with Linux. Not all computers are compatible.

And, prior to performing any operation on your hard disk that could prove destructive, you want to back up your data. You really want to back up your data.

This chapter covers the main issues you should address before you start a Linux installation. In part, this is because a Linux installation is potentially destructive to your hard disk. The first thing you need to do, though, is determine what you want to use the Linux system for, which will dictate the kind of software you need to install.

Deciding on the Kind of Installation

You can't really decide if Linux is what you want unless you know what you want to do with a Linux system. Will this be a server, desktop workstation, really hip chat system, or something else entirely? You need to decide this up front, because when you install Linux, the installation program will ask you what kind of installation you want:

- Server installation
- Personal desktop installation

▦ Workstation installation

    ▦ Custom installation

Most Linux distributions offer choices similar to these. Sometimes, you might see a choice such as Internet computer or choices that use slightly different terminology. In the end, though, the choices really revolve around the listed options.

A few distributions, such as MEPIS (`www.mepis.org/`) and SymphonyOS (`www.symphonyos .com/`), provide desktop-only software. Most common distributions, such as SUSE, Red Hat, Fedora, Debian, and Slackware, ask you to choose the kind of installation.

Don't worry too much about this question. Your choice won't determine your future, limit your education, or cost you your firstborn. Linux systems can act as both servers and desktop clients at the same time. The whole point of the choice is *appropriateness:* Make the choice that is appropriate for your needs. In addition, if you choose a particular kind of installation, you will be offered a shorter list of software to choose from, as well as create default settings most appropriate for that kind of installation.

The following sections describe each type of installation so you can make an informed choice.

Note

Chances are you have already decided, at least whether the system will be a server or desktop system. There are a few subtleties, though, so read on.

Choosing a server installation

Servers form the backbone of the Internet as well as your home network. A *server* is a broad term for computers that provide data and services to other computers. For example, a mail server transmits and stores e-mail. A file server stores files; a print server connects to one or more printers to allow you to fill up your office space with paper. And so on.

Linux has become extremely popular for use on servers. Linux combines speed, efficiency, and support for off-the-shelf hardware as well as a handy lack of licensing fees. This can dramatically reduce costs, especially if you are used to paying a fee per desktop computer just for the privilege of connecting to a Microsoft Windows server.

If you pick the server installation, you'll be presented with packages for server applications for Web, e-mail, file, printer, database, and other server tasks. You can choose the packages that support the type of server you intend to run. For example, Linux is the most-used operating system on the Internet for servers running Web sites. Apache is the most-used Web server software. If you choose the server installation, you will see packages such as the Apache Web server, along with a number of other Web-server packages such as Tux. Apache includes a number of *plug-ins,* which are add-on packages that you can pick and choose from, such as security, encryption, or special add-ons for CGI applications.

Oracle and DB2, among others, provide databases for Linux. These applications are commercial database software (meaning you have to pay for them and install them separately), but you can also choose the free MySQL or PostgreSQL database packages. Both of these databases come with most Linux distributions. In addition, you'll find even more databases available for Linux, some free and some commercial.

For application servers, you can choose commercial packages such as WebSphere or WebLogic, as well as free packages such as JBoss or Tomcat. All of these packages require a Java runtime environment.

Note

If you use Linux as a server in an environment that includes Microsoft Windows systems, you will want to install antivirus software. This software works to prevent Windows viruses from getting into your network. In general, Linux systems do not suffer from the terrible onslaught of malware, so you install antivirus software to protect the more vulnerable Windows systems on your network.

This is not to say that Linux systems are immune from malware. Refer to the sections in Chapter 15 on updating your software packages, and Chapter 20 for more general security information. Linux distributions usually include one or more Web sites where you can download security and general-purpose software updates. Always ensure that the security patches are up-to-date on your Linux systems.

Choosing a personal desktop installation

Personal desktop installations include a graphical desktop environment, the OpenOffice.org office suite of applications, Web browsers, e-mail clients, music players, and other user-oriented software packages. Choose a personal desktop installation if you primarily use your computer to perform tasks such as creating documents, browsing the Web, listening to music, or playing games.

The Linux desktop looks surprisingly like the Windows desktop. If you are familiar with Windows, you should have little problem navigating around the Linux desktop. Linux, though, includes many choices (as you've probably guessed by now). This also applies to desktop environments. The main Linux desktop environments include GNOME, KDE, and XFCE. Most Linux install programs ask you to select one of these environments to use for your desktop. If you are new to Linux, you should choose the default desktop for your Linux distribution. As with Windows, you can customize your screen background, add widgets to the front panels (similar to the Windows task bar), and choose themes, fonts, and colors for your display.

Cross-Reference

Chapter 9 offers more information on Linux desktops and some common desktop applications, and Chapter 10 explains how to customize your desktop.

Linux systems provide choice for applications, more so than most Windows systems. While you do have choice on Windows, such as WordPerfect or Microsoft Word for creating documents, the vast majority of users run Microsoft Word. On Linux, though, you can choose from AbiWord, OpenOffice.org Writer, and a plethora of other applications including KWrite, Siag Office, and more. You can choose among these programs to use the ones that suit you best. In addition, many Linux distributions include the Thunderbird e-mail client and the Firefox Web browser, both of which also run on Windows and Mac OS X. This allows you to run the same applications on multiple systems, a great help as you migrate to Linux. If you are familiar with Outlook, you may want to install Evolution, a Linux e-mail and scheduling client application.

For office applications, the OpenOffice.org suite was designed to act as an alternative to Microsoft Office. The OpenOffice.org suite can read and write Office file formats, used by applications such as Word, Excel, and PowerPoint. The suite also supports the standard OpenDocument file format, or ODF, mandated by some government institutions. The OpenOffice.org suite runs on Windows and Mac OS X, so you can migrate your documents to OpenOffice.org prior to migrating to Linux.

You'll also find games galore, as Linux distributions usually include about 50 or so simple games. (Of these, KShisen is one of the most innovative and addicting.)

Choosing a workstation installation

Think of the workstation installation as being like the personal desktop installation plus tools for software development. Why a special category for software developers? Aside from the fact that we're good-looking and fun to be around, software developers usually require special tools and applications, enough special applications to warrant creating a new category for installation. Besides, quite a few Linux users are software developers.

Software development tools include text editors such as the old-school Emacs and Vim applications, along with modern editors such as Kate, gedit, and jedit. Text editors quickly morph into full-blown integrated development environments (IDEs) such as Eclipse for Java, C, C++, Python and Ruby development, or MonoDevelop for .NET (Mono) development.

Software development for Java, C, and C++ requires *compilers,* applications that convert the program source code to an object format used by Linux. The GNU compilers, such as gcc for C and C++ or gcj for Java, are the most common compilers on Linux. Because software developers work with source code, special applications such as CVS and Subversion allow you to keep track of source code versions and manage releases.

You'll find a plethora of packages available for software development. Choose the workstation installation if your primary task on the computer is developing software applications.

Choosing a custom installation

Since you chose Linux, you're a trendsetter. You're not a part of the crowd. This also means that these arbitrary installation categories may not fit your needs. Don't worry, you can always choose the custom installation. The custom installation allows you to pick and choose among all the packages. This means, for example, that you can choose to install a graphical desktop environment, a variety of server programs, and software development tools.

For most Linux distributions, the custom installation will present you with over a thousand packages from which to choose. Luckily, you should find the installation program has helpfully divided the packages into groups, such as office applications or Web servers.

Note

If you don't know whether to install a given package, especially with the custom installation, you can usually fall back to the default choices. The packages most users install should be preselected for installation. Just stick to those choices and you should be fine. You can always install more packages later.

Choose the custom installation if the previous choices don't work for you. The custom installation is also for those experienced with Linux.

Once you've picked the kind of installation you want, the next step is to determine if your system is supported on Linux. To do this, you need to determine what hardware is installed on your computer. This may be one of those moments where you say "doh," but you'd be surprised by the huge amount of variation in PC hardware components.

Getting System Information

Generally, PC manufacturers build systems using components from a variety of vendors. Even in the same PC product line, the hard disks, graphics cards, and system boards may come from different vendors, but most vendors must assure that their parts work with Microsoft Windows.

For Linux, the situation differs. Even though millions of PCs run Linux, most system and part vendors concentrate on Windows alone. So, when you decide to install Linux on an existing PC, you need to ensure that all the components in your PC work with Linux, and specifically, the version of the Linux distribution you intend to install.

To do this, you need to first determine what components are in your PC. Second, you need to verify that each component is listed as compatible with your version of Linux.

Note

You can avoid these tasks simply by purchasing a PC with Linux preinstalled. Preinstalled Linux systems are rare compared to preinstalled Windows systems, but if you look around, you can find PCs with Linux. If Linux comes preinstalled, you're done and can jump ahead to Chapter 6. Recent advances in Linux technology mean that Linux now installs on most PCs without problems. If you tried Linux in the past and found it difficult to resolve hardware incompatibilities, you'll find that Linux has advanced a lot since the grim old days.

What do you need to know?

The main components you need to check include the following:

- The processor
- RAM
- Graphics and video hardware
- Hard disks and hard disk controllers
- Sound cards
- Network adapters

The more your hardware follows the mainstream desktop PCs, the less likely you are to have problems. Atypical components such as multicore processors or RAID disk controllers fall outside the mainstream and are more likely to be an issue with Linux than the components found in most desktop PCs.

The following list describes the main hardware issues you might face.

- **Processor:** Linux runs fine on most processors: Intel, AMD, ARM (XScale), PowerPC, and most other processor families can run Linux. Linux runs on mobile phones, PDAs, PCs, Macintosh systems, all the way up to monster-sized servers and supercomputers.

  - The only issue you may face is if you have a very new processor from a new architecture. For example, systems with multiple dual-core processors may be too new to run Linux. Even so, it is just a matter of time until Linux gets ported to these systems.

  - You also want to verify that your processor is fast enough to run the Linux distribution you intend to install. Just about every computer that still runs should be fast enough to install Linux.

- **RAM:** Check the minimum requirements of your Linux distribution based on the kind of installation you want to install. For example, you may want more RAM on a server system than on a desktop system. As a good rule of thumb, if your PC currently runs Windows XP and the amount of RAM is acceptable for XP, you have enough RAM to run Linux.

- **Graphics and video hardware:** Linux doesn't always support the latest and greatest graphics adapters. Most mainstream adapters should work just fine, though. Most graphics cards sport chips from just a few vendors, and most of these cards are pretty much the same from the Linux point of view. If you work with TV tuner cards, however, you'll need to check very carefully for compatibility.

- **Hard disks:** Linux supports most hard disk controllers and hard disks. (The disk controller, not the disk itself, is the main worry.) You'll find that Linux just works out of the box with most hard disks in most PCs. For example, most ATA/ATAPI hard-disk controllers should work just fine.

  - In general, you will likely face problems only if you have a RAID disk controller, a setup mostly used for servers. The most common RAID adapters used by Dell, for example, are often problematic on Linux.

- **Sound cards:** Linux doesn't support all the latest sound cards. Linux does support the older SoundBlaster modes. Since most new cards also support these SoundBlaster modes, you should be able to play sound from most hardware. As mentioned previously, you need to check with your Linux distribution vendor to verify compatibility.

- **Network adapters:** Linux supports most network adapters. The main issues you may find include the following:

  - Proprietary network adapters installed on laptop systems. To save on weight and cost, many vendors include proprietary network adapters, especially on laptop systems. In many cases, Linux developers have not been able to get the detailed specifications necessary to support Linux. Usually, though, this is a matter of time until you see special drivers for this type of hardware.

- Network adapters installed on the system board of desktop systems. Many desktop systems include networking built in on the system board. In such cases, most newer systems are supported by Linux, but many older systems have proven problematic.

- Wireless networking cards built for desktop systems. One area where hardware has not yet standardized is in the area of wireless networking adapters made for desktop systems. You may find the desktop adapter is really a laptop PC Card network adapter placed onto a desktop card, such as a PCI card.

Sleuthing your system hardware from Windows

If you are currently running Windows, you can sleuth your system's hardware by using the Windows control panel facility. From the Windows XP control panel, choose Performance and Maintenance (not Printers and Other Hardware). Then, choose See basic information about your computer. The Windows System Properties dialog appears. From this dialog, you can determine what is installed on your system. You can also click on System from the Control panel to get to the same System Properties dialog.

The General tab shows the processor type, speed, and the amount of RAM you have installed.

The Hardware tab provides a button to call up the Device Manager. This miniapplication shows the main components installed.

Caution

This System Properties information is not always correct. For example, I've seen some single-processor systems that falsely report multiple CPUs.

Armed with this knowledge, you can then look up Linux information online to see what Linux supports.

Finding compatible hardware lists

Your best bet for determining which hardware your Linux distribution supports is to look online at your Linux distribution's Web site. Each distribution differs (usually only slightly, but differs none the same). You need to insure your hardware works with the Linux distribution you plan to install. Table 3-1 offers a guide to online Linux compatibility lists.

Table 3-1 Linux Compatibility Lists

Linux Version	Site
Any	www.linuxcompatible.org/compatibility.html
Debian GNU/Linux	www.tldp.org/HOWTO/HOWTO-INDEX/hardware.html

Continued

Table 3-1 Linux Compatibility Lists *(continued)*

Linux Version	Site
Fedora Core Linux (also see Red Hat)	http://fedoraproject.org/wiki/HCL
Red Hat Enterprise Linux	http://bugzilla.redhat.com/hwcert/
SUSE Linux	http://hardwaredb.suse.de/index.php?LANG=en_UK
Ubuntu Linux	https://wiki.ubuntu.com//SupportedHardware/ view?searchterm=hardware%20compatibility

Most lists stick to hardware for a particular Linux distribution. Some lists, such as the Linux Compatible site, attempt to cover all major distributions.

Note

In addition, see `www.linux-on-laptops.com/` for specifics for installing Linux on most laptops.

Again, Linux supports most off-the-shelf components used in desktop systems.

Backing Up Your Data

When you install Linux, you need to create at least two new partitions on your hard disk, one for swap space and one for all your Linux applications and data. If you already have Windows installed (and chances are you do), you need to adjust the size of the Windows partition to free up space for the Linux partitions. Because this operation can potentially destroy your Windows partition, you need to back up your data prior to installing Linux. You can get around this issue by installing a new hard disk to use for Linux. In this case, the Linux partitions won't affect the Windows partitions. Even so, some Linux distributions, in an effort to be friendly, format your hard disks, all of them, for Linux.

Caution

Always double-check what the Linux installation program plans to partition and format. See Chapter 5 for more on partitioning your hard disk and Chapter 8 for building a system to dual boot Windows and Linux.

Why back up your system?

Back up your data. Back it up now. Backing up is the *right thing to do*. Why? Because computers and computer data storage is far too fragile. A backup of your data provides an extra level of protection in case anything goes wrong. If all goes well, you will never need to use your backups. But, if all does *not* go well, your backup may save your keister.

Hard disks fail. In addition, if you need to repartition your hard disk, you may lose everything. Your system may wipe out all files on the disk. This is not supposed to happen, of course. But it may.

Note

Most people don't make regular backups until something goes wrong. Then, they realize the purpose of making backups. Of course, most people (the author included) learned this lesson the hard way and too late. Go ahead. Don't back up. I dare you.

Gathering the installation and restore disks

Windows PCs should have come with a set of CDs intended to restore your system in case of system failure. This will likely include at least one restoration CD from the system vendor, such as Dell or Hewlett Packard, a Windows CD with a certificate of authenticity, and one or more CDs of the applications that came with your PC. If something goes wrong with your Linux installation experience, you'll need these disks to restore the system to its original Windows-only glory. Find these disks now, so that should you need them, they are on hand.

In addition, these disks may have special CD keys and strings of text and numbers that provide the magic code to unlock Windows and Windows applications.

Making backups on Windows

Windows XP Professional includes a backup program in the System Tools submenu under the Accessories menu. (Select Start ✿ Programs ✿ Accessories ✿ System Tools ✿ Backup.) Windows XP Home includes a backup program on the Windows CD.

Microsoft maintains a page describing how to make backups on Windows at `www.microsoft` `.com/athome/security/update/howbackup.mspx`. In addition, you can find lists of backup utilities at `http://directory.google.com/Top/Computers/Software/Backup/` and `http://dmoz` `.org/Computers/Software/Backup/`.

Note

If all this seems too complicated, you can generally take advantage of a sort of poor-man's backup by burning CDs of the data files on your system. You just need to back up the data files you've created, because your restore disks allow you to reinstall Windows. Ta-Da! You're done. This won't save any settings you have made from the defaults on Windows, though. That's why it is best to make a real backup, unless you feel you can reproduce your Windows settings without requiring a backup.

So, if you haven't backed up your data yet, stop reading and do so right now. Then come back, read the next chapter, and feel good about yourself.

Summary

This chapter covers the steps to take prior to installing Linux.

Before you install Linux on your computer, you should decide what kind of installation you want. (Whether you decide or not, the installation program will likely ask you anyway.) Each Linux distribution differs, but most offer choices such as a server installation, a desktop client installation, a software development (or workstation) installation, and, the most interesting, the custom installation.

After choosing the kind of installation, the next step is to determine your system hardware and verify this hardware runs on Linux, especially on the Linux distribution you want to use.

Finally, but most importantly, back up your data before you install Linux. This is just in case something goes wrong.

The next chapter covers how to get Linux and provides an overview of the major Linux distributions.

Part II

During Installation

Chapter 4

Getting Linux and Starting to Install

Once you have gathered all the information you need to install Linux, the next step is acquire a Linux distribution and then, you guessed it, install. Once a process fraught with errors and actual danger to your computer, installing Linux simply isn't that hard anymore. That's because Linux has advanced dramatically over the years, especially in the area of support for PC hardware. PC hardware has also standardized to quite a degree, further helping the situation.

This chapter covers how to get your hands on Linux, and the first steps towards installing, which include dealing with some of the remaining hardware issues.

Getting Linux

Chapter 2 covered the most popular Linux distributions. Once you get the installation software for a given distribution, you need to get that software on some kind of installation media, such as a CD, the most common choice. If you purchased a CD, then you're ready to go. If, however, you down-loaded the installation software, you then need to copy, or burn, the software to a CD or other installation media.

The following list shows the most common forms for installation media:

- Three or four CDs for a full installation

- One CD for a live CD

- One CD with an installer that downloads the rest of the software from the network

- One DVD-ROM for a full installation

- A USB drive or other disk-based installation package

Most users will need three or four CD-ROMs with the full installation software. You need that many CDs to hold the full set of software that comes with most Linux distributions.

Note

This book comes with the Knoppix distribution, a live CD containing Linux. You can also download or purchase other Linux distributions, as explained in "Download, buy, or acquire."

Download, buy, or acquire?

To get the CDs you need, you can download the data, creating your own CDs, or you can acquire the CDs from somewhere else. For example, you can purchase CDs from most Linux vendors or from a number of third-party sites such as `cheapbytes.com`. You can purchase Linux CDs at some computer stores. If your friends already have Linux CDs, you can use those. Except in rare instances, Linux software should be available under a very liberal license that explicitly allows for copying. This is nothing like illegal file sharing. Instead, this type of sharing is what the whole software freedom movement is all about. Workers of all countries unite!

In addition to the free or very inexpensive Linux distributions, you can also purchase Linux with full enterprise-level support from companies such as Red Hat and Novell.

If you don't have CDs readily accessible, you can download the installation software. See Chapter 2 for a listing of the most common Linux distributions with their Web addresses. Based on the distribution you chose, download the necessary installation files.

Note

Whether you acquire CDs or download the data and burn your own CDs, you need to ensure you get the version of Linux for your processor and system architecture. In most cases, this will be an x86 Intel-based PC architecture. Linux, though, runs on everything from small devices to huge supercomputers. So, you may find a popular Linux distribution such as Debian supports SPARC, PowerPC, ARM, and other processor architectures in addition to the common PC x86 architecture.

In most cases, Linux distributions provide the installer software as one or more ISO files. Each ISO file corresponds to the full file system on one CD. That is, the ISO file not only includes the installation software but also the description of where the data is laid out on a CD-ROM. Thus, each ISO file essentially holds the raw bits that need to get written to a CD-ROM or a DVD. DVD ISO files, though, tend to be much larger than CD ISO files, due to the much larger capacity of DVDs.

Note

The term ISO comes from the International Standards Organization. ISO files refer to ISO-9660, the standard for CD-ROM file formats.

ISO files provide a convenient means to get Linux CDs. For example, a four-CD installation such as Fedora Core Linux requires you simply to download four ISO files and create a CD-ROM from each one. You can also create the ISO files by hand if needed.

Note

Typically, ISO files hold more than 600MB of data. That's because a CD-ROM holds approximately 660MB. Thus, four installation CDs, in the form of four ISO files, fill up a lot of space on your hard disk (and take a long time to download).

Creating CDs from ISO files

In this chapter, I assume you don't have Linux installed yet, so you will likely be using Microsoft Windows to create the ISO files. On Windows, you can use a number of applications to burn ISO files to CDs. These applications include the following:

- ISO Recorder
- CDrWin
- Easy CD
- CDBurn
- Nero
- WinOnCD

Note

CDBurn is part of the Windows Server 2003 Support Tools from Microsoft.

Use one of these packages to burn an ISO file to a CD-ROM under Windows. In other environments, you may be able to create a CD by using a graphical file manager, such as the Nautilus on Linux, and Finder on Mac OS X.

Note

You need a CD-R or CD-RW drive to burn CDs, or a DVD-R, DVD-RW, or DVD+R drive to create a DVD. Create a CD for each ISO file you downloaded. If you have a drive for these media on a Windows PC, chances are it came with a software package for burning CDs.

One of the easiest packages to use is called ISO Recorder and is available for download at `http://isorecorder.alexfeinman.com/isorecorder.htm`. To burn an ISO file with ISO Recorder, follow these steps:

1. Download the ISO files you need. Each ISO file corresponds to a separate CD.

2. Insert a blank CD-R or CD-RW in your drive.

3. From the Windows Explorer, select the ISO file to burn.

4. Right-click on this file name.

5. Click on the Copy Image to CD menu choice to launch the ISO Recorder wizard.

6. Follow the steps provided by the wizard.

Note

ISO Recorder works only with files having an .iso file-name extension.

As mentioned previously, each ISO file corresponds to a separate CD. Thus, for four ISO files, you'll need to create four separate CDs. Remember that you are trying to create CDs from the raw data in the ISO files. You are not trying to merely make backup CDs of the ISO files.

Note

If you burn a CD and then just see one large ISO file on the CD (just one file with .iso suffix), this is a symptom that the file was merely copied to the CD. Instead, you want to create the CD from the raw bits in the ISO file. In this situation, you need to create another CD. Look in the software you used to burn the previous CD for an option named something like *Create CD from Disk Image* or *Burn CD from Image*. You need to set such an option.

Creating ISO files for later burning

Linux includes a number of programs that can help you create an ISO file from the software packages and programs that make up an installation disk. Creating these files should be considered an advanced topic. On Linux, look at the documentation for the `mkisofs` command, short for *make ISO file system*, or `cdrecord`, another command that can create an ISO file. In addition, most Linux programs that provide a graphical application to control CD burning support creating ISO files.

To create the ISO files to install Linux, you need lay out all the software you need under a separate directory for each ISO file. This requires you to know about how to create a bootable CD and exactly which software packages are needed to install Linux. That's why this is considered an advanced topic.

Once you have all the contents for each ISO file placed on disk, you can then convert the directories of files into ISO files. And then, write, or burn, each ISO file to a separate CD.

Note

You can find a lot more information on how to create ISO files at www.linuxiso.org.

Understanding the Boot Process

The boot process is what happens when a PC starts up. When a PC starts up, it finds and runs, or *boots,* an operating system. The boot process becomes important because you need to be able to boot Linux. Furthermore, Linux installation programs are typically scaled-down versions of Linux, so you need the ability to boot Linux on your PC in order to install Linux. Circular? Yes, but useful to know.

Note

All systems have some form of boot process. The process covered here describes the Intel-architecture boot process used in PCs.

PC systems provide low-level hardware control through what is called the *BIOS,* short for basic input/output system. When a PC starts, or restarts, the BIOS tries to find a program called a boot loader. Once found, the BIOS runs the boot loader. The boot loader program then is responsible for loading and running the operating system, such as Linux or Windows.

For Linux, you can choose from a number of boot loader programs, the most common of which are LILO and GRUB. Fedora Core Linux defines GRUB as the default boot loader, for example. In most cases, choose the default boot loader that comes with your Linux distribution. The boot loader searches for an operating system, such as Linux, and then starts the OS it finds.

The BIOS was defined to look in certain places for a boot loader program. By default, the BIOS looks for the first floppy disk drive, disk A: to old-time DOS users. Next, the BIOS looks for the default hard disk, disk C: under DOS. Most modern PCs don't include floppy disk drives anymore. In addition, most PCs can boot from a CD-ROM drive, if configured to do so.

This becomes important, as most Linux distributions are meant to install from a CD. Typically, you insert the CD listed as the first installation disk into your CD drive. Shut down and restart your PC, with the CD still in your CD drive. If your PC, your BIOS, is configured to boot from the CD drive, then the Linux installation program will start, beginning your Linux journey, with lots of happy ponies. On the other hand, if your BIOS is not configured to boot from the CD drive, then your previous operating system, typically Windows, will run.

Caution

Most PCs turn off the ability to boot from a CD drive for security reasons. On Windows, CDs can run a program when you insert them into the CD drive of an already running PC. (These are called autorun CDs.) An autorun CD could then restart your Windows system, starting an operating system stored on the CD. In most cases, you do not want this behavior, hence the desire to disable booting from CDs. After installing Linux, be sure to disable booting from CDs.

To enable or disable booting from CDs (or other media such as USB drives), you need to change the configuration of the BIOS.

Accessing the BIOS

The PC BIOS stores low-level system configuration data, such as the date and time or the system boot order, in CMOS memory.

Note

Few people know what CMOS means, but you'll often find this term used for the settings stored in your BIOS. CMOS, short for *complementary metal oxide semiconductor*, just defines the type of memory. PC systems store the system data in CMOS memory with a battery to maintain the data over time.

To modify a BIOS setting, you need to reboot your PC and then access the BIOS during the relatively short period of time the PC is performing the POST, or *power-on self-test*. This is the short time before the PC starts booting. Usually you'll see a message such as the following, indicating you can access the BIOS, a process often called *setup*.

```
Press DEL to enter SETUP
```

Since this time may be relatively short, you need to be prepared to press the proper key or key combination. Otherwise, you'll need to restart the PC again. Which key or key combination to use depends on the BIOS vendor. The key or key combination to press should be listed when your computer boots.

Setting the boot order

Once you access the PC BIOS, you can then define the boot order. This is the order of storage devices in which the BIOS will check to find an operating system to boot, in the form of the boot loader program listed previously. Typically, the first item, and often the only item, in the boot order is the main hard disk. This means that the BIOS should search for a boot loader program on the main hard disk.

What you need to do is to define the CD drive as the first item to check in the boot order and make the hard disk second. Each BIOS system has a slightly different means to change the boot order. You may need to search around on a number of screens to find where the boot order is located.

Note

If you are installing from a USB drive or other media, then define that media first in the boot order. Typically, a USB drive would be called a removable drive in the BIOS settings. But, not all BIOS versions support booting from a removable drive. In addition, this is also a security issue, so disable booting from USB drives after installing Linux.

Beginning the Installation

With all of this work, you should now have one or more Linux installation CDs and a PC that will boot from the CD drive first. You are now ready to install Linux. Insert the first install CD. Shut down your computer from Windows or whatever operating system you are currently running.

After the power shuts off, wait a few seconds. Start the computer. Feel the tense anticipation.

When you first boot the Linux installer, you will see text like the following (from a Fedora Core installation) with the boot prompt:

```
- To install or upgrade in graphical mode, press the <ENTER> key.
- To install or upgrade in text mode, type: linux text <ENTER>.
- Use the function keys listed below for more information.

[F1-Main] [F2-Options] [F3-General] [F4-Kernel] [F5-Rescue]

boot:
```

The boot prompt may appear after a number of other messages, product logos, and so on. For example, Fedora Core Linux includes a large blue Fedora image. At the boot prompt, you can press Enter to go on with a normal installation. You can alternatively enter in any of a number of options to control how the installation program starts. For example, enter linux text to start the installer in text mode instead of in graphics mode.

```
boot: linux text
```

Use the text mode if the installer cannot display graphics on your hardware. Otherwise, the default graphical mode should work.

Setting System Options

After many years of supporting just about every kind of PC hardware imaginable, the Linux boot prompt accepts a number of system options. If you experience problems while booting Linux, or have nonstandard hardware, you may need to set other options at the boot prompt, as described in this section. In most cases, when you determined what hardware components are installed in your PC, as described in Chapter 3, you should have found any special boot prompt options needed by the hardware.

Note

These options are used by the Fedora and Red Hat distributions. Options differ on other versions of Linux.

Boot prompt options are either a single word, such as `text`, or a *name=value* pair, such as `resolution=1024x768`. Combine the options by separating them with spaces. For example:

```
boot: linux resolution=800x600 apm=off
```

Table 4-1 lists the most common options.

Table 4-1 Common Boot Prompt Options

Option	*Use*
apci=off	Turns off APCI subsystem.
apic	Works around a bug in the BIOS for the Intel 440GX chipset.
apm=allow_ints	Changes APM system, usually used for laptops.
apm=off	Turns off APM power management.
apm=power_off	Changes APM default to power off; used mostly for systems with multiple processors.
apm=realmode_ power_off	Changes APM to power off the system in the Windows 95 way rather than the Windows NT way. Use this option if your BIOS crashes on shutdown.
dd	Prompts you for a driver disk, same as `driverdisk`.
display=IP_ Address:0	Allows you to install from a remote display, the display on the system with the given network IP address. Note that the remote system must allow connections from your PC. See the `xhost` command for details on allowing access.
driverdisk	Prompts you for a driver disk, same as `dd`.
ide=nodma	Turns off DMA, direct memory access, to your IDE hard drive. Use this option if you have problems with the IDE subsystem.
isa	Prompts you for specifics of your IDE configuration.
kbd-reset	Tells the Linux kernel to reset the keyboard at startup. The BIOS is supposed to do this, but on some systems, it does not.
lowres	Tells the installer to use the low resolution of 640 × 480. Same as `resolution=640x480`.

Option	Use
mem=numberM	Tells the Linux kernel to use the given amount of memory, in megabytes. Used to specify the real amount of memory if the BIOS cannot report more than 16MB of memory. Also used in cases where the graphics card shares memory with the processor and you want to limit the processor to a certain amount of memory, lower than the reported amount.
nmi_watchdog=1	Turns on NMIs, or non-maskable interrupts. Used to help diagnose problems with multiple processors.
noapic	Turns off APIC chip, useful for systems with a buggy BIOS or a known APIC problem.
noathlon	Tells Linux kernel not to use AMD Athlon optimizations.
noht	Turns off hyperthreading on multiple-processor systems.
noisapnp	Turns off ISA-based PnP (Plug-n-Play, often called Plug-n-Pray).
nomce	Turns off the special CPU check (machine check exception), used for older Compaq systems.
nopcmcia	Turns off the PCMCIA bus in laptops.
noprobe	Turns off hardware probing, instead asking you for the hardware information.
noshell	Turns off the shell on the second virtual console during installation.
nousb	Turns off support for USB during installation.
nousbstorage	Turns off support for USB storage; used when you face a problem with the ordering of SCSI devices.
reboot=b	Used if your system hangs during reboots. May fix the hanging problem.
resolution= WidthxHeight	Sets graphical installer to use the given screen resolution. Must be a standard resolution such as 640 × 480, 800 × 600, or 1024 × 768. Use this option if you experience problems with the graphical installer. If problems persist, try the text mode.
root=/dev/device	Specifies the device to use as the root file system for the installer to boot from, such as /dev/hda1, for the first IDE hard disk, or /dev/fd0 for the floppy A: drive. Use this option if the installer cannot find the root disk.
skipddc	Skips DDC monitor probe.
text	Runs text-mode installer instead of the normal graphics mode installer.

Most of these boot prompt options serve to turn off a normal part of Linux processing for those systems that face issues, such as systems that experience problems if Linux tries to probe the hardware. As you can see, each option was created when users faced a particular problem, sometimes a very obscure problem. So, don't use these options unless you see a particular error, such as an IDE-specific error for the ide=nodma option, or if you found hardware documentation describing your system and particular hardware problems with Linux. Otherwise, don't specify any options.

In addition, you need to provide the boot options fairly quickly. After about a minute, the installer continues as if you had pressed the Enter key at the boot prompt.

Note

See the Linux Boot Prompt How-To document at `www.tldp.org/HOWTO/BootPrompt-HOWTO.html` for more on these options.

If everything has gone well, you should be on your way to installing Linux. You should see a number of easy starting questions, such as which language to use for the installation program, and what layout type your keyboard has (typically U.S. English, for example). You will need to choose the type of installation, such as workstation, server, custom, and so on, as described in Chapter 3. These initial questions should be easy to answer.

Summary

This chapter covers the first steps to getting your hands on a Linux distribution and starting to install this wonderful operating system.

The first step to installing Linux is to get a Linux distribution on some sort of storage media, typically one or more CDs. You can purchase CDs, or download the software. Be sure to download the software for your PC's architecture. The vast majority of PCs use the Intel-based x86 architecture.

If you download the CDs, you will get one to four ISO files. Each ISO file corresponds to one CD, and holds the raw data bytes that should get written to a CD. You can write the data to a CD using any of a number of software packages, including applications for Windows and Mac OS X. The assumption here is that you don't already have Linux installed.

The initial CD in the set provides the ability to boot your PC into the Linux installer. This installer is actually a stripped-down version of Linux intended to provide enough of an infrastructure to install Linux to your hard disk. You need to insert the CD to your PC's CD drive, and then shut down your PC. Restart your PC and it should boot into the Linux installer.

You may need to access your system BIOS to enable booting from the CD drive. To access the BIOS, you need to press a special key or key combination during the initial power-on self-test of your PC. For many PCs, the special key is the Delete key. Press the special key or key combination to get into the BIOS settings, also called the CMOS settings. You need to enable booting from the CD, and place the CD drive first in the boot order. Save this data and continue booting.

When the Linux installer starts, you'll see a logo, some information, and a bare boot prompt. Press the Enter key to boot into the graphics mode installer for most distributions. Type in the text option to run the installer in text mode. You may also require other options should you face hardware issues running the Linux installer.

The next chapter covers how to partition your hard disk to provide space for Linux to install. This has proven one of the hardest parts of installing Linux, and it can impact your system's performance later on.

Chapter 5

Partitioning Your Hard Drive

Partitioning is a way of making logical separations on a hard disk drive. Windows users will be familiar with the `C:`, `D:`, `E:`, and other lettered drives. These letters can represent entire physical drives or partitions (slices) of a single drive. Linux doesn't use drive letters but rather a hierarchical file system with a root, designated as `/`, and other file systems (or simply directories) off the root file system. Windows users will find that the root file system on Linux is roughly analogous to `C:\`. Many users who are new to Linux ask, "Why should I partition my hard drive at all when just one big partition will meet my needs?" There are two general answers to this question: You should partition if you want to run more than one operating system on the same hard drive (known as *dual booting*), and you should partition your hard drive to separate data from system files.

Dual booting means that two (or more) operating systems can occupy the same hard drive, but only one may boot at a time. You will want to partition your hard drive if you currently have a Windows system and want to install Linux in a dual-boot situation. Dual booting is a good way to use your computer in a unique way without losing your applications and destroying all of your data or buying a new computer for a second operating system. If you want to know more about dual booting and what is involved, refer to Chapter 8.

As far as separating data from system files, you partition the drive mainly for protection — protection from would-be attackers, mistakes that cause a disk to fill up, and users who like to store too much data in their home directories. On any multiuser operating system, you should create partitions to separate data, applications, and system files from one another. Ordinary users of a system do not need access to certain parts of the system, where they might (accidentally or intentionally) destroy essential data. There should be common areas on an operating system, and private areas where access is restricted to those who need it. Partitioning makes housekeeping and system administration much easier.

Linux actually does a good job of protecting operating system files from regular users as only the administrative user (root) has the ability to edit or remove them. Ordinary users have access only to the `/tmp` directory and their `home` directory by default. By limiting the size of `/tmp`, `/home,` and some other key directories, you ensure that the root file system remains free of clutter and has adequate space required for normal operation. You also provide protection from applications or processes that can inadvertently cause `/tmp` or `/var` to fill to capacity and thereby render the root file system and possibly the whole operating system to an unusable state.

For a single-user workstation, you can use fewer partitions (a minimum of two), but creating multiple partitions on advanced operating systems is common practice. As mentioned, you should create at least two partitions when you install Linux: a root file system, designated as /, and a swap partition. The root file system in this case will hold all of the files and directories related to your Linux installation. The swap partition is a reserved space, not accessible by the user, that is used by the operating system for virtual memory. (A more detailed explanation of swap space is given at the end of this chapter.)

The main point to remember when installing any advanced operating system like Linux is to separate system files, user files, and swap space with partitions.

In this chapter, you learn about partitioning your hard drive(s), mounting and unmounting drives and partitions, swap space, and automatic partitioning schemes. The instructions in the chapter lead you through using an automatic partitioning tool to partition your hard drive.

Mount Points

Mount points are a new concept if you are coming from a Windows world. A *mount point* is a local directory on your hard drive where you map resources as if they are part of your basic system. Once a resource is mounted or mapped, you can cd (the command to *change directories*) into it as you would any other directory on your system. Once a partition is created, it must be mounted so that it can be used by the system and users. All partitions created during installation will be automatically mounted.

Physical media versus mount points

To illustrate the concept of mount points in contrast to physical media, let's use a familiar Windows example. On a Windows system, you have a C: drive that holds all of your directories such as \temp, \program files, \windows or \winnt, \Documents and Settings, and so on. The C: drive represents a whole physical hard drive that we will call IDE0. IDE0 means that this is the first physical Integrated Drive Electronics (IDE) hard drive on the system. (Remember in the computer world, you begin with 0 as the first of anything — except partitions.) For this Windows system, the physical drive, IDE0, is *mounted* on C: so that we can use it. In Linux, IDE0 is typically referred to as hda, or *hard disk a*. The a tells you that Linux sees this as the first hard drive. Further, there is a file that represents this first hard drive, appropriately named hda. This file is in your /dev (device) directory along with hundreds of other files that refer to physical devices of all kinds. In this directory, you will find files that represent IDE hard drives, SCSI hard drives, modems, mice, CD-ROM/DVD-ROM drives, USB devices, and so on.

To see the physical media and the mount points, you use the mount command, as follows:

```
#  mount  <ENTER>

/dev/mapper/VolGroup00-LogVol00 on / type ext3 (rw)
/dev/proc on /proc type proc (rw)
/dev/sys on /sys type sysfs (rw)
/dev/devpts on /dev/pts type devpts (rw,gid=5,mode=620)
/dev/hda1 on /boot type ext3 (rw)
/dev/shm on /dev/shm type tmpfs (rw)
none on /proc/sys/fs/binfmt_misc type binfmt_misc (rw)
sunrpc on /var/lib/nfs/rpc_pipefs type rpc_pipefs (rw)
```

```
automount(pid1646) on /misc type autofs
(rw,fd=4,pgrp=1646,minproto=2,maxproto=4)
automount(pid1697) on /net type autofs
rw,fd=4,pgrp=1697,minproto=2,maxproto=4)
```

The `mount` command tells you about the physical media and the mount points on your system. In this example, the first entry tells you that `/dev/mapper/VolGroup00` is mounted on `/` and has the file system type `ext3` and is mounted as `read/write`. The file system has type `ext3`, which is how the partition is formatted. (You may be familiar with `NTFS-` or `FAT32`-type file systems in Microsoft Windows). The other entry of interest in is `/dev/hda1` on `/boot type ext3 (rw)`. This tells you that the first partition on the drive is mounted on `/boot` with `ext3` file system and is mounted `read/write`. The other entries are for system use and will become important as your experience grows with Linux, but for now you may ignore them as they have no associated physical media. You may be wondering where the entry for the swap partition is since it is not listed here. Earlier, I stated that it is a non-user-accessible partition that is used by the operating system. If it were mounted in the traditional sense, you would see it here and have access to it. The `mount` command shows only those file systems, as mount points, that you have access to.

Mounting and unmounting file systems

Mounting a file system provides access to that file system for users and applications. Mounting a file system is very easy. You simply use the `mount` command with the device and the mount point where the device should be mounted for access. The file system type is also usually specified in the command. The `mount` command to mount a CD-ROM in your CD drive is issued as follows (`iso9660` is the file system type of a CD-ROM):

```
# mount -t iso9660 /dev/cdrom /mnt
```

You will receive the following response:

```
mount: block device /dev/cdrom is write-protected, mounting read-only
```

Your CD-ROM is now available for you to use. You may `cd` to it as you would any other directory on your system.

Unmounting a file system (or device) is usually done for system maintenance or to temporarily prevent access to a file system for some other reason. Unmounting a CD-ROM allows you to eject the CD in the drive. Otherwise, it will remain in the drive until the next reboot. It is very simple to unmount a mounted file system. To unmount the CD-ROM that you just mounted, issue the `umount` command specifying either the device or the mount point to unmount:

```
# umount /dev/cdrom or umount /mnt
```

You may receive the following message if you have changed directory onto the CD-ROM:

```
umount: /mnt: device is busy
```

This message is telling you that you are in the /mnt directory. You will have to cd out of /mnt and then reissue the umount command. (Although it looks like a misspelling, umount is correct.)

Note

Typically, only the root user may mount and unmount file systems.

Logical versus Physical Partitions

On any hard disk, you can create only four primary physical partitions. If you need more than four partitions, they have to be created as *logical* partitions within an extended partition. An extended partition is simply a primary physical partition, designated as extended, that can be divided into multiple logical partitions. This is true of any operating system and is not a function of Linux or Windows. Suppose you have a 40GB hard drive and need seven partitions configured as follows:

/boot: 100MB

/tmp: 500MB

/usr: 6,000MB

/var: 800MB

/home: 25,000MB

/opt: 6,600MB

swap: 1,000MB

This would not be possible if you tried to create all of the partitions as primary, but through the magic of extended and logical partitions, you can successfully create the partitions with the desired sizes. It is easy to create the partitions during installation; you really don't have to worry about primary, extended, and logical partitions because the partitioning tool — for example, Disk Druid on Fedora Core or Red Hat systems — takes care of the details. You simply click on the free space and then click Add to create a new partition in the free space with the desired size and mount point.

Note

Disk Druid will allow you to create a single partition as / without a swap partition. You will receive a warning about omitting the swap partition; it is possible, but not recommended, to do so.

Disk Druid is generally available in Red Hat Enterprise Linux and Fedora Core Linux only (including distributions based on Red Hat or Fedora). It is not available in other distributions. Other distributions use similar tools for partitioning your drive(s) during installation. You will be provided with prompts for automatic or manual partitioning with all distributions.

How Much Space?

You may be wondering just how much space is needed for a Linux installation and a full complement of applications, and how that space needs to be divided among the partitions. The answer depends on your needs, the type of installation you want, and the distribution you choose. A typical distribution with the X Window System and most of the desktop applications installed uses about 3GB of space on your hard drive. You should set aside at least 5GB of space if you are installing Linux on a shared system. For a dedicated system, you will need at least a 5GB hard drive. I have installed server systems that are dedicated Web and database application servers that occupied about 800MB of space. And these days, with 80GB hard drives being standard, there shouldn't be any issues with space, even if you install every package on all of the distribution CDs.

In general, dedicating space for a workstation install can be done in an automatic fashion as discussed earlier. A server installation that is going to support several, or perhaps even hundreds of users, should be installed with a bit more thought. A server installation should be installed via custom fashion and each package should be selected or deselected based on the proposed use of the server.

Caution

Never, ever do an automatic install for a server system because many packages get installed that can pose security risks to your system.

The official Fedora site states the following space requirements for each type of installation. (See your distribution's Web site to get similar information for your distribution.) Note that these numbers are for installed software only. Swap space and the /boot partition will use additional space. By default the /boot partition is 100MB, and the swap partition is set to twice the amount of RAM your computer has, in megabytes.

Custom installation (minimal): 620MB

Server: 1.1GB

Personal desktop: 2.3GB

Workstation: 3.0GB

Custom installation (everything): 6.9GB

Table 5.1 shows suggested sizes and mount points for a server system. As you gain more experience, you can alter them for your own needs.

Table 5-1 Suggested Sizes and Mount Points for a Server System

Mount Point	Size in MB
swap space	2 × RAM
/tmp	400–500MB
/var	800MB
/boot	100MB
/usr	6,000MB+
/home	~50% available space
/opt	Varies (Many third-party applications are installed here.)

Remember space is always at a premium. You can always add more disk space later if needed.

What Is Swap Space?

I briefly mention swap space at the beginning of this chapter, where I state that the operating system uses part of your disk space as extra memory. Microsoft Windows users will recognize a similar concept in the term *pagefile*. Windows uses a single file (or multiple files) for additional memory, and Linux/Unix uses a dedicated space on the hard drive for paging dormant processes and applications that can't fit into RAM (standard memory). Generally, you want to set your swap space partition to be twice as large as the amount of RAM you have. If you have 256MB of RAM, then your swap partition should be 512MB. Database and some application servers would be exceptions to this rule. There are complex algorithms — beyond the scope of this book — for computing the correct amount of swap space for those applications. For most purposes, stick with the old rule of twice the amount of RAM.

Caution

The instructions provided in this chapter will overwrite your current disk, the operating system, and all files that you currently have. If you are installing Linux on a computer with Windows, and you want to keep your Windows installation intact, please refer to Chapter 8 for information on setting up a dual-boot system and Chapter 14 on backing up your data before proceeding.

Automatic Partitioning Schemes

Most distributions of Linux will offer to automatically partition your hard drive for you. Fedora Core 4 autopartitioned my 3GB hard drive in the following way: approximately 100MB /boot partition,

768MB swap partition, and 2.2GB as the / (root) partition. This partitioning scheme is sufficient for a first-time installation or a personal workstation. For other types of installations, like a network server, I have seen the installer create moderately sized partitions for /boot and root (/), a standard sized swap (twice RAM), and then a very large (up to half of the free space) /home partition /home. The home directory, where you land when you first log in to the operating system, can be its own separate partition or just a directory off the root directory. This scheme makes sense from the standpoint of how it is used. Most of the data on the system will be kept in the user's home directories and therefore most of the space should be allocated to it.

Figure 5-1 shows the Disk Partitioning Setup screen of the Fedora Core 4 installation where you can choose automatic or manual partitioning. I chose automatic partitioning for this example and strongly suggest it for your first few installations.

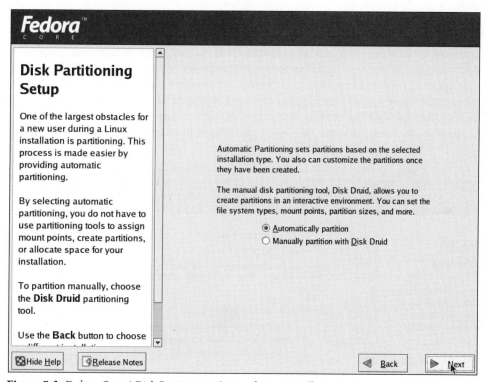

Figure 5-1: Fedora Core 4 Disk Partitioning Screen during installation.

Figures 5-2 through 5-4 show the subsequent screens that you step through in the Fedora Core installation with automatic partitioning. In Figure 5-2, you are asked to choose one of the following options:

> **Remove all Linux partitions on this system:** This option removes all *ext2*, *ext3*, and *Linux swap* partitions from all hard disks.

- **Remove all partitions on this system:** This option removes *all* partitions from all hard disks.

- **Keep all partitions and use only existing free space:** This option uses only the unpartitioned space on the hard disk(s) to install Fedora Core.

Caution

Keep in mind that removing all partitions (the second option) *deletes any data on your system.* Select this option only if you intend to completely replace an existing operating system with the new Linux installation. If this is the case, you should back up any files or data to an external storage source before you partition.

Check the box next to Review (and modify if needed) the partitions created. This allows you to see the details of how your drive will be partitioned before the partitioning occurs and makes changes if you are not satisfied. After making sure this box is checked, select the desired option.

Most of the time, unless you are upgrading or repairing a system, you will choose Remove all partitions on this system, as shown in Figure 5-2. One other circumstance in which you would *not* want to remove all partitions is when you are creating a dual-boot system by adding a second operating system to a computer with an already existing system, for example, running both Microsoft Windows and a Linux distribution on the same machine. See Chapter 8 for more detail on dual-boot systems.

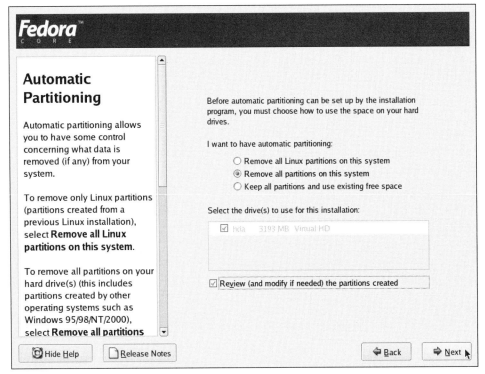

Figure 5-2: Automatic Partitioning screen during a Fedora Core 4 installation.

Next, select any disks you wish to use for Linux partitions. If your system contains only one disk, that disk is automatically selected. Any disks you select are used for Linux partitions according to the option you selected. The option selection is global, and you may not select a different option for each disk. Click Next, and you will see the Warning shown in Figure 5-3. If you click Yes, you are indicating that the automatic partitioning tool should delete everything on your hard drive, so make sure you've made working backups of all your data

Figure 5-4 shows what your hard drive looks like after automatic partitioning has taken place. You can see the layout graphically and by partition. Notice that your hard drive, `/dev/hda`, is split into two parts: `/dev/hda1` and `/dev/hda2`. The `/dev/hda1` partition is mounted on `/boot` and `/dev/hda2` is mounted on `VolGroup00`.

A Fedora Core Linux system has at least three partitions, if configured automatically: a data partition mounted on `/boot`, a data partition mounted on `/`, and a `swap` partition. In Fedora's new partitioning scheme, there is always a `/boot` partition because `/boot` contains the boot files (including the Linux kernel) for your Linux system. These special boot files cannot be mounted via logical volumes (see the following section), but must be in a separate partition.

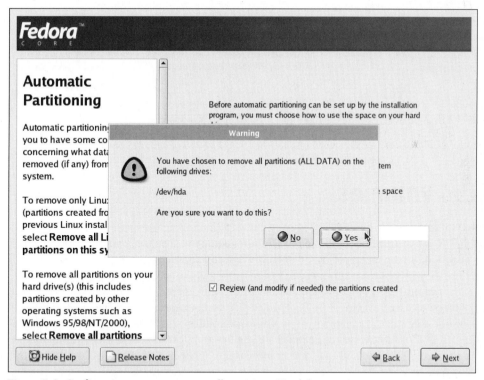

Figure 5-3: Confirmation screen to remove all partitions. Heed the warning!

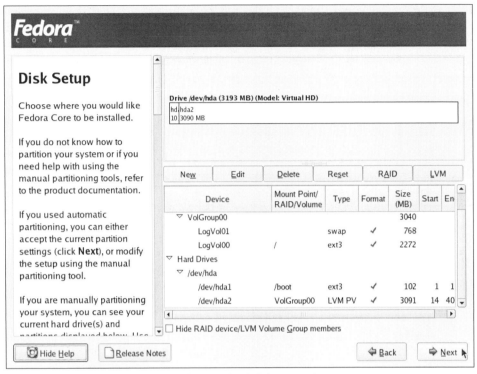

Figure 5-4: Final autopartition screen showing the disk layout and mount points.

Logical Volumes

Fedora Core 4 introduces the concept of logical volumes to Linux as the default for file systems and mount points. Logical volumes have existed in Linux for some time, but only with the introduction of Fedora Core 4 have they been set up by default. Logical volumes are standard fare in the Unix world and they truly bring Linux into a new era of scalability and flexibility as a data center operating system. This means that Linux is now on equal footing with veteran Unix flavors such as Solaris (Sun Microsystems), AIX (IBM), and HP-UX (Hewlett-Packard). Logical volume management (LVM) partitions provide a number of advantages over standard partitions. LVM partitions are formatted as *physical volumes*. One or more physical volumes are combined to form a *volume group*. Each volume group's total storage is then divided into one or more *logical volumes*. The logical volumes function much like standard data partitions. They have a file system type, such as ext3, and a mount point.

Logical volumes allow administrators to grow or shrink logical volumes without destroying data. This cannot be done with standard file systems. Here's a good example: Suppose you have a Linux computer at work that you allow 10 users to connect to and use for various tasks. One day a department head comes to you and requests access for 20 more users, but all of your available space is allocated to your current 10. Without LVM, you would have to purchase, install, and set up a new hard drive; then format, mount it, copy all of the /home files to it; and then mount it as /home. With LVM, you would simply shrink a volume that has extra space, then grow the volume that contains /home to fit the additional users. Logical volumes are a great asset to large-scale, multiuser computing and to Linux.

Summary

Mount points, file systems, and hard disks are referred to in very foreign ways in Linux and Unix. Don't be put off by this. It just takes a little time to become familiar with the terminology and differences. You don't have to configure a new hard drive, swap space, or partitions every day and even experienced people have to look up reference material on these subjects from time to time. Doing things correctly is not that easy on any operating system, but on the other hand, it isn't very difficult either. This chapter gives you some general guidelines for installing and setting up Linux partitions, swap space, hard drives, and mount points. It provides some great reference material from a Fedora Core 4 Linux perspective, but realize that, other than the installation screens, the information is applicable to any distribution of Linux. Good luck and happy partitioning.

Chapter 6

Using Accounts

When Patrick McGoohan, playing the title role in the classic TV show *The Prisoner,* is dehumanizingly renamed Number 6, he shouts at his captor, "I am not a number. I am a free man!" Unfortunately, computers find numbers a heck of a lot easier to deal with than free men, so as far as your Linux operating system is concerned, you *are* a number. To add insult to injury, you are probably number 500 or 1000 rather than 6, for reasons that are explained later in this chapter.

However, unlike the villains of *The Prisoner,* Linux is not out to erase your identity. It uses numbers only for its own internal needs. Linux also allows users to be organized into groups for various purposes. Like individual users, groups are known to the system by numbers but also have human-friendly names. This chapter explains how Linux's user and group numbering works and how the system translates those numbers into people-friendly names, and how you can use these concepts to administer and secure your computer.

Users, System Users, and Groups

Linux was designed from the beginning to allow multiple people to work on one computer. As in Windows, each user gets some system resources to call his or her own. Each user gets his or her own folder (called the home folder) populated with some basic configuration files (configuration files in the home folder override system-wide defaults). As users use and customize new software, more configuration files are added to their home folders. The graphical environment they choose to use may also add folders for documents. They each get a mailbox for incoming e-mail and the ability to send outgoing e-mail from their own unique address. They may have a special directory for hosting Web pages. There are Linux systems that serve thousands of users like this.

But even if you are the only person who ever logs in and your machine currently isn't doing anything except displaying a blank screen, you are not the only "user" of your computer. There are programs (known as *daemons* in Linux jargon) that run system services in the background, called into action by Linux as needed. Some examples would be a mail or Web server, needed only when an e-mail message or a request for a Web page is received, or the crond utility, an event scheduler. Typically, each daemon runs as a separate user that owns only the special data files it needs and no others. This mechanism is more secure; if someone breaks into your Web server, he might be able to deface or delete your Web pages, but at least he won't be able to access any other information that might be on the same system. Other system users are for specific roles such as backup operator or mail server administrator. Yet others are for "owning" specific peripherals such as a fax modem or CD burner. In each case, the reason for the existence of these users is the same: keeping the privilege to perform actions that affect the stability of the whole system as fine-grained and easy to keep track of as possible.

The user database: /etc/passwd

Linux keeps track of who owns what on a computer by giving each user, real or system, a number called a user ID (UID). Account information on UIDs can be stored in many places but typically are stored in a file called /etc/passwd.

The following code shows the /etc/passwd file from the Knoppix distribution. (It will be slightly different in other distributions.)

```
root:x:0:0:root:/root:/bin/bash
daemon:x:1:1:daemon:/usr/sbin:/bin/sh
bin:x:2:2:bin:/bin:/bin/sh
sys:x:3:3:sys:/dev:/bin/sh
sync:x:4:65534:sync:/bin:/bin/sync
games:x:5:60:games:/usr/games:/bin/sh
man:x:6:12:man:/var/cache/man:/bin/sh
lp:x:7:7:lp:/var/spool/lpd:/bin/sh
mail:x:8:8:mail:/var/mail:/bin/sh
news:x:9:9:news:/var/spool/news:/bin/sh
uucp:x:10:10:uucp:/var/spool/uucp:/bin/sh
proxy:x:13:13:proxy:/bin:/bin/sh
majordom:x:30:31:Majordomo:/usr/lib/majordomo:/bin/sh
postgres:x:31:32:postgres:/var/lib/postgres:/bin/sh
www-data:x:33:33:www-data:/var/www:/bin/sh
backup:x:34:34:backup:/var/backups:/bin/sh
msql:x:36:36:Mini SQL Database Manager:/var/lib/msql:/bin/sh
operator:x:37:37:Operator:/var:/bin/sh
list:x:38:38:Mailing List Manager:/var/list:/bin/sh
irc:x:39:39:ircd:/var/run/ircd:/bin/sh
gnats:x:41:41:Gnats Bug-Reporting System (admin):/var/lib/gnats/gnats-db:/bin/sh
mysql:x:100:103:MySQL Server:/var/lib/mysql:/bin/false
postfix:x:102:65534:Postfix Mailsystem:/var/spool/postfix:/bin/false
knoppix:x:1000:1000:Knoppix User:/home/knoppix:/bin/bash
nobody:x:65534:65534:nobody:/nonexistent:/bin/sh
sshd:x:103:65534:SSH Server:/var/run/sshd:/bin/false
partimag:x:104:65534::/home/partimag:/bin/false
telnetd:x:101:101::/usr/lib/telnetd:/bin/false
distccd:x:105:65534::/:/bin/false
bind:x:106:108::/var/cache/bind:/bin/false
sslwrap:x:107:1001::/etc/sslwrap:/bin/false
messagebus:x:109:113::/var/run/dbus:/bin/false
fetchmail:x:110:65534::/var/run/fetchmail:/bin/sh
arpwatch:x:111:114:Arpwatch user,,,:/var/lib/arpwatch:/bin/bash
bacula:x:112:112:Bacula:/var/lib/bacula:/bin/false
saned:x:116:116::/home/saned:/bin/false
vdr:x:108:117:VDR user,,,:/var/lib/vdr:/bin/false
gsmsms:x:113:1002::/var/spool/sms:/bin/false
nx:x:114:65534::/var/lib/nxserver/home:/usr/lib/nx/nxserver
```

Each line represents a user account and contains a number of fields separated by colons. The line that starts with `knoppix` is for a human user (you, the person using Knoppix). The other lines are for system user accounts.

Take a look at one of those lines to see what the fields mean:

```
knoppix:x:1000:1000:Knoppix User:/home/knoppix:/bin/bash
```

The first field, `knoppix` in this example, is the account name. When a user logs in or is sent mail or needs to be identified in any way, this is the name that is used. The account name used to be restricted to eight characters or fewer, but modern varieties of Linux no longer have that restriction. Still, account names tend to be short if for no other reason than convenience in typing.

The second field, `x`, is used to hold the user's password. In fact, the presence of passwords is the reason the user database file is called `/etc/passwd`. But nowadays, you'll just find an `x` in this field. Being able to read `/etc/passwd` is essential for any program that needs to convert usernames to UIDs and back again, but only a few programs need to know a user's password. Although the passwords were encrypted, it was too easy for malicious hackers to get passwords and attempt to crack them at their leisure. So now, passwords are kept in a separate file, `/etc/shadow`, which has more restricted access, whereas `/etc/passwd` remains available to all programs.

The third field contains the account's UID (`1000` in this example). It's this number that Linux uses internally to keep track of users. System accounts by convention have UIDs under 1000 (or 500 on some distributions.) The special user `nobody` has the highest possible UID, 65534. Any accounts created for real people will have UIDs in between those numbers. There is one more, special UID, 0, whose significance is explained later in this chapter.

Users can also be organized into groups. Every user belongs to at least one group, and the fourth field is the name of the user's primary group.

The fifth field (`Knoppix User` in this example) is known for historical reasons as the GECOS (from the General Electric Comprehensive Operating System) field. It contains the account holder's proper name or a description of what this field does in the case of system accounts. This field is also often used to hold such contact information as office location, telephone number, and so on. If such information is included, a comma is used to separate the subfields.

The sixth field (`home/knoppix`) is the account's home directory. When the account logs in, this is the place where it will start. For daemons, the home directory is either the location of their public data or some out-of-the-way directory where a break-in will not result in any important files being accessed.

The seventh and last field (`bin/bash`) is the account's shell. When the account logs in, this program runs first. Most accounts use an interactive shell such as `bash` (see Chapter 11), but any program can be the shell. This is useful for accounts that have a restricted purpose. For instance, if you want to give your friend access to your computer so he can check his e-mail, but you don't want him to have the full power and responsibility of a Linux account, you could make an account for him with an e-mail program as the shell. When he logs in, he would automatically be placed in the e-mail program. When he has finished checking his e-mail and exits the e-mail program, he will automatically be logged out.

Groups

You may want to give access to a particular system resource to only a subset of the users on the system. Take the example of a tape storage drive: You might want to give more than one person the responsibility of backing up the system to tape, but you don't want just anybody to be able to mess with this highly important task, so you arrange to make access to the tape drive possible only by accounts in the `tape` group. Or you may have several users working on a project together who need to share documents with each other but don't want other users to pry. You can create a group just for them and make their files unreadable to others.

Note

When you create a user account, a group with the same name is created for it by default with the new user as its only member. The user can use this group to share files with others by adding and removing users from the group as she see fit and changing ownership of the files she wants to share so group members can read and write them.

The group database: /etc/group

Like the user database, the group database can be stored in several ways; typically, however, it is kept in a file called /etc/group. This is the /etc/group file on Knoppix. (As with /etc/passwd, it will look slightly different in other distributions.)

```
root:x:0:
daemon:x:1:
bin:x:2:
sys:x:3:
adm:x:4:
tty:x:5:
disk:x:6:backup
lp:x:7:lp
mail:x:8:
news:x:9:
uucp:x:10:
proxy:x:13:
kmem:x:15:
dialout:x:20:knoppix,gsmsms
fax:x:21:knoppix
voice:x:22:knoppix
cdrom:x:24:knoppix,vdr
floppy:x:25:knoppix
tape:x:26:knoppix,backup,bacula
sudo:x:27:knoppix
audio:x:29:knoppix
dip:x:30:knoppix
majordom:x:31:majordom
postgres:x:32:
```

```
www-data:x:33:
backup:x:34:
msql:x:36:
operator:x:37:
list:x:38:
irc:x:39:
src:x:40:
gnats:x:41:
shadow:x:42:
utmp:x:43:telnetd
video:x:44:knoppix,vdr
staff:x:50:
games:x:60:knoppix
users:x:100:knoppix
lpadmin:x:102:
mysql:x:103:
postfix:x:104:
postdrop:x:105:
usb:x:106:knoppix
knoppix:x:1000:
nogroup:x:65534:
partimag:x:107:
sasl:*:45:
telnetd:x:101:
man:*:12:
bind:x:108:
ssh:x:109:
sslwrap:x:1001:
scanner:x:110:knoppix
crontab:x:111:
messagebus:x:113:
arpwatch:x:114:arpwatch
bacula:x:112:
camera:x:115:knoppix
saned:x:116:
plugdev:*:46:
vdr:x:117:
gsmsms:x:1002:
fuse:x:118:knoppix
```

As with the user database, each line of /etc/group is made up of fields separated by colons. This is a typical line:

```
scanner:x:110:knoppix
```

The first field is the group name. The second field used to be for group passwords stored in encrypted form. These are rarely used now, but if you want to add an extra layer of security when a user changes groups (as explained later in the chapter) you can use this feature. Like user passwords, group passwords have now been moved into their own file, /etc/gshadow, and all you will see here is an x. If the field is completely empty, it means no password is needed to change to this group.

The third field is the group's GID. Linux uses this number internally to refer to groups. As with UIDs, GIDs below 1000 (or 500 in some distributions) by convention refer to system groups.

The last field is a comma-separated list of users who belong to a group. In this case, only user knoppix is a member of the scanner group. If there were a scanner attached to the PC, only he would be able to access it. Needless to say, one user can be the member of several groups, though only one — the one mentioned in field four of the user's /etc/passwd entry — is considered the user's primary group.

Storing User and Group IDs

The text files /etc/passwd and /etc/group are the usual way account and group information are stored, but text files are not always the best choice, so you may want an alternative.

If you have a lot of users and groups, the files can get very large. As each database has to be read in full every time UID or GID information is needed, this can slow down the system's performance. In such cases it might be better to use a full-blown database server like MySQL or Oracle that is optimized for fast random access.

If you have a network of many machines and want to give a user access to all of them, it is a pain to have to edit files on each system and keep them in sync whenever an account or group is added, removed, or changed in some way. In that scenario, it would be easier to look up the information in a master directory server implementing a protocol such as NIS (Network Information Services) or LDAP (Lightweight Directory Access Protocol).

Linux supports these and other lookup methods in a way that is transparent to programs, but implementing them is beyond the scope of this book, and the default method is adequate for most users anyway.

However, because there is a chance that user and group databases on your system could be coming from some alternative source, you should not use commands such as cat or less to examine /etc/passwd or /etc/group when you want database information. Instead, use the getent command as follows:

```
$ getent passwd
$ getent group
```

getent is smart enough to get the information from the right place.

The Superuser

As mentioned previously, UID 0 is special. This account is known as the *superuser account,* and it has the power to override any other user or group restrictions. Because of this feature, it is the account that is used for systems administration tasks such as installing and removing software, stopping and starting the system, and every other job that requires powers beyond that of a standard user. The superuser is traditionally named `root`, so you will also hear it referred to as the *root account.* There is nothing special about the name `root`. You could name the superuser account `notroot` and it would still be the superuser account. Or you could create a new account called `root` with UID 8192. It still wouldn't be a superuser. (And you would run into trouble creating it if your real superuser account is also named `root`, as you cannot have two accounts with the same name.) Only assigning a UID of 0 makes an account a superuser account.

The unbound power of the root account makes it very dangerous. One runaway command executed as `root` could damage the system beyond repair. If access to the root account gets into the wrong hands, the system is wide open and defenseless against any nefarious purpose. (Being hijacked in this way is referred to as *getting rooted.*)

Needless to say, as few users as possible should be able to use the root account. Even those who can use it should not do so for mundane activities such as compiling programs, reading e-mail, or surfing the Web. Rather, they should have a separate user account for those types of things and switch to the superuser account only when performing essential administration tasks.

Cross-Reference

See Chapter 13 for more information on the superuser.

Administering Users and Groups Graphically

Now that you understand the basics of users and groups, you may want to add some to your system. With the exception of live CDs like Knoppix, which come preconfigured, all Linux distributions will set up at least the root account during installation. Figure 6-1 shows a screen from the Fedora Core 4 installer. Because most of the features of the root account such as the name, user and group IDs, and home directories are standardized, the only information the installer needs from you is a password (which you have to enter twice to guard against typos).

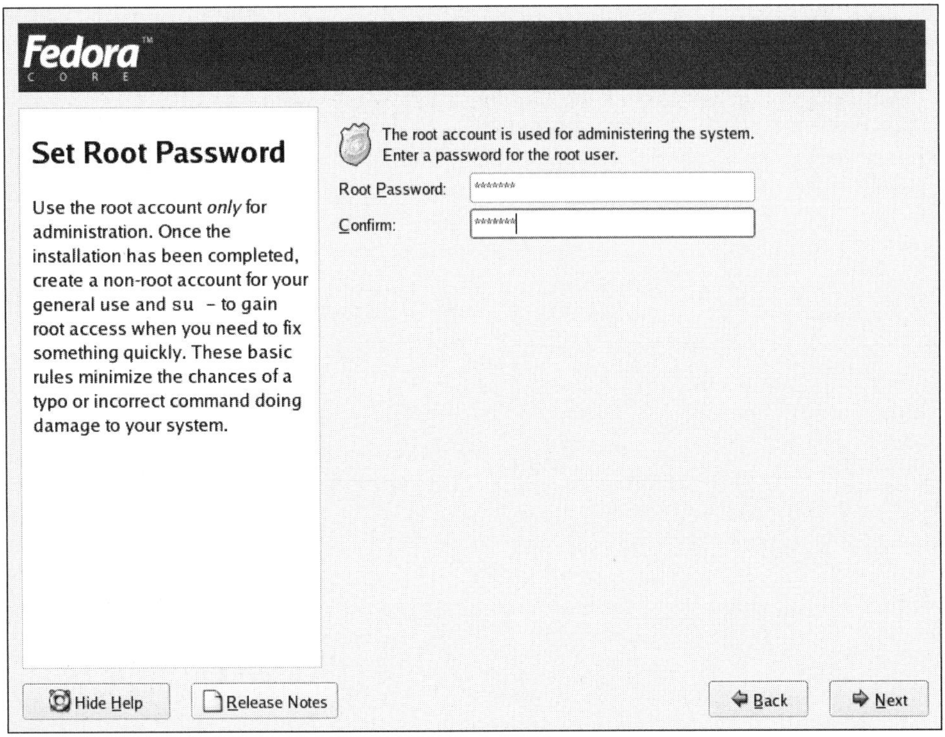

Fedora™
CORE

Set Root Password

Use the root account *only* for administration. Once the installation has been completed, create a non-root account for your general use and su – to gain root access when you need to fix something quickly. These basic rules minimize the chances of a typo or incorrect command doing damage to your system.

The root account is used for administering the system. Enter a password for the root user.

Root Password: *******

Confirm: *******

Hide Help   Release Notes   Back   Next

Figure 6-1: Setting the root account password during the installation of Fedora Core 4.

Some distributions also let you create one or more user accounts during installation. Fedora Core 4 doesn't, but you can easily do it after installation with the `system-config-users` program. You can run this program either from the command line or from the GNOME menus; select Desktop → System Settings → Users & Groups. You will see a screen that looks like Figure 6-2.

Figure 6-2: The system-config-users program.

There are two tabs, one that lists user accounts and one that lists groups. You can perform the following actions, either through the menus, the toolbar buttons, or in the case of editing user or group properties, by double-clicking on the appropriate line in the user or group tabs:

- **Add User:** This creates a new user or group on your system. Figure 6-3 shows the Create New User dialog. You enter a username, the user's real first and last names, and an initial password. If the Create home directory box is checked, the program creates a home folder for the new user. Clicking on the Home Directory text box provides a default location for this folder, or you can type in your own. If the Create a private group for the user box is checked, as it is by default, a new group is created with the same name as the new user and with the new user as its only member. As mentioned earlier, this group can be used to implement file sharing with other users. If this box is unchecked, the new user's primary group becomes Users. You may have noticed that on Fedora user accounts start from user ID 500; whereas on Knoppix, they start from 1000. As mentioned, different Linux distributions have different policies on this subject. If you want to assign a particular user ID, perhaps because you have your own numbering scheme, check the Specify user ID manually box and enter the user ID into the text box marked UID. Press OK when you are done and the new user is created.

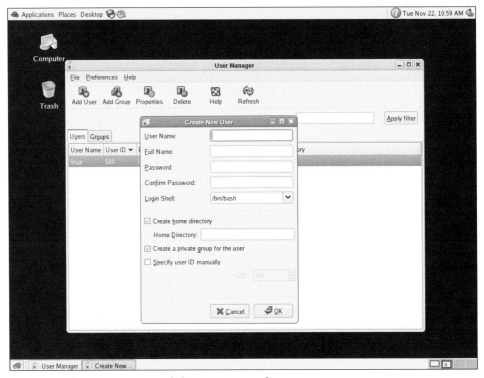

Figure 6-3: The Create New User dialog in system-config-users.

- **Add Group:** Adding a new group is similar to adding a new user account but even easier as there are not as many options in the Create New Group dialog.

- **Properties:** Here you can edit an existing user or group. The dialog for editing the properties of a user gives you some extra options for account and password info, which are unlikely to be of interest to home users. The user can also be added to additional groups in this dialog. The dialog for editing group properties lets you change the name of the group and also lets you add extra users to the group.

- **Delete:** Highlighting a line in the users or groups tabs and selecting the delete option removes that user or group from the system. Files and folders belonging to that user or group will not be deleted unless you specifically request it.

- **Help:** Some basic help on using the program is provided via your Web browser.

- **Refresh:** Use this operation to rescan the lists of users and groups so they reflect the latest changes.

Note

Note

By default, you can create and edit real users and groups only, not system users and groups. You can change this behavior from the Preferences menu, but make sure you know what you are doing if you edit system users or groups because you may render part or all of your system unusable.

One last feature of the `system-config-users` program I should mention is the search filter. On large systems with hundreds or even thousands of users and groups, it can get very cumbersome trying to search for the one you want to edit. By typing a few letters and then clicking the Apply Search Filter button, the list in the tab will be reduced to only those entries that start with the search string.

While this graphical administration tool will probably suffice for the majority of your user and group management needs, it is also useful to know how to perform the same tasks from the command line, as explained in later sections of this chapter.

Determining Your Account Information

If you want to know your UID, GID, and which groups you belong to, you can use the `id` command:

```
$ id
uid=1000 (knoppix) gid=1000(knoppix) groups=20(dialout),21(fax),22(voice),
24(cdrom), 25(floppy),26(tape),27(sudo),29(audio),30(dip),44(video),60(games),
100(users),106(usb),110(scanner),115(camera),118(fuse),1000(knoppix)
```

Note

Recall that Linux automatically creates a single-member group with the same ID and name as the user. In the preceding example, the UID and GID are both 1000 (knoppix).

You can also give `id` a username as a parameter to get similar information for that user.

If you want to know only one piece of the account information, `id` has three options, `-u`, `-g`, and `-G`, that give you the UID, GID, or groups respectively in numeric form. Adding the `-n` option gives the name instead of the number, as you can see in the following code:

```
$ id -u
1000
$ id -g
1000
$ id -G
```

```
20 21 22 24 25 26 27 29 30 44 60 100 106 110 115 118 1000
$ id -un
knoppix
$ id -gn
knoppix
$ id -Gn
dialout fax voice cdrom floppy tape sudo audio dip video games users
usb scanner camera fuse knoppix
```

Switching Users with the su Command

As mentioned previously, installing new software on the system is an example of the kind of task that can be performed by the superuser only. You can switch from your normal user account to the superuser account using the su (for *superuser*) command. (Actually, you can su to switch to any user account if you know the password for that account; see Chapter 13 for more details.) Basic usage of su is simple:

```
$ su
Password:
```

When you run su, you are asked for root's password and if you enter it successfully, you are now the superuser. You can confirm that your identity has changed with the id command:

```
# id
uid=0(root) gid=0(root) groups=0(root)
```

Note how the prompt has changed from a dollar sign ($) to a hash mark character (#) as a visual reminder you are in a special role. As soon as you are finished installing the new software, you can type exit to return to your former identity.

Becoming another user is just as easy. If there is an account on the system called linus, you can become it simply by running

```
$ su linus
```

and entering linus's password. (The all-powerful superuser can become any user without having to know the appropriate password.)

Cross-Reference

Chapter 13 covers the su command and related topics in more detail.

Passwords

When you are using a live CD like Knoppix, you can get away with not having a password on your account as nothing gets saved on the CD and everything is reset when you reboot. But if you install Linux on your hard drive, it would be suicidal to leave your account unprotected by a password and even more so for the root account. During the installation process of most distributions, you are prompted to pick a password for root and any user accounts you create but you can also add, remove, and change passwords after installation with a program called passwd.

Changing your own password and account information

Normal users can change their own passwords only. Here's how a user logged in as linus would change his password to yogurt:

```
$ passwd
Changing password for linus
(current) UNIX password:
```

After entering the old password, the following prompts appear. (If the account previously had no password, this step is skipped.)

```
Enter new UNIX password:
Retype new UNIX password:
```

Now linus enters yogurt. The program requests he enter it twice as a precaution against typos. But the passwd program rejects yogurt:

```
Bad: new password is too simple
```

Oh no! What happened? Depending on the system administrator's policy, the passwd program may check the new password to see if it is strong enough. (system-config-users does the same check.) Simple dictionary words like *yogurt* are considered weak passwords because they are easy to guess. (See the "Choosing Good Passwords" section later in the chapter.) For now, linus decides to use yo-plait instead.

```
Enter new UNIX password:
Retype new UNIX password:
```

Again, he has to type the new password twice.

```
passwd: password updated successfully
```

It seems passwd has no objections to yo-plait, so the password is changed.

Earlier, I mentioned that the GECOS field of /etc/passwd can be subdivided into comma-separated fields to hold contact information. You can change this information with the -f option to passwd. Here's how linus might change his GECOS information:

```
$ passwd -f
Password:
Changing the user information for linus
Enter the new value, or press ENTER for the default
        Full Name:  Linus Torvalds
        Room Number []: 101
        Work Phone []: (212) 555-1212
        Home Phone []: (123) 456-7890
```

No error checking is done; you can put anything in this field. The line for the linus account in /etc/passwd might now look something like this (and should appear all on one line):

```
linus:x:1001:1001:Linus Torvalds,101,(212) 555-1212,(123)
456-7890:/home/linus:/bin/bash
```

Administering passwords and account information as root

The superuser can change passwords and other account information for any user simply by adding the username as the last parameter to one of the forms shown in the previous section. If he runs passwd without specifying a username, passwd changes his own account. passwd bypasses all security checks for root, so extra vigilance for typos, weak passwords, and the like is essential. The superuser can also manipulate passwords in special ways. For example, the -d option to passwd deletes the password from the named account entirely:

```
# passwd -d linus
```

After running this command, anyone can log in as user linus without challenge. As you can imagine, this is very dangerous and should be used only when you are sure the user will be promptly setting a new password. If you want to force a user to change passwords, it is usually a better idea to use the -e option to expire the password:

```
# passwd -e linus
```

After this command is run, the password for linus becomes invalid, and the next time he tries to log in he will be prompted to select a new one.

If you want to temporarily lock out a user (perhaps he is going on vacation or hasn't paid his Internet bill), you can use the -l option to passwd:

```
# passwd -l linus
```

Now linus will not be able to log in until you use the -u option to unlock the account again.

```
# passwd -u linus
```

The passwd command has several other options a system administrator can employ to control password usage, but they are not likely to be very useful to the home user. If you are interested, look at the manual page for the passwd command (type man passwd).

Note

The system-config-users command allows you to set password usage options in a graphical way.

Group passwords

I mentioned that groups can have passwords, though they rarely do. The gpasswd command manipulates group passwords. This command can be used by root or she can use the -A option to designate this power to group administrators. For example, the following command makes user knoppix an administrator of the users group.

```
# gpasswd -A knoppix users
```

Now knoppix (or root) can use the commands in Table 6-1 to control passwords for the users group.

Table 6-1   Example gpasswd Commands

Command	Usage
gpasswd users	Set or change the group password.
gpasswd -r users	Remove the group's password.
gpasswd -a linus users	Add user linus to the users group.
gpasswd -d linus users	Remove user linus from the users group.

Choosing good passwords

Selecting an easy-to-guess or weak password can render the most intricate security schemes useless. If you are a home user, you might wonder whether strong passwords are really important. Well, even if no one save yourself ever sits down at your keyboard, chances are you have an Internet connection, and if you do, the whole world is potentially a user of your system. Apart from the technical merits of the operating system, one reason Linux users are relatively immune to the hacking attempts that plague Windows users is that historically they have been more aware of good password practices and other security measures. Don't put yourself and the good name of Linux at risk by being sloppy and making it easy to get hacked.

Here are some examples of what are universally considered to be bad passwords:

- Words that can be found in a dictionary, like `yogurt` in the earlier example. Hackers use large electronic dictionaries to attempt to guess passwords.

- Words from foreign languages. The hackers have dictionaries for those too. Even esoteric languages.

- Personal information such as telephone or social security numbers, your login name, names of family members, and other personal information. (Try searching your name on a search engine like Google sometime. You'd be surprised how much personal information is publicly available on the Internet.)

- Names of fictional characters or other cultural references (especially names from Tolkien books or *Star Trek*).

All these passwords could easily be discovered by a hacker.

The more random a password is, the harder it is for a hacker to guess it. Here are some criteria for strong passwords:

- It should be at least six characters long. It can be more, but the longer a password gets, the harder it gets to remember and type correctly.

- It should contain a mix of upper- and lowercase letters, numbers, and nonalphabetic characters.

- It should be memorable enough that its owner can type it quickly, lessening the chance someone is observing you type it.

The problem is that a password that is very hard to crack will also likely be hard to remember. This could tempt you to write the password down somewhere, which in turn can lead to it being stolen or left where it can be read by strangers. Here are some strategies often used for making a password easier to remember without reducing its strength:

- Making it up from the first (or last or third) letter in each word of a phrase. For example, the first letters of "Sing Muse of the wrath of Achilles" results in `SMotwoA`.

- Combine two words alternating a character from each word. For example, "apple" and "grape" combined make `agprpalpee`.

- Combine two words, separating them by some punctuation or digits. For example, `foot?Gold`.

You can probably think of other combination schemes along these lines.

Another way to enhance security is to change your password on a regular basis, say, once a month. This can be a problem because some users find this task onerous, and when security becomes a burden, it often falls by the wayside. But if you recognize and accept the value of security, changing passwords regularly is a very good measure.

Summary

Even on a system used by a single person, there are multiple user and group accounts. Linux maintains an internal representation of these accounts but has features that allow people to deal with them in a more human-friendly way. User and group information is usually stored in text files in the /etc directory, but alternative lookup methods are also available.

The superuser or root is an account that has privileges other users do not. It is possible to switch user and group identities. Some programs can run as a specific user or group identity regardless of the identity of whoever started them. Users can change their passwords and other personal account information, and root can do this for any account. Picking a good password that is hard to guess but easy to remember is very important for the security of your system.

Chapter 7

Setting Network Information

Networked computers seem like less of a luxury and more of a necessity nowadays. Just 10 years ago, it was somewhat rare to have a network unless you worked in a large company, but these days it is just as rare not to be connected to a network. Many people have networks at home that combine wired and wireless connections. A networked world is just a fact of contemporary life.

Understanding your network situation is becoming as much a required skill as being able to operate and program your DVD player or cellphone. Attaching a Linux computer to a network is fairly straightforward. You don't have to be a networking expert to be able to connect to and use a network with Linux; Linux was born on the Internet and networking is part of its very essence. You can certainly use Linux without ever being connected to any kind of network, but like any Unix-type computer, its strengths are apparent when networked.

Windows and Linux both speak the same network language, called TCP/IP (Transmission Control Protocol/Internet Protocol). The setup of network information is also very similar. Linux developers know that the majority of users come from a Windows world; they have made a concerted effort to ensure that the graphical elements and navigation to the tools are intuitive and familiar.

This chapter shows you how to configure your network information automatically and manually during installation. Chapter 19 illustrates how to set and adjust network information after installation. You also learn how to configure your Linux computer for cable/DSL access, LAN access, and even dial-up access via modem after installation. The chapter begins with an introduction to networking terminology and then segues into a how-to section on the various types of network settings for your specific needs.

Networking Fundamentals

The following sections offer a quick primer on the basic terms and components of networking.

Routers and gateways

A *router* is a computer or piece of special equipment that provides a gateway from your LAN to other networks and/or the Internet. In network configurations, you may see your network router referred to as *default gateway, gateway, router,* or *default router.* You can think of a router or gateway with the following analogy: You and several other people are in a room together (your LAN), and you have only one door in the room. That door is your gateway to the rest of the world. You can communicate within the room, but any messages or communications that you or anyone else in the room sends out or receives must go through that gateway.

The type of router or gateway you have on your network is really not that important; you need to know only the IP address of its LAN interface. The IP address of each device on the network is unique but must be related to the IP address of the LAN interface, as explained in the following section.

Understanding IP addresses

You don't need to understand the mysteries of IP addresses if you configure your network settings dynamically. However, if you need to manually configure your network settings, it will help if you understand your LAN's IP addressing scheme.

Note

Chapter 19 provides a more extensive explanation of TCP/IP and IP addresses. If you want to know even more about TCP/IP, pick up a copy of *TCP/IP For Dummies, 5th Edition* (Wiley Publishing, 2003). It is a great book for explaining the entire TCP/IP suite of protocols, their functions, and how everything fits together.

You can think of IP numbers or addresses as being similar to a telephone number for a device, such as a printer or desktop computer. Like telephone numbers, no two can be the same, at least on the same network. For example, everyone knows that the number for information within any area code is the area code plus 555-1212. For each area code, you have the same phone number, but the area codes are different. The Internet works the same way. You may, at some point, realize that at your home or office, your workstation has an IP address of 192.168.0.15 and your friend has the same IP address at her office. Continuing with the telephone analogy, your friend has a different area code in her office. She has a router with a *unique* IP address, and all of the IP addresses within her office are seen as that one IP address as far as the Internet is concerned. Inside her network, however, the IP address for each device has to be unique. Her computer is the only one on her network that can have the IP address of 192.168.0.15. Likewise, yours is the only one on *your* network that can have that particular IP address.

The IP address in this example, 192.168.0.15, is a typical IP address. The dots within the address separate the numbers based on their functions. 192 is the class number. A *class* is a defined range of IP addresses. 192 is included in what is known as the Class C address space range. Certain addresses were set aside by the Internet Network Information Center (InterNIC) and reserved for private use only. The InterNIC was the original controller of Internet domain names and IP addresses. The 192.168 part of the address tells you that this address is a private address in the Class C range, not for use on the Internet but only for transmitting messages within the LAN.

The number following the second dot, 0 in this example, is called the *subnet address*. The subnet address for each device on your network has to match your gateway's subnet address. For instance, if you put an IP address of 192.168.0.15 on your workstation, but your router (default gateway) has an address of 192.168.1.254, your IP address will not work. You would have to assign 192.168.1.15 for your workstation to successfully connect to your network's resources and the Internet through your gateway. The fourth number in the address (15 in the example) is the host address that uniquely identifies your workstation for your subnet.

DNS settings

DNS (domain name service) is how computers find each other on the Internet. It is a phone book of sorts where IP addresses are *mapped* to computer names, just as your name and address are associated with your phone number. Your Internet provider will give you two or three IP addresses that you can use for configuring your network manually. With those numbers entered, your network configuration is complete. You should now be able to open your favorite Internet browser application, type in www.wiley.com, and your favorite book publisher's site will magically appear in the browser window.

This works because your Web browser sends a DNS request for www.wiley.com. The IP address for www.wiley.com is found, and the information you requested is returned to your Web browser. Once the Web browser has this IP address, it sends an HTTP request for the Web page to the server attached to the IP address returned from DNS.

Manual versus dynamic settings

This chapter includes examples of manual settings for static addresses, and automatic network settings for your dynamic LAN and Internet connections. Entering static network information (that is, IP addresses that don't change over time) is a manual process, while choosing to have your network information automatically configured yields dynamic results. That is to say, that if your settings are dynamic, they will change periodically. There are advantages and disadvantages of both types. For workstations, dynamic settings seem to be the most appropriate because of the ease of setup and low maintenance involved in their use. Most ISPs use dynamic settings to alleviate support calls associated with setup. Dynamic network configuration requires that a Dynamic Host Configuration Protocol (DHCP) server exists on the network that you connect to. This service must be set up and maintained by you, your network administrator, or your ISP. Many inexpensive routers for home and small office use come equipped with DHCP services installed and enabled by default. A DHCP service is a server that hands out network information when requested by a client (a computer or other network-connected device). This information usually includes the IP address, gateway address, DNS addresses, and host name. The DHCP server supplies all of the information to the client that it needs to be able to connect to network resources and the Internet, if available.

Manual or statically configured settings are often used in network configurations for servers, printers, routers, and other networking equipment. Some network administrators manually set up all computers with static network information to enable remote administration. Manual settings require intervention, recordkeeping, and maintenance but make remote administration and static services available in a very convenient fashion. Using manual settings for network components like workstations and printers make administration easier because the LAN administrator can map out the network and all of its components. This makes for a very reliable and stable situation for the administrator. The downside of this situation is that the administrator will not be able to *hotplug* a new piece of network hardware into the LAN. She will have to issue the new device a static IP address manually. This is time-consuming on the front end of administration, but in the long run locating the device on the network will be easier.

Note

If you are adding a computer to a company network, your network administrator will probably take care of these settings in accordance with company policy. These instructions are provided to you for connecting a computer at home or in your office where you are the designated administrator.

Connecting to the Internet

Whether you are connecting one computer directly to the Internet or adding a machine to a network of desktop computers, printers, and server, Linux provides tools to make connecting relatively easy. The following sections lead you through the setup process for direct connections and connections via a local access network.

Note

If you don't already have an agreement with an Internet Service Provider (ISP) or are not part of an existing network, you'll need to establish service with an ISP in your area to get an IP address before you can connect to the outside world.

Connecting to a local area network

LAN is the acronym for local area network, which refers to the computers, cables (wires), hubs, switches, patch panels, and network interface cards that are connected to form a closed data loop. The term *local* can mean a network in a home, small office, a 50-story high-rise office complex, or a college campus. We typically think of a LAN as being something very small and limited in scope, but LANs can service thousands of users. Just because a network spans several buildings does not mean that it is not a LAN.

Note

In contrast to a LAN, a *WAN*, or wide area network, refers to two or more LANs that are connected via a high-speed communications link like a T1. A T1 is a telephone company virtual service line that, in this case, is used to connect two LANs together over great distances. The line is *virtual* in the sense that it is not a single wire connected to the LANs on each end, but rather a series of connections made through the telephone company's array of switches and routers.

The Network Interface Card

If your computer does not have a network interface card (NIC), don't worry. Locating a Linux-compatible NIC is very easy. Any office supply store, discount store, or online store will have what you need. Look for the term NE2000-compatible or simply choose a NIC with a recognizable brand name such as Netgear, Linksys, 3Com, or Intel. The NIC should come with instructions for physically installing the card in your computer.

To connect your computer to a LAN, you need three things: a network interface card (NIC), a patch cable, and an IP address. Most new computers come with a NIC already installed. I am assuming for this chapter that you have a NIC and a network to plug into. Unless you are connecting to a wireless network, you will need a cable, sometimes referred to as a *patch cable*, to connect your NIC to an outlet either in a wall or a hub or switch. This cable can be purchased at office supply stores, computer stores, and even large discount stores. Once you are physically connected to the network, you still have to use communications software so that your computer can talk to other computers on the network and the Internet.

CONNECTING AUTOMATICALLY

The instructions in this section lead you through the network setup as if you were setting it up for the first time while installing Linux. (Chapter 19 explains how to set your network information if you have already installed Linux.) The instructions in the following section show you how to manually enter the necessary network information during the installation process.

Figure 7-1 shows the screen that appears during installation for setting up network information automatically.

Note

The figures and instructions in this chapter reflect Fedora Core 4, but the dialogs for other distributions should appear very similar to the ones provided.

The default choices are all you need to continue with automatic network settings. Click Next to continue.

Figure 7-2 shows the next network information screen, asking if you want to enable a firewall. Use the default settings, Enable firewall and using SE Linux (Security Enhanced).

Fedora™
C O R E

Network Configuration

Any network devices you have on the system are automatically detected by the installation program and shown in the **Network Devices** list.

To configure the network device, first select the device and then click **Edit**. In the **Edit Interface** screen, you can choose to have the IP and Netmask information configured by DHCP or you can enter it manually. You can also choose to make the device active at boot time.

If you do not have DHCP client access or are unsure as to

Network Devices

Active on Boot	Device	IP/Netmask
☑	eth0	DHCP

Edit

Hostname

Set the hostname:
◉ automatically via DHCP

○ manually [   ] (ex. "host.domain.com")

Miscellaneous Settings

Gateway:
Primary DNS:
Secondary DNS:
Tertiary DNS:

[Hide Help] [Release Notes]   ◀ Back   ▶ Next

Figure 7-1: Network configuration screen showing automatic network configuration.

Take a look at Chapter 20 for more information on customizing your security settings. Your automatic network configuration is now complete.

MANUAL NETWORK CONFIGURATION

Now take a look at a *static* network configuration. Figure 7-3 shows how to set static network information for your IP address and netmask during installation. These settings need to match your current network settings. To find similar settings for your network, go to a computer running Microsoft Windows and select Start → Run. In the command-prompt window that opens, type **ipconfig** and press Enter and the network settings will be displayed for you. They will look similar to the following.

```
Windows IP Configuration

Ethernet adapter Local Area Connection:

   Connection-specific DNS Suffix  . :
   IP Address. . . . . . . . . . . . : 192.168.0.30
   Subnet Mask . . . . . . . . . . . : 255.255.255.0
   Default Gateway . . . . . . . . . : 192.168.0.254
```

Fedora
C O R E

Firewall Configuration

A firewall sits between your computer and the network, and determines which resources on your computer remote users on the network are able to access. A properly configured firewall can greatly increase the out-of-the-box security of your system.

Choose the appropriate security level for your system.

No Firewall — No firewall provides complete access to your system and does no security checking. Security checking is the disabling of access to certain services. This

A firewall can help prevent unauthorized access to your computer from the outside world. Would you like to enable a firewall?

○ No firewall
◉ Enable firewall

You can use a firewall to allow access to specific services on your computer from other computers. Which services, if any, do you wish to allow access to ?

☐ Remote Login (SSH)
☐ Web Server (HTTP, HTTPS)
☐ File Transfer (FTP)
☐ Mail Server (SMTP)

Security Enhanced Linux (SELinux) provides finer-grained security controls than those available in a traditional Linux system. It can be set up in a disabled state, a state which only warns about things which would be denied, or a fully active state.

Enable SELinux?: [Active ▾]

[⊘ Hide Help]   [🗋 Release Notes]   [⇐ Back]   [⇒ Next]

Figure 7-2: Firewall configuration screen.

With these numbers, you can fill in your own network settings. On this screen, uncheck the Active on Boot box and then click Edit. The Edit Interface eth0 dialog box shown in Figure 7-3 appears for you to fill in your network configuration numbers.

Note

If there are no Windows computers (or network administrator) on your network from which to gather and compare network settings, use the automatic settings shown in Figure 7-3.

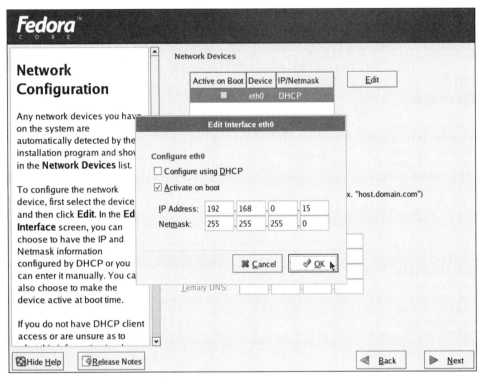

Figure 7-3: Manual network configuration settings.

Uncheck the Configure using DHCP box, but leave the Activate on boot box checked. Fill in your information and click OK. You can now enter the rest of the information as shown in Figure 7-4.

The gateway number above is the same as the default gateway number from your Windows computer. The only number in this group that must be different is the IP address that you entered in Figure 7-3. The primary DNS and secondary DNS numbers should be supplied to you by your ISP or your network administrator. The numbers shown in Figure 7-4 are public DNS server numbers. (DNS is briefly explained earlier in this chapter and is covered in greater detail in Chapter 19.) Your network configuration is now complete and you may continue your installation.

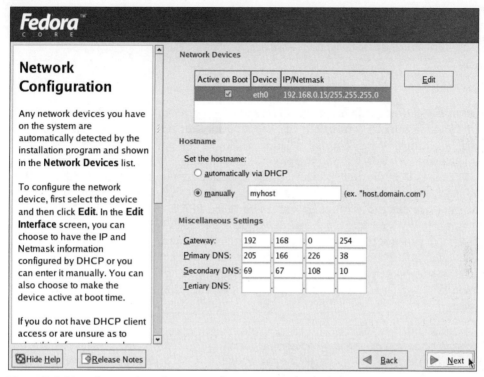

Figure 7-4: Manual network configuration information complete.

Direct Internet connections

By *direct Internet connection,* I'm referring to the typical setup for a home user connecting one machine directly to the Internet via digital subscriber line (DSL) or a cable modem. Broadband connections such as DSL and cable are very simple to set up as a direct connection to a Linux computer. You need an active working connection to either a DSL or a cable Internet provider, a broadband modem, a patch cable, and your computer with an installed network interface card (NIC). You should have an instruction manual, replete with graphics, to show you how to connect your DSL/cable modem to your computer physically. Those instructions are operating-system independent, so they should guide you through connecting your Linux machine just fine. A word of caution here: You may be on your own setting up your Linux computer for DSL/cable access because few, if any, communications-support personnel can or will assist you, so pay close attention to this and Chapter 19.

Note

If you are using a dial-up connection rather than broadband, refer to the "Dial-up connections" section later in this chapter.

The kind of service you are connecting to will determine, in part, how much effort you will have to put forth to get an Internet connection with DSL or cable. For my particular setup (cable), the process was very simple. When I installed Linux, I allowed the automatic assignment of an IP address to my computer via DHCP and the process was complete. I was online immediately upon getting an IP address from the cable provider. This is the simplest case and really no different than the LAN connection in the previous section. More often, especially for DSL connections, you will be configuring your computer to connect by something called PPPoE (Point to Point Protocol over Ethernet). This is really just a fancy, high-speed, dial-up connection. The modem connection is still going to give you a dynamic IP address but requires a username and password given to you by your provider. Setting up a DSL connection is not difficult, but it does require a different setup.

Open the Internet Configuration Wizard by clicking Applications → System Tools → Internet Configuration Wizard. Figure 7-5 shows the dialog box that appears. Select xDSL connection and click Forward.

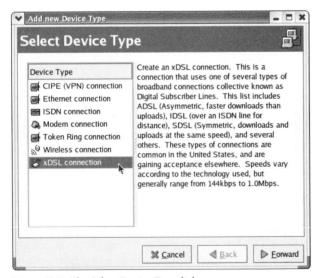

Figure 7-5: The Select Device Type dialog.

Note

Notice that there is also an Integrated Services Digital Network (ISDN) connection choice on this dialog. xDSL also refers to IDSL or ISDN with an external modem. If you have an ISDN line with an external modem that you connect to with a patch cable, use the selected dialog. If your ISDN modem is connected internally to your computer or externally with a serial cable, use the ISDN connection dialog.

Figure 7-6 shows the dialog to configure your machine to connect to your ISP. Your ISP will provide the correct settings. Enter the required information and click Forward.

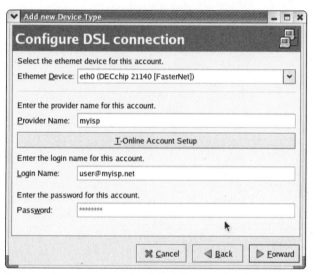

Figure 7-6: Enter your ISP-provided connection information.

Note

Do not enter any information into the T-Online Account Setup area (accessed by clicking the large button in the middle of the dialog box) unless you are instructed to do so by your ISP.

Figure 7-7 shows the confirmation dialog for your xDSL connection.

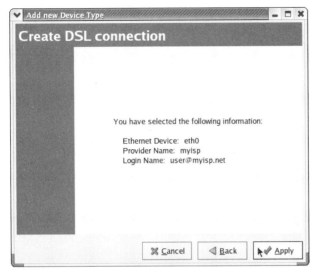

Figure 7-7: DSL connection information confirmation dialog.

Click Apply to finish with the wizard. You may have to open your Internet browser for the connection to initiate, but it will do so very quickly, and you will be connected to the Internet.

Dial-up connections

In these days of broadband, LANs, and wireless connectivity, I am surprised at the number of dial-up connections still being made. But for someone who needs Internet access only occasionally for e-mail or light browsing, this may be just the inexpensive solution you are looking for. National companies offer dial-up solutions for as little as $9.95 (or less) per month.

To connect to the Internet with your modem via dial-up, return to the Internet Configuration Wizard shown in Figure 7-5. Choose Modem connection on the Internet Configuration Wizard dialog and click Forward to begin the modem and dial-up account setup shown in Figure 7-8.

Enter your ISP's area code, phone number, provider (ISP) name, login name, and password for your dial-up account. Your ISP should provide all of this information. Ignore the country information in the left panel, unless of course, you are in one of those countries. After entering the information, click Forward to continue the setup. Figure 7-9 shows the IP Settings dialog.

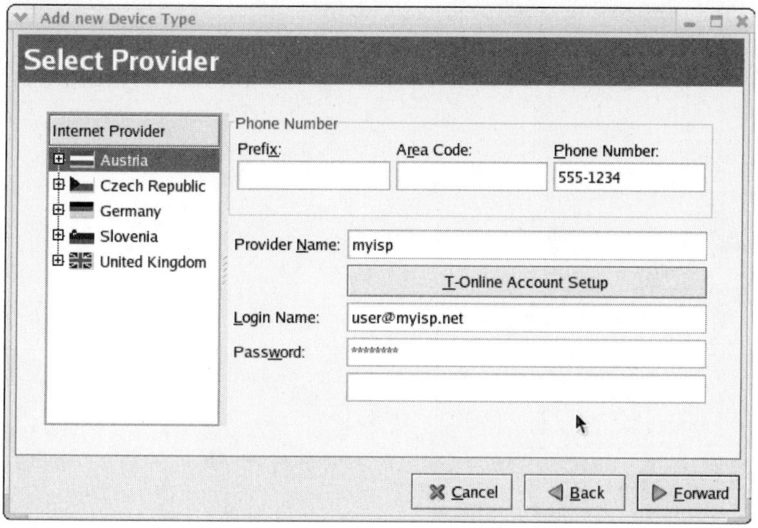

Figure 7-8: Select Provider dialog.

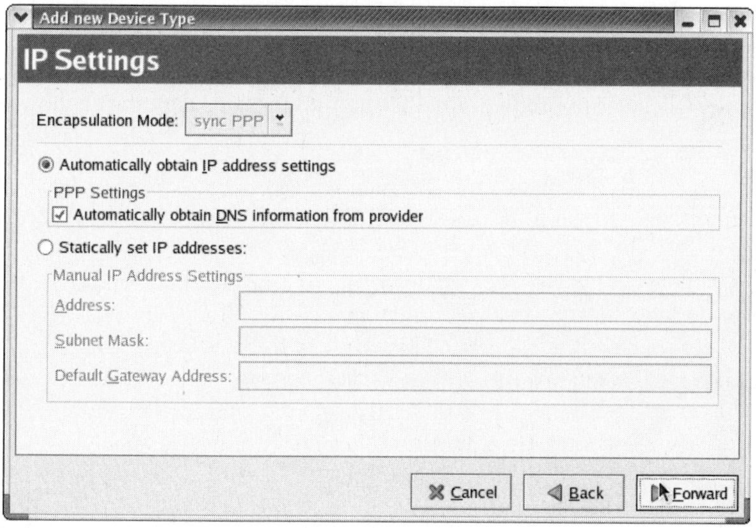

Figure 7-9: IP Settings for your dial-up account.

You should accept the defaults given in the IP Settings dialog unless your ISP tells you otherwise. The next screen asks you to confirm your entries or make changes as needed. After you confirm and apply your settings, the dialog shown in Figure 7-10 appears.

Figure 7-10: Network Configuration dialog.

In this dialog, you see that your newly created modem connection is inactive. This means that you have yet to dial the connection for the first time. Click the Activate button to save your modem connection profile and begin the account activation process. A pop-up message asks if you want to save your changes and continue. Click Yes to proceed. Another pop-up message appears, as shown in Figure 7-11.

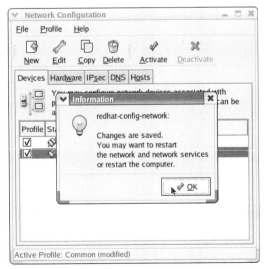

Figure 7-11: Confirmation that your modem connection profile has been saved.

Before clicking OK, make sure your modem is connected to a telephone line so that your modem can dial your ISP for confirmation of your settings. Your modem will connect, log in, and then disconnect.

Your modem setup is now complete. To use your connection, you need only to open your Internet browser, or any Internet service, and your modem automatically dials your ISP.

Wireless connections

Manual network configuration of a Fedora system is often not required. Many networks have a Dynamic Host Configuration Protocol (DHCP) service that automatically supplies connected systems with configuration data. By default, Fedora Core activates all network interfaces on your computer and configures them to use DHCP.

Wireless interfaces using DHCP join an open wireless network once it is in range. Many wireless networks are restricted and accept only those systems that have the correct security credentials. If you are setting up a wireless connection after installation, follow the steps shown previously to bring up the Select Device Type dialog and choose Wireless Connection. Step through the wizard and supply the *mode* as Ad-Hoc, *SSID* (Service Set ID), and *channel* in the appropriate blanks. Set the *transmit rate* to Auto. If your wireless network requires a WEP (Wireless Encryption Protocol) key, type it in the blank labeled Key. To find the SSID and channel, you have to ask the network administrator or, in the case of a small office/home office network, you have to use your router's Web interface to find these identifiers.

You Can Always Do It Later

All distributions of Linux allow you to set up your network configuration during the installation process, but if you don't have a NIC, aren't connected to a network, or are connected to one network and then move the computer to a different one for use, you will have to configure or reconfigure the network settings later. There are several ways to do this regardless of distribution. You have your choice of command-line tools like `ipconfig`, character-based tools such as Fedora Core/Red Hat's `setup` or `netconfig`, SUSE's `YaST2`, and Debian's `etherconf` or `netenv`, or the fully graphical tools included in GNOME or KDE, such as Network Configurator or the Internet Configuration Wizard that can be employed for network configuration. To learn how to configure, or reconfigure, your network settings at a time other than installation, please refer to Chapter 19.

Summary

Network computing has become a very important part of our everyday lives; you have to learn something about networking and how networks work to be able to use the vast resources of LANs, WANs, and the Internet. As you can see from the information in this chapter, you don't have be a network expert to be able to connect to and use a network. Whether you are connecting to a LAN or to an ISP via a DSL or cable connection or a traditional dial-up modem, you should now be comfortable doing so with Linux.

Chapter 8

Dual-Boot Installation

Dual booting is the term used to describe computer systems that can run more than one operating system (though not at the same time). This chapter explains how to configure a new or existing Windows system to also boot Linux using freely available Linux software. The only requirement for doing this is that you have sufficient space on your computer's drives to hold both operating systems and their associated applications. In addition, you'll need to have a copy of the Knoppix live CD that comes with this book and the installation CDs for the version of Linux that you've decided to install.

The Boot Process in Detail

One of the steps in installing Linux in general is configuring the Linux boot loader. This is even more important in dual-boot scenarios, as you learn in the "Installing Linux on the New Partition" section later in this chapter. First, let's explore the system boot process in a bit more detail so that you understand how a boot loader works and where it fits into the computer boot process.

As explained in Chapter 4, when you turn on your computer system, its BIOS settings specify the order in which your hard drive, CD-ROM, DVD, or other media are searched to find something that the computer can execute. The first program that the system loads is known as a *boot loader*, which is a small program that is usually stored on the first few blocks of your hard drive, bootable CD-ROM, or other bootable media. At this point, your system doesn't know anything about the geometry of your hard disks or other storage devices, but it can always find the first few blocks on any device to identify whether the drive is bootable. If so, the system loads the boot loader from that device and begins to execute it.

Once the boot loader is loaded into memory and running, it reads a configuration file located on the device that contains the boot loader and displays any available options for booting the computer system. On computer systems that run only one operating system, your boot options are straightforward and limited to ways of starting that single operating system. On systems that can boot multiple operating systems, the boot loader options are very similar but are slightly more complex, including all of the available operating systems on your computer. Instead of offering multiple ways of booting a single operating system, the options, such as they are, typically enable you just to choose among operating systems.

This sequence of executing a boot loader, which then loads and starts a more complex operating system, is known as *booting your system* because the system is performing actions that are analogous to the old expression of "pulling yourself up by your bootstraps."

Linux and Windows Together

As you learn in this chapter, it's quite easy to configure your system to run your choice of operating systems. You can easily configure your system to boot Windows when you need to read mail from your Exchange server or use Windows applications but boot Linux when you need to do more-complex, server-oriented tasks or want to explore the power of a true multitasking, multiuser operating system. Configuring a system that dual boots Windows and Linux is a great way to get familiar with Linux without having to completely give up familiar Windows applications. Once you've become friends with Linux and have learned how to do everything you need on your Linux system, you can choose to move to Linux permanently. Setting up a dual-boot system is also a great way to learn Linux if you only have one computer system and aren't willing or able to simply take the plunge and move to Linux full time.

Note

This chapter explores how to add Linux to an existing Microsoft Windows system. You can also add Windows as a second operating system on an existing Linux system, a topic outside the scope of this book.

Chapter 5 explains how and why you should create multiple partitions on your hard drive, each of which stores different parts of the files and directories that make up the Linux file system. Microsoft Windows also uses partitions but usually creates a single partition only per disk drive when you install Windows. This simplifies things but makes it tricky to add another operating system to that same computer system. You generally have two choices:

- Add another hard drive to the computer system and install Linux there.

- Change the existing partitions on your computer's hard drive to provide space in which you can create another partition, where you can then install Linux.

The first of these is usually an option in desktop computer systems, assuming that you have room inside your machine for another drive, have sufficient funds to buy another disk drive, and are dedicated and technical enough to open up your computer and add a hard drive correctly. However, if you have sufficient free space available on your system's existing drive, the second option is cheaper, faster, and easier. As discussed in Chapter 5, most full Linux installations require around 5GB of available disk space, which is sufficient space in which to install the operating system and a standard set of applications, and enough room to create and store a reasonable amount of your files and other personal data.

Changing the existing partitions on your computer system is known as *repartitioning* your system. A number of free and commercial software packages are available that make it easy to repartition existing disks. However, the first part of software is the word *soft*, which in this case means that something can go wrong, so make sure that you back up your critical Windows data before proceeding, as explained in the next section.

Note

The rest of this chapter assumes that you have only one hard drive in your computer system and therefore want to install Linux on that disk without removing your current Windows installation or files. The process is very similar if you have the funds and technical expertise to add a second disk to your system and install Linux there, except that you don't need to do any repartitioning; you just have to ensure that Linux is actually installed to the correct hard disk. In that case, you should still back up your Windows files as described in the next section — just in case — and then skip ahead to the section entitled "Installing Linux on the New Partition."

Backing Up Your Windows Data

Several free and commercial packages make it easy to repartition an existing disk drive. In 99 times out of 100, repartitioning an existing disk drive is completely safe and will not damage or lose any of the existing programs or data on your Windows partition. However, preventing the pain associated with that one remaining time is worth the effort that it takes to back up your important data before making any changes to your disk partitions. If you're tempted to skip this step and just go ahead with repartitioning, stop and think for a moment what it would be like if you lost your computer system or it was destroyed. None of the saved e-mail that you've exchanged with friends and family, none of those letters you've written, none of your digital photographs, none of your music collection, the great American novel — all gone. Are you really willing to take that chance? If so, you're braver than I am.

Explaining how to use various Microsoft Windows backup utilities is outside the scope of this book. The critical part of backing up your data is to back it up onto removable media, such as a CD-ROM, DVD, or external USB or FireWire hard disk. The key to doing backups is to write them to a device other than the one that you're backing up. Simply making a copy of important files and directories on your existing hard drive doesn't help at all if that hard drive is damaged. Make sure that you copy your important files and directories to some removable media, and then remove and reinsert or reattach it to make sure that it actually contains readable copies of your files before repartitioning the disk where they were originally stored. In most cases, you won't need them, but the one time that you do, you'll be ecstatic that you took the time to play it safe.

Depending on the software you choose and how your system is configured, you can either use a dedicated software package to back up your files or simply drag important files and directories onto your writable CD-ROM, writable DVD drive, or your external disk. However you do it, make sure that you back up any directories where you stored your important files. This is usually your My Documents folder, which may also contain folders called My Music, My Pictures, and so on, that also contain important data that you've created on your system. You may also want to examine the files on your desktop. In theory, your desktop usually contains just shortcuts to files that are actually stored in your personal folders, but many people also store working copies of their files there. You should also check the top level of your C: drive, because many people often create personal folders there and use them to organize their data. Remember, you're making backups of important data — this is no time to cut corners or do a fast job simply to get it over with.

Note

This section focuses on backing up your personal data, not critical parts of Windows itself. Locating and backing up the right Windows system files is a black art that is best left to software designed for Windows backups. If you've installed custom drivers and software on your system, you should back up any directories containing anything that you've downloaded and installed. You should also use regedit, the Windows Registry Editor, to make a backup copy of your Windows registry in case the unthinkable happens and you have to reinstall Windows.

Making Room for Linux

After you've done backups of your important files and verified that the backups are readable, it's time to move on to actually repartitioning your disk to make room for Linux. The first step in doing this is to defragment your disk, which packs the disk space associated with all of the files and directories on your Windows partition as closely together as possible. Disks become fragmented as you create and delete files. There's nothing that you can do about that except to clean things up occasionally. When you repartition your disk, you're essentially slicing off a portion of an existing partition disk so that you can use it for something else. You can't just remove a portion of an existing partition if it contains parts of files that your are using.

Disk storage on a computer is allocated in terms of *blocks*, which is just the term for the smallest chunk of space that the file system can allocate so that it can be used by a file. When you create a file on a computer system, the underlying file system that holds the file tries to allocate the blocks associated with that file together so that they can be either read or written as a unit or at least read relatively quickly. Unfortunately, over time the blocks associated with a file tend to end up spread out all over a disk partition as new blocks are allocated and old blocks are released when a file is edited, appended to, deleted, and so on. When you read a file on a computer, the computer needs to read its data in logical order, which is not necessarily the same order as the data are laid out on available blocks throughout the disk. Figures 8-1 and 8-2 show how allocation works and how fragmentation occurs over time.

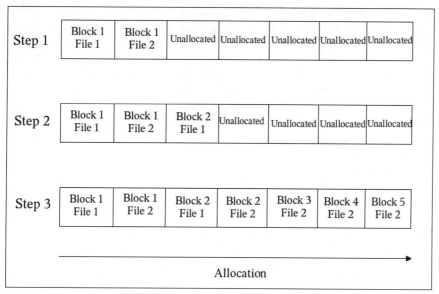

Figure 8-1: Watching fragmentation occur as files are created and edited.

In Step 1 of Figure 8-1, all is well when files are created and initial disk storage is assigned to them. Unfortunately, Steps 2 and 3 show that nonadjacent blocks usually begin to be allocated as soon as files are edited and require additional data storage. This situation can get even worse as existing files are deleted and the storage associated with them is returned to the system's list of free storage, as show in Figure 8-2, which continues from Figure 8-1.

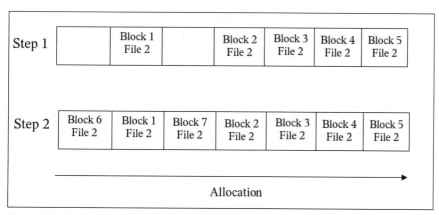

Figure 8-2: Continuing fragmentation as files are deleted and new files are created.

In Step 1 of Figure 8-2, the first file has been deleted, returning the blocks that were associated with it to the system's list of available blocks. In Step 2, what was originally the second file has grown again and claimed the space formerly associated with File 1 in as inefficient a manner as possible.

Though the blocks are contiguous on the disk, they're not in the order that the system will have to read them when reading the data that they contain, which is inefficient and implies extra system overhead.

Microsoft Windows provides a built-in defragmentation utility, which you can start by selecting (for example) the Accessories → System Tools → Disk Defragmenter menu item on a Windows 2000 system, shown in Figure 8-3. In this utility, first select the drive letter associated with the disk partition that you want to reduce in size in order to make room for Linux, and then click Defragment. The Disk Defragmenter does its work and displays a before and after picture of fragmentation on that partition once it completes.

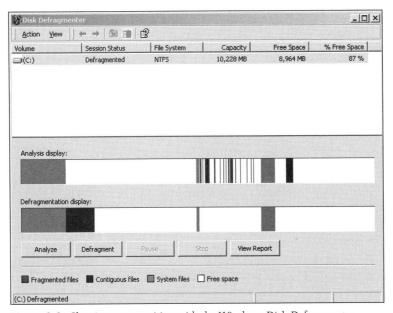

Figure 8-3: Cleaning up a partition with the Windows Disk Defragmenter.

You may wonder why Figure 8-3 shows some system files that haven't been moved closer to the beginning of the disk. Microsoft Windows system files, such as the paging file, aren't relocated by the defragmenter because these files are used internally by Windows and shouldn't be modified after they are created. However, these files are recreated if any problems are found in them, so they will be recreated even if they are located in the part of the disk that is being repartitioned for use by Linux.

After you've made sure that your disk is not fragmented, the next step in creating space for Linux is to repartition your disk using the tools found on the Knoppix live CD as discussed in Chapter 2.

Partitioning Your Hard Drive

After defragmenting your disk, insert a copy of the Knoppix live CD, such as the one that comes with this book, and reboot your system, making sure that your system is configured to boot from the

CD-ROM drive, as explained in Chapter 4. Booting from the Knoppix CD takes a little while, as it probes your hardware, configures the devices attached to your system, starts the Linux kernel and associated services, and so on. Eventually, you'll see a screen similar to the one shown in Figure 8-4. Congratulations, by the way — you're now running Linux without making any changes to your computer system!

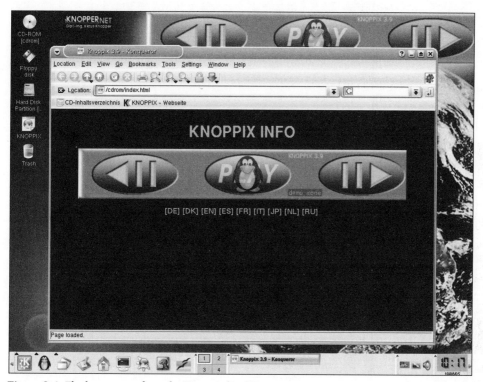

Figure 8-4: The boot screen from the Knoppix live CD.

Next, you can use a standard Linux disk partitioning utility to change the size of your existing Windows disk partition so that free space is available on the disk, in which you can then install Linux. To start this utility, click the KDE icon in the lower-left corner of the screen to display the menus for the KDE desktop environment used by Knoppix. Select the System menu item, and click the QTParted menu item. This starts a Linux partition editor that was written using the QT graphical toolkit, hence the name. The utility probes your system for hard drives and then displays its main screen, as shown in Figure 8-5.

Once this screen displays, select the disk drive that you want to partition from the Device window on the left of the screen. My system contains two drives, so it offers me two choices — you will probably see only one. After selecting /UNIONFS/dev/sda, which is the disk that contains my Windows installation, the QT partition editor displays information about the disk's current partitioning and the amount of space that is actively in use in the Details window at right, as shown in Figure 8-6.

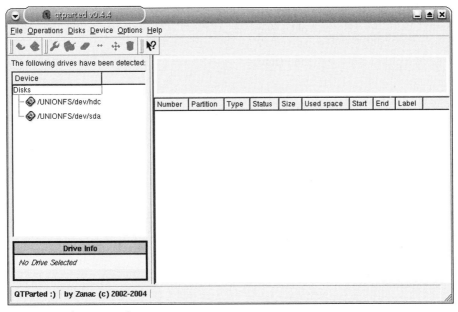

Figure 8-5: The QTParted startup screen.

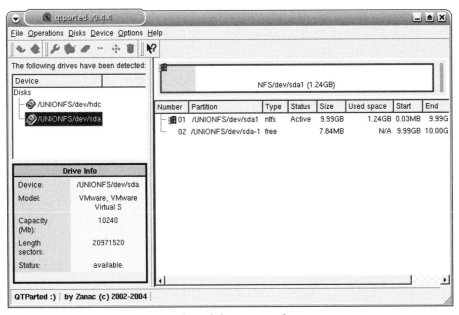

Figure 8-6: Information about a Windows disk in QTParted.

In my case, the disk actually contains an NTFS partition that holds my Windows installation and a small amount of free space, though many older Windows systems may use FAT32 partitions. To begin the repartitioning process, right-click on the NTFS (or FAT32) partition and select the Resize command from the pop-up menu. The dialog shown in Figure 8-7 appears.

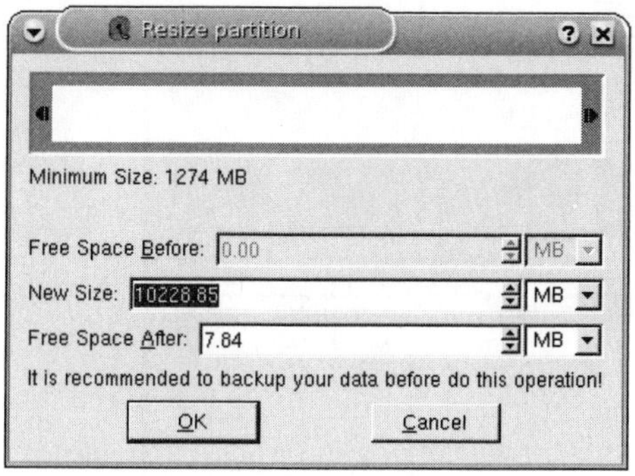

Figure 8-7: QTParted's Resize partition dialog.

To resize the selected partition, drag the arrow at the right end of the empty area at the top of this dialog to the left to represent moving the end of the partition. Don't make the partition any smaller than the Minimum Size that QTParted displays, and be sure that you still make the partition larger than the minimum value to leave some free space so that you can create new files on your resized Windows partition. As you drag the arrow, you'll the see the numbers in the bottom of the dialog change to reflect the proposed new size of your partition. This isn't actually making any changes to your disk, it's just setting things up to do so, so there's no problem if you drag the end of the partition with your mouse button, let go, and then want to make additional changes. Just grab the right arrow and drag it again to make those changes. Do not move the arrow at the left of this dialog—it won't really hurt anything, but it will end up wasting some space on your hard drive, which is never a good thing. Figure 8-8 shows this dialog after I've resized my disk so that the New Size of my Windows partition will be around 5GB, leaving approximately 5GB available for installing Linux.

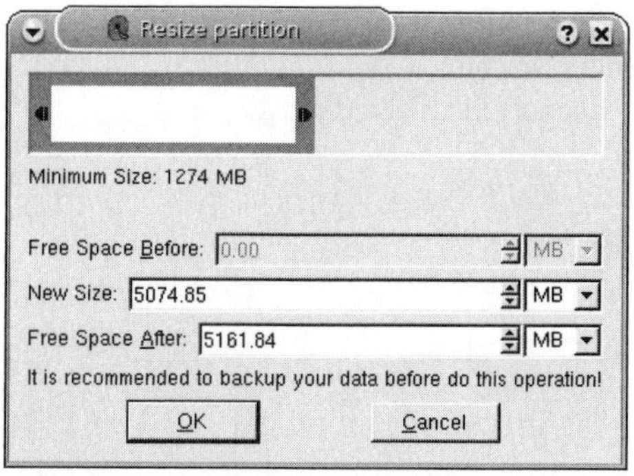

Figure 8-8: The Resize dialog after resizing a partition.

Click OK to accept the changes that you want to make to your partition. The Resize partition dialog closes and the main QTParted screen displays, looking a bit different, as shown in Figure 8-9. Note that no changes have been made to your disk yet; like the Resize dialog, the main QTParted screen just shows the proposed changes to the selected partition.

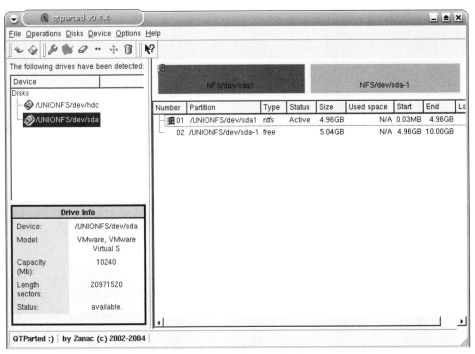

Figure 8-9: Proposed partition changes in QTParted's main dialog.

To actually make the changes that you've proposed, click the File menu and select the Commit command, which commits the changes to your disk and begins the repartitioning process. As a friendly warning, QTParted displays the warning dialog shown in Figure 8-10, which reminds you that this makes physical changes to your disk and warns you about the need for backups. Knoppix doesn't actually mount your partitions, so you can safely ignore the generic warning about unmounting partitions. The idea of mounting and unmounting partitions is a Linux concept explained in Chapter 5.

Figure 8-10: A final warning about the need for backups when repartitioning a disk.

Because you already made backups, as described in the previous section, you should be in fine shape, so just click Yes to actually begin the repartitioning process. The dialog shown in Figure 8-11 displays as the repartitioning process begins.

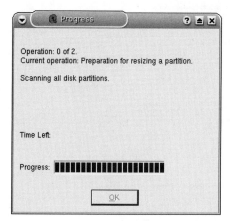

Figure 8-11: The QTParted dialog displays while repartitioning.

When the repartitioning process completes, this dialog is updated with the message `Operation completed successfully` displayed in red in the middle of the dialog shown in Figure 8-11. Next, click OK to close this dialog and redisplay QTParted's main dialog. Note that the information about the partitions on the selected disk has been updated to show the repartitioning. Your existing Windows partition is still listed, but now is much smaller, and a much larger amount of free space is listed as being available. Congratulations! You can now quit the QTParted utility by selecting the File menu's Quit command.

I've never had a problem using QTParted, but I always prefer to double-check things, just in case. To verify that all is well, reboot your Windows system at this point to ensure that things are working correctly. To do so, shut down Knoppix and restart your system by clicking the KDE menu item in the lower-left corner of your screen and selecting the Logout menu item. Select Restart the System from the pop-up dialog that displays. Knoppix shuts down and ejects the CD from your system. To reboot your system into Windows to double-check that your Windows installation is still fine, press the Return or Enter key on your keyboard.

The first time that you boot Windows after repartitioning a partition, Windows notices that your disk parameters have changed and runs its CHKDSK utility to correctly set Windows's idea of partition size and to recreate the paging file if necessary. During the Windows startup process, you will see the screen shown in Figure 8-12. Don't worry, just let Windows do its thing—Windows simply checks the disk partition, adjusts its internal parameters, and then starts Windows correctly.

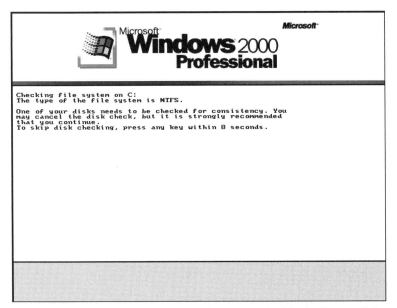

Figure 8-12: After repartitioning, Microsoft Windows double-checks your disk.

Once Windows is running, you can feel more comfortable about the repartitioning process that you just completed. You're now ready to begin your grand, dual-boot Linux adventure!

Installing Linux into a partition on an existing disk is almost identical to the installation process described in Chapter 4, except that the disk partitioning and boot loader configuration steps are different. The next section highlights these differences in the context of the Fedora Core Linux installer and explains what to expect in order to help insure that your new dual-boot system correctly starts either Microsoft Windows or Linux.

Installing Linux on the New Partition

To install Linux in the free space that you just liberated from your Windows partition, locate your Linux installation CDs, put the first CD in your CD-ROM drive, and restart your system to begin the Linux installation process. I use the Fedora Core Linux installer for the examples in this section, but the process is very similar for SUSE, Mandrake, TurboLinux, or any other Linux distribution that is designed for installation on a hard drive.

After walking through the first few Fedora Core installation screens, the screen at which differences from the standard installation process begins is the Disk Partitioning Setup Screen, shown in Figure 8-13.

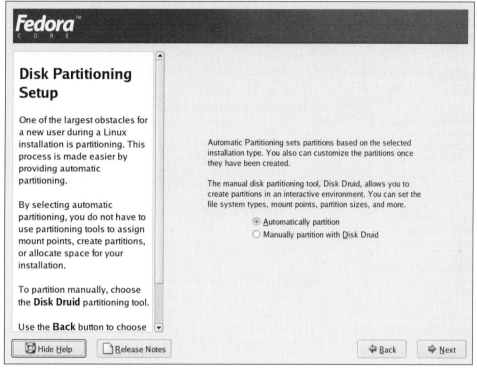

Figure 8-13: The Fedora installer's Disk Partitioning Setup screen.

Unless you really want to manually partition your disk, you should leave the Automatic Partitioning radio button selected and click next to proceed. The Automatic Partitioning screen, shown in Figure 8-14, is displayed.

On the Automatic Partitioning screen, select Keep all partitions and use existing free space. You must select this option to guarantee that the installer does not delete your existing Windows partition. You should also select Review (and modify if needed) the partitions created. This option causes the installer to display an additional screen that shows its planned changes to your disk, so that you can verify that your existing Windows partition (identified as an NTFS or FAT32 partition) will be preserved. Click Next to proceed. The screen shown in Figure 8-15 is displayed.

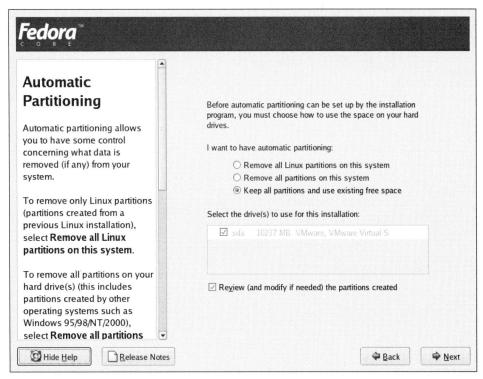

Figure 8-14: The Fedora installer's Automatic Partitioning screen.

The screen shown in Figure 8-15 provides a scrollable region at the bottom-right that enables you to see how the installer will partition and use the free space on your disk. By default, Fedora Core Linux allocates the free space on your disk into space that it can then allocate to logical volumes; this allocation scheme provides a more flexible model for Linux partition creation and maintenance than simply creating physical partitions does. Logical volumes were touched upon in Chapter 5.

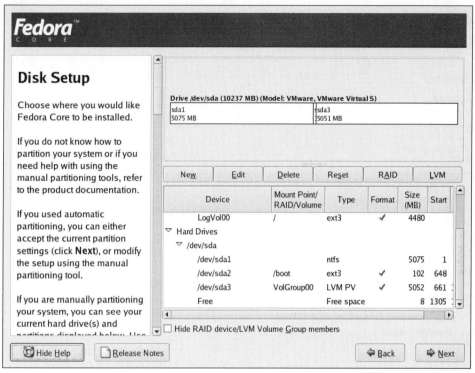

Figure 8-15: The Fedora installer's Disk Setup screen.

You will probably need to scroll down in the Device pane of the Disk Setup dialog to see the entries for your physical hard drive. Figure 8-15 shows the setup for my hard drive — as you can see, my Windows partition (/dev/sda1, in Linux terms) is an NTFS partition and will not be changed by the installation process. A second physical partition, /dev/sda2, will be created to hold the Linux /boot directory, which contains the Linux kernel, files used by the boot loader, and other files related to the boot process. Most of the space that we freed up earlier in this chapter is allocated to the new partition /dev/sda3, in which the logical volumes mentioned earlier will be created.

After you've verified that your system will be partitioned correctly (the critical thing is making sure that an NTFS or FAT32 file system is still present on your hard disk), click Next to proceed. The screen shown in Figure 8-16 is displayed.

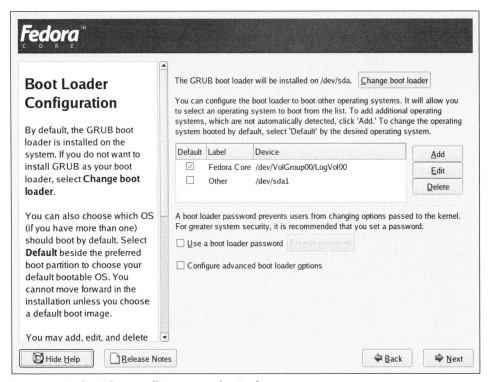

Figure 8-16: The Fedora installer's Boot Loader Configuration screen.

As you can see from this screen, the installer recognizes that your disk will contain two bootable operating systems once the Fedora Core installation completes: Fedora Core and an unknown operating system referred to as Other. As you can see from Figure 8-16, this operating system is located on the partition /dev/sda1, and (in my case) is my installed version of Windows. (The names of your disk partitions will probably be different, but the same principles apply—if you see another operating system listed here, it's almost certainly your existing Windows installation.)

This screen enables you to determine which of your operating systems boot by default when you turn on your system. Part of the process of the Fedora Core installation process is to install the Fedora Core boot loader, known as GRUB, which stands for the GRand Unified Boot Loader. GRUB is a powerful, flexible boot loader that makes it easy to boot your system in different ways, including into different operating systems. As you'll see in the next section, part of this flexibility is meant to make it easy for you to choose which system to start whenever you restart your computer. GRUB will always start one of your installed operating system by default if you don't do anything. If you want to start Linux by default and start Windows only when selecting it from a boot menu, leave the options on this screen as they are. If you want to boot Windows by default and start Linux only when selecting it from a boot menu, click the checkbox to the left of the Other entry.

Those are the only dialogs that differentiate dual-boot configuration from the standard Fedora Core installation process. Click Next to proceed with the remainder of the installation process.

Note

At this point, the Fedora Core installer still hasn't actually made any changes to your disk — it's just showing you what it plans to do. The last query dialog in the Fedora Core installer, the About to Install dialog, asks if you really, really want to proceed with installing Fedora Core. The changes that you've specified will take place only if you click Next on this screen.

Once the Fedora Core installation process completes, your system ejects the CD and you are instructed to remove the CD so that the installer can restart your system from the hard drive. The instructions in the next section explain how to select which operating system you want to run on your new dual-boot system.

Selecting an Operating System at Boot Time

As discussed in the previous section, part of the Linux installation process is to install a Linux boot loader, which is almost always GRUB nowadays. (An older Linux boot loader, LILO, still exists but is rarely used.)

When you turn on your dual-boot system, the first screen that the GRUB boot loader displays is a screen like the one shown in Figure 8-17. If you chose Fedora Core as your system's default operating system, the second line displays the version of the kernel that your system will start This will almost certainly be different on your screen, but that's OK — a newer kernel version just means that your system has been updated more recently than mine has been.

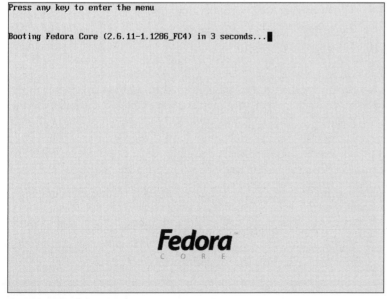

Figure 8-17: The GRUB boot screen.

As you can see from this screen, the boot loader on my system is configured to automatically start Fedora Core after waiting a few seconds for me to specify another operating system. This is a nice feature if, for example, the power goes out at your house, but you want your computer system to be available 24 hours a day. Booting a default operating system after a short pause ensures that your computer will always restart in the event of a transient problem such as a power flicker.

The previous section explains how to specify which operating system to boot by default. In my case, this is Linux. If you configured your Fedora installation the same way, you can either wait a few seconds for Fedora to boot automatically, or press any key and then press Return or Enter when you see the screen shown in Figure 8-18.

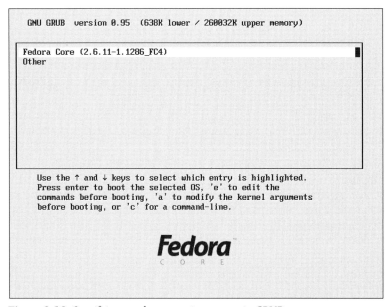

Figure 8-18: Specifying another operating system in GRUB.

To select another operating system, use the up- and down-arrows to position the cursor to the right of the operating system that you want to boot, and press Return or Enter on your keyboard. The selected operating system will start.

Note

The GRUB boot loader is extremely powerful and highly configurable. Unfortunately, discussing every nuance of configuring it is outside the scope of this book. For more information about configuring GRUB, see a book on Linux system administration or see GRUB's online documentation, which is available at `www.gnu.org/software/grub/manual/html_node/`. You must configure GRUB while running Linux if you want to make permanent changes, because the GRUB configuration file is located in the Linux /boot file system.

Summary

Configuring a computer system so that it boots both Linux and Windows is quite easy to do, thanks to the powerful tools provided with Linux. This chapter explains the basic steps, which are to free up space on your disk for Linux, install Linux in that space, and configure the system to boot the operating system of your choice. With those steps in place, selecting which operating system you want to run requires three keystrokes when you boot your system. That's not too shabby considering that your machine can not only run your familiar Windows applications but can also run Linux to serve as a modern, high-powered computing platform whenever you'd prefer to take advantage of the true capabilities of your existing computer system.

Part III

Running Linux

Chapter 9

Desktop Solutions

The typical user-oriented Linux distribution comes with one of two major desktop environments: GNOME or KDE. In many distributions both environments are provided and the user can choose which she wants to use, but there is generally a default desktop, which is what the developers of that distribution intend to be used. The specific desktop one used was, at one time, an object of almost religious adherence; there were enough technical and licensing differences between the two to fuel endless arguments. As of this writing, however, there has been a great deal of convergence and cross-pollination between the two.

What exactly is a desktop environment? Briefly, the desktop environment provides many services that can easily be taken for granted. We've become so used to doing things like dragging files from one folder to another that it's easy to forget that these are not core functions of an operating system. The desktop environment provides a consistent look and feel for applications, controls the way windows are displayed, and provides an infrastructure for managing files and activities. GNOME and KDE also offer suites of applications that interoperate gracefully.

Note

Although KDE and GNOME rule the roost when it comes to desktop environments, they're not the only game in town. There are a number of other systems available. Most of these systems do not have all of the bells and whistles that have made GNOME and KDE so popular, but they find a niche among users who want basic graphic-based functionality without the intensive memory and CPU usage that comes with the more fully featured systems. If you are interested in finding out more about alternatives to GNOME and KDE, go to `http://freshmeat.net` and click Browse and then Desktop Environments.

In this chapter, I get you started on the GNOME and KDE desktops and take you on a quick tour of some of the most essential applications you'll need.

The X Window System

It wasn't all that long ago that Linux didn't have a graphical user interface at all. Linux was developed to be a system that worked like Unix, and most Unix users were used to entering commands textually. Developing a GUI simply wasn't a priority in the early going. However, once Linux's user base began to expand and GUIs for personal computers became increasingly common, Linux developers began to take on the task of creating a viable desktop on Linux. Unsurprisingly, they began by adapting systems that were already in existence, beginning with the X Window System.

By far the most popular graphical interface in the Linux world is the X Window System, or X (but never X Windows), originally developed at MIT but now maintained by the X.Org consortium (www.x.org/). X has an interesting architecture. Programs designed to work with it (called *X clients*) do not actually draw their elements, such as icons, windows, or menus, but defer such actions to a program called an *X server*. The X server interfaces with graphics cards, mice, and other hardware and sends client requests to them. X clients and servers don't even have to run on the same machine; they can run over a local area network or even the Internet.

X also separates out the task of window management. Moving, resizing, and otherwise manipulating windows is left to a special X client called a *window manager.*

GNOME

GNOME is an acronym for *GNU Object-Model Environment.* It originated as an effort to create a free software desktop environment from scratch. Over the years it has developed into a good-looking and robust system, with a full-featured suite of applications. From the beginning, GNOME's emphasis has been on usability rather than huge numbers of features. Consequently, GNOME applications have tended to be small and simple. On the other hand, there are a lot of them.

GNOME, like KDE, sits on top of the X Window System, and uses the infrastructure provided by X to accomplish many of its functions.

GNOME is the default system on Fedora Core, which is used for the examples in this section. Fedora's desktop isn't pure GNOME. Like almost anything else in the Linux world, GNOME can be configured in an almost infinite number of different ways, and the Fedora developers have tweaked GNOME to suit their own preferences. In fact, the only way to get pure GNOME is to download the packages and install them yourself. This is tedious, time consuming, and more often than not, rather difficult. And even if you were to do it, all you'd get is the GNOME developers' idea of what a GNOME desktop should look like, which is likely no better than the distribution's.

Cross-Reference

In Chapter 10, I show you how to customize your desktop to create something that looks and works the way you want it to.

The GNOME desktop

Your GNOME session begins when you log in. As with any other multiuser system, you will need to enter your username and password at the greeting screen. When you first start your GNOME session, you should see a desktop similar to the one shown in Figure 9-1.

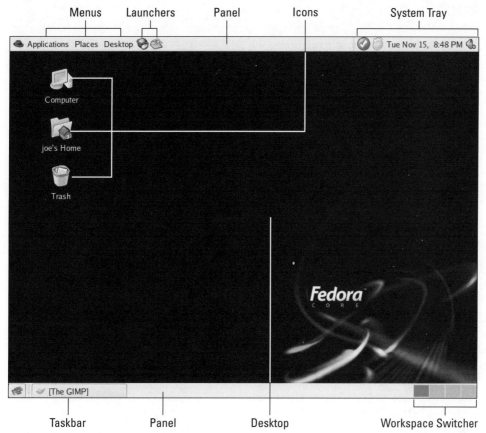

Figure 9-1: The GNOME Desktop.

As with any operating system, there are a number of features with which you'll want to be acquainted.

Note

The figures in this chapter, which reflect the Fedora Core 4 distribution, may or may not be identical to what you see on your screen. The exact details of the desktop's appearance vary depending on your distribution, the particular version of your distribution that you're using, and the type and details of the particular installation. Don't worry if, for example, you've got an extra icon or you don't see an icon that's listed or if you have slightly different entries in your menus and so forth. You can always add or remove things. In fact, once you get used to working with your desktop, you'll probably customize it to the extent that it doesn't look like anyone else's anywhere.

THE DESKTOP

When users casually refer to the *desktop*, they are usually referring to their desktop's *background*. That is, the majority of the screen, which has nothing on it. If you're using Fedora Core, the default background picture contains the Fedora Core logo. Other distributions may make use of other background images. This background image can be changed or eliminated. You can use an image of your choice, or you can set the background to be a solid color or gradient. You learn how to change the background in Chapter 10.

One of the more useful features of the desktop appears when you right-click on it. This brings up a pop-up menu, as shown in Figure 9-2.

This menu gives you the capability to create documents, folders, or launchers (a *launcher* is an icon that launches a program when clicked), or to open a terminal window (see Chapter 11 for information about how to use the terminal window). It also gives you options for organizing your desktop or changing its appearance.

Figure 9-2: The desktop pop-up menu. Notice that the background has been changed from the default choice.

ICONS

Depending on your distribution, you may or may not have a few icons on your desktop. By default, Fedora Core has icons for Computer (the root, or / directory), your home directory, and a Trash directory. If there is a CD-ROM mounted on your machine, there will also be an icon for that. Clicking on any of these directories opens the Nautilus file manager and shows the contents of that directory, as shown in Figure 9-3.

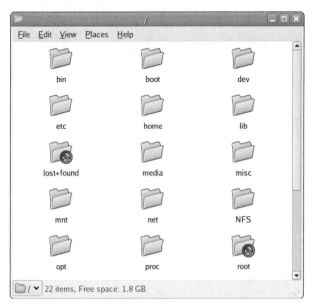

Figure 9-3: Nautilus, showing the contents of the root directory.

You can open files by double-clicking on them. (You can configure Nautilus to open a file with a single click if you prefer that.)

THE PANELS

Depending on your distribution's default configuration, you will have one or two panels on your screen. A panel is a long, narrow strip running along the top or bottom of the screen. Panels can be configured to the left or right edge as well, but top or bottom is the more common configuration.

On Fedora Core, there are two panels: one along the top and one along the bottom. The upper panel, shown in Figure 9-4, contains the Applications, Places, and Desktop menus (addressed in the next section); launcher icons for Web browser and e-mail programs (this may vary, depending on the type of installation you chose); and a system tray containing various informational features, such as the time and date, as well as an icon for the Red Hat Network and a volume control for your audio applications. (Red Hat Network is Red Hat's software update service, which is actually not available for Fedora Core; I presume it's there as an enticement to check out Red Hat's Enterprise products.)

Figure 9-4: The upper panel, with menus and various icons.

The lower panel, shown in Figure 9-5, contains the Show Desktop button (click this icon to toggle between hiding and displaying the open windows), a taskbar, which contains icons for all windows (click on a window's icon to bring it to the front), and a workspace switcher. (GNOME allows the user to have multiple desktops. By clicking on the corresponding icon in the workspace switcher, you can page between desktops.)

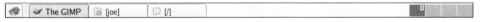

Figure 9-5: The lower panel shows the applications you have open.

Note

Remember that the arrangement of these features in the panels is arbitrary. The number, placement, and contents of the panels can be configured by the user, as detailed in Chapter 10.

THE MENUS

The Applications, Places, and Desktop menus located in the upper panel are your primary access to the programs available on your computer. If you're familiar with the menu system used on Microsoft Windows, you should have no problem adapting to GNOME's menus. The Applications menu contains a number of subcategories, and within each subcategory, a number of programs. Clicking on any of these links launches its program. The Applications menu is shown in Figure 9-6.

The Places menu (shown in Figure 9-7) gives you quick access to a number of directory locations on your computer.

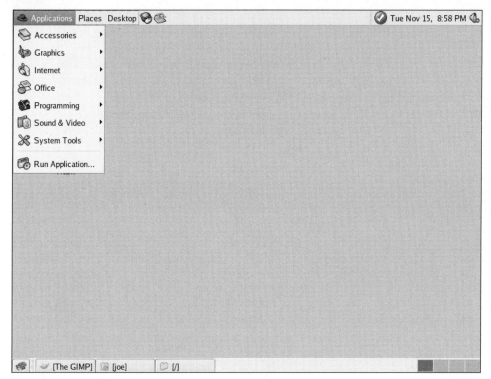

Figure 9-6: The Applications menu.

The Home Folder and Computer menu items are the same as the *user*'s Home and Computer icons on the desktop. If you don't like having icons on your desktop, you can still have quick access to those locations by clicking on the corresponding menu items. The Desktop item corresponds to the Desktop folder that resides in your home directory. The Connect to Server menu item opens a dialog (shown in Figure 9-8) that allows you to connect to a number of different types of servers (FTP, SSH, WebDAV, or user defined).

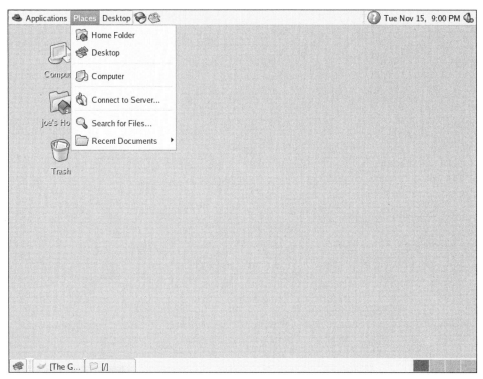

Figure 9-7: The Places menu.

Figure 9-8: The Connect to Server dialog.

The Search for Files option (shown in Figure 9-9) allows you to search your computer for a file based on text in the title or other options.

The Desktop menu (shown in Figure 9-10) gives you quick access to a number of useful functions. Most basically, you have the options to Log Out, which ends your GNOME session, or Lock Screen, which activates the screen saver and requires you to enter your password before you can start using the machine again.

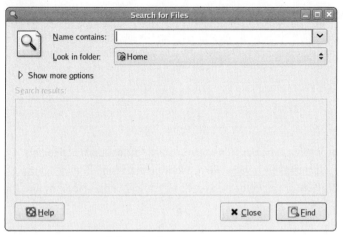

Figure 9-9: The Search for Files function.

There are two submenus in the Desktop menu: The Preferences submenu gives you access to functions that will help you configure your GNOME environment. I cover these functions in more detail in the next chapter. The Systems Setting submenu gives you access to functions that allow you to configure various basic system-wide settings on your machine.

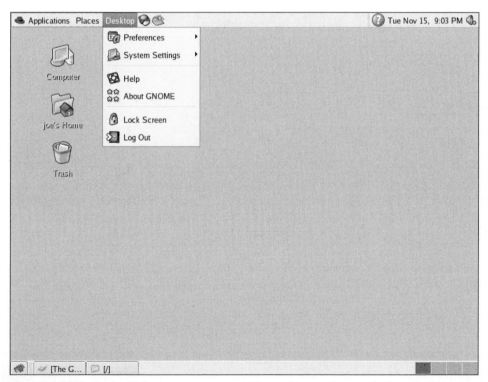

Figure 9-10: The Desktop menu.

Using the Nautilus file manager and Web browser

GNOME's native file manager is called Nautilus, and it incorporates many of the features that users have come to expect from a file manager on any operating system. Double-click on one of the icons on the desktop, or one of the folder options in the Places menu, and a Nautilus window (shown in Figure 9-11) opens showing the contents of that directory.

Note

The exception to this is the Computer icon or menu item. This icon doesn't actually access the root directory. Rather, it shows a number of options representing the various file locations on the system. These options might include the network, the floppy or CD-ROM drives, or the file system. Double-clicking on the Filesystem icon then takes you to the root directory

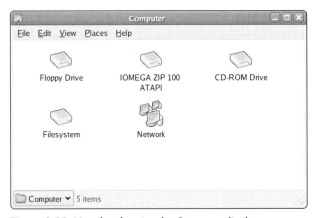

Figure 9-11: Nautilus showing the Computer display.

As with any typical file manager, you can navigate through the directory tree by clicking on entries within the Nautilus menu. Clicking on files rather than folders opens that file in a program that depends on the file type; text files open in a text editor, HTML files open in a Web browser, and so on.

Note

Nautilus is also a Web browser. You are not limited to viewing files on your local machine. Enter a Web site address, and you will see that Web page. Nautilus is not as fully featured a browser as, say, Firefox, but for basic browsing, it's fine.

Nautilus has a number of configuration options that allow you to customize the way in which it functions. From the main Nautilus window, click on the Edit menu and then select Preferences. This opens the File Management Preferences dialog as shown in Figure 9-12.

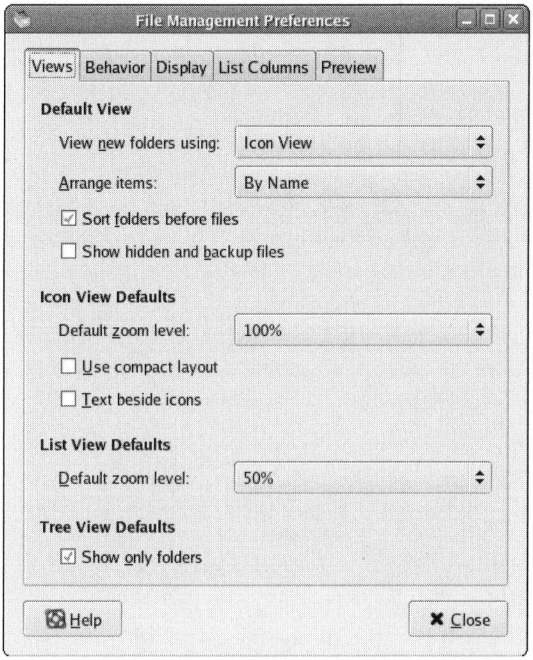

Figure 9-12: The File Management Preferences dialog.

This dialog has several tabs. The most basic is the Views tab, which contains options related to the way in which Nautilus displays information to the viewer. The first option in this tab allows you to select whether you'd prefer an icon view or a list view. Icon view shows files and directories as a set of icons arranged left to right across a window, while list view shows them arranged in a vertical list.

Whether you're using list view or icon view, files and directories (folders) are listed in alphabetical order, with directories listed before files. This behavior can be changed using the Arrange items option. As in Microsoft Windows, this option allows you to select an arrangement based on name, size, file type, date of last modification, or emblem. (Emblems can be added using the Backgrounds and Emblems option found under the Edit menu.)

Most of the other options and tabs are largely self-explanatory, and a little experimentation should yield a configuration that works well for you.

Window behavior

One of the things that GNOME controls is the way that windows behave. In this section, we look at the default way in which windows behave. If you are familiar with window behavior in Microsoft Windows, this will all be second nature.

Cross-Reference

For more information on configuring window behavior, see Chapter 10.

A typical window has a title bar across the top edge. In addition to the window's title (which is usually the name of the file being worked on and/or the name of the application in which that file is open), you will also see small icons in the left- and right-hand corners. The title bar changes color when its window is the active one. The *active window* is the one that is being used. It is usually the one that is topmost on the desktop. Clicking on a window brings it to the front and makes it active. Typically, the active window has a darker title bar than the inactive windows, as in Figure 9-13.

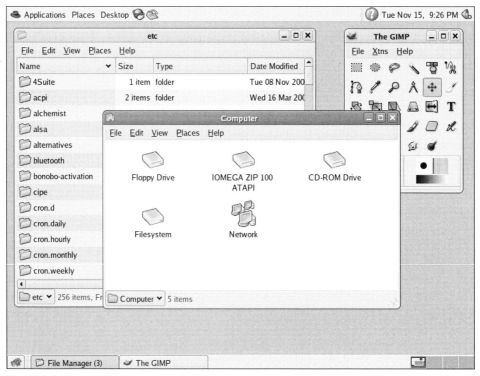

Figure 9-13: Active and inactive windows.

Clicking the icon in the left-hand corner of a window brings up a menu containing various functions related to that window. Using this menu, the window can be minimized (sent to the task bar), maximized (enlarged to fill the entire screen), placed on top, moved, resized, or closed. In addition, there are several options related to the workspace on which the window appears. The window can be moved to another workspace, or it can be designated that it will always appear on the visible workspace.

In the right-hand corner, there are three buttons that provide one-click access to three of the above functions. Using these buttons, the window can be minimized (the icon with the single horizontal line), maximized (the square), or closed (the X).

Managing multiple workspaces

As identified in Figure 9-1, there is a workspace switcher on the right-hand side of the lower panel. In the default configuration, four workspaces are shown in the switcher. You can think of a workspace as being a second (and third and fourth, and so on) iteration of your desktop. It's as if you have four identical desktops upon which you can work. Only one workspace is active at any given time, and this is what you see on your screen. The workspace switcher shows which workspace is active (the darker section), and which are not. You can switch from one workspace to another by clicking on one of the inactive workspaces. This allows you to run different sets of applications for different purposes while keeping your desktop uncluttered. Unless you specify otherwise, applications stay on the desktop on which they were opened. With a little practice, you will see how keeping your functions segregated can really streamline your work.

KDE

The acronym KDE stands for *K Desktop Environment*. If the *K* ever stood for anything, it has been lost in the mists of time. For some time, the status of KDE was controversial because although KDE itself was distributed as free software, Qt (Q toolkit, a set of programming functions) on which it was based was not free software. This led to many arguments about whether it was appropriate to use KDE on otherwise free Linux systems and probably delayed interoperability between KDE and GNOME by many months, if not years. All of this changed when the owners of Qt changed the license and made it free software.

Now that a great deal of interoperability between GNOME and KDE has been achieved, KDE is not substantially different from GNOME for most practical purposes. They may look different and there may be some cases in which their behavior might differ, but when viewed from the perspective of the broad strokes, they provide the same core functions: a visual desktop, windows, a file manager, menus and icons, and a means to configure all of this.

This section provides a brief look at the installation of KDE that is available on Fedora Core and compares it with its GNOME counterpart on the same system. The chapter then focuses on KDE as it is implemented on Knoppix.

The Fedora Core KDE desktop

The default configuration of the KDE desktop on Fedora Core looks like Figure 9-14.

Figure 9-14: The Fedora Core KDE desktop.

The major differences that you will notice from GNOME are that there is only one panel and that there are no "named" menus. That is, there are not the textual clues to alert you that menus are there. In fact, the main menu, shown in Figure 9-15, is accessed by clicking the red hat icon on the left end of the panel.

You will notice as you look through the menu items that many of the applications listed are different from the applications listed in the GNOME Applications menu. These applications are those that are bundled with the release of KDE. Certain important applications, such as Firefox and Evolution, are available via these submenus, but on the whole, the Fedora developers reason that if you're using KDE, you probably want to use KDE applications as well.

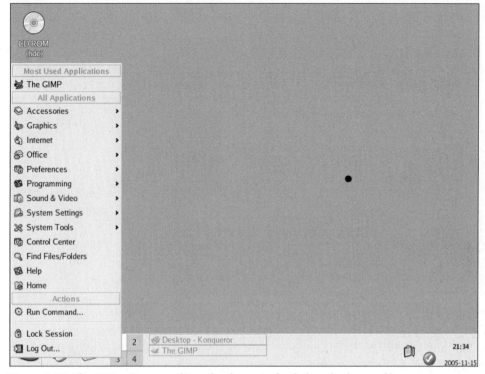

Figure 9-15: The KDE main menu. (Note the change in the desktop background.)

Beyond these considerations, if you're thinking that things that look similar will behave in similar ways, you're probably not too far off the mark. Double-clicking on a directory icon opens a file manager to that directory (although in this case, the file manager is Konqueror, rather than Nautilus), clicking on launchers starts applications, and right-clicking on the desktop brings up a menu with a number of actions available to you. (These actions are slightly different from the ones in GNOME, but not so much to be confusing.)

KDE on Knoppix

Now is a good time to try out the Knoppix live CD that accompanies this book. The great thing about Knoppix is that it runs entirely off CD. Put the CD into your computer, reboot (make sure your BIOS settings enable you to boot from a CD-ROM drive), and Knoppix starts up as shown in Figure 9-16. When you are finished exploring, you can just remove the Knoppix CD and reboot. Your previous operating system will start as usual. This is a good way to test-drive Linux with a minimum amount of disruption.

Figure 9-16: Booting into Knoppix.

As you can see from Figure 9-16, Knoppix puts up a splash screen and prompts you for boot options. You can see the full range of options by pressing F2 or F3. Most users will be able to continue without adding special options by just pressing Enter.

Knoppix next starts up the Linux kernel, which in turn begins the process of detecting hardware and launching all the programs that begin at boot time (see Figure 9-17). The first major difference from Windows you'll notice is that the system starts up in text mode, rather than with a graphical interface as in Microsoft Windows. Many arcane messages fly by. (Knoppix does at least liven up their appearance by making them multicolored.)

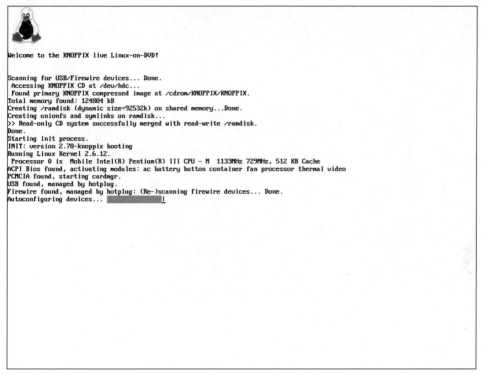

```
Welcome to the KNOPPIX live Linux-on-DVD!


Scanning for USB/Firewire devices... Done.
 Accessing KNOPPIX CD at /dev/hdc...
 Found primary KNOPPIX compressed image at /cdrom/KNOPPIX/KNOPPIX.
Total memory found: 124884 kB
Creating /ramdisk (dynamic size=92532k) on shared memory...Done.
Creating unionfs and symlinks on ramdisk...
>> Read-only CD system successfully merged with read-write /ramdisk.
Done.
Starting init process.
INIT: version 2.78-knoppix booting
Running Linux Kernel 2.6.12.
 Processor 0 is  Mobile Intel(R) Pentium(R) III CPU - M  1133MHz 729MHz, 512 KB Cache
ACPI Bios found, activating modules: ac battery button container fan processor thermal video
PCMCIA found, starting cardmgr.
USB found, managed by hotplug.
Firewire found, managed by hotplug: (Re-)scanning firewire devices... Done.
Autoconfiguring devices...          |
```

Figure 9-17: Hardware detection at boot time on Knoppix.

Linux has such a wide range of uses; you can find it installed on corporate servers providing computing power to an office full of workers or embedded into an MP3 player. To handle this diversity, the core system has to be as simple as possible. An MP3 player, for instance, doesn't even have a keyboard or monitor, while the server might have dozens of terminals attached. Thus, this text mode is the lowest common denominator approach to displaying output. Once the system is up and running, it can start up a graphical interface using the X Window System.

KDE on Knoppix differs from KDE on Fedora Core mainly in the way that things such as menus and launchers are configured. It also uses a different desktop theme — a set of visual elements (icons, window borders, and the like) — to provide a slightly different look. The default KDE-on-Knoppix desktop is shown in Figure 9-18, with the main menu and Konqueror browser open.

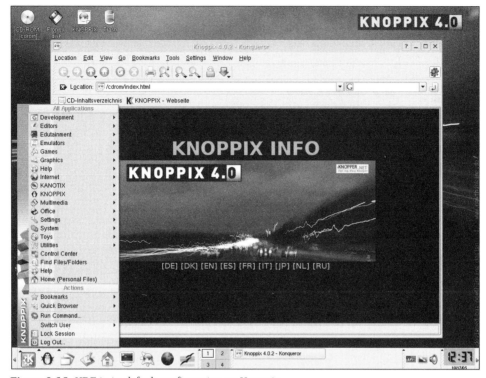

Figure 9-18: KDE in its default configuration on Knoppix.

THE DESKTOP

As with GNOME, what users commonly refer to as the *desktop* is actually the *background* of the screen, that is, the majority of the screen, which has nothing on it. On Knoppix, the default background image contains the Knoppix logo. (Other distributions may make use of other background images; the Fedora developers have added a background picture that contains the Fedora Core logo.) As with GNOME, this background image can be changed or eliminated, as explained in Chapter 10.

As with GNOME, right-clicking on the desktop brings up a pop-up menu, as shown in Figure 9-19.

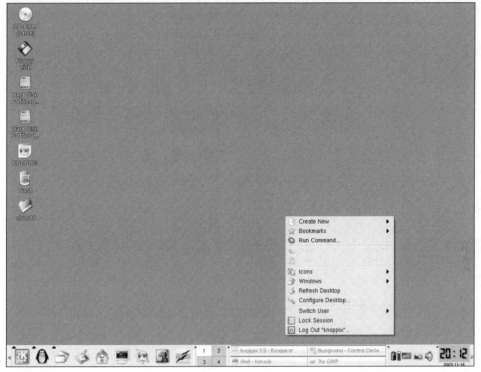

Figure 9-19: The desktop pop-up menu. (Note the change from the default background.)

This menu gives you the capability to create documents, folders, or launchers, to run a command, log in as a different user, lock the screen, or log out. It also gives you options for organizing your desktop or changing its appearance.

ICONS

Your Knoppix KDE desktop should show a few icons. As with GNOME, there is a trashcan, as well as icons representing the CD-ROM and floppy drives (assuming your system has them). There may also be icons representing partitions on your hard drive. These icons are determined by the particular partitioning scheme on your hard drive. Because Knoppix is most often used from a live CD, those partition icons will probably represent Windows partitions, or whatever else you may have on your system. Clicking on any of these directories opens the Konqueror file manager and shows the contents of that directory, as shown in Figure 9-20.

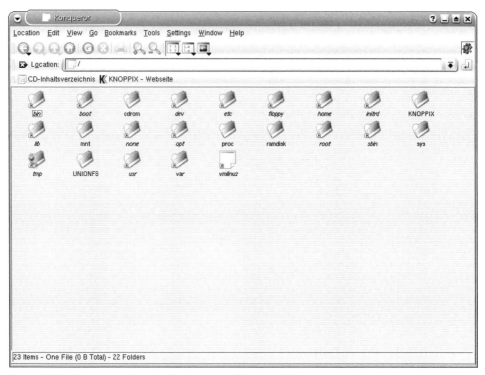

Figure 9-20: Konqueror, showing the contents of the root directory.

You can open files and directories by clicking on them.

THE PANEL

There's only one panel in KDE's default configuration, shown in Figure 9-21. As configured in Knoppix, it is located along the bottom of the screen.

Figure 9-21: The KDE panel.

The panel contains, from left to right, the K menu (the main menu), the Knoppix menu, the window list, the show desktop icon, a home directory icon, launchers for the terminal, Konqueror, Firefox, and OpenOffice, the workspace switcher, the task list, and the system tray, which contains various applets.

THE MENUS

There are three menus on Knoppix's implementation of KDE. They are accessed by clicking the three leftmost icons in the panel. The small black arrows in the corner of each icon indicate that a menu will appear when the icon is clicked.

The first menu is the K menu. The *K* in this case doesn't stand for anything. It simply designates that this is the main menu from which most applications and options can be selected.

The K menu contains a number of subcategories that can help you find the exact application that you're looking for. Some of the subcategories have subcategories of their own, as shown in Figure 9-22.

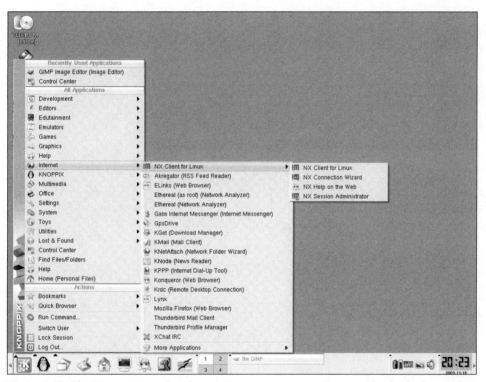

Figure 9-22: The K menu, opened to show the Internet category with several levels of subcategories.

The Knoppix menu, found in the second position and indicated by a penguin icon, gives you access to certain system functions. You can configure hardware, network functions, or services, run certain system utilities, or open a *root shell* (a terminal logged into the superuser account). Figure 9-23 shows the Knoppix menu.

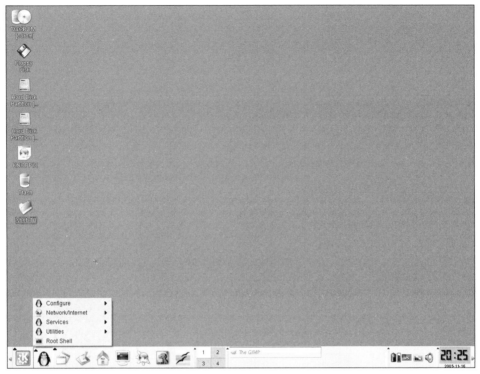

Figure 9-23: The Knoppix menu.

The window list, found in the third position, gives you quick access to any of the programs currently running (see Figure 9-24). Simply click on the name of the window you want to access and it is moved to the front. (In this way, it operates much like the taskbar, about which more in a moment).

If the window you need is located on another workspace, you are taken to that workspace.

Figure 9-24: The window list.

KDE window behavior

Like GNOME, KDE provides window control and behaviors comparable to Microsoft Windows systems. Chapter 10 shows you how to configure the window behavior to suit your preferences.

Using Konqueror's file manager and Web browser

KDE's file manager is called Konqueror. In addition to being a file manager, Konqueror also functions as a Web browser. You bring up a Konqueror window by clicking on a directory or drive icon or by clicking on the Konqueror icon in the panel. If you do the former, Konqueror opens showing the contents of that directory. If you do the latter, the Konqueror appears showing a start screen, as in Figure 9-25.

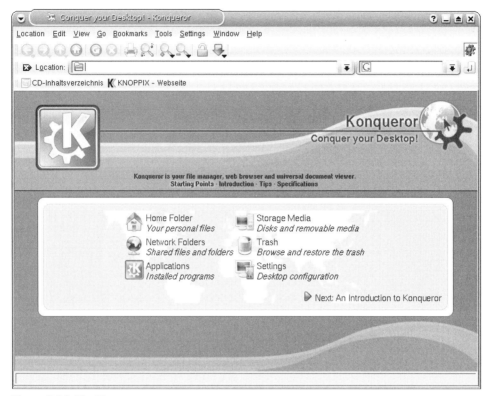

Figure 9-25: The Konqueror start page.

Clicking any of the links on the start page takes you to a relevant area. You'll notice that some of the links recapitulate menus or icons on your desktop. Clicking on these items displays the same thing that clicking on the menu or icon would. For example, if you click on the Applications link on the start page (which is associated with the same icon as the K menu in the panel), you see the same choices that exist in the K menu.

You can display a particular file or directory in Konqueror by typing the path name in the location bar at the top of the screen. (The location bar also accepts a URL to a remote Web page.)

Like Nautilus, you can change the way Konqueror displays the contents of a directory. Click on the View menu and select View Mode for a list of formatting options including icon, list, tree, multi-column list, or others.

GNOME and KDE Interoperability

As mentioned at the start of this chapter, there has been a great deal of convergence between GNOME and KDE. At this point, it's relatively easy to use GNOME-based applications on KDE and vice versa. Fedora Core in particular (and indeed Red Hat distributions more generally) has made interoperability a priority and has developed configurations that make GNOME and KDE look almost identical. A KDE application running on Fedora Core's GNOME configuration, for example, does not look substantially different from a similar GNOME application, as you can see in Figure 9-26.

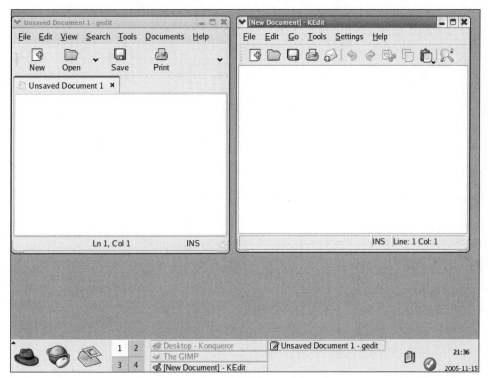

Figure 9-26: gedit and kedit side by side on Fedora Core.

Not all distributions provide this degree of integration between the two desktops, but it's worth noting that it can be done.

The Essential Applications

To wrap up this chapter, here's an introduction to a few of the most essential utilities available on the Linux desktop: office applications, Web browsers, and e-mail applications.

OpenOffice.org

Both GNOME and KDE contain office applications, but the premier Linux office suite is OpenOffice.org (`www.openoffice.org/`). OpenOffice.org started life as a German product called StarOffice. Sun Microsystems bought StarOffice, and while continuing to sell it as a commercial product with support available, they generously decided to also release an open source version, OpenOffice.org. OpenOffice.org is now found in virtually every major Linux distribution. Several major applications make up the OpenOffice.org suite (along with some utilities that expand its abilities even further):

- **Base** is a simple database application similar to Microsoft Access. It can be used to create standalone databases along with fancy reports, queries, and charts in conjunction with Calc and Writer.

- **Calc** is the OpenOffice.org spreadsheet. It can open up and save Microsoft Excel spreadsheets, even those that contain Visual Basic macros. It can connect to Base and other databases and create charts in a wide variety of styles.

- **Draw** is a program for creating vector (line-based) images and diagrams. These can then be embedded into other OpenOffice.org applications.

- **Impress** is a presentation application similar to Microsoft PowerPoint. It has all the styles and visual effects a presentation junkie could wish for and can export its slides into HTML and PDF formats as well as PowerPoint.

- **Writer** is the OpenOffice.org word processor. It has all the formatting and layout features you would expect in a modern word processor, a thesaurus and spell checker for many different languages, and, most importantly for Linux adopters, pretty accurate (though not, alas, perfect) import and export filters for Microsoft Word documents. Writer can also create HTML pages for the Web.

- **Math** is an equation editor, used for accurately typesetting complicated mathematical formulas. It works well with Writer and other OpenOffice.org applications and as a standalone application.

Figure 9-27 shows an application from the OpenOffice.org suite, Impress.

Although I've emphasized the compatibility of OpenOffice.org with Microsoft Office, I hope its own native formats will become industry standards in their own right. Because OpenOffice.org is open source and cross-platform (with versions available for Windows and Mac OS as well as Linux) and because information about its file formats is fully available, using it is good insurance for making sure your data stays *future-proof*. Unlike Microsoft Office users, with OpenOffice.org, you can upgrade to a new version without worrying about compatibility, and without opening your wallet.

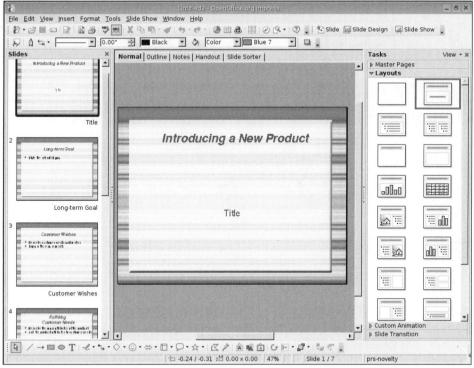

Figure 9-27: The OpenOffice.org Impress presentation application.

Mozilla Firefox

Firefox began life as Netscape Navigator and was later rechristened in an open source version as Mozilla Navigator. More recently, the open source community took the somewhat ponderous Mozilla Navigator and pared it down into a sleek, powerful Web browser called Firefox. In less than two years, not only has Firefox caught up with Microsoft's Internet Explorer, it has surpassed the older program in many ways with features such as support for the latest Web standards, built in pop-up blocking, and greater emphasis on security. Figure 9-28 shows Mozilla Firefox in action.

Firefox does not support ActiveX controls (a type of Web extension used only in Microsoft systems), but it can use Netscape-compatible plug-ins. Available plug-ins include Macromedia Flash, RealAudio, and Adobe Acrobat. Some Linux distributions include these, but others don't for licensing reasons, so you have to download and install them yourself.

Figure 9-28: The Mozilla Firefox Web browser.

Firefox has its own architecture for extensions. A few examples of the many available extensions include the following:

- **webdeveloper** contains useful tools for professional Web designers and programmers.
- **bugmenot** fills in forms on Web sites that demand registration with random information.
- **greasemonkey** allows you to add dynamic HTML scripts to any Web page so you can drastically alter its appearance or behavior.

To add an extension, click on the Tools menu and select Extensions. The Extensions window opens. Click the link marked Get more extensions. This takes you to the home page for Firefox Add-ons. Browse the page and find the add-on that you want to add. Click on the extension's link, and then scroll down until you see a link marked Install Now. Click on that link. A window opens prompting you to confirm the installation. Click Install Now, and the extension is added. You will need to restart Firefox before the extension starts working.

Firefox is not just a great browser; it has significance for all users of the Web. Years of Internet Explorer monopoly caused stagnation in the adoption of new Web technologies. The Mozilla project has been at the forefront of developing and using the latest advances in the field. Mozilla Firefox is available for Windows and Mac OS as well as Linux. Now that Web designers have to cater to more than one browser, standards compliance is increasing, which makes the Web easier to use and build upon for everyone.

E-mail programs

E-mail is the killer application of the Internet, and Linux has many power e-mail programs. Three of the most popular are:

- **Evolution** is the official GNOME e-mail client. If you use the GNOME desktop, you'll probably want to use this program as it integrates well with other GNOME applications. One useful feature unique to Evolution is an add-on called Exchange connector, which allows Evolution to access and synchronize with a Microsoft Exchange server.

- **KMail** is the official e-mail client of the KDE desktop. Like Evolution, the chief benefit of using KMail is integration with its desktop.

- **Mozilla Thunderbird** is an e-mail client from the people who brought you the Firefox Web browser. It lacks integration with a desktop, but because it is cross-platform like Firefox, it could be a good choice in an organization where people use several different operating systems.

Figure 9-29 shows the Evolution e-mail client.

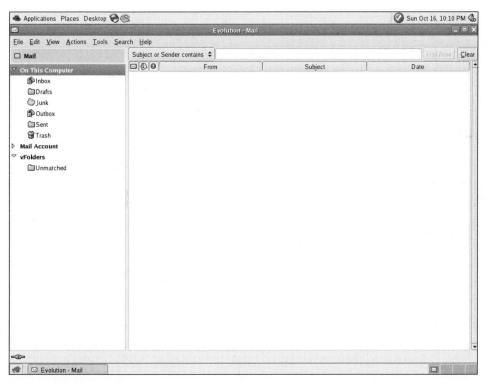

Figure 9-29: Evolution.

Cross-Reference

See Chapter 12 for more information on various e-mail programs.

Summary

Although graphical user interfaces are relatively new on Linux, they've actually been around the Unix world even longer than Windows or Mac OS. GNOME and KDE are the two major competing desktops on the Linux platform; they provide the Linux user with many of the same functions as the desktop environments on other platforms. In fact, desktop environments in general have matured enough so that a common set of functions is found on most systems, and users familiar with one should have little trouble adapting to another. Most distributions prefer one or the other as their default desktop, but many distributions provide both. Many aspects of the two systems are the same, and to some extent, there are no compelling reasons to prefer one to the other.

Chapter 10

Customizing GNOME and KDE

The default settings for GNOME and KDE, no matter what distribution you're using, provide an attractive and easy-to-use interface, but let's face it: it's a lot more fun to work on a desktop that you designed. Both GNOME and KDE can be customized and tweaked in a variety of ways that can provide you with a user experience that is unique to the way you want to work. You can change the background picture, or do away with it all together, move panels and icons, add launchers to your panel, customize menus, change the way windows look and behave — on and on.

In this chapter, I show you the basics of how to customize your desktop environment. There are so many options that I can't possibly cover everything, but I hit the highlights and give you a point of departure. Half the fun of customizing your desktop is discovering new settings along the way.

Customizing GNOME

Depending on your distribution, you may have a unified GNOME Control Center listed among your configuration options. On Fedora Core, you do not have this in your menus (although you can access it by selecting Applications→Run Application and then giving the command `gnome-control-center`). Rather, Fedora Core gives you direct access to various configuration options under the Desktop menu, located in the upper panel. This menu contains the same options as the GNOME Control Center, as you can see by comparing Figures 10-1 and 10-2.

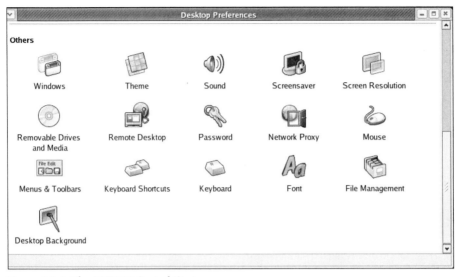

Figure 10-1: The GNOME Control Center.

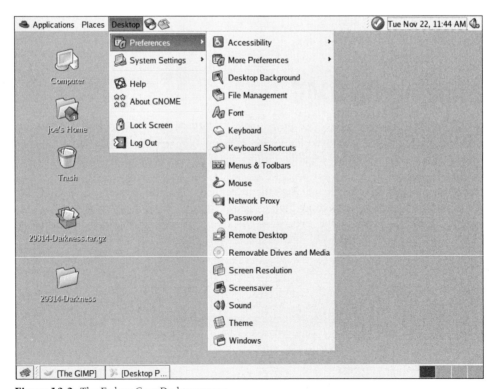

Figure 10-2: The Fedora Core Desktop menu.

Once you've established the location of either of these things, you're ready to start customizing.

Customizing your desktop background

The desktop background is one of the easiest customizations available. Some people like a plain, neutral background, while others like a pretty picture or crazy design. The default background for Fedora Core is a spare, dark-blue image with a small abstract design and the Fedora Core logo in the lower-right corner. If you like this image and want to keep it, you need do nothing. However, if you want to change it, select Desktop → Preferences → Desktop Background (or Desktop from the GNOME Control Center), and the Desktop Background Preferences window opens as shown in Figure 10-3.

Figure 10-3: The Desktop Background Preferences window.

The main panel of this window shows you the wallpaper that's available for your desktop. Simply click on the wallpaper you want to use, and it will be immediately applied to your desktop. You can choose another, if you like, to see how it looks; when you're happy with your choice, click Close to close the Desktop Background Preferences window.

ADDING NEW WALLPAPER

If none of the available wallpaper choices thrill you, you might want to find some new wallpaper or add a picture of your own. To do this, you need to have a picture that you want to use already on your computer. You can either download one off the Internet or import one of your own pictures from a CD or other media. Once you've copied the file to your computer, put it somewhere accessible, such as your home directory. (For this example, we'll imagine that you've copied an image to your home directory and named it `wallpaper.jpg`).

Next, from the Desktop Background Preferences window, click the Add Wallpaper button. This will open the Add Wallpaper window, as shown in Figure 10-4.

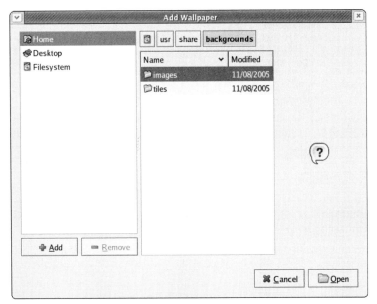

Figure 10-4: The Add Wallpaper window.

In the left-hand panel, double-click the entry marked Home. In the right-hand panel, you see a list of the files in your home directory. Select the `wallpaper.jpg` file and click Open. The Add Wallpaper window closes, and you now see the image you selected listed among the available wall-paper images. It should already be selected, but if it isn't, click on it, and you should see the image on your desktop.

DESKTOPS WITH NO WALLPAPER

Of course, using an image on your desktop is not required. The very first item in the Desktop Background Preferences window is No Wallpaper. If you select this option, you will need to decide what to do with your background. You have three choices: a solid color, a vertical gradient, or a horizontal gradient. (A gradient is a set of two colors with the first blending into the second over the range of the desktop: the vertical gradient blends top to bottom, while the horizontal gradient blends left to right.)

When you select No Wallpaper, the Desktop Colors section of the Desktop Background Preferences window becomes active. (If your previous desktop image was not large enough to cover the whole screen, the Desktop Colors section may already be active, so that you can select the color that will be used for your desktop's border.) The area that reads Solid Color can be clicked and a menu opens allowing you to choose Solid Color, Vertical Gradient, or Horizontal Gradient. If you selected Solid Color, you see a box next to your selection. Clicking on this box opens the Pick a color window as shown in Figure 10-5.

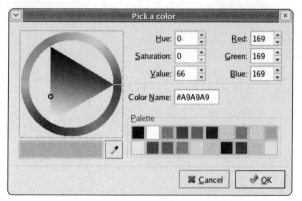

Figure 10-5: The Pick a color window.

This window allows you to select the color that appears on your desktop. Your selection is represented by the small circle. You can move this circle anywhere within the triangle. If you click on the outer ring, you will change the position of the triangle, which, in turn changes the range of colors within it. A little practice shows you how easy it really is. Once you've selected your color, click OK. The window exits, and the new color appears on your desktop.

If you selected Vertical or Horizontal Gradient (such as that shown in Figure 10-6), you will have two color boxes next to your selection. These boxes represent the two colors that will form the ends of the gradient. Click on each box to bring up the Pick a color window. When you have made your selections, the resulting gradient will be the range of colors between the two colors you selected. A word of caution: Not all color combinations makes good gradients. Turquoise and dark lime green, for example, will not appeal to most people.

Once you have arranged the desktop background as you like it, click Close on the Desktop Preferences Window. Your new desktop is now saved and appears in this configuration every time you log in, until you change it.

Desktop themes

Perhaps the easiest way to customize the look of your desktop is to use themes. A theme is a set of visual elements (title bars, window corners, icons, borders, and so on) that combine to give everything on your desktop a consistent look.

To access the theme controls, select Preferences → Theme from the Desktop menu. This opens the Theme Preferences window as shown in Figure 10-7.

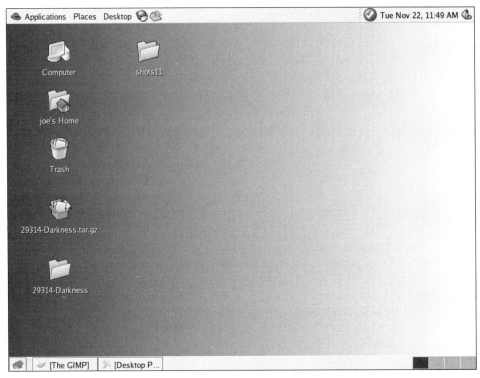

Figure 10-6: A horizontal gradient on the desktop.

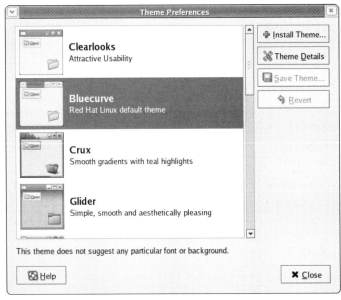

Figure 10-7: The Theme Preferences window.

In the main panel, you can see a number of themes listed. As with the Desktop Background Preferences window, you can select a theme simply by clicking on it. The visual elements of your desktop change when you do. (This may take a few seconds.) If you like the new theme and decide you want to keep it, simply click Close to exit the Theme Preferences window. If you'd like to try something else, click on that instead. Your theme changes every time you click on a new one.

INSTALLING NEW THEMES

A default installation of Fedora Core comes with only a few themes, and for the most part, they're fairly spare. These themes are designed for simplicity and ease of use. There are, however, literally hundreds of themes available; they run the gamut from spare and useful to themes that are extremely entertaining, if tough on the eyes.

The central clearing house for GNOME themes is in the Art section of the GNOME Web site, located at `http://art.gnome.org`. The themes are broken out into several types:

- **Application:** These are themes that control what buttons and checkboxes look like, what color windows and panels are, and so on.

- **Window Border:** These themes control the outlines of windows. That is, they determine whether corners are square or rounded, what color active and inactive title bars are, and more.

- **Icons:** Here you can find sets of icons that give a unified look.

- **Login Manager:** Login Manager themes determine what the initial login screen looks like.

- **Splash Screen:** Splash screen themes control what you see while your GNOME session is starting up.

There is also a sixth category: GTK+ Engines. These themes are primarily of use to theme developers. That is, if you decide you want to create themes from scratch, you might want to investigate these, but the casual user can ignore this category.

You will often find that themes in several categories have the same name. In cases like this, you can be reasonably assured that they form parts of an overarching theme. That is, an application theme with a particular name is designed for use with a window border theme of the same name.

To install an application theme, first download the theme. Do not extract the archive — it needs to be in the archived, compressed format. Open the Theme Preferences window and click the button marked Theme Details. This opens the Theme Details window as shown in Figure 10-8.

The Theme Details window should be open to the tab marked Controls. If a different tab is selected, click on the Controls tab. Next, find the icon for the theme that you downloaded. (If you didn't download it to the desktop, open a Nautilus window and navigate to it.) Click on the icon and drag it onto the Theme Details window. Your installation of the theme is confirmed. Click OK to dismiss the confirmation window. You should now see the name of the theme you downloaded in the pane on the left side of the Theme Details window. It may already be highlighted. If it's not, you can click on it to highlight it. Once highlighted, the controls on your applications should change to display the new theme's artwork.

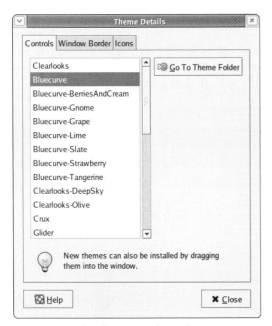

Figure 10-8: The Theme Details window.

Installing a window border theme works in exactly the same way as installing an application theme, except that when you open the Theme Details window, you need to click on the Window Border tab before you drag the icon onto it.

Installing icon themes is a bit trickier. There is a bug in the version of the Theme Preferences program used on Fedora Core 4 that does not install the theme file into the proper location. Therefore, you must do it manually, using the terminal.

First, download the theme file. The file should be in the format `<theme-name>.tar.gz`. Open a terminal window. (Do this by right-clicking on the desktop and selecting Open Terminal from the pop-up menu.) In the terminal window, type the following commands:

```
mv <theme-name>.tar.gz .themes
cd .themes
tar xzf <theme-name>.tar.gz
```

At this point, you can close the terminal window, and the theme should be installed.

To install a Login Manager theme, first, download the theme package, then click on the Desktop menu, and then select System Settings → Login Screen. You are prompted for the superuser's password. This opens the Login Screen Setup window as shown in Figure 10-9.

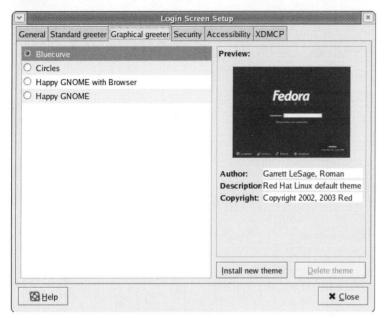

Figure 10-9: The Login Screen Setup window.

Click on the tab marked Graphical Greeter, and click the button reading Install new theme. A navigator window opens. Use this window to navigate to your theme's package file. Click on the file to highlight it, and then click Install. The window closes, and you should see your new theme listed in the pane on the left side of the Login Screen Setup window. Click on your new theme to highlight it (its preview appears in the right-hand pane), and then click Close. You should see the new login screen the next time you log in.

To install a splash screen theme, download the theme. In this case the theme is not an archive file but rather a graphic file such as a PNG or JPG image file. After you download the file, put it in the directory that you intend to use to store it. In this case, let's imagine that your storage directory is `/misc/gnome/splash`, and the file is `/misc/gnome/spash/newsplash.png`. Next, click on the Applications menu and select System Tools →Configuration Editor. This opens the Configuration Editor as shown in Figure 10-10.

In the left pane, click on the disclosure triangle next to the apps folder and scroll down the list of subfolders until you find gnome-session. Click the disclosure triangle to the left to expand the category. Then click the options folder to highlight it. In the upper-right pane, you should see an entry marked splash image (Figure 10-11). Double-click on this.

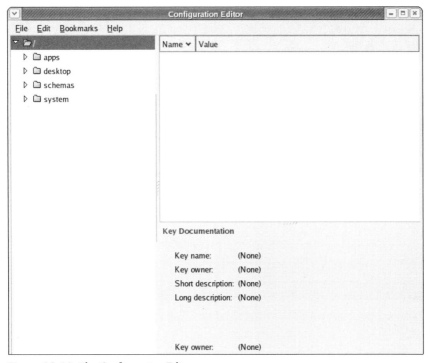

Figure 10-10: The Configuration Editor.

Figure 10-11: The Configuration Editor showing the selections for changing the splash screen.

When you click on splash image, the Edit Key dialog opens (Figure 10-12).

Edit Key

Name: /apps/gnome-session/options/splash_imag

Type: String

Value: splash/gnome-splash.png

✖ Cancel   ✓ OK

Figure 10-12: The Edit Key dialog.

In the Value field, type the name of the file, in this case /misc/gnome/splash/newsplash.png, then click OK. The Edit Key dialog closes, and you should see the new value listed in the Configuration Editor. At this point, you can close the Configuration Editor, and your new splash screen should appear the next time you log in.

Customizing the panel

One place where you might care to add a few personal touches is on one or more of the panels. On Fedora Core, most of the bottom menu is given over to the taskbar and the workspace switcher, but the top panel has a reasonably large space to which you can add launchers or applets. In addition, you can also change the size and behavior of the panel.

ADDING APPLETS AND LAUNCHERS

You can easily add an applet or a launcher to the panel by right-clicking on the panel and selecting Add to Panel from the menu that pops up. This opens the Add to Panel window as shown in Figure 10-13.

In the Add to Panel window, you can see several applets and functions that can be added to the panel. An *applet* is a small program that can run inside the panel. A good example of an applet is the Weather Report program. Weather Report pulls weather data from a server and displays the current conditions and temperature as an icon in your panel. (Obviously, a network connection is required for this applet to work.)

Tip

You can configure the Weather Report applet by right-clicking on it and selecting Preferences from the pop-up menu. At the very least, you'll need to set your location before the applet can get your weather. In general, any applet that has configuration options can be configured by right-clicking and selecting preferences.

Figure 10-13: The Add to Panel window.

A *launcher* is an icon that launches a program when it's clicked. You can add a launcher to your panel by selecting Custom Application Launcher or Application Launcher from the Add to Panel window. Use Application Launcher if you want to add a launcher for a program that is already listed in the system menus, or Custom Application Launcher if the application you want to add is not listed.

If you choose Custom Application Launcher, the Add to Panel window changes into the Create Launcher window as shown in Figure 10-14.

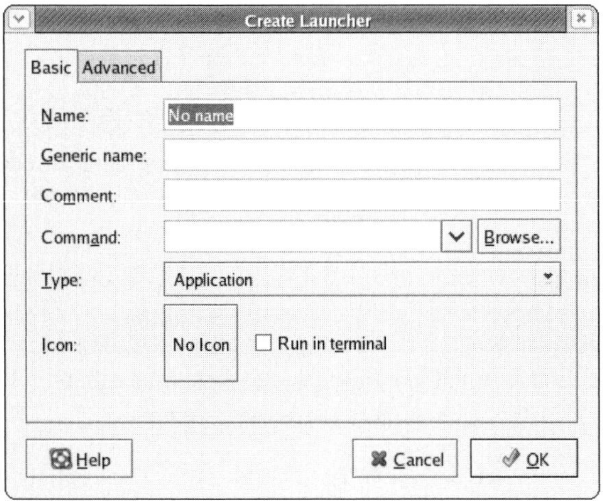

Figure 10-14: The Create Launcher window.

Fill out the information as requested in the window. The Name and Comment fields can be filled with anything you like. The Command field must be filled with the command that you would give if you were going to launch the program with a text command. (See Chapter 11 for more information about using text commands.)

In the area marked Icon, click on the square labeled No Icon and you will see a set of available icons. Select the one you want and click OK. The icon that you chose will now be displayed in the square. Click OK and your launcher is added to the panel.

If you choose Application Launcher from the Add to Panel window, the Add button changes to a Next button. Click this button, and you are presented with a list of categories from which to choose. (Notice that these categories exactly mirror the categories in the Applications menu. Click the disclosure triangle next to the category of your choice, and the category expands to show all the entries within it. Select the item you want to add and click Add. Your item then appears in the panel.

CONFIGURING PANEL PROPERTIES

To configure the panel's properties, right-click on the panel and select Properties from the pop-up menu. This opens the Panel Properties window as shown in Figure 10-15.

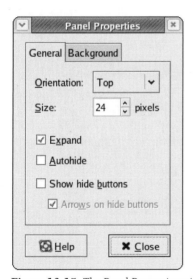

Figure 10-15: The Panel Properties window.

The Panel Properties window has two tabs. In the General tab, you can configure such attributes as orientation (top, bottom, left, right), size, and expandability characteristics. In the Background tab you can configure the background of the panel. The default selection for the panel background is None (use system theme). This means that the theme you selected for the overall desktop look will also control the panel's background. If you prefer, you can configure the panel to use a solid color (with an adjustable level of opacity) or an image file.

Customizing KDE

Customizing KDE is not enormously different from customizing GNOME, as many of the same concepts apply. Customizing the desktop background, for example, is done in much the same way. You have the choice of a background image, or of solid color, vertical, or horizontal gradient. However, you also have several other choices such as Pipecross Gradient (a sort of X-shaped gradient), Elliptic Gradient, as well as various two-color pattern options. The specifics of these choices are not terribly important — if you're interested, you can look at them and decide if you like them or not. The point is that the procedure is more or less the same, and the concepts laid out in the GNOME section of this chapter will often transfer with slight adaptations.

The KDE Control Center

KDE's customization options are accessed from within the KDE Control Center. Unlike Fedora Core's approach to GNOME (individual customization modules), KDE has a unified control panel that allows you to make multiple adjustments in one session.

To access the KDE Control Center, look in KDE's main menu for the Control Center option, and click it. (This is true regardless of whether you're using Fedora Core or Knoppix.) This opens the main Control Center window as shown in Figure 10-16.

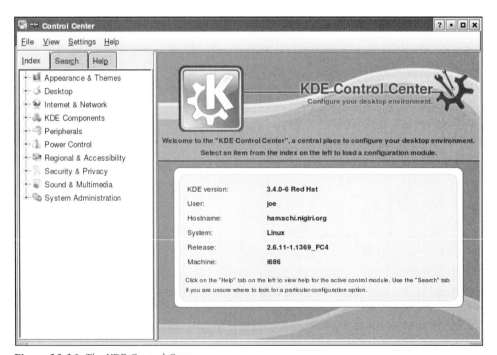

Figure 10-16: The KDE Control Center.

In the left-hand pane, you can see a number of entries, each with a small plus sign (+) next to them. Clicking on the plus sign expands the category, so that you can see the entries within it. For present purposes, we are interested in the Appearance & Themes category, so click on the plus sign and expand it. As you can see, the entries inside this category represent a number of options familiar from the previous discussion of GNOME configuration.

Click Theme Manager, and the large right-hand pane shows the Theme Manager, as shown in Figure 10-17.

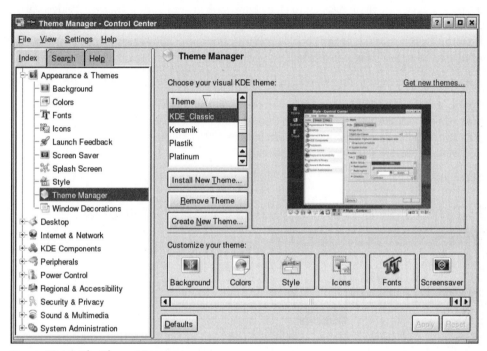

Figure 10-17: The Theme Manager.

The Theme Manager encompasses several other options as well, as you can see from the presence of the Background, Colors, Style, Icons, Fonts, and Screensaver buttons across the bottom. This makes the theme manager a good jumping-off point for customizing your environment.

In the upper-left corner of the Theme Manager, you can see a pane that lists a number of themes. If you select a theme, you can see a preview of it in the right-hand pane. Unlike GNOME, the changes will not occur immediately. You must click Apply before any changes are made to your desktop.

CUSTOMIZING YOUR THEME

As mentioned earlier, a set of buttons along the bottom of the Theme Manager allows you to alter certain aspects of your desktop theme without affecting others. These buttons do the following:

■ **Background:** Background allows you to change the desktop background or wallpaper. This functions similarly to the corresponding function in GNOME.

■ **Colors:** The Colors button allows you to change the color scheme of your theme. When you click this button, a window opens showing you an example of the current color scheme. It also gives you several other schemes from which you can choose. When you select a scheme, the example changes to reflect the scheme you chose. Click Apply to apply these changes to your desktop.

■ **Style:** The Style option allows you to change the look of your various *widgets*. Widgets are things like tabs, radio buttons, checkboxes, progress bars, and the like. Select your style from the drop box in the upper pane. A preview shows in the lower pane. As always, click Apply to make the changes take effect.

■ **Icons:** The Icons button allows you to choose which icon set will be used.

■ **Fonts:** The Fonts option allows you to choose the fonts that will be used for various purposes on your desktop. By clicking the Choose button next to any font function, you will pull up the Select Font window, as shown in Figure 10-18. Select the font, style, and size you want. A preview is shown in the lower pane.

■ **Screensaver:** This option allows you to choose the look and behavior of the screensaver.

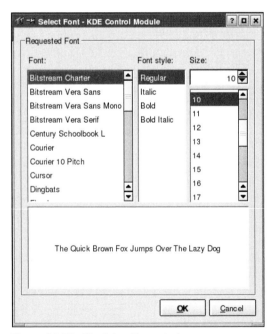

Figure 10-18: The Select Font window.

INSTALLING NEW THEMES

The process for installing new themes on KDE is only slightly different from that for GNOME.

To install a new theme, you must first download a theme package. Click the link marked Get new themes... in the upper-right corner of the Theme Manager. This opens a Web browser to the Web site www.kde-look.org. On the left-hand side of the page, click Themes/Styles, and then select the version of KDE that you are using. (In this case, my version of KDE is 3.4, so I clicked the KDE 3.2 – 3.5 link.) At this point, you can browse for new themes. When you find one you want, download the file. For this example, assume that you've downloaded the file to the directory /home/stan.

Open a terminal window by right-clicking on the desktop and selecting Konsole from the pop-up menu. Type cd /home/stan. Now type ls. You should see the package file in the directory listing.

At this point, type tar xvfz packagename, where packagename is the name of the file you just downloaded. The file expands. Usually, this creates a new directory.

Note

Some packages may be compressed using the bzip2 program rather than gzip; these files will end with the suffix .bz2. To extract these files use the command tar xvfj packagename.

Now, go back to the Theme Manager, and click Install New Theme. This opens a navigator window as shown in Figure 10-19.

Figure 10-19: The navigator window.

Click on the Home Folder button. In the large pane, you should see the folder that was just created. Double-click that folder, and you should see a file with the suffix .kth.

Note

Not every package listed on kde-look.org is a theme for KDE as a whole. Some of these packages are themes for various applications, or just simply background art. Read the comments for each package before you decide if you want to download it. If you do not find a .kth file, read all the documentation to make sure that you have an actual KDE theme.

Select that file, and click Open. The navigator window closes, and you should see the theme listed among those in the Theme Manager. You may now select it and click Apply to use it on your desktop.

Note

You may find that some of the themes on kde-look.org are in different file formats. Often the makers of themes will create or package themes especially for particular Linux distributions. For example, you may find that there are theme RPM files for Fedora Core or Red Hat Linux systems. These will have their own installation procedures. You should be able to find documentation at the site.

Summary

GNOME and KDE offer similar solutions to the same needs, but they differ in some ways. GNOME's customization system, at least on Fedora Core, relies on a distributed set of controls, accessed from the Desktop menu. KDE opts for a more centralized Control Center. With both systems, desktop backgrounds, colors, fonts, and widgets can be configured to create a look as unique as the user.

Chapter 11

Using the Terminal

I f you told some people that you were thinking about trying Linux, they may have warned you that you would need to learn a lot of arcane commands. Generally, the progress made on the various desktop environments has relieved users of the need to use text commands for most everyday tasks. Nevertheless, Linux's command-line interface is still very much alive and kicking. For many people, the very idea of using text commands seems almost charmingly retro. Weren't we all too happy to get rid of our DOS machines back in the early 90s? Certainly now that we've reached the 21st century, if not actually talking to our computers like Captain Kirk, we should at least not be typing commands into them!

The fact of the matter is that there are several very good reasons to keep the command-line interface around. One is historic: The command-line interface (CLI) was the first interface that Unix had, and believe it or not, there are still a few programs kicking around from back-in-the-day. If you want to use an old, old piece of software, you need a way to run it.

But the CLI exists for reasons beyond the mere legacy. There are actually situations in which a command-line interface makes more sense than a graphical one. One of the tenets of the Unix philosophy is to avoid *captive user interfaces*. This means that whenever possible, you want programs to be able to present a way by which they can be used by another program, rather than a human user. Obviously, another program can't extend an arm from the screen and wiggle the mouse around. It's got to be able to send commands in a way that's available to it. For this reason, many programs — even if their main interface is graphical — have an alternative text-based interface. If you need to use a certain function of the program, you (whether *you* are a human user, or another program) can simply give the command.

A third reason to keep the CLI around is automation. Many Linux functions can be automated by means of the `cron` utility. This utility is an example of a program that uses other programs. If a program has a command-line interface, it can be run automatically using `cron`.

Furthermore, the Unix command language is more than just a set of commands. It also comprises an actual programming language. Unix commands are entered by means of a *shell,* which is a command interpreter. In addition to simple program invocation commands, the shell can also understand certain programming language commands such as `if-then` constructs. Using these constructs, you can create programs to serve a variety of needs.

Finally, note that the shell command syntax is very rich and complex. Even if you aren't full bore into writing programs, you can still use the shell command language to do such things as redirecting program input and output (if you want, for example, to redirect the output of a program to a file, rather than to the screen) or to pipe the output of one command into another.

This chapter gives you a look at all of these uses for text commands (with the exception of the `cron` utility, which is discussed in Chapter 17). You will see that far from being a relic of the past, the Linux command-line interface is actually one of the reasons that Linux is so advanced!

The Unix Shell

Some people use Linux without ever looking at a graphical interface. Their environment is composed entirely of text, and they do their work simply by entering commands and using text-based programs. They are able to do this by making use of the shell. The shell is a command interpreter that accepts commands from the user and translates them into actions to be executed by the system. A user who is well versed in the shell command language can do almost anything a graphical interface user can do, and a few other things, besides.

As if that weren't enough, the shell is also a programming environment. It is possible to write programs using the shell's command language and execute those programs with a single command.

So why is it called a shell? The answer has to do with the propensity of Unix programmers to give things whimsical names. A *kernel* — be it Unix, Linux, or any other — is so called because it constitutes the inner core of the system. A kernel is never really designed to be used by humans. Rather, it is designed so that programs can have access to system functions. A *shell* is designed so that human operators can interact with a system. Thus, from the operator's perspective, the shell is something that seems to surround and protect the kernel.

Thus far, I've been talking about "the shell" as if it were a monolithic entity. Actually, there are a number of different shells, each with its own features and qualities. Some are better suited to certain tasks than others, but to a certain extent, they all manage to accomplish the same tasks. Which shell you use is largely a matter of personal preference. Here's a brief look at four of the most popular shells:

- **The Bourne shell** is the original Unix shell. Almost every Unix or Unix-derived system has some variant of the Bourne shell installed on it. Indeed, the Bourne shell is so basic that its program name (the command which one would give to start it) is `sh`.

- **The Bourne-again shell** or BASH is the free software version of the Bourne shell that was created for the GNU project. Originally, BASH was written to be identical in function to the Bourne shell, but as it has developed, it has taken on new features of its own. BASH is the variant of the Bourne shell found on most Linux systems and is probably the most popular shell among Linux users. BASH's extra features mean that shell programs written for the Bourne shell usually run on BASH without modifications, but the reverse is not always true. Because of this, you may want to check for compatibility issues if you're trying to use a Bourne-style program written for another system. The examples in this book use the BASH shell. The Bourne-again shell's program name is `bash`, but on many systems, it can also be invoked with `sh`.

- **The Korn shell** (`ksh`) was the first shell to have such features as command-line editing (the ability to use editing functions from within a command), the ability to recall earlier commands, and integer arithmetic (the ability to do arithmetic in the shell without having to invoke an external calculator program). The Korn shell was also the first shell to allow the user to manage multiple processes from the command line. In other words, the Korn shell allows the user to switch back and forth between running processes — something that users of graphical interfaces take for granted, but which, if you think about it, would not seem to be so easy in a text-based environment.

Were it not for BASH, the Korn shell (`ksh`) would probably have eclipsed the Bourne shell in popularity. BASH took a number of features, notably those listed previously, from the Korn shell and incorporated them into an overall Bourne shell–type environment. To some extent, this stole some of the Korn shell's thunder.

■ **The C shell** was developed for the purpose of having a Unix shell with a programming language that is similar in syntax to the C programming language. The C shell can do just about anything the Bourne, BASH, or Korn shell can do, but it frequently does it in a different way. Often when a user tries to do something on an unfamiliar system and runs into problems, it's because the C shell has been set as the default shell on that system, and the user is not aware of it. Because of this, it's often a good idea to double-check the shell you're using. You can check your shell by giving the command `echo $SHELL`. The C shell is usually known by the program name `csh` but may also be known as `tcsh`, depending on which version you have installed.

Note

You can check your shell by giving the command `echo $SHELL`.

Finding the Terminal

At this point, you may be staring at your Linux machine saying, "Okay, where do I enter these commands?" To use the shell, you need to be using a terminal. In the era before personal computers became popular, it was common for computer users to be sitting at a *dumb* terminal, which was connected to a mainframe computer by a bulky cable. These were called dumb terminals because they did no computing functions on their own. They provided the display screen and the keyboard, and they relayed signals back and forth between the user and the mainframe.

With the advent of the personal computer, people began doing more of their computing functions on their local machines. When they needed to log into another machine, they still needed the functionality of the old dumb terminals. To do this, they used *terminal emulation* programs. Simply put, a terminal emulator is a program that gives you a terminal-in-a-window on your desktop.

On most systems you can get a terminal window by right-clicking on the desktop and choosing New Terminal, New Shell, Terminal Window, Console, or something similar from the menu that pops up. If there's nothing like that available, look in your Start menu under System Utilities or the like. Popular terminal emulation programs have names like Xterm, Gterm, Kterm, Konsole, or something along those lines. Once you've found the program launcher and clicked it, you should get something that looks like the window in Figure 11-1.

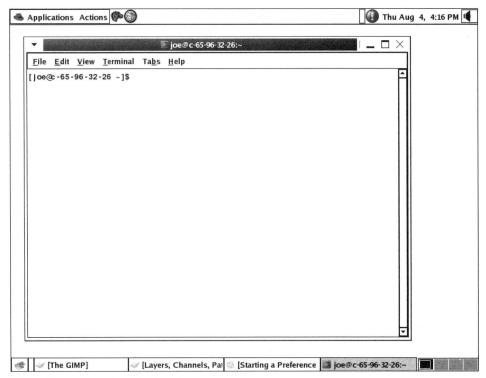

Figure 11-1: A typical terminal window.

As you can see, there's not much to it — just a blank window with a single line of text. That text you see is the *shell prompt,* and anytime you see it, the shell is telling you that it's ready to accept your input. The shell prompt may look different on your system. Most shell prompts — the BASH shell in particular — are configurable, and the designers of your particular distribution have probably configured your prompt in a particular way. Under the BASH shell, the prompt ends with a dollar sign ($) if you are logged in as a regular user and with a hash mark (#) if you are logged in as the root, or superuser. This is important because it's possible to issue commands as the superuser that can damage your system. If you find that you are logged in as the superuser when you hadn't intended to be, log out, and log back in under your regular user account.

Having found the prompt and made sure that you're not logged in as root, you're ready to begin giving commands.

Anatomy of a Command

Every Unix command invokes a unique program or a shell function. Even the simplest, most mundane commands invoke programs. Consequently, there can be some inconsistencies in the way that commands are used because the way in which a command is read by the program that it invokes is, to some degree, at the whim of the programmer. Most commands follow a format that, although it may not appear so at first glance, is very consistent and logical. The syntax looks like this:

```
command -option(s) target(s)
```

The `command` part is the name of the command, for example, `ls` (the *list* command) or `cat` (the *concatenate* command). This is the command's program name and is often the only required part of the command. (That is, it is possible to invoke some commands with only the program name—although this is not true of all commands.) The second part of the command, designated `-option(s)`, can be used to give certain options to the command that can affect its behavior. (Options are sometimes also referred to as *flags* or *switches*.) Examples of options might include `-v` (for verbose) and `--help` (to get information about the command). Notice that most single-letter options are preceded by a single dash, while word-length options are generally preceded by double dashes. The `target(s)` is the thing(s) upon which you want the command to act. Depending on the command, this can be a directory, a file, or other object of the action. There can be multiple targets if the command requires it. For example, the `mv` command, which is used to move a file, requires both the name of the file being moved, and the desired new location of the file as targets.

Note

Command options and targets are sometimes collectively referred to as *arguments.*

A simple example command

Let's look a command in detail to get a slightly better idea of what's going on here. The `ls` command is used to get a listing of the contents of a directory. (It's roughly equivalent to the old DOS `dir` command.) This command can be invoked purely as is, by simply typing **ls** at the command prompt.

```
[joe@hotategai bin]$ ls
[                           magnifier
411toppm                    Mail
4rdf                        mail.local
4ss                         mailmail
4ssd                        mailq
4ss_manager                 mailq.postfix
4versa                      mailq.sendmail
4xml                        mailsettings
4xpath                      mailstat
4xslt                       make
4xupdate                    makedb
a2p                         make_driver_db_cups
a2ping                      make_driver_db_lpr
```

```
a2ps                              make_encmap
ab                                makeindex
ac                                makeinfo
aclocal                           makekdewidgets
aclocal-1.4                       makemap
aclocal-1.5                       makempx
aclocal-1.6                       makempy
aclocal-1.7                       makeobj
```

As you can see, when given in this way, the output of the command is a list of the files in the current directory. (In this case, the current directory is /usr/bin, as shown in the shell prompt, and I have truncated the output for space.) This is the *default behavior* of the command. That is, when no option or target is provided, this is how the command works. There are a few things to notice here. The first is that the listing given is that of the *current directory*. That is, whichever directory you are in when you give the command is the one for which you get the listing. (I show how to change directories later in this chapter.) Second, the listing is given in a columnar format, with the names of the files printed in columns across the area of the screen. Third, only the names of the files are printed, with no other information about them given. Fourth, the file names are printed in alphabetical order. Fifth, only the names of *normal files* are printed. (There are special files that are not displayed, as you will see shortly.)

Adding options

Now, let's see how you can change some of these behaviors. First, suppose that you want the file names displayed as a comma-separated list rather than in column format. Do this by using the -m option, like this:

```
[joe@hamachi bin]$ ls -m
[, 411toppm, 4rdf, 4ss, 4ssd, 4ss_manager, 4versa, 4xml, 4xpath, 4xslt,
4xupdate, a2p, a2ping, a2ps, ab, ac, aclocal, aclocal-1.4, aclocal-1.5,
aclocal-1.6, aclocal-1.7, aclocal-1.9, aconnect, acpi_listen,
activation-client,adddebug, addftinfo, addr2line, addr2name.awk,
afs5log, ainit, akregator, aleph,allcm, allec, allneeded, alsacard,
alsalisp, alsamixer, amidi, amixer, amstex,animate, anytopnm, aplay,
aplaymidi, apm, apmsleep, appletproxy, apropos, ar, arecord,
arecordmidi, ark, artscat, artsc-config, artsd, artsdsp,
artsmessage,artsplay, artsrec, artsshell, artswrapper, as, asciitopgm,
ascii-xfr, aseqdump,aseqnet, aserver, aspell, aspell-import, assistant,
at, atktopbm, atq, atrm,attr, audiofile-config, audit2allow,
authconfig, authconfig-gtk, autoconf,autoheader, autoipd, autom4te,
automake, automake-1.4, automake-1.5,automake-1.6, automake-1.7,
automake-1.9, autoreconf, autoscan, autoupdate,autovbox, awk, b2m,
bamstex, bashbug-32, batch, bc, bdfindex, bdftops,
```

Note that you are still in the /usr/bin directory, as in the example from the previous section.

Next, how can you change the directory whose contents are being displayed? You do this by giving the name of another directory as a target, like so:

```
ls /etc
a2ps.cfg              init.d                quotatab
a2ps-site.cfg         initlog.conf          racoon
acpi                  inittab               rc
adjtime               inputrc               rc0.d
alchemist             iproute2              rc1.d
```

This will give you the contents of the /etc directory instead of the current directory. (Unless /etc is the current directory, in which case the result will be the same.) If you want to display the /etc directory's contents as a comma-separated list, simply combine the option and the target, like so:

```
ls -m /etc
4Suite, a2ps.cfg, a2ps-site.cfg, acpi, adjtime, alchemist, aliases,
aliases.db,alsa, alternatives, anacrontab, asound.state, at.deny,
auditd.conf, audit.rules,auto.master, auto.misc, auto.net, auto.smb,
bashrc, blkid.tab, blkid.tab.old,bluetooth, bonobo-activation,
cdrecord.conf, cipe, cpuspeed.conf, cron.d,cron.daily, cron.deny,
cron.hourly, cron.monthly, crontab, cron.weekly,csh.cshrc, csh.login,
cups, dbus-1, default, dev.d, dhclient-eth0.conf
```

If you want to display information about the files other than the names, you can do so by using the -l option, which displays the contents in *long* form. Use the following command:

```
ls -l
```

For the /etc directory use the following:

```
ls -l /etc
total 3740
drwxr-xr-x    2 root root     4096 Nov  8 18:00 4Suite
-rw-r--r--    1 root root    15289 Mar 23  2005 a2ps.cfg
-rw-r--r--    1 root root     2562 Mar 23  2005 a2ps-site.cfg
drwxr-xr-x    4 root root     4096 Mar 16  2005 acpi
-rw-r--r--    1 root root       46 Nov  8 16:49 adjtime
drwxr-xr-x    4 root root     4096 Mar  3  2005 alchemist
```

If you want certain "special" files to be listed (for example, files whose names begin with a dot, such as the .profile file are not listed by default), you would use the -a option (note the., .., and .pwd.lock files):

```
ls -a
.                     httpd                 profile.d
..                    idmapd.conf           protocols
4Suite                im_palette.pal        pwdb.conf
a2ps.cfg              im_palette-small.pal  .pwd.lock
```

Options can be combined. For example, if you want all files (including special files) to be displayed in long format, you would use both the -l and the -a options together, like so:

```
ls -la
total 3768
drwxr-xr-x  89 root root   12288 Nov 24 04:05 .
drwxr-xr-x  25 root root    4096 Nov 15 20:30 ..
drwxr-xr-x   2 root root    4096 Nov  8 18:00 4Suite
-rw-r--r--   1 root root   15289 Mar 23  2005 a2ps.cfg
-rw-r--r--   1 root root    2562 Mar 23  2005 a2ps-site.cfg
drwxr-xr-x   4 root root    4096 Mar 16  2005 acpi
-rw-r--r--   1 root root      46 Nov  8 16:49 adjtime
drwxr-xr-x   4 root root    4096 Mar  3  2005 alchemist
```

Note that where more than one option is used, the preceding dash need be typed only once, not before each individual option.

The options for any given command are unique to that command. The -l option for the ls command would not necessarily do the same thing for any other command. Although you learn some of the more common options for certain commands in this chapter, the best way to find out all the options for any given command is to read the manual page for that command. For example, running the command man ls shows that there are no fewer than 34 options for the ls command. Some of these options are sure to be obscure to the casual user, but they do exist and a description of each of them is found in the manual page.

Sources and destinations

Earlier I mentioned that sometimes there is more than one target for a command. Typically, the use of multiple targets takes the form of a *source* and a *destination* target. As an example, look at the mv command, which is used to move a file from one location to another. Assume that you have a file called /home/fred/bedrock, meaning the file called bedrock is located in the directory /home/fred (Fred's home directory). Now imagine that you want to move it to the directory /home/wilma. Do that by giving the command in this form:

```
mv /home/fred/bedrock /home/wilma
```

After this command runs, the file would be designated as /home/wilma/bedrock. If you wanted to rename the file at the same time that you moved it, you could have given the command like so:

```
mv /home/fred/bedrock /home/wilma/gravel
```

Then the file would become known as /home/wilma/gravel. This command can also be used to rename a file but leave it in the same directory:

```
mv /home/fred/bedrock /home/fred/gravel
```

This would leave the file in /home/fred but would change the name from bedrock to gravel.

In each of these cases, you can see that the command uses the first target as the object to be acted upon (the *source*) and the second as the desired result of the action (the *destination*). In most cases, the source will come first and the destination second. As usual, the manual page is the final authority for the proper locations of the source and destination.

Some Common Useful Commands

Now that you've seen the proper way to give a command, here are a few common commands that you will probably find yourself using on a day-to-day basis. These commands are really the bare minimum for getting by in a text-based environment.

pwd

The pwd command is given by itself without options or targets. The command's name stands for *print working directory*, and the command does just that. It tells you the directory that you're currently in.

```
[joe@hamachi etc]$ pwd
/etc
```

cd

The cd (change directory) command takes as an argument the name of the directory to which you wish to move. So, for example, if you're in your home directory, and you want to move to the /etc directory, you'd give the command

```
cd /etc
```

After you've done this, assuming there are no problems (such as trying to move into a directory that doesn't exist or that you don't have permission for), the directory that you've used as the target will become the new current (working) directory.

Note

To understand the pwd and cd commands, it's helpful to understand the concept of the *current directory*. Sometimes called the *working* directory (as per the pwd command), the current directory is the directory that you are *in* at any given time. When you first log into your account, or open a terminal window, you'll usually be in your home directory. The precise location of your home directory may vary from system to system, but usually it will be something along the lines of /home/username or /user/home/username or something like that. (username in this context represents your username — the name that you use to log into you computer.) To *be in* a directory means that any command you give assumes the current directory as a point of reference. If you give the ls command without arguments, for example, you will get a listing of the current directory.

Note

Under the file system convention that Linux has inherited from Unix, files can be specified in either an absolute or a relative way. For example, assume that your home directory is located at /home/dennis and you create a subdirectory called /home/dennis/letters. If you are in your home directory, and you want to move into the letters subdirectory, you can give the command cd letters. You could also give the command in the form cd /home/dennis/letters. The first form is the relative, and the second is the absolute. It is important to note that the relative form is always *relative to the directory you are in at any given time*. For example, if you are in the /etc directory, and you give the command cd letters, the shell assumes that you mean /etc/letters. If no such directory exists, you'll get an error message. From /etc, you'd have to use the absolute format to get to /home/dennis/letters.

ls

The ls command, as discussed earlier, gives a listing of whichever directory is given as the command's target. If no target is given, it produces a listing of the current directory. Here are some of the most common options for the ls command:

-l   Prints the directory listing in *long* format. This means that in addition to file names, you get such information as the permissions associated with the file, the user who owns the file, the group that owns the file, the size of the file, the date that the file was last modified, and so on.

-a   Lists all files, including files whose name begins with a dot (not listed by default).

-F   Displays the file type. Directories will be designated by a trailing slash, executable files (programs) with an asterisk, symbolic links (file names that point to other files) with an at sign (@), and others. Note that this option is a capital F. Case matters.

-t   Sort files by time stamp. (The *time stamp* is the piece of data that tells the date and time that the file was last modified.)

cat

The cat command displays the contents of a file. Obviously, this is most useful with text files. Using the cat command dumps the output to the screen without any sort of page breaks. The cat command takes the name of one or more files as a target. Here are some of the more common options for cat:

-n   Prints the number of each line.

-b   Does the same thing as -n but does not number blank lines.

-v   Displays nonprinting characters such as carriage returns, control characters, and so on.

less and more

The less and more commands do nearly the same thing as cat; namely, they are pagination programs. Sometimes the cat command is not suitable because a file takes up more than one screen of space. When this is the case, the text at the start of the file scrolls off the screen before the user can read it. By using the less or more command, the machine displays the contents of the file one screen at a time and then pauses. When the user has finished reading, he presses the space bar, and the next screen is displayed. Depending on which version of these commands is installed, the user may be able to page backwards by pressing the B key. Both of these commands take the name of a file as a target. There are options for these commands, but they are not widely used. The curious can find them by reading the manual pages.

There are differences between less and more, most notably that less allows you to move backwards through files. I recommend that you try them both and see which one you like better.

Advanced Command Writing

Unix shells, and BASH in particular, allow for some fairly advanced ways of using commands. These functions go beyond the scope of any particular command but don't quite rise to the level of programming. Beyond the basics of simple commands, there are shell functions that allow commands to work with the shell itself and to be combined into very flexible compound commands. This is where the real power of the Unix shell shows itself.

Redirecting input and output

The first shell function addressed here is *redirection*. Redirection means taking input from or sending output to some place other than the usual. Every program that takes input or produces output (which is to say, most of them) has a standard place that those things come from or go to. In the majority of cases, input comes from the keyboard, and output goes to the screen, but each program defines its own defaults. These default locations are called the *standard input* and the *standard output*. (For the remainder of this section, assume that the standard input is the keyboard and the standard output is the screen.)

REDIRECTING OUTPUT

I'll start with redirecting output, since it's the easier of the two concepts to grasp. Consider the ls command. This command generates output in the form of a directory listing. When you give the ls command, the directory listing is printed to the screen. Suppose that instead of the screen, you want this output to go to a file, which you can then read later. In this case, you could use the ls command in conjunction with the *output redirection operator,* which is the greater than character (>), and the name of the file to which you want the output redirected.

For the example, say that you (in this case, user jeff) want to list the contents of the /etc directory and store them in a file called etclist in your home directory. You would give the command in this form:

```
ls /etc > /home/jeff/etclist
```

If the file to which you've redirected your output does not already exist, the output redirection operator creates it. If the file does already exist, the output redirection operator replaces the contents of that file with output of your command. This behavior can be changed by giving the command in this form:

```
ls /etc >> /home/jeff/etclist
```

Caution

When using the > operator, it is possible to lose the contents of a file. Every time you redirect output in this way, the output from the current job overwrites the output from the previous job. Unless you are very sure about what you're doing, I recommend that you use the >> operator, which does not overwrite, but rather appends new data to the file.

By using the doubled output redirector (>>), the output of the command is appended to the end of the file instead of replacing the contents of the file. Like the single operator, the double operator creates the file if it doesn't already exist. The double operator can be useful if you want to run a command several different times and compare the output, or if you want to log the operation of several different commands.

REDIRECTING INPUT

Redirecting input is similar in concept to redirecting output. In this case, instead of sending output to a file, you take input from a file. This is usually done to feed arguments to a command. For example, suppose you have a file named ls-args that contains the line

```
/etc
```

Running the following command would output a directory listing of the /etc directory.

```
ls < ls-args
```

REDIRECTING INPUT AND OUTPUT AT THE SAME TIME

You can combine the preceding two functions like so (replacing username with your own username):

```
ls < ls-args > /home/username/etclist
```

By doing this, you are able to take the arguments to the command from the ls-args file and send the output to the etclist file.

You might be asking yourself why you'd want to do this. Remember that a part of the Linux design philosophy is to make things automatable where possible. If you can create files with an operator and take input from files with an operator, you can use files that were created automatically as input to other commands. It only takes a little imagination to see what could be done using something like this. Something like `ls etc >> etclist`, for example, might be used to feed a command like `cat < etclist`.

Pipes

There is another type of redirection operator called a *pipe*. A pipe is used to direct the output of one command to become the input to another. The pipe is designated by the vertical bar character (|), found above the backslash on many keyboards.

Suppose that you want to read the directory listing of a very populous directory. You give the `ls` command, but the listing is so long that the file names at the beginning scroll off the screen before you can read them. How can you handle this situation? Well, you could redirect the output of the `ls` command into a file and then read the file using the `more` or `less` command to page through it, but that seems rather cumbersome and would probably lead to having a lot of files cluttering up your system unless you were very conscientious about deleting them. A more elegant solution is to pipe the output of `ls` directly into your pagination program, like so:

```
ls -l /etc | more
```

By doing this, you eliminate the need for file creation, and you're able to get the result that you wanted.

The preceding is a somewhat trivial example, but piping is a very powerful function. Imagine that you have produced a long text document for your company, XYZCorp. Just as you have completed your document, the company announces that it has changed its name to ABCCorp, and all documents must be updated to reflect the change. You could go through the document and change everything by hand, but that would be tedious and take too much time. Instead, using the `sed command`, a pipe, and a redirection operator, you can just do this:

```
cat document | sed 's/XYZCorp/ABCCorp/g' > document-updated
```

Note

`sed` is a text editor that can be used in a noninteractive way to process text on the fly.

This command uses `cat` to generate the output of the file `document` and then uses the pipe to stream that output into the `sed` command, which makes the substitution. The output of the `sed` command is then redirected into a file called `document-updated`. Voila! You have just updated your file, and it only took a few seconds.

A (Very) Brief Introduction to Shell Programming

As mentioned earlier in this chapter, the Unix shell is not just a command interpreter; it's also a richly featured programming environment. Shell programming is more than just a nifty feature of a Linux system; it's a core component that makes the system work. When a Linux system first boots up, it executes a series of shell programs that start all of the crucial system functions. By adjusting these programs, a savvy administrator can exercise extremely fine control over the system.

Note

You may hear shell programs referred to as *scripts*. Indeed, I use that term at times in this book as well. For all practical purposes, scripts and programs are the same thing. The term comes from an earlier period of Unix's history, when the shell didn't have nearly as many programmer-friendly features. At that time, shell programs were indeed little more than scripts that had to be followed without much in the way of self-adaptability. These days, the shell includes many of the features that you would find in any other programming language, and so the term *shell program* is probably the more accurate one. Nevertheless, many people continue to use the term *script*, mostly as a matter of convention and habit.

Shell languages are *interpreted*. This term distinguishes them from compiled languages such as C. The disadvantage of an interpreted language is that it is typically much slower than a compiled one. Compiled languages are converted to binary before they are run. Binary is the native language that the machine speaks, and so the program is ready to run right out of the gate. Interpreted languages, by contrast, must be converted to binary on the fly. This takes time, and so the programs tend to run slower, and with greater processor requirements. Shell programs tend to be simple, and given the power and speed of today's processors, most people won't notice a difference. The advantage of an interpreted language is that it's easy to modify a program written in it. Because the program doesn't need to be recompiled after every modification, you need only edit the file in place, and the changes will be reflected the next time the program is run.

The important thing to remember about shell programs is that anything you can do at the command line, you can do in a shell program. You can invoke any program, pass arguments such as options and targets, and do input and output redirection.

With that in mind, here are a couple of things that you need to know before going further:

- **Shell programs are text files.** To create a program, you've got to use a text editor to create a file. Any text editor will do, so pick one you like. (Likely candidates can be found in Chapter 17.) I recommend that you stay away from word processors, however. A word processor such as the one included with the OpenOffice.org suite will add formatting characters to the file. These will confuse the shell. An editor such as kedit or gedit is a better choice.

- **Shell programs need to be made executable.** This means that you must set execute permission at least for yourself. You can do this with the `chmod` command, like this:

  ```
  chmod u+x <programname>
  ```

  It's very easy to forget to do this. If you write a program and it won't run, check the permissions. That's almost always the problem. (See Chapter 13 for more information about permissions.)

The magic word

All shell programs must begin with the *magic word*. The magic word is a special combination of characters that lets the system know that what follows is a shell program and should be treated as such. The magic word consists of a hash mark (#) followed by an exclamation point (!), followed by the full path name (location and file name) of the shell program. In the vast majority of cases, the shell program lives in the `/bin` directory, so, for example, the full path name for the BASH shell is almost always `/bin/bash`. So, for a BASH shell program, the magic word looks like this:

```
#!/bin/bash
```

If you ever want to say this to someone, say "hash bang slash bin slash bash." (An exclamation point is known as a *bang* in Linux, and whenever you're talking about path names, you should always include the slashes.)

Comments

A very important but frequently overlooked part of any shell program, comments are what the programmer writes to explain what's going on. Simply put, a comment is a line in a program that is ignored by the interpreter. Consequently, you can write anything you want in the comment, and it won't affect the operation of the program. In BASH shell programs, a comment is any line that begins with a hash mark (aside from the magic word).

```
# This is an example of a comment.

# If you want your comment to span multiple lines, you'll need
# to begin each line with a hash mark.
```

At the very least, in your comments you should leave the name of the program, your name, the date on which it was last modified, and the purpose of the program, like so:

```
# foobar.sh (shell programs typically take the suffix .sh)
# By Joe Merlino (joe@example.com)
# 8/3/05
# A program to foo the bar.
```

The comments do not need to be in exactly that format, but that's the general idea. I want to stress that you should include comments even if the program is very small, very simple, and intended only for your own use. It is very, very easy to write a program, only to look at it a few days or weeks later and have absolutely no idea what it is, or was meant to do. In addition, you never know when someone else might find your program useful. Keeping that information in there lets them know where the program came from. (You never know when you're going to find yourself getting an e-mail from someone you've never heard of asking a question about a program you wrote and then gave to a friend, who then gave it to a friend of his, and so on. Such a thing may sound annoying, but it's actually quite an ego boost!)

In addition, if your program has more than one section, you should leave a comment in each section explaining what that section does. You don't have to go into detail about how exactly it does it — if you're a halfway decent programmer, that should be obvious from the code — but you should at least say something like "this section prepares the bar to be foo'd."

As you look at more and more programs, you'll discover that quite a few programmers neglect commenting. There are many reasons for this. Some programmers feel that commenting is a waste of time. Others think that if you can't figure out exactly what's going on from the code, you're not worthy of knowing their secrets. Still others are just lazy and don't bother. If I can instill one attitude about good programming, it would be that comments are important and should not be neglected.

A simple shell program

In this section, we look at a simple shell program and get an idea of how exactly one is put together. I introduce a few commands that you haven't seen before, as well as some programming concepts that may be new to you. Don't worry, I explain these all fully before the section is finished. For now, just look at the program, and get a sense of the overall design and flow of it.

```
#!/bin/bash

# backup.sh - a program to back up data on your system
# By Joe Merlino, 8/3/05

#Define a few variables:

BACKUP_DIR = "home"   # The directory that needs to be backed up
REPOSITORY = "backup"   # The directory where you'll store your backups
DATE = $(date+%b%d)   # Today's date in month/day format

# Do the backup
```

```
if [ -d $REPOSITORY ] && [ -s $REPOSITORY ]     then
        tar cfz /$REPOSITORY/$DATE.tgz /$BACKUP_DIR
        echo "Backup for $DATE done."
    else
        echo "Couldn't find repository directory"

fi
```

Now, let's break this down piece by piece.

STUFF AT THE TOP
First, you have this bit:

```
#!/bin/bash

# backup.sh - a program to back up data on your system
# By Joe Merlino, 8/3/05
```

Suffice it to say that if you read the previous section, you know what this is. You have the magic word and some general comments. Moving on.

VARIABLE ASSIGNMENTS
The next section looks like this:

```
#Define a few variables:

BACKUP_DIR = "home"  # The directory that needs to be backed up
REPOSITORY = "backup"  # The directory where you'll store your backups
DATE = $(date+%b%d)  # Today's date in month/day format
```

In this section, you define some variables. What are variables? Simply put, a variable is a name to which any value can be assigned. You can think of a variable's name as a sort of empty container that can be filled with anything. This allows you to use the variable's value — the thing that you've put into the container — without necessarily knowing what it is.

The first two variable assignments are straightforward. You assign a text string — the word home or the word backup — to each of the variable names. You do this using the equals sign (=), which, in this context functions as the *assignment operator.*

You might wonder why you would need to assign these variables, since it's pretty clear from what follows that they're only standing in for some fairly standard directory names. In a very simple program like this, you probably don't actually need to do this, but if you were writing a long program that made reference to those directories many times, this move could save a lot of time. For example, if the location of your REPOSITORY directory were to change, you would need only change the variable assignment. Were you to make direct reference to it, you would need to go through the program and change every reference. Not an appealing prospect.

The third variable assignment is not quite so obvious; it's a *command substitution*. Simply put, you assign the output of the date command to the variable named DATE. The date command simply returns as output the current date. (By using the %b and %d options, you specify that you want the date in month/day format.) By enclosing the command in parentheses and preceding that expression with a dollar sign, you tell the shell that you want to use the output of that command as the value for the variable. In this way, anytime the program is run, you will get a unique value for the DATE variable. The importance of this will become clear shortly.

Note that in this section, not only do you include a comment describing what the section does, you also have a comment on each variable assignment. (You can begin a comment in the middle of a line — everything to the right of the hash mark will be considered the comment.) Some people might consider this overkill, but I find it helpful.

THE ACTION

Now that you've done the preparation, you're ready to move on to the action part of the program. This is the part where you actually give commands to the system:

```
# Do the backup

if [ -d $REPOSITORY ] && [ -s $REPOSITORY ]
then
        tar cfz /$REPOSITORY/$DATE.tgz /$BACKUP_DIR
        echo "Backup for $DATE done."
    else
        echo "Couldn't find repository directory"


fi
```

There's a lot of stuff packed into this stanza, so let's take things piece by piece. The first thing to notice is the word if. if is a *flow control* construct. Flow control constructs allow programs to make decisions about how they will execute themselves. The if statement alerts the system that there is a condition coming up and that all the code that is between the word if and the word fi (which is just if spelled backwards) will only be executed if that condition is met.

The if/fi construct is augmented by the then and else parts. then and else are actually parts of the if/fi construct. The then section specifies that the enclosed code will be executed if the condition in the if statement is met, and the else section specifies alternate code that will be executed if the condition is *not* met. You can look at the entire construct like this:

```
if [ a condition is met ]

    then
        something happens
    else
        something different happens
    fi
```

Notice that the sections that are subordinate to the if, then, and else statements are indented. This is done to make it obvious which statements are "inside" other statements. In most, if not all, programming languages, it is possible to have multiple constructs inside one another. A structure such as

```
if [ condition ]

    then
        command
        command
        if [ condition ]
            then
                command
        fi
  fi
```

is not only possible but also quite common. The indentation makes clear which section is subordinate to which. You need only align the left-hand side vertically, and the structure becomes evident.

Note also that an else section is not required.

Now that you have a handle on the construct, turn your attention to some of the other features here. Looking more closely at the if statement, you see that there are two expressions enclosed inside square brackets. Under the BASH shell, square brackets serve a special purpose. They are exactly syntactically equal to the test command. The test command is a program that is used to evaluate conditions. The statement

```
if [ -d $REPOSITORY ] && [ -s $REPOSITORY ]
```

could also be rewritten as

```
if ( test -d $REPOSITORY ) && ( test -s $REPOSITORY )
```

The test command feeds a particular value back to the if statement depending on whether the result of the test is true or false. The first of these test statements has a -d option. This is used to instruct test to ask if the target supplied—in this case, the value of the REPOSITORY variable—is a directory. (By preceding the name of the variable—REPOSITORY—with a dollar sign—$REPOSITORY, you tell the shell that you want to look at the variable's value.)

In the second test statement, the -s option tests whether the REPOSITORY directory has a size greater than zero. If the size of that directory is zero, you may have a problem. (The directory's name might exist, but there might not be a file system actually mounted there.)

Between the two `test` statements is the symbol `&&`. This is a *logical and* operator. This means that in order for the entire `if` statement's condition to be evaluated as true, both `test` statements must be true. In other words, the `REPOSITORY` directory must both exist *and* have a size greater than zero for the entire expression to be considered true. There is also a *logical or* operator (`||`) that would evaluate as true if either `test` (but not necessarily both) were to evaluate as true.

Assuming that both `test` statements are true, the `if` construct executes the code that is directly beneath the `then` statement, so let's look at that code:

```
then

        tar cfz /$REPOSITORY/$DATE.tgz /$BACKUP_DIR
        echo "Backup for $DATE done."
```

The first command is an invocation of the `tar` program. `tar` is used to create archives of files and directories. Unfortunately, the command has a strange syntax. `cfz` is a set of three options. `tar` does not use a dash to precede options. Also, the usual positions of the source and destination targets are reversed. As written above, the command will create an archive called `$DATE.tgz` (a file whose name is whatever the value of the `DATE` variable is, with the suffix `.tgz`) in the `REPOSITORY` directory. The archive will be composed of all the files, directories, and subdirectories within the `BACKUP_DIR` directory. The `c` option directs `tar` to create the archive. The `f` option allows you to specify the archive's file name, and the `z` option tells `tar` to compress the archive using the `gzip` program.

The second command uses the `echo` function to print a message to the screen telling you that the backup has been done.

Should either of the tests given in the `if` statement fail (that is, return a value of false), the construct executes the code directly beneath the `else` statement:

```
else
        echo "Couldn't find repository directory"
```

This simply prints a warning to the screen that the `REPOSITORY` directory could not be found. The program will then exit without taking any action.

And there you have it. Obviously, this program is very simple, and this section merely intended to give you a taste of the kinds of things that are possible using the shell. There are many more commands and several other types of flow control constructs.

If you are interested in learning more about shell programming, many fine books have been written on the subject. Try *Beginning Shell Scripting* by Eric Foster-Johnson (Wrox, 2005) as a start. While many commands are the same from shell to shell, some of the programming constructs — or at least the precise form of syntax used for them — can vary quite a bit. I recommend that you decide on a shell first and then look into its programming features.

Summary

Despite their primitive appearance, text commands offer a degree of subtlety and flexibility that is simply not possible with graphical program interfaces. Text commands offer a greater number of command options, noninteractive use that enables them to be used by programs, and automated execution. Features such as input and output redirection allow commands to be combined in creative and powerful ways. There are a number of shells available for Linux systems, and each has its own features and its own unique flavor. Shells can be programmed, which allows complex actions to be aggregated into manageable (and automatable) pieces.

Chapter 12

Internet Solutions in Linux

You have a computer, and you just installed a new operating system on it. You've logged in and had a look at the desktop. What do you do now? If you're like most people I know, the first thing you're going to want to do is pull up a Web page or check your e-mail. This chapter shows you how to use the basic Internet functions that come with your Linux distribution. Most distributions these days come with a number of programs that perform basic functions such as e-mail, Web browsing, instant messaging, and others.

This chapter assumes that you have a working connection to the Internet. You should have configured your network connection during installation. If you did not, or if things have changed, refer to Chapter 19 to learn how to set up your network connection.

Browsing the World Wide Web

It seems like the most popular Internet activity today is browsing the World Wide Web. The Web puts a world of information, from the most critical to the most useless, at your fingertips. We in the Linux community are lucky in that the best Web browser in the world, Mozilla's Firefox browser, runs natively on Linux. This was not always the case. The Netscape browser has always run on Linux, but for several years, Netscape was outpaced — both in terms of popularity and functionality — by Microsoft's Internet Explorer. For some time, Linux users had to content themselves with a second-fiddle Web browser.

That changed in 1998, when a foundering Netscape decided to release the code to its browser as free software. This release was the beginning of the Mozilla project, whose ambition was nothing less than the creation of the world's best Web browser. Given the high degree of overlap between the free software community in general and the Linux community in particular, it's unsurprising that they didn't leave Linux behind when they brought out Firefox.

In fact, all the components of the Mozilla project run on all of the major operating systems, including Linux, various flavors of Unix, Windows, and Mac OS.

Note

The Mozilla project produces several products. The term *Mozilla* itself refers to an integrated suite of products that includes a Web browser, e-mail client, and HTML composition tool. Firefox is a standalone browser, and Thunderbird is a standalone e-mail client.

There are other Web browsers for Linux, and I mention a few of these later in this chapter, but I think Firefox is the best.

Running Firefox

Firefox is installed by default on almost any major Linux distribution. If, for some reason, it is not, check your distribution's installation media to see if there is a package available. If there is, install it using the techniques described in Chapter 15. If not, you can download packages from www.mozilla.org. Follow the instructions on that site to install the packages.

Firefox is installed by default on both Knoppix and Fedora Core. To start Firefox on Knoppix, simply click the red-and-yellow Mozilla Firefox icon in the dock. On Fedora Core, click the Web Browser icon (the one with the globe being encircled by a fox), or select the menu path Applications → Internet → Firefox Web Browser, as shown in Figure 12-1.

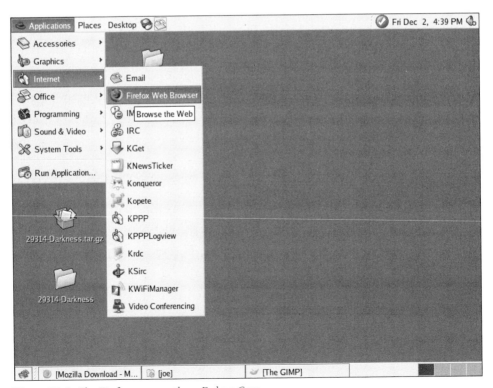

Figure 12-1: The Firefox menu path on Fedora Core.

Once you've selected the appropriate icon or menu path, the main Firefox window should appear, as shown in Figure 12-2.

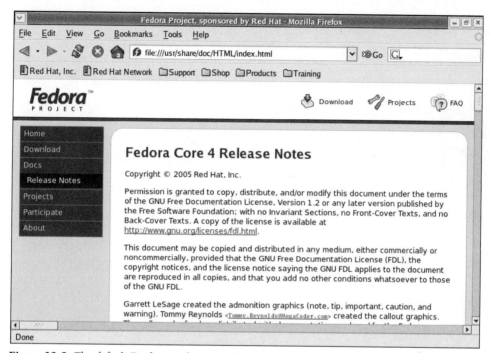

Figure 12-2: The default Firefox window on Fedora Core.

By default, the page on which Firefox starts is set by your distribution's maintainers. As you can see in Figure 12-2, the default home page for Fedora Core is the file /usr/share/doc/HTML/index.html, which contains the release notes for your version of Fedora Core. If you wish to change the default start page, you can do so from the Preferences window as described in the next section.

For now, you can pull up any Web page by entering its URL in the location bar, which is located in the upper panel of the window. From this point, Firefox acts pretty much like any other Web browser.

One of the nicer features of Firefox is *tabbed browsing*. You can have multiple Web pages open in separate tabs in the main browser window. You can open a new tab by pressing the Ctrl-T key combination. You can switch back and forth among pages by clicking on the tabs at the top. If you want to open a linked site in a new tab, hold down the Ctrl key and click on the link. (Alternatively, you can right-click on the link and select Open Link in New Tab from the pop-up menu.) Figure 12-3 shows a Firefox session with the tabs from several open windows visible immediately above the Fedora Project banner.

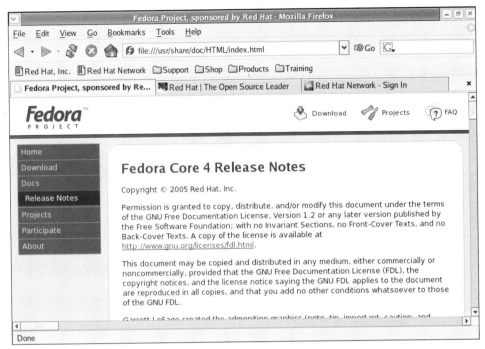

Figure 12-3: Tabbed browsing in action.

Configuring Firefox

Firefox is highly configurable, both with regard to its look and feel and with regard to how it behaves. To access Firefox's configuration options, select Edit → Preferences. The Preferences window opens, as shown in Figure 12-4.

Along the left-hand side of the Preferences window are a number of icons that represent different sets of configuration options.

- The **General** option set includes options for setting your home page, the fonts and colors in which text is displayed, the language that Firefox uses, and options for setting up a connection to the Internet via a proxy server. (See Chapter 23 for more information about proxy servers.)

- The **Privacy** option set (shown in Figure 12-5) shows various options related to the security of personal information.

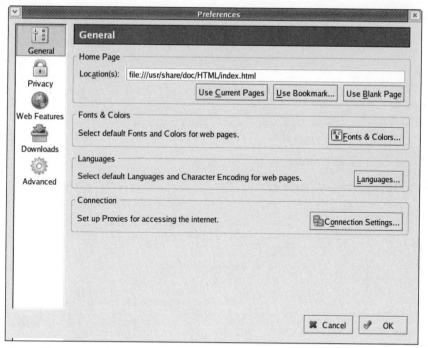

Figure 12-4: The Preferences window.

You can view details about each of these options by clicking the boxed plus sign to the left of each option.

- The **Web Features** option set contains options for configuring the way Firefox reacts to certain types of content that it may find on the Web. Arguably, the most useful option in the Web Features menu is the option to block pop-up windows. Clicking the Allowed Sites button allows you to make exceptions to this rule, in case a particular site uses pop-up windows for something useful.

- The **Downloads** category (shown in Figure 12-6) controls how Firefox will handle downloaded files.

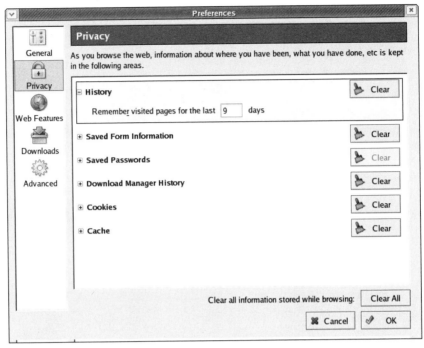

Figure 12-5: Configure privacy options.

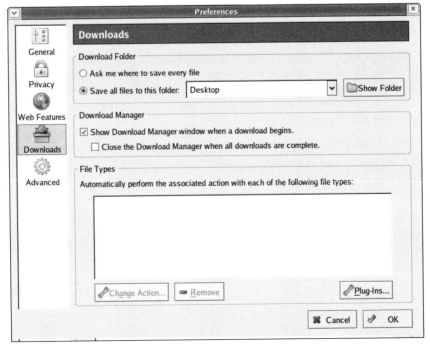

Figure 12-6: Use this screen to select your download preferences.

The **Advanced** category contains a number of options that do not necessarily fit into other categories and which may be of interest primarily to power users. These options include things like security preferences, multimedia handling options, and others. Each subcategory has a box containing a plus sign to its left; click this box to expand the category and see all of the options.

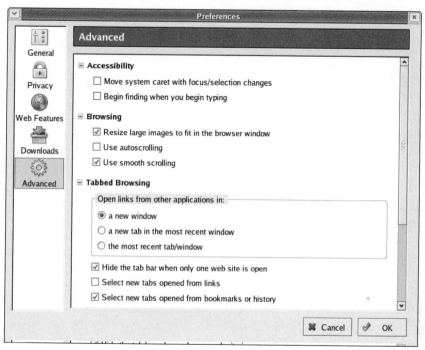

Figure 12-7: The Advanced option set.

Using Electronic Mail

If there's any Internet function that rivals the World Wide Web for popularity, it's electronic mail. It's difficult to say whether the Web or e-mail is more popular (especially since there are sites such as Hotmail that allow you to read your e-mail on the Web), but it's pretty safe to say that there are probably very few people who use the Internet who don't use e-mail.

There are quite a few e-mail programs available for Linux. This chapter covers two: Evolution and Mozilla's Thunderbird. The details for these two programs should be easily transferable to most any other client, however, because most of them tend to work more or less the same way. In fact, if you've used a Windows or Macintosh e-mail client, the odds are that most of the information presented here will be familiar, at least in its broad outline.

E-mail setup

Both e-mail programs (and most others) have wizards that make the process of setting them up easy. The wizard asks for several bits of information:

- **Your name**

- **Your incoming mail server type:** There are two main protocols used to receive mail: Post Office Protocol version 3 (POP3) and Interactive Mail Access Protocol (IMAP).

- **Your incoming mail server address:** The host name or IP address of your POP3 or IMAP server. This will typically be something like pop3.example.com.

- **Your outgoing mail server address:** The host name or IP address of your Simple Mail Transfer Protocol (SMTP) server. This is where mail actually gets sent out to the Internet from. Typically, it will be something like mail.example.com.

- **Your username on the mail servers:** This is typically the first part of your e-mail address. If your e-mail is linuxfan@example.com, your username would be linuxfan. But you might have a different username for the mail server, or you might have different names for the incoming and outgoing servers.

- **Your password on the mail servers:** As with the username, you might have the same password for incoming and outgoing mail or different ones. Each of these programs gives you the option of storing and automatically entering the password as needed, which saves some typing but leaves you at the risk of other people being able to access your mail if they get hold of your computer.

- **Mail server encryption type:** Usually conversations between your e-mail software and the server occur in plain text. It is possible for a hacker to eavesdrop on them, so some mail servers employ Secure Socket Layer (SSL) or Transport Layer Security (TLS) to encrypt communications. In this case, you must instruct your e-mail software to use the same protocol. Both Evolution and Thunderbird support SSL and TLS.

Additional features might require more information, but this is the minimum you need to know to set up an e-mail account. If you don't have this information, or are unsure about it, you should be able to get it from your ISP or from your system or network administrator.

Using Evolution

Evolution is the default e-mail client on Fedora Core, and it's a good choice. Evolution was originally a product of the Ximian Corporation, which was the brainchild of Miguel De Icaza, one of the original driving forces behind GNOME. Ximian was eventually acquired by Novell, and much of their work has been incorporated into Novell's Linux distribution. Individual components, however, do run on a standalone basis and are available as free software.

Evolution is more than just an e-mail client. It has calendar functions, as well as a to-do list, has a contact management system (sort of an address book on steroids), and synchronizes with a personal digital assistant (PDA). This section, however, focuses on its e-mail functions.

On Fedora Core, Evolution can be started by clicking the yellow Evolution icon in the dock or by selecting Applications → Internet → Email. On other systems, if Evolution is installed, it should be located in a similar menu path. It can also usually be started by giving the command `evolution` at a shell prompt.

When you start Evolution for the first time, a wizard opens to guide you through the process of setting up an e-mail account. To use this wizard, you will need the information listed earlier. Once you have all of this information, you can use the wizard.

1. The first screen is merely a Welcome screen telling you that you are about to start the wizard. Read this screen and then click Forward.

2. The next screen, shown in Figure 12-8, asks you to fill in some information about your identity. This is the information that will appear on your outgoing e-mails. Fill in the information on this screen and click Forward.

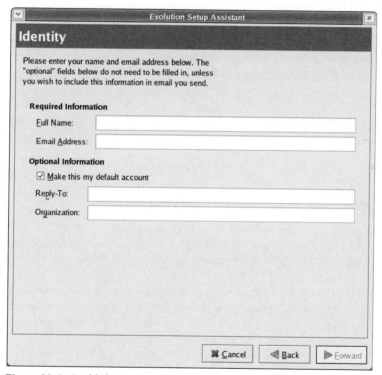

Figure 12-8: Establish your identity.

3. The next screen asks you to select the type of server that you will be using. The most common types of servers are POP and IMAP, and it's very likely that you'll be using one of these; however, the wizard also includes options for several other types of servers. When

you have made your selection, the screen changes to show fields asking for the host name or IP address of the server as well as some other information. Fill in the information and click Forward.

4. The next page asks you to select some options relating to how you want Evolution to deal with incoming mail. Check the boxes if you want incoming mail checked automatically, if you want messages left on the server, and if you want to disable POP3 extensions (not usually necessary unless you're getting your mail from an old mail server). Make your selections and click Forward.

5. The next page asks you to select the type of server to use for your outgoing mail. In all probability, this will be an SMTP server; however, you can also choose to use Sendmail. You should select Sendmail if you are using your own Linux machine as the outgoing mail server. (For more details about running mail servers, see Chapter 22.)

Note
If you're using a mail server program other than Sendmail on your machine, you can usually select Sendmail at this junction anyway. Most non-Sendmail servers can also be invoked using the `sendmail` command, so it should work anyway.

Make your selection. If you are using an SMTP server, fill in the name or IP address of the server and any other authentication information you might have, and click Forward.

6. The next screen asks you to give the account a name. Choose an easily identified name and click Forward.

7. On the next screen, select your time zone and click Forward.

8. The next screen asks if you want to import mail or address contacts from Pine. Pine is a text-based e-mail program. If you've used Pine, you can select these options. If not, make sure they're deselected, and then click Forward.

At this point, you're done. The wizard shows you a final page and asks you to confirm the settings you've entered. If you want to change anything, you can use the Back button to navigate through the series of pages until you find the setting you want to change. If not, click Apply to save your settings. The wizard exits, and the main Evolution window appears, as shown in Figure 12-9.

Evolution acts in pretty much the same way as any other e-mail client. You probably set up your account to retrieve your mail at regular intervals, but you can download your mail at any time by clicking the Send/Receive button. When you receive mail, the message title appears in the upper-right pane of the main window. Click on a message title to view it, and the body of the text appears in the lower-right pane.

To reply to a message, click the Reply button (or Reply to All if that's appropriate). An editor window opens as shown in Figure 12-10.

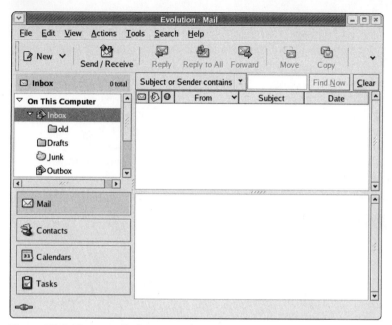

Figure 12-9: The main Evolution window.

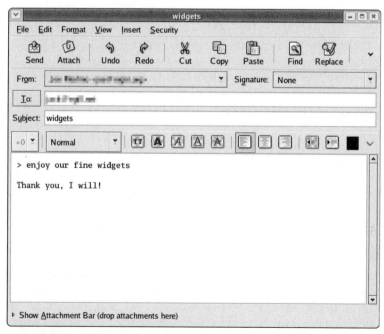

Figure 12-10: Editing an outgoing message.

Type and edit your reply, and when you're done, click Send.

The procedure for creating a new message is similar. Click the New button to open the editor window. Type your message (remember to fill out the To: and Subject: lines), and click Send when you're done.

If you want to add the sender of a message to your address book, you can do so by highlighting the title of the message and selecting Actions → Add Sender to Address Book. A window opens asking you to confirm this action. Click the button labeled Add to Contacts. To access an address from your address book, start a new message and click the To: button to open your address book (see Figure 12-11). Select the name of the person to whom you want to send the new e-mail, and click the To: button. Then click K. The Address Book window closes, and you are returned to your message, with the recipient's name filled in.

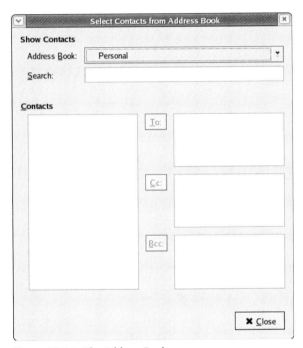

Figure 12-11: The Address Book.

Using Thunderbird

I'm not aware of any major Linux distribution that uses Thunderbird as the default e-mail client, but it's easy to install and run. In addition to e-mail, Thunderbird handles RSS feeds and newsgroups.

To install Thunderbird, download the package from www.mozilla.org, and then follow the directions on that Web site. Essentially, this involves no more than simply putting the package where you want it and then expanding it. (Alternatively, you can use your distribution's native package installation program if you prefer. For further details on precise methods of installing software packages, see Chapter 15.) Once you've got Thunderbird installed, you can start it by opening the terminal window and giving the command thunderbird. If you decide to keep Thunderbird, you can create a launcher for it as described in Chapter 10.

As with Evolution, Thunderbird starts an account wizard the first time you run it. This wizard helps you to set up your account. The wizard asks for much the same sorts of information as described in the section on Evolution. The details of the wizard are not exactly the same, but they're close enough that the astute user should be able to adapt easily.

You can use the Forward and Back buttons to navigate through the wizard. When you've entered all the information, you are presented with a confirmation screen as shown in Figure 12-12.

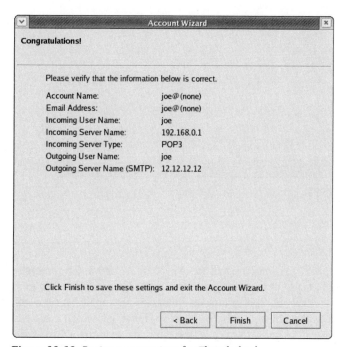

Figure 12-12: Review your settings for Thunderbird.

If all the information on this screen is correct, click Finish. You will see the main Thunderbird window as shown in Figure 12-13.

Now you're ready to use Thunderbird. You can download your mail using the Get Mail button and compose mail using the Write button. New incoming mail appears in the upper-right pane. Click on a message title to view the body of the message in the lower-right pane. Reply to a message using the Reply or Reply All buttons.

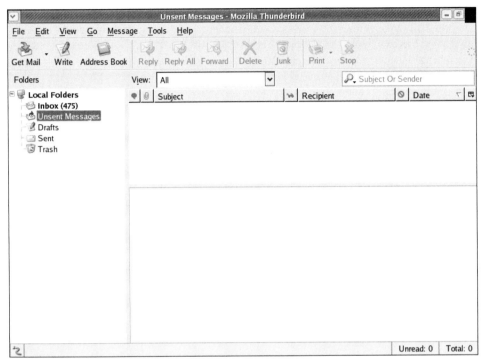

Figure 12-13: The main Thunderbird window.

Antispam features

Unsolicited e-mail, or *spam,* is a huge problem. Some people receive 20 or 30 unwanted messages for every legitimate e-mail, so some kind of system for sorting mail is a must. Many e-mail programs, including Evolution and Thunderbird, include adaptive or *Bayesian* filters for junk mail. This is a statistical method using the Bayes algorithm whereby you train the filter by showing it which messages you consider spam and which ones you want to keep. Over time, the filter adapts to the unique style of spam you receive and becomes increasingly accurate in predicting whether an incoming message is junk or something you'll actually want to read. The number of false hits in a well-trained Bayesian filter is impressively low. Unfortunately, the method is not foolproof. In the arms race between spammers and antispammers, the enemy is getting more and more devious in finding ways to make their messages seem innocuous. Still, using an adaptive filter provides welcome relief to users bombarded by junk mail.

To enable spam filtering on Evolution, open the Evolution Settings window by selecting Edit → Preferences, and then click the tab marked Junk. Click the checkbox marked Check incoming mail for junk. You are also given the option to check a box marked Include remote tests. This applies a set of tests that are maintained in remote locations and may include filtering criteria beyond what you can maintain locally. Applying these filters may make filtering slower but will also probably make it more accurate.

Make your selections and click Close.

At this point, you'll need to train your filters. As you go through your mail, when you encounter junk messages, click on them to highlight them, and then mark them as junk mail by selecting Edit → Mark as Junk. The more messages that you mark, the more accurate your filters become, and the less spam you should actually see.

Encryption

In order to encode sensitive information or just to digitally sign a message, you need some sort of encryption. Evolution has such encryption built in, and Thunderbird can use encryption with a plug-in called Enigmail (`http://enigmail.mozdev.org/`). You can also use these programs to easily check signatures or decrypt mail from other users. To make your digital identity known, you have to create a cryptographic key using a program called GNU Privacy Guard (GnuPG) and upload it to a public key server so other people can look it up when they get signed mail from you. The GnuPG Mini-Howto at `http://webber.dewinter.com/gnupg_howto/english/GPGMiniHowto.html` provides a good overview of the whole process.

CREATING AND DISTRIBUTING KEYS

To use GnuPG encryption on Evolution, you'll need to do a few things. First, you'll need to generate a key pair. Follow these steps:

1. Open a terminal window.

2. At the command prompt, type **gpg --gen-key**.

3. You are presented with a choice of key types. Unless you have a reason not to, select the first type (DSA and Elgamel).

4. You are asked to specify the size of your key. Again, unless you have a reason not to, you can select the default (2048 bits) just by hitting the Enter key.

5. You are asked to select how long your key will be valid. This is up to you. Select 0 if you don't want your key to expire. You are asked to confirm this choice.

6. You are now asked to answer a few questions in order to create a User ID for your key.

7. Next, you need to create a passphrase for your key. This is a very important step. Your passphrase can be anything, and it can include spaces. Select a phrase that you will remember.

8. The computer now generates your key. This may take awhile. You can do other things on your computer while this is going on. This is helpful because the computer uses random bits of information from things like keystrokes and mouse movements to help generate the key. When it's done, it prints some information about your key and returns you to the system prompt.

Second, upload your public key to a key server. This way, people who need to download your key can do so and use it to decrypt your messages. To do this, follow these steps:

1. Find out your key's ID number. Do this by giving the following command:

   `gpg --list-keys`

   You should see a string that looks like this:

   `pub  1024D/XXXXXXXX  YYYY-MM-DD`

   (The ID number is represented by the Xs in this example.)

2. Give this command:

   `gpg --send-keys --keyserver wwwkeys.pgp.net KEYNUM.`

   (Substitute the number of your public key for `KEYNUM`.)

In order to send encrypted mail to someone, you need to obtain his or her public key. Your would-be recipient should provide you with the ID number of his or her key. You can add this key to your keychain by giving the following command:

`gpg --recv-keys --keyserver wwwkeys.pgp.net KEYNUM`

(Again, substitute the public key ID number for `KEYNUM`.)

ENABLING ENCRYPTION

Next, you will need to enable GPG encryption in Evolution. To do this, follow these steps:

1. Select Edit → Preferences.

2. Click the icon marked Mail Accounts. Select the account for which you want to use encryption, and click Edit. The Account Editor window opens.

3. In the Account Editor window, click the tab marked Security.

4. In the field marked PGP/GPG Key ID, enter the ID number for your private key (the one labeled `sub`) and click OK.

SENDING ENCRYPTED E-MAIL

Now that you've got encryption set up, you can use it to encrypt e-mail. Remember, before you can send encrypted e-mail to people, you need to have their public key in your keyring. The public key has the recipient's e-mail address included in it. Now, compose a message to that person as you normally would, but before you send it, click on the menu marked Security. Under this menu, you are given the option to encrypt and/or sign the message. Select these options. Once you've done that, click Send. You are prompted for your GnuPG passphrase. Type it in, and the message is signed, encrypted, and sent.

DECRYPTING RECEIVED MAIL

Decrypting e-mail that you receive is very easy. When you open the message, you are prompted for your GnuPG passphrase. Type it in, and the message is decrypted. You can see a banner at the bottom indicating GnuPG's status for the message (usually something like `Valid Signature/Encrypted`).

Instant Messaging

Instant messaging is a technology that has become very popular over the past few years. Instant messaging allows you to send a message to another user (provided that they use the same instant messaging service that you do) and have it appear on their screen almost instantaneously. Most of the instant messaging services provide clients for Microsoft Windows but have largely left Linux and Mac users on their own. Fortunately, independent developers have stepped in to fill the gap.

There are several instant messaging clients that exist for Linux. In this section, I describe GAIM, the one that is bundled with GNOME, and the default client for Fedora Core and Knoppix, but almost any IM client will operate in an almost identical fashion.

Getting an account

To use an instant messaging service, you first need to get an account. To do this, you visit that service's Web site and create an account. Most services are free, and you can get an account simply by filling out some information. You will need to choose a username and password. Once you've done all that, you're ready to set up your client.

Which IM Service?

Instant messaging services are distinct from the software that allows you to use them. While it's certainly true that if you want to use, say, AOL's messenger service, you can use a client of their creation, you are not required to do so. (AOL does have a version of its messenger software for Linux.) For example, GAIM is a messenger program that works with the AOL service but is not created or provided by AOL. It's an independently produced piece of free software that does much the same thing as AOL's, but it is distinct from it. You can use any instant messenger client as long as it supports the protocol used by the service that you want to use.

Even though instant messenger services have been around for a while, and even though most of them are free, the service remains balkanized. That is to say that most of the services do not interoperate. If you have an account on the AOL Instant Messenger service (AIM) and your friend has an account on Yahoo, you will not be able to talk to each other. This means that for practical purposes, you will probably end up making your decision based on whichever service most of your friends or colleagues are on.

Fortunately, GAIM and a number of other IM clients are able to support multiple protocols at the same time. This means that you can be logged into more than one service simultaneously. If you have a number of friends spread out among disparate services, the solution may well be to simply get an account on each service and run them all together. The only drawback here is that you will not be able to set up group chats among people on multiple services.

Configuring GAIM

Once you've got an account, you're ready to use GAIM. Before you start chatting, you'll need to set it up with your account information. Start GAIM by selecting Applications → Internet → IM on Fedora Core or Main → Internet → GAIM Internet Messenger on Knoppix. (Any other distribution should have a similar menu path; otherwise, you can try giving the command gaim at a terminal prompt.)

When you first start GAIM, you see a login screen, as shown in Figure 12-14.

Figure 12-14: The GAIM login window.

This screen asks you to select an account. You can't do this before you have entered your account information, so click the Accounts button. This brings up the Accounts window as shown in Figure 12-15.

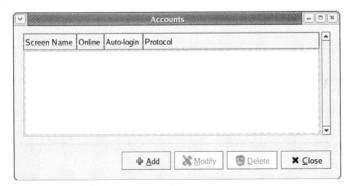

Figure 12-15: The Accounts window.

Click the Add button to bring up the Add Account window, shown in Figure 12-16.

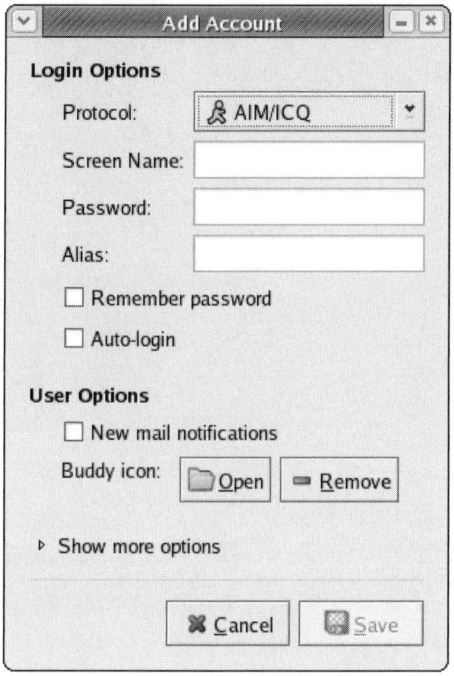

Figure 12-16: The Add Account window.

Click the Protocol dropdown box, and select the type of instant messaging account that you signed up for. Then, in the appropriate fields, fill in your screen name (login ID) and password. If you check the Remember password checkbox, you will not need to fill in your password on subsequent logins. This is a slight security risk, so if you think that might be a problem, don't do it. If you check the Auto-login box, GAIM logs you into your account as soon as you launch the program.

When you're done filling in your information, click Save. The Add Account window exits, and your newly created account appears in the Accounts window. In the Accounts window, click Close. Return to the Login window. Your account now appears in the Account field, and if you chose Remember password, your password is shown as a string of asterisks. Click the Sign on button, and you are logged into the system.

Using GAIM

Once you've got your account information set up, you're ready to start using GAIM. The first thing you need to do is establish a *buddy list*. This is a list of people with whom you regularly chat. When you first log on, you should see the Buddy List window as shown in Figure 12-17.

Figure 12-17: The Buddy List.

Add your buddies to this list. Once you've done that, you can see who is logged into the system and available for chatting. To add a buddy, click on the Buddies menu and select Add Buddy. The Add Buddy window opens. Fill in your buddy's screen name. If you like, you can also fill in an alias for your buddy. (This is useful if your buddy's screen name is something you're unlikely to remember.) When you've done this, click Add. Your buddy should now appear in the Buddy List. If he does not, he may not be logged in. Click on the Buddies menu and select Show Offline Buddies. This shows all of your buddies, whether they're logged in or not.

To chat with a buddy, click on that buddy's name to highlight it. Then click the IM button. (Alternatively, you can just double-click your buddy's name in the list.) This opens a chat window, as shown in Figure 12-18.

Figure 12-18: The chat window.

Type the message that you want to send in the lower pane. When you're done, click Send. The message is sent to your buddy. The message that you typed also displays in the upper pane. When your buddy responds, his message also appears in the upper pane. In this way, you see the conversation happen in sequence. (Obviously, your buddy needs to be logged in. You can see his status in the Buddy List window.)

If a buddy initiates a conversation with you, a window appears asking you if you want to accept the message. If you do, the chat window opens with your buddy's message in it.

When you are done chatting, click on the Conversation menu and select Close. The chat window disappears.

Summary

All of the most popular Internet functions are available to Linux users. In addition, you have a wide choice of programs that you can use to take advantage of these functions. This chapter presents several of the major Internet software packages. They are slick, fully featured implementations of the functions and rival their equivalents on any other operating system. Most of the information presented in this chapter will transfer to other programs with minor modifications, as most programs of these types behave in a similar manner.

Part IV

Basic Administration

Chapter 13

User and File Management Solutions

Linux, like the Unix systems upon which it was based, was designed from the beginning to be a true multiuser system. Unlike Windows and older versions of the Mac OS, Linux is designed to handle multiple users in a way that goes beyond a simple set of preferences or a profile. In fact, using any of the various remote login systems that exist, a Linux machine can be used by any number of users (within the limits of what its hardware can handle of course), *at the same time.*

This has several implications for a user who is unfamiliar with this type of system. Recall that when you first installed your Linux system, you created both a user account and a superuser (root) account. You must think of these two accounts as entirely separate entities. The system doesn't know that the user `susan` may also be the user `root`. You may find yourself experiencing a certain amount of frustration if you try to do "susan things" with the `root` account, or "root things" with the `susan` account.

Some of this frustration may be derived from the concept of *ownership*. Under Linux's user management system, files are *owned* by a user — usually the creator. The owner gets to decide who can read, modify, or execute (that is, run) the file (if it's a program). One of the biggest pitfalls experienced by Linux users comes from attempting to use files to which they don't have the appropriate permissions.

Single users may also belong to one or more groups. Groups of users can be designated as secondary owners of files, and permissions can be assigned based on group affiliation as well as individual identity. In this way, groups can share access to files, while keeping out anyone who isn't a member of the group.

In this chapter, I take you through the process of creating new user accounts, creating groups, assigning users to groups, and assigning permissions to files, so that they may be kept private, or shared, as you desire.

Understanding User and Superuser

You were introduced to the concept of the superuser in Chapter 6. The superuser has total control over the entire system. The superuser can access any file, run any program, create new users, and delete them from the system. For precisely this reason, you should not use the superuser account for day-to-day activities on the system, and this is why you were asked to create a user account when you installed your system.

Unlike the superuser, a regular user is limited in what she can do. This is something of a double-edged sword. You might think, "Why shouldn't I just use the superuser account all the time? That way I can do anything I need to do without being limited." The answer is simple: With the limitations of a regular user account also comes a limitation of the amount of damage you can do. Here's an example. As the superuser, you can give this command:

Caution

WARNING: Do not actually run this command! It will delete every file and directory on your system!

```
rm -rf /*
```

The `rm` command is used to delete files and directories. This command deletes every file and directory on your system. If you do this with the `root` account, you will completely decimate your system. As a regular user, you can't do this because you wouldn't have ownership of the critical system files, and the command would fail.

Keeping superuser and regular user functions separate is a safety feature, and the marginal inconvenience of switching to the superuser account is a very small price to pay for that safety.

The su command

That inconvenience is further reduced by the existence of the `su` command. The `su` command, introduced briefly in Chapter 6, allows you to switch accounts in midstream. For example, suppose you are logged in under your regular user account — `susan` — and you need to perform a superuser function. You can simply open a terminal and give the `su` command. You are then prompted for the superuser's password. When you have entered this, you will be using the superuser account, and you can perform whatever actions you want to. When you're done, simply give the `exit` command, and you will be back in your regular user account.

If that's still too inconvenient for you, you can use the `-c` option to give a one-off command as the superuser. Suppose that you want to remove the file `badfile`, but you don't have the appropriate permission. You could do this:

```
su -c "rm badfile"
```

This gives the command `rm badfile` as the superuser. You are still prompted for the superuser's password, but in this case, you will not be dropped into an interactive shell as you were when you used `su` by itself.

The way `su` works is that when a user successfully enters another account's password, the program asks Linux to change the user's old identity to the new one and then starts up a new shell and places him in it. The problem is that, by default, `su` gets that information from the user who is su-ing rather than the user who is being su-ed to. So if Susan is using the Korn shell (`/bin/ksh`) and the new user is using the BASH shell (`/bin/bash`), `su susan` leaves the new user at a BASH prompt, not a Korn shell prompt. Also, the new user won't get the benefit of any customizations Susan may have made to her login environment. (See Chapter 11 for more information on this.) That may be okay. But what if the complete experience of being Susan is required? In this case, you would run `su` like this:

```
$ su - susan
```

The - option tells `su` that you don't want to just start a new shell; you want to mimic a complete login sequence as if Susan were at the keyboard typing in her password herself.

If you want to combine this with the - option, you have to make sure - appears at the end of the command options:

```
$ su -c mail - susan
```

This would start a new login as `susan`, immediately execute the mail program to read her e-mail, and when she exited from mail, immediately log her out.

One problem you might run into when using `su -c` is that it allows only one parameter. Look what happens if you try and use it to remove a file called `/root/badfile`:

```
$ su -c rm /root/badfile
Unknown id: /root/badfile
```

Oops! It thought `/root/badfile` was the name of a user you were trying to become. The workaround for this is to put the entire command you are trying to run in quotation marks so it will be treated as one unit like so:

```
$ su -c "rm /root/badfile"
```

Much better!

"Visual" su

With the increasing popularity of graphical user interfaces (GUIs), many distributors have created various graphical administration tools for their systems. A graphical tool that, for example, would allow you to create a new user account on your system is certainly more convenient to use than a command-line program that does the same thing. Obviously, running such a program requires super-user privileges, and most programs of this type will prompt you for the superuser's password when you start them up.

These programs contain a built-in `su` command that takes effect when you start them. When you've successfully entered the superuser's password, the program runs as if it were being run directly from the superuser account. (If you are logged in as the superuser, you generally don't need to enter the superuser's password to use these sorts of programs.)

sudo

Some systems implement an alternative using su. The sudo command (pronounced *soo doo*) allows certain specified users the right to use superuser functions. For example, suppose you're logged in as susan, and you want to remove badfile. You'd give the command like this:

```
sudo rm badfile
```

You are then prompted for *your* password (not the superuser's, but susan's). At this point, the sudo program consults the file /etc/sudoers, and if susan is listed in that file, it executes the command.

su and sudo are not exclusive. It is possible for a given system to have both commands on it, but as a matter of good practice, it's probably best to choose one or the other.

Switching groups

There are comparatively fewer reasons to change your group than your user identity, but if you do choose to switch groups, the su command has counterparts in the newgrp and sg commands. newgrp allows you to change your primary group to one of the other ones you belong to. You can test this with the id command:

```
$ id -gn
knoppix
$ newgrp users
$ id -gn
users
$ exit
exit
$ id -gn
knoppix
```

Using newgrp puts you into a new shell where your default group is the one you specified. Of course, you must already be a member of that group in order to make it your default. When you want to revert to your former identity, type exit to close the shell. Like the default invocation of su, newgrp just spawns a new shell. Also, like su, newgrp has a - option to get a full login experience in the new shell.

sg does pretty much the same thing as newgrp, but it has one extra feature that can be useful: a -c option (as with su) for when you just want to change groups for one command. For example:

```
$ sg  shadow -c "cat /etc/shadow"
```

This lets you print out the contents of the shadow password file if you are a member of group shadow. (And you shouldn't be. It's a huge security risk to let anyone except a few key programs have access to the etc/shadow file.)

Creating New User Accounts

There are several methods by which you can create new user accounts, and to a certain extent, how it's done will depend on the distribution that you use. Almost all distributions have a text-mode utility called `useradd` or `adduser` that will allow you to add a user from the terminal. In addition, many systems have graphical programs that will allow you to add a user. It is the graphical programs that are likely to differ from distribution to distribution.

You will need some basic information to set up an account:

- The new user's username, that is, the name under which he or she will log in
- The new user's full name
- An initial password for the new user
- The shell that you would like the new user to have as his default
- The location of the new user's home directory
- The new user's numeric user ID

Some of these pieces of information are optional. For example, the shell, home directory, and numeric ID are given default values if you do not specify them. Generally, you would specify a numeric ID only if you had a specific reason to do so. For example, if you were moving a user's account from another machine, you might want to make sure they have the same ID number on the new machine. For the most part, though, you can let the machine assign IDs.

Note

As a rule, it's best to use numeric ID numbers above 500. Numbers below 500 are generally reserved for system-specific functions. The superuser, for example, is always user number 0. Many programs need user-ID numbers to function, and these are generally numbers below 500. `useradd` starts assigning ID numbers with 501.

Using text mode

Creating user accounts may be one area of Linux administration where using text mode really isn't any more difficult than using a GUI tool. Using the `useradd` or `adduser` utilities, you can create accounts quickly and simply. (Most systems have one of these two utilities. They function virtually identically, and on many systems, the same utility will go by both names. For example, on Fedora Core, typing the command `man adduser` brings up the manual page for `useradd`.) For practical purposes, you can consider them identical. This chapter uses `useradd` for the examples.

The `useradd` command takes a number of options as arguments. Each option corresponds to a piece of information about the new user. Imagine that you want to create a new user with the name `harry`. You want this user to have UID 552, to have `/bin/bash` as his default shell, to have `/home/harry` as his home directory, and to have `temppass` as his initial password. You'd give the command in this format:

```
useradd -u 552 -s /bin/bash -d /home/harry -p temppass harry
```

Note that the options come between the command name and the target, which in this case is the login name that you want to give the new account. Table 13-1 shows a list of common options that `useradd` takes.

Table 13-1   Options for useradd

Option	Meaning
-u	Numeric user ID
-g	Numeric default group ID
-G	One or more additional groups to which the user may belong
-d	Home directory
-s	Default shell
-c	Comment (can be used to note user's real name)
-e	Expire date (if the account should expire on a certain date)

NUMERIC IDENTIFIERS

Recall from Chapter 3 that every user on a Linux system has a unique ID number. Typically, these numbers are assigned sequentially, but as you can see from the preceding example, they can also be assigned by hand. The same holds true for groups. (Groups are discussed in more detail later in this chapter.) You can think of these ID numbers as being the *real* unique token of a particular user's identity, because these numbers are how the users are represented to the system. The login name that a user has is a convenience, since we humans respond better to names than to numbers.

THE SKELETON DIRECTORY

Sometimes, as an administrator, you may find it convenient to put a standard set of files in each user's home directory when it is created. This can be done automatically using a *skeleton* directory. This directory contains the basic set of files, and these files are copied to a new user's home directory when it is created. Here's a listing of a typical skeleton directory:

```
[joe@hamachi ~]$ ls -a /etc/skel
.  ..  .bash_logout  .bash_profile  .bashrc  .emacs  .gtkrc  .kde  .zshrc
```

Typically, the skeleton directory is located at /etc/skel, but it may vary from system to system. You can also specify a nonstandard skeleton directory by using useradd's -k option.

Using graphical tools

If graphical tools appeal to you more than command-line utilities, you'll have to do some investigation into what your particular distribution offers. Most of the major distributions sport graphical user management tools, and they're generally easy to find. On Knoppix, for example, the user administration tool is found by going to the Start menu and choosing Main menu → System → KUser (User Manager). This brings up the main KDE User Manager, as shown in Figure 13-1.

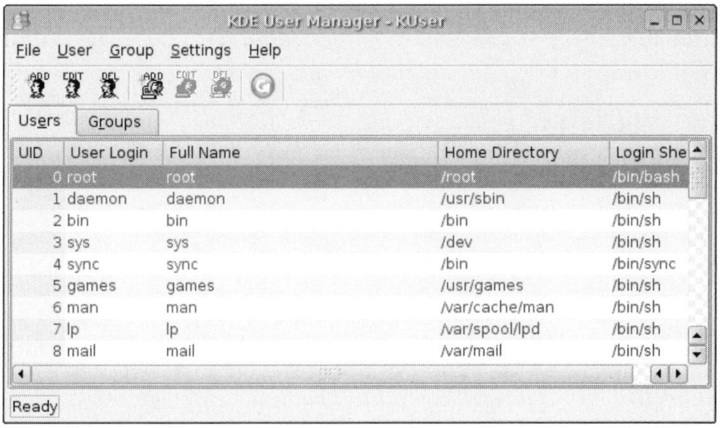

Figure 13-1: The main KUser window.

From the main KUser window, to add a new user, click the Add button, which shows an icon of a face. You are prompted to enter the name of the new user. Enter the user's login name (in this case, harry). This brings up the User Properties dialog, shown in Figure 13-2, which allows you to enter all of the relevant information.

Enter the information in this dialog. Make sure the checkbox marked Account disabled is unchecked. If you want to set an initial password for the new user, click the Set Password button and you are prompted to type and verify the new password. Then click OK.

Note

If you're running Knoppix from a live CD, such as the one included with this book, you may encounter errors if you try to create new users. This is because unless you configure the system to do so, the live CD is not really designed to be used as the core of a permanent multiuser system. You will be able to run KUser and see how it works, but you will not be able to save the changes, unless you've made these configuration changes. If you're interested in doing this, see the Knoppix Web site for instructions.

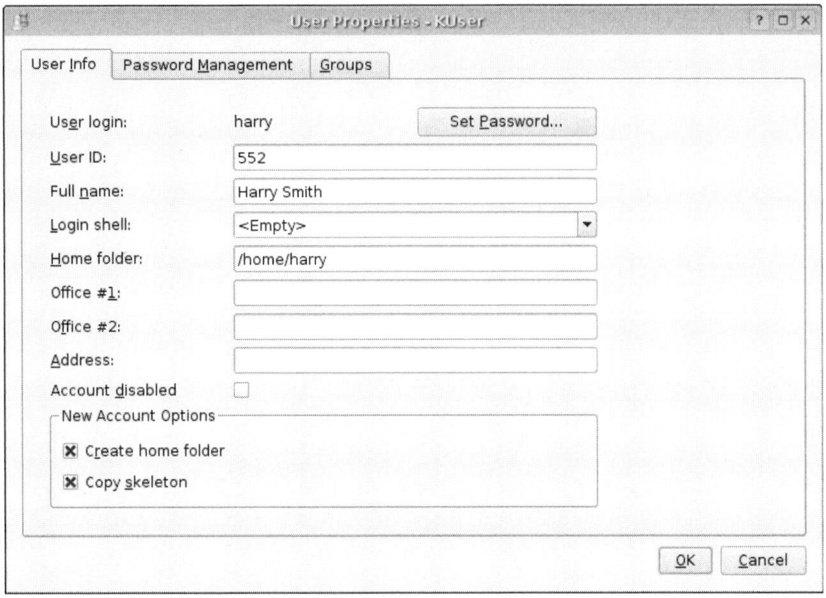

Figure 13-2: The User Properties dialog.

After you've entered all the information and clicked OK, the new account is created. At this point, you should see the new user in the list of users in the main KUser page.

Note

Who are all the other users you see in the main KUser window? You might expect to see root (the super-user), and the user account that you created for yourself, but if you look at KUser, you will see that there are a number of users already there. These are *system accounts*. System accounts exist to provide "owners" for certain processes that the system runs. Without these virtual users, all of these system processes would have to run with the superuser as their owner. This presents a security risk, because were a malicious person to gain control of one of these processes, that person would be able to act as the superuser on the system.

The procedure is similar on almost every other Linux system. (Really, there are only so many ways you can go about this.) On Fedora Core, for example, the user administration tool is called system-config-users and can be found by using the menu path Desktop → System Settings → Users and Groups. It is almost identical to KUser, except that the users shown in the main window are filtered so that only user accounts are shown. (This can be changed by selecting Preferences → Filter system users and groups.) As with KUser, there is an Add User button, which brings up a dialog box where you can enter information. Figure 13-3 shows the Fedora Core User Manager.

The differences between user managers are essentially superficial. They may look different, but they operate the same way.

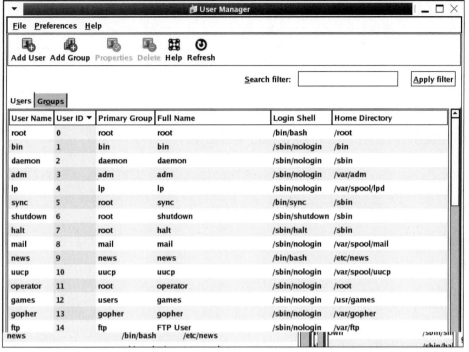

Figure 13-3: The Fedora Core User Manager.

Creating and Assigning Users to Groups

While individual users represent the most basic level of organization, Linux has inherited from Unix a secondary level—the group. You can create groups if you are the superuser, and you can assign users to them. Groups can be secondary owners of files, and each file has a set of permissions that apply to the group that owns it. This means that the user who owns a file can give access to the members of a specific group, without giving access to everyone on the system.

As an example, imagine that you are administering a Linux machine for a small company. You have some files pertaining to payroll matters, and the information contained in these files is sensitive. You could create a group called `payroll` and make only those users who are responsible for payroll administration members of that group. You can then assign the sensitive files to that group and give the group access to them. That way, the files are available to everybody who needs to see them but not to anyone else. (Incidentally, this applies to programs too. One of the forms of permission that you can grant is the right to *execute*—that is, run—a program. This permission can also be assigned to a group, so that only the members of that group would have the ability to run a given program.)

In this section, you learn how to create groups, assign users to them, and assign files to particular groups. The next section explains file permissions and how to grant various levels of access to users and groups.

Creating groups

Creating groups is not all that different from creating users. In fact, on many Linux systems, you often do both at the same time. Many distributions are set up so that anytime you create a user account, you also create a group with the same name, and the user is assigned to that group. In other words, in addition to the user jack, there is also a group called jack, and the user jack is automatically assigned to that group. You can, of course, create other groups and assign users to them as well. A user can be assigned to any number of groups.

CREATING GROUPS WITH THE TEXT MODE METHOD

Like creating users, creating groups can be done in either text mode or by using graphical utilities. To create a group in text mode, you use the groupadd command. The groupadd command functions similarly to useradd and requires you to add some additional information on the command line. A typical groupadd command might look like this:

```
groupadd -g 1015 payroll
```

This command creates a group called payroll with a group ID number of 1015. If you leave out the -g option, it automatically assigns the group a number. The number will be above 500 (groups 0–500 are generally reserved for system groups) and one greater than the highest numbered group that already exists. You must, however, supply the name of the group.

CREATING GROUPS WITH GRAPHICAL METHODS

To add a group using a graphical tool, you will generally use the same tool that you did to add a user. (Most graphical tools combine the user and group creation functions.) So, on Knoppix, you would use KUser.

In the main KUser screen, click the Groups tab to see a list of all the groups currently on the system (Figure 13-4). Notice that there are several system groups (those with ID numbers below 500) and a few higher-numbered ones. (If you are running Knoppix from the live CD, you will see several groups with ID numbers above 1000 but no actual user groups.)

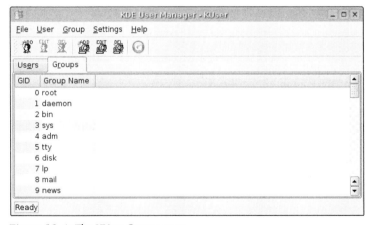

Figure 13-4: The KUser Groups pane.

To add a group, click the Add button that shows an icon of a computer and two faces. This opens the Group Properties dialog, shown in Figure 13-5.

Figure 13-5: The KUser Group Properties dialog.

You can assign the group an ID number either by hand or by using the default one given to you, and you need to enter the name of the group; for this example, name the group payroll. You can assign users to the group at this time or later, as explained in the following sections. After you've entered the group's name and ID number, click OK, and the group is created.

Assigning users to groups

After you've created your new group, it's time to assign users to it. In the following example, you add the users jack and jenny to the payroll group.

ASSIGNING USERS TO GROUPS WITH THE TEXT MODE METHOD

To assign a user to a new group, you need to modify that user's profile on the system. You can do this using the usermod command. The usermod command works in almost exactly the same way (with the same options) as the useradd command, so to assign jack to the payroll group, do this:

```
usermod -G payroll jack
```

The -G option (note that it's capital G) is used to specify additional groups to which the user belongs other than the default group to which he is assigned. Jack's default group is probably the jack group, which was created when you created his account. You need to do the same thing for Jenny:

```
usermod -g payroll jenny
```

Jack and Jenny are now members of the payroll group.

ASSIGNING USERS TO GROUPS WITH GRAPHICAL METHODS

Group assignment is one area where graphical methods are arguably easier—or at least more straightforward—than text methods.

Under Knoppix, with the KUser Group Properties window open as in Figure 13-5, you can see a list of users along the right-hand side. Click on the name of a user that you want to add to the group, and click the button marked Add. That user will be shown in the pane on the left-hand side of the window. Repeat the procedure for any other users that you want to add to the group, and click OK. The users are then added to the group.

Note

You can add users to a group at the time you create the group or at any subsequent time. To add users to an already existing group, open KUser and from the main window, click to highlight the group you want to edit, and then click the button marked Edit, which shows the group icon (the computer with two faces). This opens the Group Properties window, showing your selected group.

Setting File Permissions

Now that you understand the basic principles underlying user and group identity, turn your attention to the topic of file ownership and permission.

There are three basic classes of permissions and three types of permission in each class, making nine permissions in all. The permission classes are user, group, and all, and the permission types are read, write, and execute. Table 13-2 shows what those permissions mean.

Table 13-2   File Permission Types

Permission	*Meaning*
User	
Read	The user can view the contents of the file.
Write	The user can modify the contents of the file.
Execute	The file is a program and the user can run it.
Group	
Read	Any member of the group can view the contents of the file.
Write	Any member of the group can modify the contents of the file.
Execute	The file is a program and any member of the group can run it.
All	
Read	Any user on the system can view the contents of the file.
Write	Any user on the system can modify the contents of the file.
Execute	The file is a program and any user on the system can run it.

A file can have any combination of these permissions. For example, there may be a file on the system that is readable by any user on the system, writable only by the owner, and executable by the payroll group. Such a file would have permissions User: read, write, and execute; Group: read and execute; All: read.

Note

Setting permissions on directories is almost the same as file permissions, but the system works slightly differently. For a directory, having read permission means that you can list the directory's contents. In other words, if you give the ls command for a directory that you don't have read permission on, you will get an error message. write permission for a directory means that you can change the contents of a directory; that is, you can add files to or remove files from that directory. execute permission means that you can use that permission as your current working directory; that is, you can execute a cd command and enter that directory.

A graphical look at permissions

Using the CD that comes with this book, open Knoppix on your computer. On Knoppix, open the Konqueror file manager by clicking the house icon in the taskbar. Konqueror opens to the default home directory (/home/knoppix for users of the live CD). Click the Desktop icon. This moves you to the directory /home/knoppix/Desktop. Next, right-click on the icon marked KNOPPIX.desktop, and from the pop-up menu that appears, select Properties. This brings up the Properties window as shown in Figure 13-6.

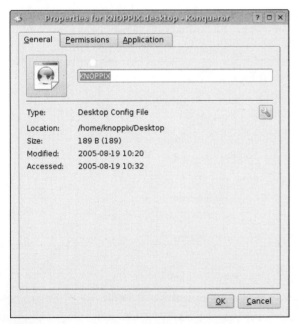

Figure 13-6: The Konqueror file Properties window.

In this window, click on the Permissions tab. In the upper pane, you can see the permissions listed, similar to those shown in Figure 13-7.

Figure 13-7: File permissions for KNOPPIX.desktop.

These permissions are described in a somewhat informal way, but you can get the idea. If you're using the Knoppix live CD, you are logged in as the user knoppix, and therefore you would be entitled to change these permissions, which you can do by clicking on the arrows to the left.

For a more systematized look at the permissions, click the Advanced Permissions button. This opens the Advanced Permissions window, shown in Figure 13-8.

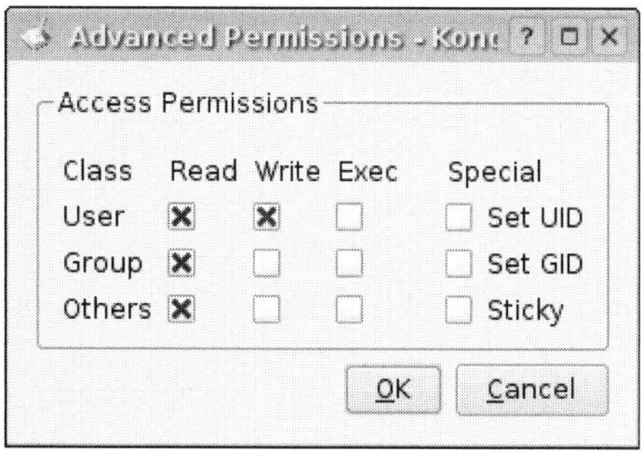

Figure 13-8: The Advanced Permissions window.

Here you can see the permissions laid out in a format more consistent with the description that you saw in the last section. (Knoppix uses the term Others where most systems use the term All.)

Checking permissions from the terminal

Permissions are also visible using text mode tools. On any Linux system, open a terminal window and give the command ls -l /etc. You should get a listing that looks something like this:

```
-rw-r--r--   1 root root   15276 Oct  5  2004 a2ps.cfg
-rw-r--r--   1 root root    2562 Oct  5  2004 a2ps-site.cfg
drwxr-xr-x   4 root root    4096 May  9 12:13 acpi
-rw-r--r--   1 root root      47 Aug  7 14:17 adjtime
drwxr-xr-x   4 root root    4096 May  9 12:16 alchemist
-rw-r--r--   1 root root    1574 Oct  8  2004 aliases
-rw-r-----   1 root smmsp  12288 Aug  7 14:22 aliases.db
drwxr-xr-x   4 root root    4096 May  9 12:18 alsa
drwxr-xr-x   2 root root    4096 May  9 14:59 alternatives
-rw-r--r--   1 root root     329 Sep 28  2004 anacrontab
-rw-r--r--   1 root root    5297 Aug  7 14:17 asound.state
-rw-------   1 root root       1 Oct  5  2004 at.deny
-rw-r--r--   1 root root     325 Oct 15  2004 auto.master
-rw-r--r--   1 root root     581 Oct 15  2004 auto.misc
-rwxr-xr-x   1 root root    1057 Oct 15  2004 auto.net
-rw-r--r--   1 root root    1182 Sep 23  2004 bashrc
-rw-r--r--   1 root root     350 May  9 13:08 blkid.tab
drwxr-xr-x   2 root root    4096 May  9 12:12 bluetooth
drwxr-xr-x   2 root root    4096 May  9 12:18 bonobo-activation
-rw-r--r--   1 root root     976 Oct 18  2004 cdrecord.conf
drwxr-xr-x   2 root root    4096 May  9 13:13 cipe
```

(This is only the first page of the listing. On most Linux systems there are many more entries in the /etc directory.)

In the very first column on the left-hand side, you see a series of characters. This set of symbols gives you a good deal of information about the file, including its permission status. The first character on the far left tells you the type of file. For most purposes, it will either be a dash (-) indicating a normal file, or a d indicating a directory. Beginning with the second character, you see the permissions. Characters two, three, and four indicate, respectively, read, write, and execute permissions for the user. If you see an r in the second space, that means the user has read permission. If you see a dash, it means that the user does *not* have read permission. Likewise, a w indicates write permission, and will be found in the third space, and an x indicates execute permission, and will be found in the fourth space.

The next three spaces — spaces five, six, and seven, correspond to read, write, and execute permission for the group, and spaces eight, nine, and ten correspond to read, write, and execute permission for all users. Consider this entry:

```
-rwxr-xr-x   1 root root    1057 Oct 15  2004 auto.net
```

What you see here is that the file auto.net is a regular file (indicated by the dash in position one). The owning user has read, write, and execute permission, the group has read and execute permission, and all users have read and execute permissions.

You can tell by looking at columns three and four that the user who owns the file is root (column three) and the group that owns the file is the root group (column four).

Note

Execute permission is a little different with directories. When you see a directory in a listing (indicated by the d in the first position), execute permission means that the relevant user class has the ability to enter that directory. So, for example, if you see this:

```
drwxr-xr-x   2 root root    4096 May  9 13:13 cipe
```

It means that the owner, the group, and all users have the ability to enter the cipe directory.

Changing permissions

Of course, the permissions system would not be very useful if you couldn't change permissions. Granting and limiting permissions, and otherwise customizing a file's level of access, is at the heart of the system. Before we get into the nuts and bolts of how exactly this is done, it's important to point out that *you must be the file's owner or the superuser to change permissions on a file*. This may seem to be an obvious point, but it's an important one, and one that's easy to forget.

CHANGING PERMISSIONS WITH GRAPHICAL METHODS

If you're using a graphical file manager, such as Konquerer or Nautilus, you can generally edit permissions directly from that program. Take another look at Figure 13-8 — Konqueror's Advanced Permissions window. You can edit a file's permissions simple by checking or unchecking the various checkboxes that you see there (again, provided you are the file's owner or the superuser). Most graphical file managers have some sort of permissions mechanism that operates in a similar fashion. If you're using a distribution other than Knoppix, consult your system's documentation to find out exactly how your file manager handles it.

CHANGING PERMISSIONS WITH TEXT MODE METHODS

Changing a file's permissions can also be done in text mode using the chmod command. The chmod (a contraction of *change mode*) command takes the name of the file as the target and the change in permission mode as an option. The options take a slightly unusual form, and it's probably easiest to grasp this through examples.

Suppose you have a file called share-file, and you want to grant read access to it for all users on the system. Initially, share-file has this set of permissions:

```
-rw-rw----  1 joe joe 0 Dec  9 15:18 share-file
```

Give this command:

```
chmod a+r share-file
```

You get a set of permissions that looked like this:

```
-rw-rw-r--  1 joe joe 0 Dec  9 15:18 share-file
```

   In this case, the a designates that you are changing the permission for all users. The plus sign designates that you are *granting* permission, and the r designates that you are granting read permission. If, after giving this command, you decided that you wanted to revoke this permission, you could do so by giving the command

```
chmod a-r share-file
```

This will revert the permissions back to

```
-rw-rw----  1 joe joe 0 Dec  9 15:18 share-file
```

Note that here you have changed the plus sign to a minus sign, indicating that you want to revoke that permission.
   Suppose that you wanted to give read, write, and execute permissions to all users. In that case, you'd give this command:

```
chmod a+rwx share-file
```

In this instance, you've designated all users, and you've included read (r), write (w), and execute (x) permissions.
   If you wanted to grant read and execute permission to members of the group, you'd give the command this way:

```
chmod g+rx share-file
```

   By now it should be evident how the command works. You can designate the user (u), the group (g), or all (a), and you can designate read, write, or execute permissions. Use a plus sign to grant a permission and a minus sign to revoke it.

Note

The only users who can change permissions on a file are the owner of that file and the superuser. Any changes in permissions are relative to the owner of the file. For example, if you give user execute permission to a file, the "user" in question is the file's owner. Likewise, group permissions apply to the group that owns the file.

Changing Ownership

Although not an issue of permission per se, a crucial part of the whole file management system is the ability to change the ownership of files. Remember that every file has two owners: a user and a group. You can change either of these. As with permissions, you can change the ownership of a file only if you are the file's owner, or the superuser.

Caution

If, as a user, you change the user owner of a file — that is, you assign ownership of the file to a user other than yourself — you will not be able to get the ownership back. Only the user to whom you assigned owner-ship, or the superuser, can assign ownership back to you.

Changing user ownership

Changing ownership is done with the `chown` command. Using the `chown` command is simple. It takes the name of the new owner as an option and the name of the file as the target. So, for example, if you wanted to assign ownership of the file `share-file` to the user `jack`, you'd give the command in this format:

```
chown jack share-file
```

Changing group ownership

Changing the owning group of a file is likewise simple and is done with the `chgroup` command. The `chgroup` command operates in exactly the same way as the `chown` command, taking the name of the group as an option and the name of the file as the target. So, if you wanted to assign the file `share-file` to the `payroll` group, you'd give the command like so:

```
chgroup payroll share-file
```

If you really want to show off, you can do them both at once, like so:

```
chown jack.payroll share-file
```

Changing ownership with graphical methods

Both user and group ownership of files can be changed using graphical methods available with the various distributions' file managers. Look back at Figure 13-7. Notice that in the Ownership pane of that window you can change the group owner by clicking on the arrow next to it. (Changing the user owner is not possible in this situation because you're using a live CD, and you are not actually the `knoppix` user. With a more traditional installation, changing the user owner would be possible.)

As with other operations of this type, there will be slight variations depending on the actual file manager program you're using, but they are generally pretty much the same.

Setuid and Setgid Programs

The `mount` command allows you to attach a new storage device or partition on a storage device to your system. Normally, this command can be run only by the superuser. To allow an ordinary user to mount, for example, a Windows share, the user must have the ability to become `root`. It would be a bad idea to give everyone the `root` password just for this task and impractical to have the administrator do it each time.

Instead, Linux takes care of this problem by means of a feature called setuid. A program that has setuid permissions enabled runs not as the user who invoked it but as the user who owns it. You can say that a program "is setuid" to a particular user; when you do, you mean that program has its setuid permission flag set and is owned by that user. Looking at `mount`'s permissions with the `ls -l` command, you can see that `mount` is setuid `root` (as indicated by the `s` instead of `x` in the first group of permissions), so any user can start it, and it will run not as that user but as `root`:

```
-rwsr-xr-x  1 root root 68496 2005-09-20 12:43 /bin/mount
```

In the same way, `setgid` programs don't assume the group of the user that started them; they always retain the group they are owned by. `crontab` is a program for scheduling actions to take place at particular times. It is setgid `crontab` so that it can create and write to files in `/var/spool/crontab`, which is where `crond`, the daemon that actually runs the scheduled actions, looks for new tasks.

The ability to change from one account to another in midexecution requires keeping track of what the original account was, or you would not be able to change back again. So, for each process Linux also maintains a record of what are called *effective* user and group IDs (EUID and EGID). `mount`'s real UID, for example, would always stays the same as the user's. But the EUID would change to 0, that is, `root`'s UID, until it completed execution. While a `setuid` program is running, operating system features that need to check the identity of the process see it as the effective value, 0 in this case. They have the ability to see the real value too if necessary. (This is why you can mount only some types of devices unless you are really `root`. `mount` checks both the real and effective UIDs and applies its own policies.)

For all their utility, `setuid` and `setgid` programs are used only sparingly. It is all too easy for a coding mistake in one of these programs to allow a malicious user more privileges than he is entitled to. It is very dangerous indeed if the error is in a program that is setuid or setgid `root`. So, Linux programmers try to avoid using this feature as much as possible. However, there are still a few situations where the use of `setuid` and `setgid` programs is unavoidable. Thus, every Linux system has at least a few.

Summary

Linux's nature as a true multiuser system presents a few challenges to the new user and administrator. Having multiple users requires that each have a unique identity and that each exercise a certain amount of control over his or her personal computing space. This is done using unique user and group ID numbers and by allowing users and groups to "own" files. The owners of files may determine who has access to them and what kind of access will be granted.

Chapter 14

Backing Up Data

W arning: You are about to read the most boring chapter in this book. It's true; making back-ups is nowhere near as fun and interesting as setting up a Web server or poring through the kernel source code. Consequently, most of us find excuses to postpone or even completely forget this chore. Until the fateful day arrives — and it will, mark my words! — when an important file gets accidentally deleted.

And if you are using Linux in your business, backing up data might not just be a good idea but the law. Regulations such as the Sarbanes-Oxley Act may require you to maintain an audit trail of every transaction and communication your company makes.

So keep reading; I show you how to keep your data safe and sound with as little effort as possible.

What Do You Need to Back Up?

To plan a proper backup regimen, you need to think about what kinds of data you are going to back up and how often you want to back it up. Backing up the operating system itself, for instance, could be a lower priority than backing up a client's account information. You might consider it sufficient to back up the former once a month, whereas the latter would be backed up every evening. On the other hand, if you are experimenting heavily with Linux and often find yourself in a situation where you've rendered it inoperable, or if you deal with your clients only once a year at tax time, you will have an opposite set of priorities. This is something you have to determine for yourself, but once you have decided the scope and frequency of your backups, you can automate the process and have the computer take care of the burden for you.

Routine backups

You can always play it safe and back up your entire system, but you will generally be wasting a lot of time and space. Much of your system consists of software provided by the vendor, which does not change that often and can be easily restored if you have the original installation media or access to the Internet. Nowadays most Linux distributions install software in units called *packages*. Fedora, for instance, uses RPM format packages (see Chapter 15 for more information about this), and you can get a list of installed packages by running the following command:

```
$ rpm -qa > mypackages.txt
```

If your distribution uses the other common format, .deb, as used in Debian or distributions derived from it like Linspire, Ubuntu, Mepis, or Xandros, this command does the same thing:

```
$ dpkg-query -show > mypackages.txt
```

In both cases, this queries the package database for a list of all installed packages and stores the output in a file called mypackages.txt, which you can print out or store somewhere and use to re-create your system if it gets trashed.

Note

Remember to regenerate the list of installed packages every time you add or remove packages.

If you have installed software outside the package system's purview (non-RPM format packages within a Fedora system or software you have compiled yourself, for example), you'll have to find some alternative method of keeping track of it. One way of making it easy for yourself is to install such software only in /usr/local, the place in the Linux file system hierarchy explicitly reserved for nonvendor software. Then you can back up that whole section of the file system and be confident you have everything. Some commercial Linux software, typically that with a Unix heritage, installs into /opt, which has a similar purpose to /usr/local; so, if you have any such software, be sure to back up /opt too.

Here are other sections of the file system that should be backed up routinely:

- **/home:** This directory is the number-one priority because /home contains the home directories where users' personal data is kept.

- **/etc:** This directory is also very important to back up as it contains system configuration data.

- **/srv:** This directory is the place in the file system where data belonging to servers goes, for example the Web sites delivered by a Web server, so this is also a prime target for frequent backups.

- **/var:** This directory is used for storing *variable* data, a mixed bag. Some subdirectories, such as /var/mail, where users' incoming mailboxes are kept, or /var/log, where the system log files are kept, are definitely worth keeping; others, such as /var/run, which contains lock files for servers, are not. My advice is to keep things simple by just backing up everything in /var.

By and large, backing up these directories should cover all the important files on your system. It's not a 100 percent guarantee because, unfortunately, some programs don't fully obey the file-system design guidelines.

Backup schedules

As mentioned in the last section, doing a full backup each time is not efficient. Still, you should do a full backup on occasion just to make sure you have a copy of every file. Depending on how much your system changes, once a week or even once a month is a good interval between full backups. Because doing a full backup can be a lengthy process, schedule it for a time when the system is being lightly used, such as a weekend or late at night. This also minimizes the chances of files changing while the backup is going on.

A partial backup of the files that have changed between your full backups should also be done on a regular basis, typically every day or, if you have a lot of activity going on, perhaps even a couple of times a day. There are two types of partial backup you can make.

Incremental backups store all the files that have changed since the last full or partial backup. In other words, if you did a full backup every Sunday and an incremental backup every other day of the week, Monday's backup would contain all the files that changed since Sunday. Tuesday's backup would contain all the files that changed since Monday, Wednesday's backup would contain all the files that changed since Tuesday, and so on. The chief advantages of incremental backups are that they are fast and use less storage space because only the minimum amount of data necessary is copied.

Differential backups store all the files that have changed since the last full backup. If you did a full backup every Sunday and a differential backup every other day of the week, each of those days' backups would store the files that have changed since Sunday. Thus differential backups will be slower and take up more storage space than incremental backups. There is likely to be a lot of overlap; a file changed on Monday could potentially be backed up as many as six times. Some administrators actually like this kind of redundancy as backups can go wrong. Having multiple copies of a file increases the chances at least one of them is good.

Bare-metal recovery

It is possible for a system to become so damaged that you cannot even start your backup procedures. However, with some planning and backing up the right directories in advance, you can still get the system up and running to the point where you can restore it from your backups without having to do a reinstall.

Keep a live CD like Knoppix handy. It will make your job immensely easier. Once you boot into Knoppix, you have a complete Linux system at your disposal. You can mount all the partitions from your crashed system and fix any problems that have occurred or start your backup software.

What if the partition table itself has been corrupted? Part of your backup procedure should be to note the number and size of all the partitions on each drive in your computer. You can list partitions with the fdisk -l command:

```
# fdisk -l /dev/sda

Disk /dev/sda: 2147 MB, 2147483648 bytes
255 heads, 63 sectors/track, 261 cylinders
```

```
Units = cylinders of 16065 * 512 = 8225280 bytes

   Device Boot       Start       End      Blocks   Id  System
/dev/sda1     *          1        13      104391   83  Linux
/dev/sda2               14       261     1992060   8e  Linux LVM
```

You also need to know where each partition is mounted and if it requires any special mount options, which is information you can get from the file /etc/fstab:

```
# cat /etc/fstab
/dev/VolGroup00/LogVol00 /                        ext3    defaults         1 1
LABEL=/boot              /boot                     ext3    defaults         1 2
/dev/devpts              /dev/pts                  devpts  gid=5,mode=620   0 0
/dev/shm                 /dev/shm                  tmpfs   defaults         0 0
/dev/proc                /proc                     proc    defaults         0 0
/dev/sys                 /sys                      sysfs   defaults         0 0
/dev/VolGroup00/LogVol01 swap                      swap    defaults         0 0
/dev/hdc                 /media/cdrom              auto    exec,noauto,managed 0 0
```

Save this information in a file and print it out or save it somewhere. (Unfortunately, you can't save it on the Knoppix CD itself.) Remember to update it if you make any changes to your partition table. Now you can use fdisk to recreate damaged partition tables if necessary.

Backup Devices

After deciding what you need to back up, the next step in your backup strategy is to decide what kind of media you will use to store your data. The answer depends on several factors, including the storage capacity, reliability, price, writing speed, and availability of media.

Tapes

You've probably seen old movies where a huge computer has a whole bank of tape machines behind it clicking and whirring away. Tapes have been around for a long time and are still in wide use today because of their reliability and speed. They are a bit expensive, however, and the cheaper kinds don't have as much storage capacity. There are several varieties:

- **DDS or SCSI DAT:** Storage capacity for these tapes is anywhere from 2 to 20GB. The tape drive uses the standard SCSI interface to talk to the Linux kernel, so compatibility is not a problem.

- **QiC/Travan:** This is the older standard of tape technology, but still in widespread use. Storage capacity is between 400MB and 10GB. A special device driver is needed by Linux to be able to access the drive, but it is included in the standard kernel and is compatible with most models.

■ **DLT/SuperDLT:** These tapes are the top of the line and boast storage capacities of up to 640GB. Those that use the SCSI interface don't usually suffer from compatibility problems, but very high-end models might require driver support for maximum performance, and that driver might not be available for Linux. (Though with the growing prominence of Linux in the server market, hardware manufacturers are becoming more likely to support these drivers.)

From the home or small-business user's perspective, DAT tapes probably provide the best price/performance ratio, but the tape drive market changes rapidly, so you would be well advised to do research on prices and storage capacity on sites such as Pricewatch (`www.pricewatch.com`) and LinuxHardware.org (`www.linuxhardware.org`) before buying.

CD/DVD

Nowadays, CD or DVD writers are standard on most desktop PCs and even some laptops. They use the SCSI or IDE interface and so do not have compatibility problems with Linux. This makes writable CDs or DVDs a handy solution for backup media. There are two problems: First, CD and DVD capacities are relatively smaller than DAT tape capacities. CDs have a capacity of only 650MB, and DVDs top out at 4.7GB. Second, CDs and DVDs can be prone to heat damage, scratching, and other factors, which make them unsuitable if you need high levels of reliability.

Zip/REV drives

Iomega Corporation originally positioned its line of removable storage drives as a replacement for floppy drives. These drives didn't quite become as ubiquitous as floppies but have a respectable following, especially in industries like publishing and advertising where large files have to be transported from place to place. Zip disks have between 100MB and 750MB of storage. REV disks store up to 35GB. The drives have a USB or SCSI interface and work well with Linux. See `www.iomega.com` for more information about these types of drives.

USB keys

These are small, solid-state devices with a USB interface. They hold from 64MB to 1GB of data. Obviously this isn't enough to back up an entire system, but it is more than adequate for the typical user's personal data. They are especially useful for the kind of user who finds himself working on several different computers.

Another hard drive

Perhaps the easiest way to back up a hard drive is to another hard drive. Disk drives are getting bigger and cheaper per gigabyte of storage every day.

A standard method of keeping two or more hard drives synchronized is called RAID (Redundant Array of Independent Disks). Most Linux distributions allow you to set up disks in a RAID formation at installation time. It is also possible to set it up afterwards.

RAID can improve disk usage and performance, but from the backup perspective, the main benefit of RAID is the redundancy. If one disk in the set fails, you still have the others that replicate the data; therefore, nothing is lost. It is less than ideal in other ways. RAID can't help you in the case of deletion of individual files. Like all changes, deletions are also replicated across the entire disk set. It is also no defense against a power failure or some catastrophic hardware malfunction that causes all the disks to crash at once.

A more promising variation on the theme is Network Attached Storage (NAS). This is a PC or a special device with a lot of disk storage whose sole purpose is to act as a file server for other PCs on a network. The NAS device can also be used to back up data from the other PCs. Once only a feature of big corporate data centers, there are a number of inexpensive NAS devices available now aimed at the home/small-business market.

Note

A good source for Linux-friendly information on hardware topics including RAID and NAS is Tom's Hardware Guide (other operating systems are covered too). The page with articles and reviews on storage products can be found at `www.tomshardware.com/storage/`.

Compression

The storage sizes given above reflect the normal capacity for each device. However, backup data can be compressed, and this can allow you to substantially increase the amount you can store. Typically, sales brochures for backup devices double the normal capacity to indicate their compressed capacity, but this is overly optimistic. In real-world usage, text and some other types of data with a regular structure compress well, whereas binary files such as images have a data structure that is far less regular, and compressing them provides only modest savings. In some cases, the compressed version may actually be bigger.

Using the tar Command

Now you need some software to perform the actual backup. One capable though somewhat spartan command-line tool is a standard part of any Linux or Unix system: tar. `tar` (usually compressed with the `gzip` program) is used as a common file distribution format for Linux files occupying the same function as `PKZip` (which uses an entirely different type of compression) does on Windows systems. These *tarballs* as they are known, usually have a `.tgz` or `.tar.gz` extension.

But before `tar` was used for distribution, it was used for archival purposes. `tar` actually stands for *tape archiver,* though it can be used with more types of media than just tapes.

Creating tar archives

To create a new archive using `tar`, use the `-c` option. The `-f` option gives the file name of the new archive to be created, and `/etc` in the following example, is the directory to be archived. Note that unlike other Linux command-line programs, the `-` before `tar` options can be omitted.

```
$ tar -cf etc.tar /etc
```

You can use a device name instead of a file for the name of the new archive. If you wanted to back up to a tape drive whose device name was /dev/tape, it might look something like this:

```
$ tar -cf /dev/tape /etc
```

Or to a Zip drive called /dev/sda5:

```
$ tar -cf /dev/sda5 /etc
```

When creating backups of system files, remember to run tar as the root user as it won't be able to add any files it cannot read.

Also, you may notice that tar gave a warning about stripping the initial / from file names stored in the archive. To suppress this stripping behavior, use the -P option:

```
$ cd /
$ tar -cPf  ~/etc.tar etc
```

Adding the -v option prints out the name of each file as it is added to the archive.

Compressing the output

You can automatically compress the tar file with gzip using the -z flag:

```
$ tar -czf etc.tar.gz /etc
```

Other compression utilities can also be used. The -j flag uses bzip2, which provides somewhat better compression than gzip at the expense of some speed.

```
$ tar -cjf etc.tar.bz2 /etc
```

The -Z flag uses compress, which is common on commercial Unix systems but relatively rare on Linux because the only implementation, called ncompress, is not free software.

```
$ tar -cZf etc.tar.z /etc
```

In order to use any of these compression options, you have to have the relevant compressor installed or you will get an error message.

Listing tar file contents

Now that you have created a tar file, you can examine its contents with the -t option. Notice the -z option is also used because the tar file has been compressed with gzip:

```
$ tar -tzf etc.tar.gz
etc/
etc/fstab
```

```
etc/pcmcia/
etc/pcmcia/ide.opts
etc/pcmcia/cis/
etc/pcmcia/cis/3CXEM556.dat
...
```

You can also add the -v option to get verbose information on the contents of the tar file:

```
$ tar -tvzf etc.tar.gz  | head
drwxr-xr-x root/root         0 2005-11-20 07:16:52 etc/
-rw-r--r-- root/root       526 2005-09-18 18:35:14 etc/fstab
drwxr-xr-x root/root         0 2005-10-03 11:00:52 etc/pcmcia/
-rw-r--r-- root/root       486 2005-09-09 12:59:35 etc/pcmcia/ide.opts
drwxr-xr-x root/root         0 2005-09-20 16:52:54 etc/pcmcia/cis/
-rw-r--r-- root/root       134 2005-09-09 12:59:35 etc/pcmcia/cis/3CXEM556.dat
...
```

Extracting files

Once you have a tar file, you can extract files from it using the -x flag like so:

```
$ tar -xpf etc.tar
```

tar will not extract files with the ownership and permissions information recorded in the archive for them unless you also use the -p option. Also, remember unless you used the -P option when creating the archive, tar has stripped the leading / in file names; so, you will actually get a directory called etc in your current directory, which is probably not what you want. The -C option changes the working directory to one you specify before starting extraction. (You can also use it with the create option, c.)

```
$ tar -xpC / -f etc.tar
```

You can also use the -z, -j, and -Z options to unpack archives with gunzip, bunzip2, or uncompress, respectively.

Adding the -v option causes tar to print the name of each file it is extracting from the archive.

Just using the -x option by itself extracts all the files in the archive. What do you do if you just want one specific file? Simply provide the full file name as stored in the archive as the final argument to tar:

```
$ tar -xf etc.tar /etc/passwd
```

This extracts passwd into a subdirectory of the current directory called etc. If you really want to overwrite /etc/passwd, use the -c option as mentioned previously.

Deleting files from a tar archive

The `--delete` option (with two dashes) to `tar` removes a file while keeping the rest of the archive intact.

```
$ tar --delete -f etc.tar etc/passwd
```

You cannot safely delete from an archive on a magnetic tape drive without first unpacking it, deleting the file, and then repacking the archive. Also, `--delete` does not work on an archive compressed with the `-z`, `-j`, or `-Z` option. Assuming /etc was backed up to a tape drive and you wanted to delete /etc/passwd from the archive, the full process would go like this:

```
$ tar xf /dev/tape /etc
```

This extracts /etc from the tape into a subdirectory of the current directory called etc. Then the command

```
$ rm etc/passwd
```

deletes the file we no longer want and the command

```
$ tar cf /dev/tape etc
```

packs it all up again.

Refreshing or replacing files in a tar archive

When you use the `-u` option to `tar` and a file name, the file is compared to the version in an existing `tar` archive (specified with `-f`). If it is newer, it replaces the version in the archive. If it is older, nothing happens. If there was no such file in the archive, it is added. If the archive itself doesn't exist, it is created.

```
$ tar -uf etc.tar /etc/passwd
```

Use this option to keep a backup up-to-date with the latest versions of files.

If you want to do a true replace, that is, update an archive with a file regardless of whether the existing version is newer, the only way is to delete the file from the archive first with the `-d` option and then use `-u`.

```
$ tar -df etc.tar /etc/passwd
$ tar -uf etc.tar /etc/passwd
```

The `-u` option won't work on archives that have been compressed with the `-z`, `-j`, or `-Z` flag.

Appending to tar files

The -u option also won't work if the archive is stored on magnetic tape because tape drives cannot randomly access a particular point on the tape. However, there is a workaround; you see, tar archives can actually contain multiple copies of the same file. The -r option appends a given file to the end of an archive (again, specified with the -f option) regardless of whether that file already exists in the archive in addition to any existing versions.

```
$ tar -rf etc.tar /etc/passwd
```

Normally, when you use -x to extract a file with multiple versions in the archive, only the most recently added or appended version (the one nearest to the end of the archive) is chosen. tar has an option called --occurrence (note the two dashes), which lets you select a particular version. So if, for instance, there are three versions of /etc/passwd in an archive, the command

```
$ tar -xf etc.tar --occurrence=2 /etc/passwd
```

would extract the second version. --occurrence by itself is equivalent to --occurrence=1.

Like -u, the -r option also doesn't work on archives compressed with -z, -j, or -Z.

Changing media

Sometimes the data you are backing up will be bigger than the available media. In this case, tar aborts with an error message unless your invocation of the command includes the -M option. In this case, you would be prompted to insert a new CD-R or other storage medium. This applies to both creating and appending or updating archives. In operations on a multivolume archive that do not require writing to it, such as listing contents or extracting files, the -M option is not needed. This is one way you could back up your entire system to a SCSI tape drive:

```
$ tar -cM -C / f /dev/tape /
```

If you want to automate the changing of media, use the -F option followed by the name of a script instead of -M. Now instead of a prompt, when it is time to insert a new storage medium, your script runs instead. Your script can be written to do something as simple as playing a sound to alert you to direct your attention to the computer or more complex tasks such as ejecting and labeling a tape or sending your boss an e-mail with a report on the status of the backup. In the following example, /usr/local/bin/alert_backup_operator is a script that might do something like page the backup operator when the tape is full.

```
$ tar -cF /usr/local/bin/alert_backup_operator -C / -f /dev/tape /
```

Keeping track of multiple volumes of backup media can be a chore. Sticky labels have a tendency to peel off. Covers or jewel cases get lost. The information you wrote on the tape with a marker gets all smudged and illegible. You're better off adding a descriptive label to the archive itself. When you use -M or -F, you can also add the -V option followed by a string. This adds a label to each volume.

```
$ tar -cM -V "Intranet server" -f /dev/tape /
```

When you examine one of these volumes with the -t option, the results will look like this:

```
$ tar -tf /dev/tape
Intranet server Volume 1
etc/
etc/fstab
etc/pcmcia/
etc/pcmcia/ide.opts
etc/pcmcia/cis/
etc/pcmcia/cis/3CXEM556.dat
...
```

You can also use the label to extract a file from a multivolume archive without having to go through each volume.

```
$ tar -x -V "Intranet server Volume 2" -f /dev/tape /etc/passwd
```

You will get an error message if the specified label doesn't exist or is spelled incorrectly.

Controlling a Tape Drive with mt

In the previous section, I alluded in a couple of places to a peculiarity of tape drives, namely that they cannot be accessed randomly, only sequentially. Another oddity is that tape drives are not mounted as part of the file system, while other backup media are. Once a USB key, for instance, is mounted, you can cd to it, use cp, mv, ls, and so on. With a tape drive you can't; you have to use a program called mt instead. The GNU version of mt is part of the cpio package, which is not installed by default in every Linux distribution, so you may have to install it yourself.

Table 14-1 describes the most common operations you can perform on a tape drive with mt. The format of the command is

```
$ mt <operation>
```

You can also give mt the -f option followed by a device name to specify a particular tape device. If the option is omitted, mt defaults to using /dev/tape.

You can find out more about mt by reading its man page.

Table 14-1   mt Operations

Operation	Usage
asf n	Position the tape at the beginning of the *n*th file from the start of the tape.
bsf n	Position the tape at the beginning of the *n*th file previous to the current position.
eof n	Write *n* end of file markers at the current position.
eom	Position the tape at the end of media, that is, at the end of the last piece of data.
datcompression 0|1|n	If 0, disable data compression on the drive. If 1, enable it. Any other number lists the current compression status. This operation works on some non-DAT drives too.
fsf n	Position the tape at the beginning of the *n*th file after the current position.
offline	Rewind and eject the tape.
rewind	Go back to the beginning of the tape.
status	Display the drive's status.

Putting It All Together

Armed with your newfound knowledge of `tar`, you can craft a set of commands to back up your data the way you like it. Run your backup script on a regular basis automatically with `cron`, and you can relax, knowing that your data is safe and sound.

Note

The `cron` scheduling utility is covered in Chapter 17. Use `cron` to run two scripts: one for your full backup every week and another for your partial backup every day. (As mentioned earlier, these are just suggested times. Both full and partial backups may need to be run more or less frequently depending on your needs.)

Here is a very basic example of a backup script:

```
#!/bin/bash

#
# Run this as root to do a full backup. (Well, directories which only
```

```
# contain system files are not included so it's not a *completely* full
# backup.)
#


PATH=/bin:/usr/bin

mydirs="/etc /root /boot /home /srv /usr/local /var/mail /var/log"

# rewind the tape to the beginning.
mt rewind

for dir in $mydirs
do
    # run tar in each of the chosen directories.  Use the gzip
    # compression option (z) to save space, the volume header option
    # (V) to give the archive a label and the verbose option (v) so
    # the operator can see how the backup is proceeding.
    tar -czV"backup of $dir `date +%D`" -vf /dev/tape $dir
done

# rewind the tape again and eject it.
mt offline
```

Undoubtedly, you will want to expand on this to create your own custom backup solution.

KDat: A Graphical Tool for Tape Backups

Although tar is pretty simple once you get used to it, some people prefer something more graphical. KDat is part of the KDE project and is a GUI front end to tar and mt and your local file system. It is designed to ease the process of backing up to tape. It simplifies using tar to make multiple archives on one tape, for instance. Or it can help you create profiles of directories and files that need to be backed up. Figure 14-1 shows you the initial screen that comes up when you start KDat.

Before performing a backup, you need to make sure your tape is mounted and formatted.

 Mounting tapes: Before you can use KDat, you need to mount a tape. Insert it into the tape drive and select Mount Tape from the File menu. KDat rewinds it and places status information about it in the tree view on the left side of the screen under the tape drive node.

When you mount a tape, KDat also creates a catalog on your computer for it. As files and archives are added or removed from the tape, the catalog is updated. This is handy if you have many tapes and can't remember which of them a particular file you want to recover is stored on.

■ **Formatting tapes:** If KDat thinks you have inserted a new tape, you are prompted as to whether you want to format it, an operation which is somewhat badly named in my opinion. KDat's format is not the same as the low-level format required by some older types of tape the first time you use them before they can accept data. If your tapes need such a low-level format, you must do it yourself before starting this process. (Your tape drive's manual will explain how.) When KDat begins its formatting, all existing data on the tape is destroyed. You will be asked for two pieces of information during the format process: a name for the tape and its estimated capacity.

You can also format or reformat a tape by selecting Format Tape from the File menu.

■ **Unmounting tapes:** When you are finished with a tape, select Unmount Tape from the File menu, and after KDat has told you it is safe to do so, you can eject it.

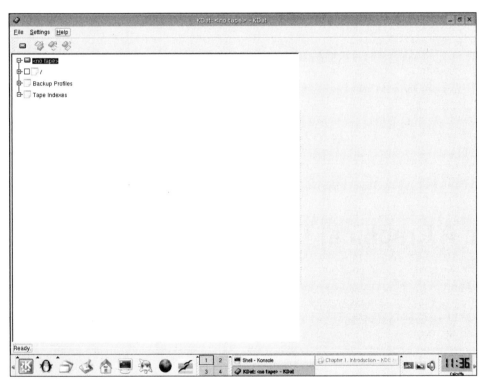

Figure 14-1: KDat.

Performing a backup

The first step is to select some files or directories to back up. KDat provides several ways of doing this. Expand the local file node in the tree view on the left side of the screen. You can see each folder and file in the root folder of your file system. Each of these folders can be expanded to show the folders and files beneath it, which can in turn display more folders and files and so on. If you highlight a file or folder, it (along with everything below it in the case of folders) is selected for backup. Also each file or folder has a checkbox next to it. You can have greater flexibility in selecting candidates for backup by checking the appropriate boxes. You cannot mix highlighting and marking checkboxes; selections have to be one style or the other. Finally, if you have set up a backup profile (as explained later), you can highlight it from under the backup profiles node of the tree view, and only files or folders listed in that profile will be selected for backup.

When you have finished your selections, choose Backup from the File menu. A dialog box pops up offering backup options. Once you confirm that everything is to your satisfaction, KDat begins the backup. The progress of the backup is shown as well as the speed of writing and estimated time to completion. KDat also prompts you to change tapes if necessary.

Verifying your backup

After making a backup, you should verify it to make sure it went as intended. If you are keeping your backups for the long term, you should also verify them on a regular basis to make sure they haven't deteriorated in any way. It's additional work, but it's better than being left in the lurch when you really need your backups. You can select files or folders for verification in the same ways as when you created the backup, by highlighting them or checking checkboxes. The only difference is that you select files from the tape drive node of the tree view rather than the local files node. After you have selected files to verify, choose Verify from the File menu. A dialog box containing verification options comes up, and after you have made any needed changes to them, the verification process begins. Just like when creating backups, KDat shows the progress of the verification and prompts you if you need to change tapes.

Restoring files and folders

Use the catalog that KDat created as part of the backup process to determine which tape contains the files you want to restore. The process of selecting files to restore is similar to selecting them for verification or backup creation. Highlight or check files and folders to restore from the tape drive node of the tree view. After you have selected the files to restore, choose Restore from the File menu. A dialog box containing recovery options comes up; you can make any changes you need here. One option in particular you might want to change is the folder into which files should be restored. The restoration process then begins, and again, KDat shows its progress and prompts you if you need to change tapes.

Creating a backup profile

KDat can help you manage different backup tasks by creating a profile for each one, such as your weekly full backup, daily incremental backup, and so on. Start by highlighting or checking files and folders from the local files node of the tree view. Choose Create Backup Profile from the File menu. You can set several options in the dialog box that appears.

- **Archive Name:** KDat doesn't use this internally, but a name makes it easier for humans to keep track of things.

- **Working Folder:** This is the folder in which backed-up files will be restored.

- **Stay on one filesystem:** If checked, the backup process will not follow symlinks (symbolic links to files) into other file systems.

- **GNU listed incremental:** If you've already done a full backup, you can save time and tape space by making subsequent backups increments of the full one. When this option is selected, a snapshot of the full backup is taken and updated with each incremental backup. Only the files that have changed since the last incremental backup are archived.

- **Snapshot file:** This is the name of the snapshot file.

- **Remove snapshot file before backup:** Checking this option effectively resets incremental backups by deleting the snapshot file before commencing.

Press the Apply button to save the backup profile.

Configuring user preferences

KDat can be configured by selecting Preferences from the Edit menu. You can set these options:

- **Default tape size:** This is the default size to use when a tape is to be formatted.

- **Tape block size:** This is the default size of a block on the tape drive.

- **Tape device:** This is the default tape device, for example, /dev/tape.

- **Tar command:** If for some reason you want to use a command other than the standard tar (it must, however, be tar-compatible), you can set the path to it here.

- **Load tape on mount:** When this option is set, KDat sends a load command to the drive before mounting a tape.

- **Lock tape drive on mount:** Setting this option disables a tape drive's eject function while a tape is mounted.

- **Eject tape on unmount:** Setting this option automatically ejects a tape from the drive when it is unmounted.

- **Variable block mount:** If this is set, KDat attempts to increase efficiency by changing the tape's block size to a variable amount if the drive supports it.

Burning CDs and DVDs

KDat is not suitable for backing up to CDs and DVDs, but KDE has another program for this purpose called K3b. When you run it for the first time, K3b autodetects your burner hardware. You can check that it made the right choices and correct any mistakes or tweak settings by selecting K3b setup from the Settings menu. Figure 14-2 shows the setup dialog.

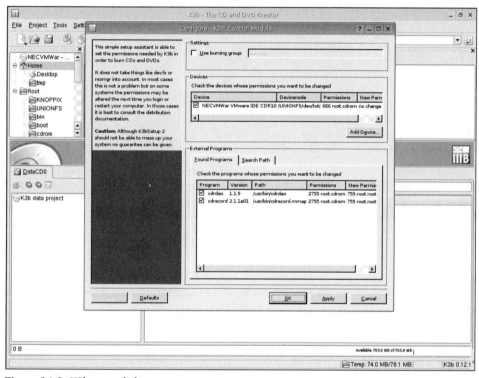

Figure 14-2: K3b setup dialog.

Now that your hardware is configured correctly, you can start using K3b. Figure 14-3 shows the main screen that comes up when you start up K3b.

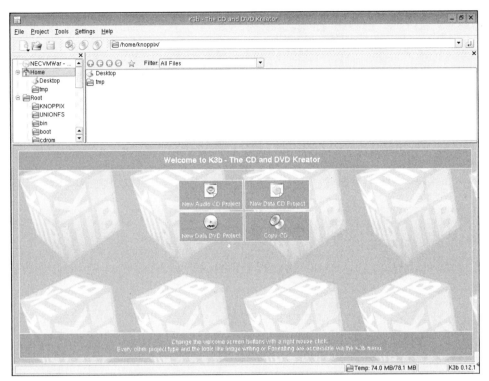

Figure 14-3: K3b startup screen.

Select New Data CD Project from the buttons in the lower half of the screen if you want to back up to a CD. Select New Data DVD Project in order to back up to a DVD. For the rest of this section, I'll assume you want to burn a CD. But the process is the same for both types of media.

When you click New Data CD Project, you see the screen shown in Figure 14-4.

K3b organizes burning sessions into projects. As the text in the window in the bottom right says, you can drag files and folders from the tree view in the upper left. The status bar keeps track of how much space is taken up by the files you've chosen.

After you have made your selections, select Burn from the Project menu, and the backup process begins. K3b displays the progress of the operation. If you want to save the project for later reuse, you can do so from the File menu.

In this section, I have only covered K3b as a backup tool. But it is a full-featured package for CD and DVD burning and capable of a lot more. From within K3b, press F1 to access the extensive online help.

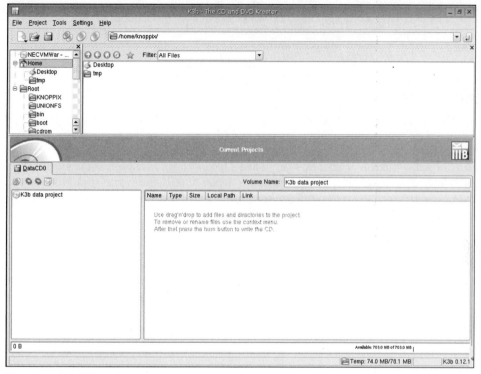

Figure 14-4: A K3b project.

Commercial Backup and Recovery Packages

The open source software mentioned in this chapter is more than good enough for average backup needs. However, if you prefer a commercial solution, a number of vendors have products for Linux. The list in Table 14-2 is not exhaustive or detailed but provides a jumping-off point for further exploration.

Table 14-2   Commercial Backup Solutions for Linux

Product	Vendor	Web Site
Arkeia Network Backup Arkeia Smart Backup	Arkeia	www.arkeia.com/
BRU	The Tolis Group	www.tolisgroup.com/
Legato Networker	EMC Legato	www.legato.com/
Storix Backup Administrator	Storix	www.storix.com/
UNiBACK	Orbit Software	www.orbitsw.com/

Solutions for Common Backup Issues

Rounding out this chapter, here are solutions to some situations you may face when backing up your system.

Undeleting files

The unthinkable happens, and an important file gets deleted. Can it be undeleted? Sadly, the answer for the most part is no. The standard Linux file system ext3 is engineered in such a way that in the event of a crash it can easily be restored to a consistent state. Normally this is a good thing — a very useful feature indeed — but the downside is that when a file is marked as deleted, it is immediately gone. Earlier file systems merely marked a deleted file as "space ready for reuse" (as did Window's FAT file system), which put the deleted file in a sort of limbo from which, if you acted quickly enough, it could be recovered. Your only hope with ext3 is to use the grep command to search through the raw data on the disk seeing if you recognize any sectors that belonged to your file and, when you do, laboriously stitch them together again. This is pretty difficult for a text file and downright impossible for binary files.

The various GUI environments available for Linux usually implement a trashcan similar to Windows or Mac OS. When you delete files using the file managers provided by those environments, the files are copied to that trashcan and truly deleted only when the trashcan is emptied. But this doesn't work if the program you used to delete the file wasn't designed for that GUI. So keep those backups current!

Backing up OpenOffice.org documents

People who use Linux at their job or school are mostly concerned with backing up the documents they create during the course of their work. If you are one of these people and you are creating documents with the popular OpenOffice.org office productivity suite, there are some options you can select to protect your work from a delete gone awry, a sudden power failure, or similar mishap. One such option is the automatic save feature. From the Tools menu, select Options→ Load/Save→ General. You will see a dialog box like the one in Figure 14-5. By selecting the Save AutoRecovery information every checkbox and selecting a time in minutes, OpenOffice.org is configured to periodically store enough information to recreate your document in the event of a crash.

Another useful option in this dialog is Always create backup copy. When this option is selected, every time you save your document, OpenOffice.org makes a copy of the old version with the same name but the extension .BAK in a directory, which by default is home directory/.openoffice.org2/ user/backup/. (You can change it by selecting OpenOffice.org→ Paths from the Options dialog.) Unfortunately, OpenOffice.org does not keep a sequence of backups; if there is already a .BAK file for the document, it gets overwritten when a new backup is made.

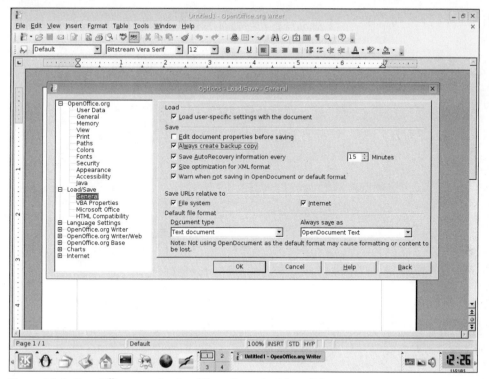

Figure 14-5: OpenOffice.org writer Load/Save-General options dialog.

Copying an entire partition

Sometimes it is useful to make an exact copy or image of an entire partition or even an entire drive. (Windows administrators often call this process *ghosting* after Norton Ghost, a utility that performs a similar task on the Windows platform.) If you need to set up many identical PCs, having an image of a standard configuration and just copying it to each new computer and then making any final adjustments is faster and easier than going through the full installation process on each one.

On Linux, you can use a utility called `partimage` to make partition images. `partimage` is included in Knoppix but may not be included in other distributions. If it is not available in yours, you can download it from `www.partimage.org/`. `partimage` requires the partition it is copying to be out of use and unmounted before it can begin, so you should boot from a Knoppix CD first and run `partimage` from there. `partimage` skips blank areas of the partition and also performs compression where possible, as shown in Figure 14-6.

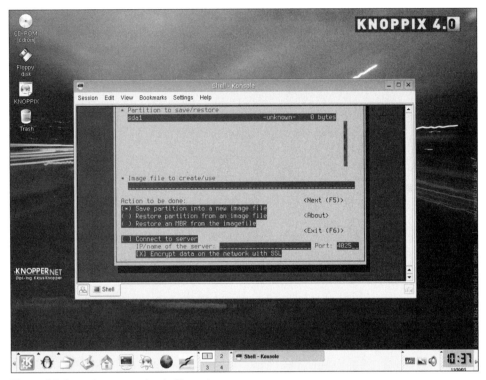

Figure 14-6: partimage running in Knoppix.

Backing up databases

Backing up databases is very important, but it presents its own problems. Most databases, for the sake of efficiency, do things like cache as much data into RAM as possible. So backing up the file system the database is on isn't enough to capture its full state. The way to work around this is to temporarily shut down the database and run a utility to dump the full contents of the database. (Most database software provides such a utility.) Then you can use your usual backup method to store the dumped data.

Summary

Backing up your Linux system is a decidedly unglamorous but vital task. To begin, you must consider what needs to be backed up and the various types of media available for backups. You can use the `tar` utility with its many options to create backup solutions. For users of tape drives, the command-line `mt` utility and the graphical KDat application are available. CD and DVD users can try the K3b application. Commercial backup software is an option, though free software is more than up to most backup tasks. Some common backup issues have nice solutions; some don't.

Chapter 15

Software Management Solutions

One area in which the Windows and Macintosh crowds have it somewhat easier than Linux users is the area of installing software. Most Windows or Macintosh software packages come in the form of binary packages that either install themselves or interface with a standard program like Install Shield.

Linux, by contrast, has two major competing package managers, both of which require some knowledge on the part of the user. The two major package management systems are RPM, which is most often found on Red Hat–derived systems, and APT, which is usually found on Debian-derived systems. In addition, it is possible to install software from source code, which is the set of raw instructions as written by the programmer.

While software management can be a bit more complicated on Linux, the major package management systems do offer some advantages over their Windows and Mac counterparts. These systems, generally, make it very simple to keep track of what's installed on your system, to install software over network connections, and to verify the integrity of software packages.

RPM

RPM originally derived its acronym from the name Redhat Package Manager, which indicates its origin as a component of Red Hat Linux. As Red Hat became increasingly popular, RPM was adopted by other systems as well, and eventually development of RPM became somewhat independent of Red Hat. These days, RPM officially stands for RPM Package Manager. Although a good deal of the development of RPM is still done by Red Hat, RPM is free software and can be used on any system.

RPM package names usually follow a strict naming convention. Generally, you'll see something like this:

```
cdrecord-2.01.1-5.i386.rpm
```

There are five parts to this package identification scheme. First is the package name, in this case, cdrecord. This is usually, but not always, the name of the program as well as the name of the package. Sometimes the name of the package differs from the name of the program; this most often happens when the package includes more than one actual program. For example, on Red Hat–based systems, there is usually a package called `binutils` that includes a number of small programs used for working with binary files. Since the programs are small, they are grouped together in one package.

The second part of the package name is the version number. In this example, the version number is `2.01.1`. Version-numbering conventions are by no means universal, and a software developer can choose any version-numbering scheme he or she wants. The only constant is that a higher number indicates a later version of the program.

Third is the build number, in this case, `5`. The build number indicates the number of times that the package has been built from the source code. In most cases, the build number is not important, but it's included in the package name because if there was a problem with a certain build, the packager may release a new one.

Fourth is an identifier for the CPU architecture, in this case `i386`. This indicates that the binary is built to run on an Intel 386 or compatible system. Now, you may be thinking that it's been a long time since anybody ran a 386 for any serious purpose, but the Intel X86 series is backward-compatible. That means that a binary built to run on a 386 also runs on a 486, Pentium, P2, P3, and so on. Also, these binaries will run on the AMD processors, which are Intel-compatible. The only caveat about architecture designations is that you should be certain that the architecture of your system is the same as or higher than the architecture designation of the package. For example, a package labeled with the architecture designation i586 will run on a Pentium or later CPU, but it will not run on a 386 or 486 machine.

Finally, you have the package suffix, rpm. This designates that the file is, in fact, an RPM package. The RPM program will not work on a file that does not have this suffix.

Acquiring the right software packages

In theory, acquiring software packages couldn't be easier: simply find a download site and download the package. In practice, it can be a little more complicated. Some software packages are built with a specific distribution, and possibly a specific version of that distribution in mind. In such cases, you'll need to make very certain that you have the correct package for your distribution. If you don't, you may have problems running, or even installing, packages.

How is this possible? There are a couple of reasons a package might not work on a given distribution. First, an RPM package usually comes not only with the program in question but also with a set of files that support that program. Often configuration files and documentation are included along with the program binary. If your distribution expects these files to go in a certain location, and the package wants to put them somewhere else, you may have trouble. Second, you may have an issue of *dependency*. Some programs rely on your having other programs or files in place for their proper functioning. These dependencies are listed in the RPM package, and when you attempt to install a package, the RPM program checks to see if all of the packages on the dependency list are installed. If one or more of these is missing, you get an error message, and the package won't be installed. (If your distribution has the YUM utility, you can avoid this problem. See the section on YUM later in this chapter.)

So how do you deal with this? The best thing to do is to find a download site that is specific to the distribution and version that you're using. For example, if you're using Fedora Core 3, you can go to `fedora.redhat.com`, look in the download section for a mirror site that carries the list of packages for Fedora Core 3, and download the package you need from there. In a pinch, you might be able to use a package from the Fedora Core 4 (FC4) set, but there's a good chance that you're going to run into a dependency issue, as the packages for FC4 may be expecting more-recent versions of supporting software. Generally, look first to the official Web site for your distribution. You can usually find what you're looking for there.

Installing and upgrading with RPM

Imagine that you've downloaded a package named `foobar-1.0-1.i386.rpm` and you're now ready to install it. In this example, `foobar` is the name of the package, `1.0-1` are version numbers, and `i386` is the architecture (in this case Intel 386, meaning PC-type processors). You can install an RPM package from any directory, but it's best to keep the packages you've downloaded in a central location. You can use an already existing directory, or you can create one just for this purpose. To install this file to a directory called `/RPM`, for example, give the `su` command to become root, and then give the following command:

```
rpm -i /RPM/foobar-1.0-1.i386.rpm
```

Note

The `/RPM` directory needs to be writable by nonroot users if you want to be able to download packages without assuming superuser powers. From a security standpoint, it's probably best not to download things as root, so make sure that you have regular user access to whatever directory you're using to download your packages into.

The `-i` option stands for *install*. If your shell prompt returns without giving you any error messages, the package was installed successfully.

A somewhat more informative response is generated by using this format:

```
rpm -ivh foobar.1.0-1.i386.rpm
```

The `-v` option is used to specify that you want *verbose* output. This is not much more than a message telling you what RPM is doing. The `-h` option tells RPM to print a line of hash mark characters (#) as the installation is progressing, similar to the progress bar you often get in graphical applications. Neither of these options is critical, but they do provide feedback to make for less suspense. Using this form of the command, you should see output that looks something like this:

```
Preparing...      ########################################### [100%]
   1:foobar        ########################################### [100%]
```

To uninstall the package, use this command:

```
rpm -e foobar
```

The -e option here stands for *erase*. The developers chose to use "erase" rather than "uninstall" to avoid confusion with the *upgrade* (-U) option. Note that in this case, you need specify only the name of the package, not the file name of the original package file you used when you installed the package. Once installed, the package's name is entered into RPM's database, and RPM keeps track of the version number and other details.

If you attempt to install a package that has already been installed on your system, your attempt fails, and generates the error message

```
Package foobar is already installed.
```

This is true even if you are trying to install a newer version of the package, so to override this, you need to use the upgrade option, -U. You can use the upgrade option with the additional options that you used with the -i option, like so:

```
rpm -Uvh foobar
```

You can do this even if a previous version of the package is not installed, in which case the -U option ends up functioning in exactly the same way as the -i option. For this reason, some people will simple use the -U option all the time, regardless of whether the package was previously installed.

Caution

Important: Don't use the -U option to install a new kernel. Always leave yourself a way to back up to an older kernel. Always install kernel packages using the -i command.

Note

The name of an RPM file need not be local. RPM can install a package file over a network—even the Internet. To use this functionality, you can you specify the RPM file as a URL. So, for example, suppose you have a download site with the URL http://www.rpms4u.com, and you want to install a file called foo.rpm that resides in the directory /newrpms. You can install this file with the following command:

```
rpm -ivh http://www.rmps4u.com/newrpms/foo.rpm
```

Now, suppose you've got foobar version 1.0 installed, and you want to upgrade to version 1.1 (which you've already downloaded). You can do it with this command:

```
rpm -U foobar-1.1-1.i386.rpm
```

In this case, the new package replaces the old one. There is no need to uninstall the old package.

Verifying a package with RPM

If you are concerned about the authenticity of a package, that is, if you want to make sure that the package you're getting is the exact one that was issued by the packager, RPM gives you a way to verify the integrity of what you download. Why should you be concerned about this? It is possible that malicious code can be inserted into a program, which could then be packaged and sent on to users. This could, for example, provide a back door for hackers to gain entry into your system or compromise your security in other ways.

How much of a threat this is depends on how sensitive your system is and on what kind of software you're installing. For example, if you're installing a word processing program on a single machine that's behind a firewall, it's probably not too much of a threat. If you're installing a proxy server on a machine that *is* the firewall, it's probably critical.

In any case, verifying software is easy, so there's really no reason not to do it.

The first thing you need to do is to import the public key of the packager. Of course, this is only possible if the packager has and provides a public key and uses it to sign packages. This is always the case with Red Hat packages. Red Hat provides its public key with its installation, and it is located at /usr/share/rhn/RPM-GPG-KEY. In the case of other distributions, you may need to download the key from a Web site or FTP server. So that you can recognize a public key when you see one, here's what Red Hat's looks like:

```
The following public key can be used to verify RPM packages built and
signed by Red Hat Software using `rpm -K' using the GNU GPG package.
Questions about this key should be sent to security@redhat.com.

-----BEGIN PGP PUBLIC KEY BLOCK-----
Version: GnuPG v1.0.0 (GNU/Linux)
Comment: For info see http://www.gnupg.org

mQGiBDfqVDgRBADBKr3B16PO8BQOH8sJoD6p9U7Yy17pjtZqioviPwXP+DCWd4u8
HQzcxAZ57m8ssA1LK1Fx93coJhDzM13O+p5BG9mYSWShLabR3N1KXdXQYYcowTOM
GxdwYRGr1Spw8QydLhjVfU1VS14xt6bupPbWJbyjkg5Z3P7B1UOUJmrx3wCgobNV
EDGaWYJcch5z5B1of/41G8kEAKii6q7Gu/vhXXnLS6m15oNnPVybyngiw/23dKjS
ZVG7rKANEK2mxg1VB+vc/uUc4k49UxJJfCZg1gu1sPFV3GSa+Y/7jsiLktQvCiLP
1ncQt1dV+ENmHR5BdIDPWDzKBVbgWnSDnqQ6KrZ7T6A1Z74VMpjGxxkWU6vV2xsW
XCLPA/9P/vtImA8CZN3jxGgtK5GGtDNJ/cMHhuv5tnfwFg4b/VGo2Jr8mhLUqoIb
E6zeGAmZbUpdckDco8D5fiFmqTf5+++pCEpJLJkkze1/32N2w4qzPrcRMCiBURES
PjCLd4Y5rPoU8E4kOHc/4BuHN9O3tiCsCP1oCrWsQZ7UdxfQ5LQiUmVkIEhhdCwg
SW5jIDxzZWN1cm1OeUByZWRoYXQuY29tPohVBBMRAgAVBQI361Q4AwsKAwMVAwID
FgIBAheAAAoJECGRgM3bQqYOsBQAnRVtg7B25Hm11PHcpa8FpeddKiq2AJ9a08sB
XmLDmPOEFI75mpTrKYHF6rkCDQQ361RyEAgAokgI2xJ+3bZsk8jRA8ORIX8DHO5U
1MH27qFYzLbT6npXwXYIOtVnOK2/iMDj+oEB1Aa2au4OnddYaLWp06v3d+XyS0t+
5ab2ZfIQzdh7wCwxqRkzR+/H5TLYbMG+hvtTdy1fqIXOWEfoOXMtWEGSVwyUsnM3
Jy3LOi48rQQSCKtCAUdV2OFoIGWhwnb/gHU1BnmES6UdQujFBE6EANqPhpOcoYoI
hHJ2oIO8ujQItvvNaU88j/s/izQv5e7MXOgVSjKe/WX3s2JtB/tW7utpy12wh1J+
JsFdbLV/t8CozUTpJgx5mVA3RK1xjTA+On+1IEUWioB+iVfT7Ov/0kcAzwADBQf9
```

```
E4SKCWRand8KOXloMYgmipxMhJNnWDMLkokvbMNTUoNpSfRoQJ9EheXDxwMpTPwK
ti/PYrrL2J11P2edOx7zm8v3gLrYOcueliSba+8glY+p31ZPOr5ogaJw7ZARgoS8
BwjyRymXQp+8DeteOTELKOL2/itDOPGHWO7SsVWOR6cmX4V1RRcWB5KejaNvdrE5
4XFtOdO4NMgWI63uqZc4zkRa+kwEZtmbz3tHSdRCCE+Y7YVP6IUf/w6YPQFQriWY
FiA6fD1OeB+B1IUqIw8OVgjsBKmCwvKkn4jg8kibXgj4/TzQSx77uYokw1EqQ2wk
OZoaEtcubsNMquuLCMWijYhGBBgRAgAGBQI361RyAAoJECGRgM3bQqYOhyYAnj7h
VDY/FJAGqmtZpwVp9IlitW5tAJ4xQApr/jNFZCTksnI+4O1765F7tA==
=3AHZ
-----END PGP PUBLIC KEY BLOCK-----
```

To import the key so that it can be used by RPM, give this command:

```
rpm --import /usr/share/rhn/RPM-GPG-KEY
```

If you are not using Red Hat's key, you can replace `/usr/share/rhn/RPM-GPG-KEY` with the file name of the key you downloaded. After you've imported the key, you can use it to check the signature on the package. Give this command:

```
rpm -K rpm-file
```

You'll need to replace `rpm-file` with the actual file name of the package you want to verify. If the package is authentic, you should see the message: `md5 gpg OK`. If you get an error message, you might want to make sure that the site you've downloaded your package from is actually the site you thought it was. You may even want to e-mail the site's administrator to make sure that he or she knows that the packages on that site are failing the integrity tests. Note that Red Hat's key, for example, works only on software that was packaged by Red Hat. If your packages come from a third party, you will need to use its key instead.

Note

It's worth double-checking the nature of the site to make sure it's the site you thought it was. For example, Red Hat's key is not going to work on a package that was not created by Red Hat, so if you thought that the site you were downloading from was an official Red Hat download or mirror site and it wasn't, you might be getting errors on otherwise good packages.

Querying a package with RPM

One of the better features of RPM is that it gives you the ability to query your system about the packages that are installed on it. Thus, if you have any questions about what's installed on your system, or you need information about the details of a specific package, you can run a query and find that information. You can find a complete listing of query options by reading the RPM manual page (give the command `man rpm`), but the following example shows you a couple of the more commonly used query options to give you a feel for what kind of queries are possible.

The most common query is this format:

```
rpm -qiv package name
```

In this case, the -q option indicates that you're running a query. The -i option specifies that you want the packages information, and the -v option indicates that you want verbose output. Don't be confused by the fact that you have an -i option here. Because the first option in the set is -q, the -i option is taken from the set of query options, not the set of installation options. This prints a good deal of information about the named package, including the name, version and description. For example, the command

```
rpm -qiv cdrecord
```

produces this output:

```
Name        : cdrecord                Relocations: (not relocatable)
Version     : 2.01.1                   Vendor: Red Hat, Inc.
Release     : 5                        Build Date: Mon 18 Oct 2004 09:56:58
AM EDT
       Install Date: Mon 09 May 2005 12:21:05 PM EDT      Build Host:
                                                tweety.build.redhat.com
Group       : Applications/Archiving   Source RPM: cdrtools-2.01.1-
                                                5.src.rpm
Size        : 1292577                     License: GPL
Signature   : DSA/SHA1, Wed 20 Oct 2004 02:35:17 PM EDT, Key ID b44269d04f2a6fd2
Packager    : Red Hat, Inc. <http://bugzilla.redhat.com/bugzilla>
    URL         :http://www.fokus.gmd.de/research/cc/glone/
                employees/joerg.schilling/private/cdrecord.html
Summary     : A command line CD recording program.
Description :
  Cdrecord is an application for recording audio and data CDs. Cdrecord
  works with many different brands of CD recorders, fully supports
  multi-sessions, and provides human-readable error messages.
```

Note

You can run this command either on an installed package or on an uninstalled package file. If you are doing the former, you need specify only the name of the package. If the latter, you'll need to specify the package's full file name.

If you are interested in finding out what files a particular package installs, you can use the command

```
rpm -qlp file name
```

For example, the command

```
rpm -qlp samba-client-3.0.14a-1.i386.rpm
```

would produce this output:

```
/sbin/mount.smb
/sbin/mount.smbfs
/usr/bin/findsmb
/usr/bin/net
/usr/bin/nmblookup
/usr/bin/rpcclient
/usr/bin/smbcacls
/usr/bin/smbclient
/usr/bin/smbmnt
/usr/bin/smbmount
/usr/bin/smbprint
/usr/bin/smbspool
/usr/bin/smbtar
/usr/bin/smbtree
/usr/bin/smbumount
/usr/bin/tdbdump
/usr/lib/samba/lowcase.dat
/usr/lib/samba/upcase.dat
/usr/lib/samba/valid.dat
/usr/share/man/man1/findsmb.1.gz
/usr/share/man/man1/nmblookup.1.gz
/usr/share/man/man1/rpcclient.1.gz
/usr/share/man/man1/smbcacls.1.gz
/usr/share/man/man1/smbclient.1.gz
/usr/share/man/man1/smbtar.1.gz
/usr/share/man/man1/smbtree.1.gz
/usr/share/man/man8/net.8.gz
/usr/share/man/man8/smbmnt.8.gz
/usr/share/man/man8/smbmount.8.gz
/usr/share/man/man8/smbspool.8.gz
/usr/share/man/man8/smbumount.8.gz
/usr/share/man/man8/tdbdump.8.gz
```

This command can be run on package files only, not on the names of installed packages. If you want to run this command on installed packages, drop the -p from the list of command options. There are many more query options, but these should suffice to give you an idea of the kinds of things that can be done with RPM's query functions. (Remember that for installed packages, you use the name of the package only, so the correct syntax would be rpm ql samba-client.)

Note

The files that get installed when you install an RPM package may not be immediately locatable using the `locate` command. This is because `locate` uses a database that is updated at regular intervals but which is not updated when you install packages. If you need to locate a particular file that was installed by the package, you can either use the package query shown in the preceding example, or you can update the database manually by giving the command `updatedb`. This command may take anywhere from a few seconds to a few minutes to run depending on the speed of your system. This command must be run as root.

Using YUM

YUM is a program that provides a very convenient front end to RPM that checks your database of installed packages against a list of available updates, download updates, resolve dependencies, and install packages. YUM is very similar to Debian's APT utility (discussed later in this chapter) and makes maintaining the software packages on your system a lot easier. YUM is installed by default on Fedora Core.

CONFIGURING YUM

If you're using Fedora Core, YUM comes preconfigured to use the official Fedora repositories. If you list the contents of the directory `/etc/yum.repos.d`, you will see the following files:

```
fedora-devel.repo
fedora-extras-devel.repo
fedora-extras.repo
fedora.repo
fedora-updates.repo
fedora-updates-testing.repo
```

Each of these files contains information about a particular repository site. So if you're a Fedora user, you don't need to do any configuration to use YUM.

If you're not a Fedora user, or if you want to customize your YUM configuration, you should start with the `/etc/yum.conf` file. The default `/etc/yum.conf` file on Fedora Core 4 looks like this:

```
[main]
cachedir=/var/cache/yum
debuglevel=2
logfile=/var/log/yum.log
pkgpolicy=newest
distroverpkg=redhat-release
tolerant=1
exactarch=1
retries=20
```

```
obsoletes=1
gpgcheck=1

# PUT YOUR REPOS HERE OR IN separate files named file.repo
# in /etc/yum.repos.d
```

In all likelihood, you won't need to change anything, but look at a few of the variables, just in case.

- `cachedir`: This is the directory where YUM keeps its database files, as well as package files that it downloads.

- `retries`: This variable controls the number of times that YUM attempts to connect to a given repository before giving up.

- `gpgcheck`: This variable controls whether YUM verifies the GPG signature on a package. A value of 0 translates to "don't verify," whereas a value of 1 translates to "do verify."

If you want to set up extra repositories in addition to the ones already listed in the /etc/yum.repos.d directory, you must create a new file for each repository. Here's the contents of a typical file in that directory:

```
[base]
name=Fedora Core $releasever - $basearch - Base
#baseurl=http://download.fedora.redhat.com/pub/fedora/linux/core/
  $releasever/$basearch/os/
mirrorlist=http://fedora.redhat.com/download/mirrors/fedora-core-$releasever
enabled=1
gpgcheck=1
gpgkey=file:///etc/pki/rpm-gpg/RPM-GPG-KEY-fedora
```

There are a couple of variables whose values are assumed here. The value of the `$releaserver` variable defaults to the version of your operating system's release. (This makes sure that you search for the appropriate packages for your distribution's version.) `$basesearch` refers to your computer's architecture (most likely i386 for PCs). From those variables, you can see how values are given to the parameters in the file. Here's a breakdown of the file, line-by-line.

```
[base]
```

This line designates the title of the file's block. In this case, it refers to the base files for Fedora Core. It could also refer to updates or something similar.

```
name=Fedora Core $releasever - $basearch - Base
```

This line designates the name of the repository. In this case, the name would be `Fedora Core 4 - i386 - Base`.

```
#baseurl=http://download.fedora.redhat.com/pub/fedora/linux/core/
        $releasever/$basearch/os/
```

This line provides the base URL for the repository. In this case, that URL is `http://download.fedora.redhat.com/pub/fedora/linux/core/4/i386/os/`. In this case, the base URL is commented out. This means that the `download.fedora.redhat.com` site will not be used. Rather, a site from the mirror list (described following) will be used instead. This keeps Red Hat's servers from being hammered constantly by thousands of YUM users.

```
mirrorlist=http://fedora.redhat.com/download/mirrors/fedora-core-
        $releasever
```

This line provides a URL to a list of mirror sites that YUM uses should the main site not be available.

```
enabled=1
```

This line allows you to designate whether or not a particular repository will be used. If the value is 1 it is used; if the value is 0 it is not used. This allows you to, in effect, turn off a given repository without deleting it.

```
gpgcheck=1
```

As in the main configuration file, this option tells you that you should check the packages' GPG signatures.

```
gpgkey=file:///etc/pki/rpm-gpg/RPM-GPG-KEY-fedora
```

This line gives the location of the file containing the GPG key that should be used to check the packages' signatures.

RUNNING YUM

The most basic operation with YUM is installing software. To install a software package, first, assume superuser powers, and then give the command

```
yum install package
```

where `package` is the name of the package you want to install. For example, if you want to install the `cdrecord` package, the command would be

```
yum install cdrecord
```

You don't need to mess around with the full file names as with RPM since the YUM configuration files take care of that for you. When you give this command, YUM connects to the appropriate repository and downloads certain information about the `cdrecord` package. If that information includes dependencies, YUM asks you whether to download and install the prerequisite packages as well.

If you already have a package installed, and you want to upgrade to a newer version of the same package, give the command

```
yum update package
```

This upgrades the package. It also checks the dependencies and upgrades the prerequisite packages if they are needed. If you're not sure if there's a newer version of a package, you can give the command

```
yum check-update package
```

This checks whether an upgrade is available.

Note

If you leave the package name off of the yum check-update command, YUM checks for updates for all of your installed packages. If you leave the package name off of the yum update command, it upgrades every package on your system for which newer versions are available.

To uninstall a package, use the command

```
yum erase package
```

or

```
yum remove package
```

There are other options for YUM, but these will get you started and are likely to be the ones you'll use most often. If you want to learn more, read the YUM manual page by giving the command man yum or see the YUM homepage at http://linux.duke.edu/projects/yum/.

APT

APT, the Advanced Packaging Tool, is the package management system that is most often found on Debian-derived systems. Like YUM, APT resolves dependencies automatically. That is, if you attempt to install a package whose functioning is dependent on another package that is not installed, APT installs that package automatically.

Like RPM, APT uses a special package format. In this case, the packages are known as *deb files* because they end with the suffix deb. As you might expect, this indicates that they are built for Debian systems, and even though not all of the systems that use the APT system are Debian systems, the suffix applies to any system using APT.

There are several ways that you can use APT. The most common is to use APT to install packages over the Internet. One function included with APT is the `apt-get` utility, which finds packages, resolves their dependencies, and installs them. You can also use APT on local files and CD-ROMs, however, with equally good results.

Setting up for APT

Before you start using APT, you might want to take a few minutes and make sure it's set up the way you want it. With some distributions, the default setup may be fine for your use; with others, you may want to do some tweaking. The main area of customization is the `/etc/apt/sources.list` file. As its name suggests, this file is a list of sources — specifically it refers to places, both on the Internet, and on your local system, where `.deb` files can be found. When you run APT, it looks in this file for information about where to look for packages.

A typical `/etc/apt/sources.list` file might look like this:

```
# See sources.list(5) for more information, especially
# Remember that you can only use http, ftp or file URIs
# CDROMs are managed through the apt-cdrom tool.
deb http://http.us.debian.org/debian stable main contrib non-free
deb http://non-us.debian.org/debian-non-US stable/non-US main contrib non-free
deb http://security.debian.org stable/updates main contrib non-free

# Uncomment if you want the apt-get source function to work
#deb-src http://http.us.debian.org/debian stable main contrib non-free
#deb-src http://non-us.debian.org/debian-non-US stable/non-US main contrib non-
#free
```

Here you see that the available sources are listed in the form of URLs. As the comments indicate, you can use URLs of the type `http://`, `ftp://`, or `file://`. If you are planning to use packages on a CD-ROM, you need to use a different feature of APT, discussed later in this chapter.

In the preceding example, there are three Debian mirrors listed. Look closely at this line:

```
deb http://http.us.debian.org/debian stable main contrib non-free
```

This line is the first place that APT looks for package files. The first entry in the line, `deb`, tells APT that it is looking for `.deb` files. The second part, `http://http.us.debian.org/debian`, is the base URL for the site. The remaining entries, `stable main contrib non-free`, are subdirectories that APT searches for a particular package. If APT cannot find the package in any of these subdirectories, it moves on to the next entry in the file.

You can add lines in the preceding format to the file to add any mirror or download site that you want. If you know of a particular site that tends to be very fast and reliable, you might want to put it first, or at least very high up in the list, whereas if you have a site that tends to be slow, you might want to put it low on the list.

You might prefer to download the packages manually and install them directly from your hard drive. To do this, create a directory that you want to keep the files in. For this example, we'll call it `/debs`. Then add this line to your `/etc/apt/sources.list` file:

```
deb file:/debs
```

You'd probably want to place this line first in the file so that APT looks in the local directory, going to the Internet only if necessary.

Installing packages with APT

Once you've got the `/etc/apt/sources.list` file set up, you're ready to install packages. Installing packages, either from files or from the Internet, is done with the `apt-get` command. For example, to install the package `cdrecord`, simply give this command:

```
apt-get install cdrecord
```

APT downloads (if necessary), resolves dependencies (again, if necessary), and installs the package. If the package has dependencies, those are downloaded and installed as well. (If this is the case, you get a message informing you of the other packages that need to be installed and asking if you want to continue. Most of the time there shouldn't be a problem with saying "yes," but if you don't want to install a particular package, you have the option to abort the procedure.)

Updating with APT

Like RPM, APT maintains a database of packages that are installed on your system. You can check this database against the list of available packages by running the command

```
apt-get update
```

When you give this command, APT checks your list of installed packages against the lists maintained at the sites in your `/etc/apt/sources.list` file. If there are new packages available, you are informed and given the opportunity to update your system.

Note

I'm distinguishing here between *updating*, by which I mean checking your system against a list to see if there are newer versions of some programs available, and *upgrading*, by which I mean installing a newer version of a specific package (or your entire system if that's applicable).

Upgrading packages with APT

APT makes it very easy to upgrade the software on your system. Simply give the command

```
apt-get upgrade
```

and APT returns a list of all the packages that have new versions available. You are then given the option to upgrade those packages.

APT can even be used to upgrade your entire system if a new version of your system becomes available. You can do that by giving the command

```
apt-get dist-upgrade
```

(This particular command can take a long time to finish running, and, as one might expect, downloads can take a long time if you're trying to do this very soon after a new release is announced.)

Removing packages with APT

Now that you've seen how `apt-get` handles installation and upgrading, it will probably come as no surprise that removing packages is equally simple. To remove a single package, give this command:

```
apt-get remove package
```

replacing `package` with the name of the package you want to remove.

This removes the program files, but leaves any configuration files in place. This can be useful if you need to keep them for any reason, but it can be annoying if you're trying to get rid of everything related to a particular package. If you want to remove everything related to a given package, you can give the command in this form (note the double dash before `purge`):

```
apt-get --purge remove <package>
```

Using a CD-ROM

The development of APT was originally done under the assumption that users would download files off the Internet. This was fine when systems were relatively small, but today's Linux distributions often fill multiple CDs. This can be a nightmare to install over the Internet if you've got a slow connection. Consequently, the developers have added special functions to APT to enable you to install packages from CD-ROMs. For the most part, this works in the same way as what you've already seen. The difference is that there is a particular procedure involved in adding the CD-ROM to the `/etc/apt/sources.list` file. This is done with the `apt-cdrom add` command.

Using this command assumes that your CD-ROM drive is properly configured and listed in the `/etc/fstab` file. If you can see the contents of the CD-ROM that you put in the drive, this is probably the case. If not, refer to Chapter 16 for instructions on how to make sure your drive is configured properly.

Once your drive is properly configured, you can give the command

```
apt-cdrom add
```

and the location of your CD-ROM drive is added to the `/etc/apt/sources.list` file. This enables APT to search any CD that's inserted in your CD-ROM drive for packages. If it doesn't find the package it's looking for there, it moves on to other sources listed in the `/etc/apt/sources.list` file.

Querying packages with APT

Although not as extensive as related RPM tools, APT does provide a few utilities for getting information about packages on your system. Suppose you want some basic information about the lilo package. You would give this command:

```
apt-cache show lilo
```

which would produce this output:

```
Package: lilo
Priority: important
Section: base
Installed-Size: 271
Maintainer: Russell Coker <russell@coker.com.au>
Architecture: i386
Version: 1:21.7-3
Depends: libc6 (>= 2.2.1-2), debconf (>=0.2.26), logrotate
Suggests: lilo-doc
Conflicts: manpages (<<1.29-3)
Filename: pool/main/l/lilo/lilo_21.7-3_i386.deb
Size: 143052
MD5sum: 63fe29b5317fe34ed8ec3ae955f8270e
Description: LInux LOader - The Classic OS loader can load Linux and others
This Package contains lilo (the installer) and boot-record-images to
install Linux, OS/2, DOS and generic Boot Sectors of other OSes.
.
You can use Lilo to manage your Master Boot Record (with a simple text screen)
or call Lilo from other Boot-Loaders to jump-start the Linux kernel.


Package: lilo
Status: install ok installed
Priority: important
Section: base
Installed-Size: 190
Maintainer: Vincent Renardias <vincent@debian.org>
Version: 1:21.4.3-2
Depends: libc6 (>= 2.1.2)
Recommends: mbr
Suggests: lilo-doc
Description: LInux LOader - The Classic OS loader can load Linux and others
This Package contains lilo (the installer) and boot-record-images to
install Linux, OS/2, DOS and generic Boot Sectors of other OSes.
.
You can use Lilo to manage your Master Boot Record (with a simple text screen)
or call Lilo from other Boot-Loaders to jump-start the Linux kernel.
```

Notice that there are two lilo packages here. The first one is the package that is available at the first location in your /etc/apt/sources.list file. The second one is the package that is currently installed on your system.

To learn what packages the lilo package depends on, you can use the command:

```
apt-cache depends lilo
```

To find out which package a particular file belongs to, you can use this command:

```
apt-file search filename
```

where filename is the name of the file whose owning package you want to find.

To find out the names of all the files that a particular package contains, use the command:

```
apt-file list package
```

where package is the name of the package about which you want the file list.

Note

You can find an excellent description of APT's capabilities at www.debian.org/doc/manuals/apt-howto/. You can also find complete documentation by giving the command man apt.

Summary

Both RPM and APT provide package management systems that allow the administrator to install, remove, upgrade, and query software packages. Both of these systems are roughly equivalent in terms of functionality. Which system you use is largely a question of the lineage of your system. If your system is Red Hat derived, you'll probably use RPM. If it's Debian derived, you'll probably use APT.

## Chapter 16

Installing and Removing Hardware

It would be great if every computer system came with all of the peripherals and add-in cards that you'd ever need. Unfortunately, the reality of modern computing is that as soon as you buy a computer system, someone will announce some new printer, scanner, USB device, or internal card that you simply must have. Assuming that your computer system is sexy enough to last you for a few years, at some point you'll also want to upgrade something that's already inside it. Whether this means getting a fancier video card or faster Ethernet card, or adding support for FireWire (IEEE 1394) or Bluetooth so that you can connect to your video camera or phone, you're going to have to change things.

The ability to attach new hardware and have it "just work" with a personal or business computer system is one of the best features of modern versions of operating systems such as Microsoft Windows and Mac OS X. This is typically referred to as "plug and play" support, which some less optimistic users often refer to as "plug and pray" — you attach a new device or add a new card, turn on your machine, and pray that Windows or OS X will locate and correctly identify the newly connected hardware. Long thought to be the best feature of Microsoft Windows and generations of Apple's Macintosh operating system, this same capability is provided by today's Linux distributions.

The remainder of this chapter explores how Linux distributions identify, register, and interact with new hardware. I show you how to work with cases (such as disk drives) where simply recognizing new hardware isn't enough, and then explore some of the most popular built-in software that Linux provides to help you get information about the hardware in your system, should you ever need to do so manually.

How Linux Handles Hardware

All internal and external peripherals use what are known as *device drivers* to enable the Linux kernel to locate, identify, and exchange information with them. Device drivers are small pieces of system software that are the operating system's conceptual equivalent of the print drivers that you're probably used to when configuring your system to print to a new printer.

Linux device drivers can either be compiled into the Linux kernel or loaded whenever the kernel needs them. Modules that are loaded on demand are known as *loadable kernel modules* and are stored in a subdirectory of the /lib/modules directory on your Linux system. Because Linux makes it easy for you to upgrade the Linux kernel whenever new capabilities are available, the loadable kernel modules for a specific version of the Linux kernel are stored in a subdirectory whose name matches the release of the kernel that they're associated with. You can identify the release of the Linux kernel that is running on your system by executing the uname -r command, as in the following example:

```
$ uname -r
2.6.11.4-21.9-default
$ ls /lib/modules
2.6.11.4-20a-default    2.6.11.4-21.9-um            2.6.8-24.10-default
2.6.8-24.14-default     scripts
2.6.11.4-21.8-default   2.6.11.4-override-default  2.6.8-24.11-default    2.6.8-
24.16-default    2.6.8-24-default
2.6.11.4-21.9-default   2.6.11.4-override-um       2.6.8-24.13-default
2.6.8-24.17-default     precompiled
```

The output of the uname -r command shows the kernel on my system is based on the 2.6.11 Linux kernel, with a minor patch level of 21 and 9 subsequent patches. The -default at the end is an optional version string that anyone who compiles a kernel can add to provide additional information. On my system, this is the default kernel provided from the distribution vendor. The system on which I ran this example actually offers a number of different kernels, so its /lib/modules directory contains subdirectories of loadable kernel modules for each of the available kernels. However, there is always a subdirectory that matches the release name of the version of the Linux kernel that is currently running on your system.

The decision to compile a device driver into the kernel or build it as a loadable kernel module is largely left up to the vendor who provides the Linux distribution that you are using. Some device drivers, such as the device drivers that the kernel needs to read the type of disks that your system contains (IDE, SATA, SCSI, and so on) and the device driver for the type of file system used to organize information on the partitions on your disks, must be built into the kernel. Device drivers for other types of devices, such as Ethernet cards, USB devices, FireWire devices, and so on, are often provided as loadable kernel modules because this keeps the kernel as small as possible, while still providing the flexibility to enable your Linux system to access and use those devices.

The ability of Linux systems to use device drivers that are provided as loadable kernel modules is analogous to the Microsoft Windows systems ability to install device drivers from CDs (or even floppies) that accompany many hardware and peripheral purchases. Loadable device drivers are not just a good idea in terms of effectively using system resources by keeping the kernel as small as possible. Being able to load device drivers on demand is also a good idea for hardware vendors because this enables them to ship drivers for their devices that are independent of a specific Linux distribution. Many hardware manufacturers enable you to download device drivers in source or binary formats from their Web sites, which enables them to provide updates without requiring that you rebuild your system's kernel

---

Where Do Device Drivers Come From?

It's in the best interests of any hardware manufacturer to supply device (and print) drivers for all popular operating systems when they release a new card or external peripheral. It takes time and money to develop and perfect these drivers, which often means that the driver CD that falls out of the box that your new printer came in provides drivers only for Microsoft Windows and Apple's Mac OS X. Since Linux is still viewed as an up-and-coming operating system, few hardware vendors are savvy enough to provide out-of-the-box drivers for Linux. A problem? Not really? It's simply time to toot the horn of open source again.

Not everyone wants to develop device drivers but happily, many motivated Linux fans do. Both Linux users who have the same hardware that you do and the Linux distribution vendors who want Linux to become increasingly popular are highly motivated to provide support for almost any modern card or peripheral. I've been using Linux systems for over 10 years, and the last few years have been a true joy in terms of instant, built-in support for almost every piece of new hardware that I've added to my systems. I hope that your experience will be the same.

Loading device drivers at boot time

When Linux systems boot, they probe the hardware located in your system and then run a command known as modprobe (*probe for modules*) that performs various functions including loading the device drivers associated with your system's hardware and peripherals. On modern Linux systems (those running a version of the 2.6 Linux kernel), the set of actions to perform and device drivers to load are listed in the file /etc/modprobe.conf. On older Linux systems, this information was stored in a file called /etc/modules.conf, which is usually still present on modern Linux systems in case older system applications look for it. (In the modern versions, this file is always empty.)

The /etc/modprobe.conf file is a text file that contains entries that are associated with various logical and physical system devices. Most Linux distributions automatically create an appropriate /etc/modprobe.conf file for you during the installation process, but it's still useful to understand the format of this file just in case you ever need to modify it. A small section of an example /etc/modprobe.conf is the following:

```
alias   eth0          3c501
options 3c501         io=0x280 irq=5
```

The first of these entries tells the modprobe command to associate the driver 3c501 (a driver for an older 3Com Ethernet card) with the system's primary Ethernet device, eth0. The second tells it to associate specific options with that device driver when loading it.

The /etc/modprobe.conf file contains many other types of entries, but discussing all of them is outside the scope of this book. For more information, you can examine the /etc/modprobe.conf file on your Linux system, which often contains useful comments that explain various entries. For more details, you can use the man modprobe.conf command from a terminal window to view the system's online reference information about the format of this file.

Accessing devices

Linux systems access devices through what are known as device nodes. Device nodes are special types of files that identify the device driver that should be used to access each device and provide an entry point for accessing that device. Device nodes are stored in the /dev directory on any Linux or Unix-like system. This directory can be listed using the ls command, like any other directory on a Linux system, as shown in the following example:

```
# ls -l /dev
total 161
crw-rw----  1 root video   107,   0 2005-03-19 17:01 3dfx
crw-------  1 root root     10, 157 2005-03-19 17:01 ac
crw-rw----  1 root root     56,   0 2005-03-19 17:01 adb
crw-rw----  1 root root     10,  10 2005-03-19 17:01 adbmouse
crw-------  1 wvh  audio    14,  14 2005-03-19 17:01 admmidi0
crw-------  1 wvh  audio    14,  30 2005-03-19 17:01 admmidi1
crw-------  1 wvh  audio    14,  46 2005-03-19 17:01 admmidi2
crw-------  1 wvh  audio    14,  62 2005-03-19 17:01 admmidi3
...
```

The /dev directory on most desktop Linux systems can contain hundreds of device nodes, each of which reflects a device that could possibly be attached to that system. These files are small, but having hundreds of them still accounts for some amount of disk space. Some Linux distributions, such as those used in small Linux systems designed for embedded computing and consumer electronics, create device nodes dynamically when you boot the system, but most desktop Linux distributions simply preallocate them all when you install Linux so that they're already present if you ever attach and want to use a specific type of device.

Linux device nodes follow certain naming conventions that make it easy to know how to access well-known types of hardware. For example, as shown by the following output from the Linux df (*disk free*) command, disk drives and the partitions that they contain are generally identified with names beginning with /dev/sd (SCSI drives) or /dev/hd (standard IDE hard drives):

```
# df
Filesystem      1K-blocks       Used Available Use% Mounted on
/dev/sda1        10490040    5882836   4607204  57% /
/dev/sda3          257012      42880    214132  17% /boot
/dev/sda8       160010472  154613964  5396508  97% /home
/dev/sda5         4200824     856640   3344184  21% /tmp
/dev/sda6        31462264   25145952   6316312  80% /usr
/dev/sda7        31454268   26412580   5041688  84% /usr/local
/dev/hdf1       240362656  226340964   1811892 100% /opt2
/dev/hde1       240362656  222295728   5857128  98% /mnt/music
```

As you see in the next section, Linux systems do a great job of identifying and configuring hardware both at boot time and when new devices are attached to a running system. However, understanding underlying concepts like device drivers and device nodes can still be quite handy when problems occur or you simply want to look under the hood and see exactly how things work on your computer system.

Finding new hardware dynamically with hotplugging

In addition to automatic hardware detection during installation and at boot time, modern Linux systems use a mechanism known as *hotplugging,* which enables your system to dynamically detect and automatically configure new devices as they are attached to a running system. Hotplugging is integrated into the device drivers used by Linux 2.6 and later kernels and is supported on buses such as PCI, USB, PCMCIA, FireWire (IEEE 1394), the buses used for docking laptops, and so on. A *bus* is any shared connection between the different functional units in your computer system — common examples are FireWire (IEEE 1394), PCI, SCSI, USB, and the basic bus for system input devices such as your keyboard. Whenever any hotplug event occurs on a supported bus, the hotplug system examines the event and attempts to load or configure any device drivers associated with that event.

Most modern Linux systems use a version of hotplugging to check their hardware configuration at boot time. Because this is being done at boot time, this is often referred to as *coldplug* because the machine was cold (that is, off) when the system started. In order to expedite hardware checks at boot time, modern Linux systems also maintain configuration information about the hardware that the system contains. When you first install a Linux distribution, each distribution uses its own, dedicated piece of software to probe your system's hardware and capture its current configuration. This software and its archived information are then reused by the coldplug system as part of the boot process each time you boot your Linux system.

Two of the best examples of the hardware scanning and identification software available on different Linux distributions are the software used by Novell's SUSE Linux and the system that is shared between the Fedora Core and Red Hat Enterprise Linux distributions. SUSE Linux provides an integrated suite of system administration modules with various capabilities known as YaST (Yet another System Tool), which includes a hardware detection module. Red Hat Enterprise Linux and Fedora Core use a hardware detection tool and associated library known as kudzu. These are complex and different enough that discussing them in detail is outside the scope of this book — the important thing is that each Linux distribution provides a built-in mechanism for locating and identifying the hardware that it contains and that each distribution stores and reuses this information each time you boot your Linux system to make sure that the system comes up and initializes its hardware correctly.

Basic hotplug support is included in almost all current distributions of GNU/Linux, including Red Hat, Debian, Fedora Core, Mandriva, and SUSE. Some distributions provide dialogs that notify the user when new devices are detected during boot time through coldplugging or dynamically through hotplugging and automatically offer to configure the new device. For example, Figure 16-1 shows a pop-up notice from a SUSE 10.0 system, reporting that a new hard disk was detected.

In this case, clicking Yes displays a graphical user interface for disk partitioning and formatting that is every bit as friendly and powerful as that provided by such popular operating systems as Microsoft Windows. See the SUSE example shown in Figure 16-2. Most modern Linux distributions provide graphical utilities for disk partitioning and formatting.

Figure 16-1: A new hardware message from SUSE Linux.

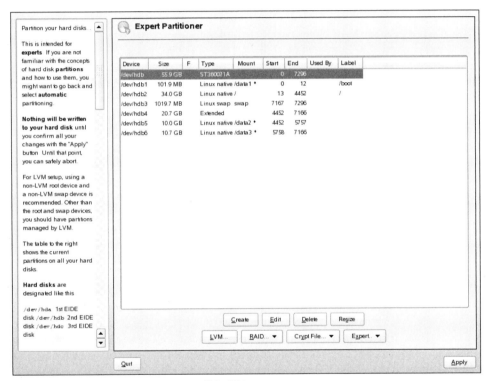

Figure 16-2: Disk partitioning on a Novell SUSE Linux system.

Getting Information About Your Hardware Manually

As mentioned earlier in this chapter, the installation utilities provided by the various Linux distributions do a good job of detecting, configuring, or helping you configure the hardware found in any system on which you are running Linux. Combined with Linux hotplug support, you rarely have to do much manual hardware configuration or identification. However, things weren't always this friendly. Therefore, over the years, Linux has accumulated a good number of utilities that probe various aspects of your system and report what they find. These utilities were originally developed to help you both identify the hardware communicating through various buses and interfaces in your system and provide status information that helps you determine whether that hardware is actually doing more than just saying "yes, I'm out here."

The next few sections highlight some of the best-known hardware-related utilities that are provided with most Linux distributions. Because most of the hardware-related Linux utilities are associated with a specific system communication bus or interface, the following sections are organized by interface type.

Locating, listing, and activating PCI devices

Most of the slots inside modern computers are PCI (Peripheral Component Interconnect) slots, but many older PCI drivers may not be fully integrated with the hotplug subsystem discussed earlier in this chapter. If you're lucky, after shutting down your system, opening it up, inserting a new PCI card, closing everything up, and rebooting, your Linux system will recognize the new card and activate the associated driver. However, if your system can't identify the card correctly or was not built with support for the associated driver, you will need to get some information about the device.

Linux provides two primary utilities for identifying the PCI devices found in your system: the lspci and scanpci utilities. These two utilities and the differences between them are discussed in the next two sections.

LISTING PCI BUS DEVICES

The lspci utility scans the PCI bus and lists all of the devices that it finds. The lspci utility does a good job of locating and identifying PCI devices in a user-friendly fashion, as you can see from the following sample output:

```
0000:00:00.0 Host bridge: VIA Technologies, Inc. VT8385 [K8T800 AGP]
    Host Bridge (rev 01)
0000:00:01.0 PCI bridge: VIA Technologies, Inc. VT8237 PCI bridge [K8T800 South]
0000:00:07.0 FireWire (IEEE 1394): VIA Technologies, Inc. IEEE 1394
    Host  Controller (rev 80)
0000:00:08.0 RAID bus controller: Promise Technology, Inc. PDC20378
    (FastTrak  378/SATA 378) (rev 02)
0000:00:09.0 Multimedia video controller: Brooktree Corporation Bt878 Video
    Capture (rev 11)
0000:00:09.1 Multimedia controller: Brooktree Corporation Bt878 Audio Capture
    (rev 11)
0000:00:0a.0 Ethernet controller: Marvell Technology Group Ltd. Gigabit Ethernet
    Controller (rev 13)
0000:00:0b.0 Unknown mass storage controller: Promise Technology, Inc. PDC20268
    (Ultra100 TX2) (rev 02)
0000:00:0f.0 RAID bus controller: VIA Technologies, Inc. VIA VT6420 SATA RAID
    Controller (rev 80)
0000:00:0f.1 IDE interface: VIA Technologies, Inc.
```

```
VT82C586A/B/VT82C686/A/B/VT823x/A/C \
     PIPC Bus Master IDE (rev 06)
0000:00:10.0 USB Controller: VIA Technologies, Inc. VT82xxxxx UHCI USB 1.1
     Controller (rev 81)
0000:00:10.1 USB Controller: VIA Technologies, Inc. VT82xxxxx UHCI USB 1.1
     Controller (rev 81)
0000:00:10.2 USB Controller: VIA Technologies, Inc. VT82xxxxx UHCI USB 1.1
     Controller (rev 81)
0000:00:10.3 USB Controller: VIA Technologies, Inc. VT82xxxxx UHCI USB 1.1
    Controller (rev 81)
0000:00:10.4 USB Controller: VIA Technologies, Inc. USB 2.0 (rev 86)
0000:00:11.0 ISA bridge: VIA Technologies, Inc. VT8237 ISA bridge [KT600/K8T800
    South]
0000:00:11.5 Multimedia audio controller: VIA Technologies, Inc.
VT8233/A/8235/8237 \
     AC97 Audio Controller (rev 60)
0000:00:18.0 Host bridge: Advanced Micro Devices [AMD] K8 [Athlon64/Opteron]
     HyperTransport Technology Configuration
0000:00:18.1 Host bridge: Advanced Micro Devices [AMD] K8 [Athlon64/Opteron]
     Address Map
0000:00:18.2 Host bridge: Advanced Micro Devices [AMD] K8 [Athlon64/Opteron]
     DRAM Controller
0000:00:18.3 Host bridge: Advanced Micro Devices [AMD] K8 [Athlon64/Opteron]
     Miscellaneous Control
0000:01:00.0 VGA compatible controller: Matrox Graphics, Inc. MGA G400 AGP (rev 05)
```

The first portion of each line provides the PCI bus identifier for each PCI device, followed by information about the type of device found, the manufacturer of that device, and the specific device that was detected. For example, in the first entry in this sample output, 0000:00:00.0 is the PCI identifier of the device, Host bridge is the type of device, VIA Technologies, Inc. is the manufacturer, and VT8385 [K8T800 AGP] Host Bridge (rev 01) is the specific device that was detected. The lspci utility gets this information by looking up the low-level information that it actually detects in a PCI database, which is contained in the file /usr/share/pci.ids on most Linux systems.

When examining the output from the lspci command, it helps to have a basic understanding of the PCI cards in your system and the PCI devices that are built into your motherboard. For example, in the previous sample output, all of the VIA Technologies PCI devices are built into the motherboard on the sample system where I ran this command, while devices such as the "Multimedia video controller: Brooktree Corporation Bt878 Video Capture" and "VGA compatible controller: Matrox Graphics, Inc. MGA G400 AGP" devices are add-in cards on my system. The first is a video capture card that I use for watching and recording television in a separate window on my monitor, while the latter is this system's video card. In each case, the information given by the lspci command identifies the manufacturer, the type of card, and even the firmware revision of the card, which is usually sufficient for identifying the driver that I need to load in order to take advantage of the capabilities of the card. Note that the lspci output for the video capture card is followed by an entry for the audio capture feature of the card, "Multimedia controller: Brooktree Corporation Bt878 Audio Capture."

If you need additional information about any PCI device in your system, the `lspci` command also provides a verbose option, `-v`, which causes the `lspci` command to display more-detailed information about each PCI device. For example, the section of the output from the `lspci -v` command for my system's video card (the last entry in the previous sample output) is the following:

```
0000:01:00.0 VGA compatible controller: Matrox Graphics, Inc. MGA G400 AGP
             (rev 05) (prog-if 00 [VGA])
        Subsystem: Matrox Graphics, Inc. Millennium G400 MAX/Dual Head 32Mb
        Flags: bus master, medium devsel, latency 64, IRQ 11
        Memory at f2000000 (32-bit, prefetchable) [size=32M]
        Memory at f6e00000 (32-bit, non-prefetchable) [size=16K]
        Memory at f6000000 (32-bit, non-prefetchable) [size=8M]
        Expansion ROM at f6d00000 [disabled] [size=64K]
        Capabilities: [dc] Power Management version 2
        Capabilities: [f0] AGP version 2.0
```

As you can see, this probably isn't all that interesting to most people, but it does provide some useful information about the AGP and power management capabilities of the card. This level of information can therefore be useful when fine-tuning your system for best performance. However, if that isn't enough information for you, you can also specify the `-vv` option (*very verbose*), which provides even more detail.

SCANNING THE PCI BUS

The `scanpci` utility is similar to the `lspci` utility in terms of its capabilities. Like the `lspci` utility, it examines the PCI bus and provides information about the cards and onboard devices that it finds. This utility does a good job of probing the PCI bus but (by default) does a somewhat poorer job of identifying the cards and bridges that it finds. Sample output from running this command on the same system where I ran the previous examples is the following:

```
pci bus 0x0000 cardnum 0x00 function 0x00: vendor 0x1106 device 0x3188
  VIA Technologies, Inc.  Device unknown
pci bus 0x0000 cardnum 0x01 function 0x00: vendor 0x1106 device 0xb188
  VIA Technologies, Inc.  Device unknown
pci bus 0x0000 cardnum 0x07 function 0x00: vendor 0x1106 device 0x3044
  VIA Technologies, Inc. IEEE 1394 Host Controller
Corporation Bt878 Video Capture
pci bus 0x0000 cardnum 0x09 function 0x01: vendor 0x109e device 0x0878
  Brooktree Corporation Bt878 Audio Capture
pci bus 0x0000 cardnum 0x0a function 0x00: vendor 0x11ab device 0x4320
  Galileo Technology Ltd.  Device unknown
pci bus 0x0000 cardnum 0x0b function 0x00: vendor 0x105a device 0x4d68
  Promise Technology, Inc. 20268
pci bus 0x0000 cardnum 0x0f function 0x00: vendor 0x1106 device 0x3149
  VIA Technologies, Inc.  Device unknown
pci bus 0x0000 cardnum 0x0f function 0x01: vendor 0x1106 device 0x0571
```

```
VIA Technologies, Inc. VT82C586A/B/VT82C686/A/B/VT8233/A/C/VT8235  \
  PIPC Bus Master IDE
pci bus 0x0000 cardnum 0x10 function 0x00: vendor 0x1106 device 0x3038
  VIA Technologies, Inc. USB
pci bus 0x0000 cardnum 0x10 function 0x01: vendor 0x1106 device 0x3038
  VIA Technologies, Inc. USB
pci bus 0x0000 cardnum 0x10 function 0x02: vendor 0x1106 device 0x3038
  VIA Technologies, Inc. USB
pci bus 0x0000 cardnum 0x10 function 0x03: vendor 0x1106 device 0x3038
  VIA Technologies, Inc. USB
pci bus 0x0000 cardnum 0x10 function 0x04: vendor 0x1106 device 0x3104
  VIA Technologies, Inc. USB 2.0
pci bus 0x0000 cardnum 0x11 function 0x00: vendor 0x1106 device 0x3227
  VIA Technologies, Inc.  Device unknown
pci bus 0x0000 cardnum 0x11 function 0x05: vendor 0x1106 device 0x3059
  VIA Technologies, Inc. VT8233/A/8235 AC97 Audio Controller
pci bus 0x0000 cardnum 0x18 function 0x00: vendor 0x1022 device 0x1100
  Advanced Micro Devices [AMD] K8 NorthBridge
pci bus 0x0000 cardnum 0x18 function 0x01: vendor 0x1022 device 0x1101
  Advanced Micro Devices [AMD] K8 NorthBridge
pci bus 0x0000 cardnum 0x18 function 0x02: vendor 0x1022 device 0x1102
  Advanced Micro Devices [AMD] K8 NorthBridge
pci bus 0x0000 cardnum 0x18 function 0x03: vendor 0x1022 device 0x1103
  Advanced Micro Devices [AMD] K8 NorthBridge
pci bus 0x0001 cardnum 0x00 function 0x00: vendor 0x102b device 0x0525
  Matrox Graphics, Inc. MGA G400 AGP
```

This information comes from running the `scanpci` command on the same system on which the `lspci` command was run and isn't quite as concise as that provided by `lspci`. On the other hand, like the `lspci` command, the `scanpci` command provides a verbose option, `-v`, which provides a great deal of detailed information that can be useful in debugging or implementing drivers. For example, the following is the verbose output for the last driver detected in the previous `scanpci` listing:

```
pci bus 0x0001 cardnum 0x00 function 0x00: vendor 0x102b device 0x0525
    Matrox Graphics, Inc. MGA G400 AGP
  CardVendor 0x102b card 0x2179 (Matrox Graphics, Inc. Millennium G400
    MAX/Dual Head 32Mb)
  STATUS    0x0290  COMMAND 0x0007
  CLASS     0x03 0x00 0x00  REVISION 0x05
  BIST      0x00  HEADER 0x00  LATENCY 0x40  CACHE 0x40
  BASE0     0xf2000008  addr 0xf2000000  MEM PREFETCHABLE
  BASE1     0xf6e00000  addr 0xf6e00000  MEM
  BASE2     0xf6000000  addr 0xf6000000  MEM
  BASEROM   0xf6d00000  addr 0xf6d00000  not-decode-enabled
  MAX_LAT   0x20  MIN_GNT 0x10  INT_PIN 0x01  INT_LINE 0x0b
  BYTE_0    0x20  BYTE_1  0x41  BYTE_2  0x04  BYTE_3  0x50
```

Locating, listing, and activating USB devices

Linux provides the `lsusb` utility to scan the USB bus and list all of the devices that it finds. The `lsusb` is similar in use and capabilities to the `lspci` utility discussed previously and does a good job of locating and identifying USB devices in a user-friendly fashion, as you can see from the following sample output:

```
# lsusb
Bus 005 Device 001: ID 0000:0000
Bus 004 Device 001: ID 0000:0000
Bus 003 Device 001: ID 0000:0000
Bus 002 Device 001: ID 0000:0000
Bus 001 Device 007: ID 05e3:0700 Genesys Logic, Inc. SIIG US2256
     CompactFlash Card Reader
Bus 001 Device 001: ID 0000:0000
```

As you can see from this example, I only have a single USB device attached to this sample system at the moment. If I attach another (in this case, a printer), I see output like the following (with the new line in bold):

```
# lsusb
Bus 005 Device 001: ID 0000:0000
Bus 004 Device 001: ID 0000:0000
Bus 003 Device 001: ID 0000:0000
Bus 002 Device 001: ID 0000:0000
Bus 001 Device 008: ID 04b8:0005 Seiko Epson Corp. Stylus Printer
Bus 001 Device 007: ID 05e3:0700 Genesys Logic, Inc. SIIG US2256
CompactFlash Card Reader
Bus 001 Device 001: ID 0000:0000
```

As you can see, the `lsusb` utility provides an accurate picture of the USB devices that are currently attached to a Linux system and even does a good job of identifying them. Like the `lspci` and `scanpci` commands, the `lsusb` command provides a verbose (`-v`) option, which provides more-detailed information about the USB devices that are attached to your system. This is most useful when used in conjunction with the `-s` option, which lets you specify a certain USB device by giving its USB bus ID and (if necessary) its device number. For example, to get way too much information about the printer that I just attached to my system, I could use the command `lsusb -v -s 001:008`. A sample of the output of this command is the following:

```
# lsusb -v -s 001:008
Bus 001 Device 008: ID 04b8:0005 Seiko Epson Corp. Stylus Printer
Device Descriptor:
  bLength                18
  bDescriptorType         1
  bcdUSB               1.10
  bDeviceClass            0 (Defined at Interface level)
```

```
  bDeviceSubClass          0
  bDeviceProtocol          0
  bMaxPacketSize0          8
  idVendor           0x04b8 Seiko Epson Corp.
  idProduct          0x0005 Stylus Printer
  bcdDevice            1.00
  iManufacturer            1 EPSON
  iProduct                 2 USB Printer
  iSerial                  3 L11P10505280955070
  bNumConfigurations       1
  Configuration Descriptor:
    bLength                9
    bDescriptorType        2
    wTotalLength          32
    bNumInterfaces         1
    bConfigurationValue    1
    iConfiguration         0
    bmAttributes        0xc0
  ...
```

Note that when using the -s option to specify a bus ID and device number, you must provide the leading zeroes or the command will not work correctly.

Getting hardware information from the /proc and /sys file systems

Because they are powerful, multiprocessing operating systems, Linux systems need to maintain and manage a great deal of information about active processes and various types of resources. The resources about which the Linux kernel needs to maintain information ranges from internal, kernel status information to information about how both the kernel and user processes are accessing physical resources on the system. Linux systems provide convenient ways of identifying and examining process and system resource information by using two in-memory file systems that are mounted at the /proc and /sys directories. In-memory file systems are simply portions of preallocated memory that have been formatted as a type of file system and which are then mounted and accessed like any other file system. The in-memory file system that is mounted on /proc is a file system of a type known as *proc*, while the in-memory file system that is mounted on /sys is a file system of a type known as *sysfs*. Because these file systems live only in your system's memory, they are re-created each time you reboot your system and are constantly updated to contain up-to-the-clock-tick information about different aspects of your Linux system.

The Linux /proc file system contains entries that act as interfaces to the kernel's internal data structures and therefore provide information about the status of all running processes on your system. This information includes general status information for all of the devices, file systems, and resources that the system is using and how the system is using resources such as memory, locks, and so on. The /proc file system was introduced in the 2.4 series of Linux kernels and is used by commands such as ps (*process status*), vmstat (*virtual memory statistics*), and many others to provide accurate and up-to-date information about what's happening on your system.

Introduced with the 2.6 Linux kernel, the /sys file system contains entries that provide information about the kernel's view of your system's hardware and the kernel modules used to manage those physical resources. Prior to the 2.6 kernel, this information was also stored in the /proc file system, but the Linux kernel developers introduced the /sys file system to provide a clear separation between process- and system-related information. Unfortunately, because the /sys file system is relatively new to Linux, some of the system information that you'd expect to find there is still found in the /proc file system — it's tricky to change where 10 zillion different utilities look for system-level information. A good rule of thumb to use when looking for system hardware information (which is, after all, what we're looking for in this chapter) is: You should consult the /proc file system for high-level information, consult the /sys file system for low-level system information, and always look in the other if you can't find the information that you're looking for in one of them. How's that for a hard-and-fast rule?

The contents of the /proc and /sys file systems and how the kernel uses the entries in those file systems is complex enough to merit its own book and is therefore certainly too complex for this chapter. For most Linux users, the information in the /sys file system is too low level to be of much use when trying to debug hardware identification problems. The high-level information that you need to see how your Linux distribution and running processes identify your hardware is still located in the /proc file system.

The following items are some of the highlights of contents of the /proc file system that you can use when trying to identify the hardware in your system and how the system is trying to use it:

- **/proc/bus:** This directory contains subdirectories for each bus found in your system. Each of these subdirectories contains a file called devices that contains summary information about the devices that were detected on that bus and other subdirectories that provide status information about each of these devices. For example, the file /proc/bus/input/devices on one of my systems provides information about my keyboard, PS/2 mouse, and the generic speaker that is built into every PC:

```
# cat /proc/bus/input/devices
I: Bus=0010 Vendor=001f Product=0001 Version=0100
N: Name="PC Speaker"
P: Phys=isa0061/input0
H: Handlers=kbd event0
B: EV=40001
B: SND=6

I: Bus=0011 Vendor=0001 Product=0001 Version=ab41
N: Name="AT Translated Set 2 keyboard"
P: Phys=isa0060/serio0/input0
H: Handlers=kbd mouse0 event1
B: EV=120017
B: KEY=40000 402000000 3802078f840d001 f2ffffdfffefffff
    fffffffffffffffe
```

```
B: REL=140
B: MSC=10
B: LED=7

I: Bus=0011 Vendor=0002 Product=0005 Version=0000
N: Name="ImPS/2 Generic Wheel Mouse"
P: Phys=isa0060/serio1/input0
H: Handlers=mouse1 event2
B: EV=7
B: KEY=70000 0 0 0 0
B: REL=103
```

/proc/cpuinfo: This file contains information about the type and status of the system's CPU. On one of my test systems that uses a 64-bit processor, this file provides the following information:

```
# cat /proc/cpuinfo
processor        : 0
vendor_id        : AuthenticAMD
cpu family       : 15
model            : 12
model name       : AMD Athlon(tm) 64 Processor 3200+
stepping         : 0
cpu MHz          : 2202.833
cache size       : 512 KB
fpu              : yes
fpu_exception    : yes
cpuid level      : 1
wp               : yes
flags            : fpu vme de pse tsc msr pae mce cx8 apic sep mtrr
                   pge mca cmov pat pse36 clflush mmx fxsr sse
                   sse2 pni syscall nx
mmxext lm 3dnowext 3dnow
bogomips         : 4325.37
TLB size         : 1024 4K pages
clflush size     : 64
cache_alignment  : 64
address sizes    : 40 bits physical, 48 bits virtual
power management: ts fid vid ttp
```

/proc/devices: This file provides a high-level view of all of the devices that are available in your system. Linux (and Unix) systems separate devices into two classes — character devices, which are accessed as a stream of input characters, and block devices, which are accessed in a structured fashion using larger data units (blocks). *Character devices are things like your keyboard, mouse, and data buses such as FireWire and USB. Block devices* are things like disk drives and other devices that contain file systems. A section of this file from one of my test systems is the following:

```
# cat devices
Character devices:
  1 mem
  2 pty
  3 ttyp
  4 /dev/vc/0
  4 tty
  4 ttyS
  5 /dev/tty
  5 /dev/console
  5 /dev/ptmx
  6 lp
  7 vcs
  9 st
 10 misc
 13 input
 14 sound
 ...
171 ieee1394
180 usb
188 ttyUSB

Block devices:
  1 ramdisk
  2 fd
  7 loop
  8 sd
  9 md
 11 sr
 33 ide2
 34 ide3
 65 sd
 ...
```

▓ **/proc/meminfo:** This file contains information about the memory that is available in your system and how your system is using it. The contents of this file on a sample system are the following:

```
# cat /proc/meminfo
MemTotal:      1023660 kB
MemFree:          9420 kB
```

```
Buffers:          39300 kB
Cached:          305648 kB
SwapCached:      243568 kB
Active:          710216 kB
Inactive:        168280 kB
HighTotal:            0 kB
HighFree:             0 kB
LowTotal:       1023660 kB
LowFree:           9420 kB
SwapTotal:      6297472 kB
SwapFree:       5327564 kB
Dirty:             3328 kB
Writeback:            0 kB
Mapped:          592672 kB
Slab:             62180 kB
CommitLimit:    6809300 kB
Committed_AS:   2045916 kB
PageTables:       24704 kB
VmallocTotal: 34359738367 kB
VmallocUsed:      16256 kB
VmallocChunk: 34359721695 kB
HugePages_Total:      0
HugePages_Free:       0
Hugepagesize:      2048 kB
```

/proc/version: This file contains information about the version of the Linux kernel that your system is running. On one of my test systems, this file contains the following (its contents would normally be on one line but are spread across two here for readability):

```
# cat /proc/version
Linux version 2.6.11.4-21.9-default (geeko@buildhost)
     (gcc version 3.3.5 20050117 \
(prerelease) (SUSE Linux)) #1 Fri Aug 19 11:58:59 UTC 2005
```

/proc/pci: This file lists all of the devices found when probing the system's PCI bus when the system booted. A sample section of the /proc/pci file on one of my systems looks like the following:

```
PCI devices found:
  Bus  0, device   0, function  0:
    Host bridge: Silicon Integrated Systems [SiS] 620 Host (rev 2).
      Master Capable.  Latency=32.
      Non-prefetchable 32 bit memory at 0xe8000000 [0xebffffff].
        Bus  0, device   0, function  1:
    IDE interface: Silicon Integrated Systems [SiS] 5513 [IDE] (rev
        208).
  Master Capable.  Latency=22.I/O at 0xffa0 [0xffaf].
    Bus  0, device   1, function  0:
```

```
    ISA bridge: Silicon Integrated Systems [SiS] 85C503/5513
        (rev 179).
Bus  0, device   1, function  1:
  Class ff00: Silicon Integrated Systems [SiS] ACPI (rev 0).
Bus  0, device   2, function  0:
  PCI bridge: Silicon Integrated Systems [SiS] 5591/5592 AGP
        (rev 0).
    Master Capable.  No bursts.  Min Gnt=12.
Bus  0, device   9, function  0:
  Ethernet controller: Intel Corporation 82557 [Ethernet Pro 100]
        (rev 8).
    IRQ 3.
    Master Capable.  Latency=64.  Min Gnt=8.Max Lat=56.
    Non-prefetchable 32 bit memory at 0xefffb000 [0xefffbfff].
    I/O at 0xde00 [0xde3f].
    Non-prefetchable 32 bit memory at 0xefe00000 [0xefefffff].
      Bus  0, device  11, function  0:
  Ethernet controller: Davicom Semiconductor, Inc. Ethernet 100/10
        MBit (rev 1 6).
    IRQ 10.
    Master Capable.  Latency=64.  Min Gnt=20.Max Lat=40.
    I/O at 0xdc00 [0xdc7f].
    Non-prefetchable 32 bit memory at 0xeffffaf80 [0xefffafff]
        Bus  0, device  15, function  0:
  Multimedia audio controller: C-Media Electronics Inc CM8738
        (rev 16).
    IRQ 12.
    Master Capable.  Latency=64.  Min Gnt=2.Max Lat=24.
    I/O at 0xd800 [0xd8ff].
```

The first few entries in this file show that the system from which I got this information uses an SiS motherboard and describes the bridges that connect the PCI and ISA buses to the system's primary data bus, identifies the motherboard as providing a built-in IDE interface, and then begins to identify specific controllers that were found in the system, such as (in this excerpt), my Ethernet controllers and the multimedia controller. You need to know the specific device controllers that are located in your system (Ethernet, multimedia, video, communication, and so on) in order to make sure that the kernel that you are building contains or has access to the drivers necessary for Linux to use that hardware.

■ **/proc/cpuinfo:** This file describes the characteristics of the central processing unit(s) in a computer system. The contents of this file on one of my test systems is the following:

```
processor     : 0
vendor_id     : GenuineIntel
cpu family    : 6
model         : 6
model name    : Celeron (Mendocino)
```

```
stepping        : 5
cpu MHz         : 501.137
cache size      : 128 KB
fdiv_bug        : no
hlt_bug         : no
f00f_bug        : no
coma_bug        : no
fpu             : yes
fpu_exception   : yes
cpuid level     : 2
wp              : yes
flags           : fpu vme de pse tsc msr pae mce cx8 sep mtrr pge
                  mca cmov pat pse36 mmx fxsr
bogomips        : 999.42
```

While you can always compile a Linux kernel for the 386 processor family (which will therefore run on any modern x86 processor), being able to identify the specific processor in your system enables you to take advantages of optimizations and processor-specific zconfiguration options that can help you build the fastest, most powerful kernel possible for your system.

Getting Information from System Logs

One of the best sources of information about the hardware that your system identifies when it boots is the system log, which is the text file /var/log/messages on all Linux systems. Each time you boot a Linux system, all of the messages displayed by the basic boot processes are concatenated to this file, which therefore contains a bewildering, but complete, collection of information about all hardware detection and system initialization. A sample section of this file is the following:

```
Sep 25 10:20:47 64bit kernel: klogd 1.4.1, log source = /proc/kmsg started.
Sep 25 10:20:47 64bit kernel: Adding 6297472k swap on /dev/sda2.  Priority:42
    extents:1
Sep 25 10:20:47 64bit kernel: bootsplash: status on console 0 changed to on
Sep 25 10:20:47 64bit kernel: NET: Registered protocol family 10
Sep 25 10:20:47 64bit kernel: IPv6 over IPv4 tunneling driver
Sep 25 10:20:47 64bit kernel: bootsplash: status on console 0 changed to on
Sep 25 10:20:47 64bit kernel: eth0: network connection up using port A
Sep 25 10:20:47 64bit kernel:     speed:           100
Sep 25 10:20:47 64bit kernel:     autonegotiation: yes
Sep 25 10:20:47 64bit kernel:     duplex mode:     full
Sep 25 10:20:48 64bit kernel:     flowctrl:        symmetric
Sep 25 10:20:48 64bit kernel:     irq moderation:  disabled
Sep 25 10:20:48 64bit kernel:     scatter-gather:  enabled
Sep 25 10:20:48 64bit kernel:     tx-checksum:     enabled
```

```
Sep 25 10:20:48 64bit kernel:     rx-checksum:     enabled
Sep 25 10:20:48 64bit ifup: No configuration found for sit0
Sep 25 10:20:52 64bit rcd[7114]: Loading system packages
Sep 25 10:20:55 64bit kernel: eth0: no IPv6 routers present
Sep 25 10:21:16 64bit rcd[7114]: Done loading system packages
Sep 25 10:21:18 64bit sshd[7346]: Server listening on :: port 22.
Sep 25 10:21:18 64bit sshd[7346]: Generating 768 bit RSA key.
Sep 25 10:21:18 64bit sshd[7346]: RSA key generation complete.
Sep 25 10:21:19 64bit last message repeated 3 times
Sep 25 10:21:19 64bit rcd[7114]: Starting heartbeat
Sep 25 10:21:19 64bit kernel: ACPI: Power Button (FF) [PWRF]
Sep 25 10:21:19 64bit kernel: ACPI: Sleep Button (CM) [SLPB]
Sep 25 10:21:20 64bit kernel: powernow-k8: Found 1 AMD Athlon 64 / Opteron
    processors (version 1.00.09e)
Sep 25 10:21:20 64bit kernel: powernow-k8: BIOS error - no PSB
Sep 25 10:21:20 64bit kernel: Floppy drive(s): fd0 is 1.44M
Sep 25 10:21:20 64bit kernel: FDC 0 is a post-1991 82077
Sep 25 10:21:20 64bit /etc/hotplug.d/block/50-hwscan.hotplug[7587]
...
```

This is a small section of the messages that are written to /var/log/messages when booting a sample Linux system. To find information about a specific device, you need to use a Linux utility such as grep, which looks for text strings in a text file. For example, to see any messages associated with a hard drive, you can search for some part of the drive's name in the /var/log/messages file. For example, since IDE hard drives are typically attached to a system with names beginning with *hd*, you could use the command grep hdf /var/log/messages to see if the system found a hard drive attached as /dev/hdf and to see what partitions it contains:

```
# grep hdf /var/log/messages
Oct 10 18:38:06 64bit kernel:  hdf: hdf1
Oct 10 18:38:06 64bit /etc/hotplug.d/block/50-hwscan.hotplug[8777]: new block
    device /block/hdf/hdf1
Oct 10 18:38:08 64bit kernel:  hdf: hdf1
Oct 10 18:38:08 64bit /etc/hotplug.d/block/50-hwscan.hotplug[8832]: new block
    device /block/hdf/hdf1
```

These messages show that the hotplug system found the drive /dev/hdf and that it contains one partition, /dev/hdf1.

The /var/log/messages file is useful for getting information not only about devices attached to the system but also about developing hardware problems on your system. For example, the following messages (ironically, about the same hard drive) show the types of messages that you may see when a hard drive begins to go bad:

```
Oct 10 19:12:36 64bit kernel: hdf: drive_cmd: status=0x51 { DriveReady
    SeekComplete Error }
```

```
Oct 10 19:12:36 64bit kernel: hdf: drive_cmd: error=0x04 { DriveStatusError }
Oct 10 19:17:18 64bit kernel: hdf: dma_intr: status=0x51 { DriveReady
    SeekComplete Error }
Oct 10 19:17:18 64bit kernel: hdf: dma_intr: error=0x84 { DriveStatusError
    BadCRC }
Oct 10 20:45:34 64bit kernel: hdf: DMA disabled
Oct 15 13:47:31 64bit kernel: hdf: drive_cmd: status=0x51 { DriveReady
    SeekComplete Error }
Oct 15 13:47:31 64bit kernel: hdf: drive_cmd: error=0x04 { DriveStatusError }
```

Oh well, time to reformat and potentially replace that disk drive! While nobody likes to see hardware fail, it's at least nice that Linux systems provide a mechanism for noticing the problem in advance, giving me the opportunity to copy my data off the drive before it actually fails.

Summary

Today's Linux systems do a good job of identifying and configuring your system's hardware when you first install a Linux distribution. The days of having to be a computer nerd to configure and use a Linux system are long gone. Linux systems also provide dynamic mechanisms for detecting newly attached hardware that are every bit as powerful and friendly as those found on operating systems such as Microsoft Windows.

Admittedly, this user-friendly hardware detection is relatively new to Linux systems. However, as shown in this chapter, the command-line-oriented roots of Linux mean that a large number of powerful tools are also available should you have problems with any of the hardware in your system. These can help you get more-detailed information about your system's hardware to make the most of that hardware, can help you identify problems if they begin to occur, and (if you're lucky) can enable you to resolve or address those problems before you lose data.

Chapter 17

Automation and Timed Execution

As the saying goes, "necessity is the mother of invention." Back in the days when processors were slow and time online had to be scheduled, it was not always possible to do certain tasks whenever you wanted to. A user who wanted to run a long and processor-intensive operation would often face the prospect of coming in after hours to use the machine when it would otherwise be idle. "Wouldn't it be great," those users thought, "if we could program the operation ahead of time and have it run automatically at a time we specify?"

Of course, in the world of information technology, when someone has an idea that's likely to save time or effort, eventually it is put into practice; so, Unix and its derivatives enable their users to schedule tasks to be executed at specific times. These days, it's not so much a matter of allocating processor time as it is having a way to execute repetitive or tedious tasks automatically. To be sure, the system is still used to schedule tasks that are best run when system usage is low. For example, many system administrators schedule backups to run in the wee hours because users are less likely to be online making changes to files.

On a single-user system, such considerations are less critical. Nevertheless, you may find a scheduler useful for some tasks, whether it's making backups or just to remind you of a meeting at a particular time.

Overview of Scheduling Options

There are two main ways of scheduling a task for future execution. For the simplest situations, you can use the `at` command. This command does exactly what its name implies: It executes a command *at* a specific time. The `at` command is best used for simple jobs that are going to be run only once. The following section details the method and syntax for using this command.

The other method is to use the `cron` program. The `cron` program is a daemon program that is always running in the background. `cron` is used by several other programs that are fairly important to the running of any system, so it is generally installed and configured to start automatically as part of the base of most systems. This is true of just about any Linux system, and you shouldn't have to start it.

To use `cron`, you must place the command that invokes your task in a file called the *crontab file*. Crontab files exist for the system as a whole (usually located at `/etc/crontab`), and other crontab files exist for each user. Each entry in a crontab file contains a specific date and time designation, and when the specified time is reached, the command is executed.

The advantage of using `cron` is that you can schedule tasks to be run on a cyclical basis. That is, you can schedule a task to be run every Tuesday at 2 a.m. or on the 12th of every month. The disadvantage is that the syntax for designating times is somewhat unintuitive and can be confusing. The advantage of using `at` is that the syntax for designating times is very simple and flexible. As a rule, use `at` for simple, one-shot tasks and `cron` for more-complex things that need to be done on an ongoing basis.

Using at

The basic syntax of the `at` command is very simple. It takes this form:

```
at <time> <command>
```

Here `<time>` of course represents an expression that designates the time at which you'd like to have your command run, and `<command>` is the command you want to run. Suppose that you've written a script (called `/home/susan/backup.sh`) to do a system backup, and you want to run it at 6 p.m. You could give the command in this format:

```
at 18:00 /home/susan/backup.sh
```

In this example, the date that the command should be run is assumed to be today. (In reference to the `at` command, the term "time" means both the date and the time of day.) The time is given as 18:00, which expresses 6 p.m. in 24-hour notation. What makes the `at` command so flexible is that it has several different formats in which you can express the time. For example, the preceding command could also have been written as follows:

```
at 6pm /home/susan/backup.sh
```

If the current time is 2 p.m., you could write the command as

```
at now + 4 hours /home/susan/backup.sh
```

If you want to run the command tomorrow at 6 p.m. you could use the following format:

```
at 6pm tomorrow /home/susan/backup.sh
```

Similarly, any of the following would be valid (though they don't always refer to the same date and time):

```
at midnight /home/susan/backup.sh

at noon tomorrow /home/susan/backup.sh

at teatime + 3 days /home/susan/backup.sh

at 7am Jun 23 /home/susan/backup.sh

at 7am 02/27/06 /home/susan/backup.sh
```

As you can see, there are many possible formats for specifying the time, and the odds are that even without being an expert, you can specify the time intuitively in a format that at will recognize.

Using at interactively

If you have multiple jobs that you want to run at the same time, or if you just prefer, you can use at interactively. Suppose that you have several jobs that you want to run at 2 p.m. Give the command

```
at 2pm
```

and hit the Enter key. You are presented with a prompt that looks like this:

```
at>
```

At this prompt, you can enter any command, and that command will be executed at the designated time. When you press the Enter key, you get the same prompt again. To exit this interactive mode, press Ctrl+D. You are returned to your shell prompt.

A sample interactive at session might look like this:

```
$ at 2pm
at> ls /etc
at> w
at> <EOT>
job 3 at 2005-10-19 14:00
```

(Note that all of these commands are grouped together as job 3. In this case, a job refers to all of the commands entered in a single session.)

Viewing the queue

You can view a list of pending jobs using the atq command. You will not be able to see the exact commands that you specified, but you can see a list of job numbers and the time they are scheduled to be executed. Job numbers displayed here are the same numbers that are output in the last line after an interactive at session. Here's a sample atq list:

```
$ atq
5          2005-10-19 17:00 a joe
6          2005-10-20 14:00 a joe
4          2005-10-19 14:00 a joe
```

Canceling jobs

If you want to remove a job from the `at` queue, you can do so by using the `atrm` command. For example, running the command

```
atrm 5
```

would remove job number 5 from the queue. You can remove multiple jobs by listing them with a space separating each job, like so:

```
atrm 4 5
```

Restricting access to at

As the administrator of a system, you may decide that you don't want certain users to have access to the `at` command. For example, you may find that one of your users is using `at` to schedule huge downloads of personal materials to run late at night. You can deny that user access by creating a file called `/etc/at.deny` and placing her username into it. This file is a simple text file, with usernames listed one per line. Any user whose name appears in this file will not be allowed to use the `at` command.

Alternatively, you can create a file called `/etc/at.allow`. If this file exists, *only* those users whose names appear in it will be allowed to use `at`. All other users will be denied access to it.

Using cron

A somewhat more complex alternative to `at`, `cron` is the natural choice for running jobs on a cyclical basis. Using `cron`, you can specify the minute, hour, day, month, and/or day of the week on which you want any given command to run. If, for example, you direct `cron` to run a command on the 15th of the month, that command will run on the 15th of every month until you remove the command from `cron`'s to-do list, described in the next section.

The crontab file

The to-do list is actually a file called a *crontab*. A crontab file contains a list of commands along with the dates and times that they are meant to be run. There is a master crontab file for the entire system, usually located at `/etc/crontab`, along with individual crontab files for each user. Although they are simple text files, because of the way `cron` works, they should not be edited directly. Instead, they are created, edited, and installed using the `crontab` command. If you want to schedule a `cron` job, give the command

```
crontab -e
```

This command opens the crontab file in a text editor.

Note

The editor used by the `crontab -e` command will be whichever editor is listed as the value of the `EDITOR` environment variable. On most Linux systems, the default value for this variable is the `vi` editor, but as with any environment variable, the value can be changed. This should, however, be a text-based editor, such as `vi`, `emacs`, `joe`, `jed`, `pico`, or the like.

Once the editor is open, you can add entries to the file. The entries must be in a specific format, which looks like this:

```
<minute> <hour> <day> <month> <day of week> command
```

It is not necessary to fill in every field. You can use the asterisk character (*) in any field to mean "all possible values." So, for example, you could have a crontab entry that looks like this:

```
0 4 * * * ls /etc
```

This line runs the command `ls /etc` at 4 a.m. every day. The zero in the first position indicates that the command is to be run at zero minutes past four. If the first position had been an asterisk, the command would be run 60 times. Once at 4:00, once at 4:01, once at 4:02, and so on. The asterisks in the third, fourth, and fifth positions mean that the command will be run at 4 a.m. each day of each month and on each day of the week. That may seem somewhat redundant, but those values can be used to narrow down the days a command might run. For example,

```
0 4 1,15 2 0 ls /etc
```

would run the command at 4:00 on every Sunday, as well as on the 1st and 15th of February. (When counting days of the week, 0 is Sunday, 1 is Monday, etc.)

Once you have finished making your entries, exit the editor, and the new crontab file is installed into the proper location.

Some tips for using cron effectively

The `cron` function is a very useful one, and I'm sure that you will find plenty of work for it; however, its usefulness is greatly expanded if you keep in mind some basic ideas about how to deploy it effectively.

- **Know where your output is going.** Some jobs, for example a backup operation, might not produce much in the way of output. Other jobs produce a lot of verbiage. The example of ls /etc used earlier does nothing but produce text output. If you do not specify an output location, your output will generally be e-mailed to you. If you want the output placed in a file, use output redirection (see Chapter 11) to accomplish this.

- **Keep your crontab clean.** Nothing is removed from your crontab file until you delete it. If you're using cron frequently, make sure you keep an eye on your crontab file, and delete items that are no longer needed.

- **Remember that cron is cyclical.** If you have a job set to execute on November 15, that job will execute on November 15 again next year if you don't take it out of your crontab file.

- **Use scripts for complex operations.** Instead of trying to cram complex operations onto a command line, consider making a script file (see Chapter 11) that can be executed by cron. This practice provides you with a lot of flexibility and allows you to design as complex an operation as you care to, while still making it easy to include as a line in the crontab file.

- **Use full path names.** Commands executed by cron are generally run in the system's default shell, with default values for environment variables. Generally, this doesn't present a problem, but if you have a heavily customized PATH variable, you may have become accustomed to dropping the full path names on files that would not normally be recognized. To avoid this, it's often a good idea to use full path names for files and commands. It's not always necessary, but it can help.

- **Test your commands first.** There's nothing more frustrating than setting up a spiffy new cron job, only to find out later that it failed. To avoid this, test any command you plan to use before setting it up to run automatically. Make sure your syntax is correct and all of your command-line arguments are doing what they're supposed to do. Once you've got it verified, you can put it in your crontab with confidence.

- **When in doubt, check your logs.** The cron program logs all of its activity. This log is usually found at /var/log/cron. If your system uses the logrotate program (most do), you should also find files with names like /var/log/cron.1, /var/log/cron.2, and so on. These are older log files. The higher the number, the older the file. These files are rotated on a daily basis, so /var/log/cron is today's log, whereas /var/log/cron.1 is yesterday's. If anything has gone wrong with one of your cron jobs, odds are the logs will at least give you a clue of where to look for the problem.

Other cron and crontab functions

The crontab -e format is the most common way of using the crontab command, but there are others as well.

- **crontab -l** lists your crontab file, without invoking an editor.

- **crontab -u** *<username>* allows you to view another user's crontab file. (You must have superuser privileges to use this form.) You must follow this with one of the other options. For example, `crontab -u jenny -l` lists Jenny's crontab file.

- **crontab -r** erases your crontab. This is useful if you want to clean everything out.

- **crontab -i** does the same thing as `crontab -e` but prompts you for a confirmation first. This is helpful in preventing the accidental loss of a crontab file.

Controlling access to cron

Access to `cron` is controlled in a way similar to that used to control access to `at`. If you wish to deny a user access to the cron program, create a file called `/etc/cron.deny`, and put that user's name in it. Similarly, you can create a file called `/etc/cron.allow`, and only those users whose names appear in that file will be allowed to use cron.

The batch Command

The `batch` command is an alternative to `cron` and `at`. Instead of running a program at a specific time, it runs the program whenever the system load drops below a particular level. If you're on a busy system and planning to run a job that will use a lot of system resources, you *could* run the job using `at` to start the job at a time at which you believe the system load will be low. Alternatively, you can use `batch` to run the job at the first opportunity that the system load is low. The advantage of using `batch` is that you know what the actual system load will be when you start the job. The advantage of using `at` is that you know exactly when the job will start.

To use `batch`, give your command in this form:

```
batch <command>
```

It should be noted that `batch` is really just a front end to `at`. When you use the `batch` command to schedule jobs, it goes into a queue just like any other `at` job and can be viewed with the `atq` command.

Summary

Timed execution can really alleviate the tedium involved in certain repetitive tasks. It can also make system-intensive jobs much less onerous to others using the system. The `at` and `batch` commands and the `cron` utility allow the user to schedule jobs at future times or when system resources permit. The `at` and `batch` commands are best suited to one-time operations, while the `cron` utility is better suited to situations where you need to run a command periodically. The `cron` utility is managed by means of the `crontab` command.

Chapter 18

File Sharing Solutions

One common use of Linux is to serve files on a network. Linux makes an excellent file server, capable of serving files to Windows machines, other Linux (and Unix in general) machines, and Macintosh machines, all with free software. With these capabilities, Linux can make a very compelling choice for a central file server on a mixed-platform network.

Linux-to-Windows File Sharing

Many users will be primarily interested in sharing files between a Linux server and one or more Windows clients. The file sharing protocol used by Windows systems is called System Message Block, or SMB. Most major Linux distributions ship with an implementation of the SMB protocol called SAMBA. SAMBA is a file server that operates on SMB, in effect fooling Windows clients into thinking it's a WindowsNT or Windows 2000 file server.

In addition, the most recent version of Apple's Macintosh operating system, Mac OS X, has built-in support for SMB, which means that a central Linux server running SAMBA can share files with both Windows and Macintosh clients (and, of course, other Linux machines).

Preparing to set up a SAMBA server

There are a couple of things to consider before you go ahead and set up your SAMBA server. The first and perhaps most important is what it is that you're actually going to share. SAMBA is configurable enough so that you could plan for various scenarios. You could, for example, share all users' home directories. This would present some security problems, but it is possible to restrict access so that each user could access his or her own home directory only. A more common scenario, the one presented in this chapter, involves setting up a directory that could be shared among all users or among a selected group of users. This type of shared central repository is a very simple arrangement and serves as a jumping-off point for discussions of more-elaborate arrangements.

Note
A SAMBA *share* refers to a shared directory.

Installing the software

The first step in getting a SAMBA server up and running is to install the software. Depending on the options you chose when you installed your Linux system, you may already have SAMBA installed. You can check this by going into whichever directory on your system is used to house the startup scripts for the various servers on your system and looking for a script called `samba` or `smb`. For example, on a Fedora Core system, the appropriate directory would be `/etc/rc.d/init.d`. There you will find the file `/etc/rc.d/init.d/smb`, which is the main startup script for the SAMBA server program.

Another method might be to use your distribution's package management system. On Fedora Core, for example, you can use the YUM tool to see if Samba is installed by giving the command `yum list samba`. If Samba is installed, you should see output that looks like this:

```
Setting up repositories
Reading repository metadata in from local files
Installed Packages
samba.i386                          3.0.14a-2              installed
```

If you don't find those scripts, you need to install the software, using whichever package management system is installed on your distribution. (Package management systems are discussed in Chapter 15.) If you're using any of the major distributions, you should be able to find the SAMBA package on one of the installation CDs or on your distribution's download site.

Note

Again, if you're using Fedora Core, you can use the YUM tool to install SAMBA. You can accomplish this simply by giving the command `yum install samba`.

If you can't find the software there, or if you want to check to see if there are any newer packages available, check `www.samba.org`. The SAMBA team maintains a repository of packages for many Linux distributions, as well as source code packages that you can compile and install yourself, if you prefer. Different distributions sometimes put files in nonstandard locations, and a source code installation lets you decide for yourself where you want to put things.

Configuring the SAMBA server

Once the SAMBA package is installed, you need to do some configuring to get it ready to run. There are several ways to do this:

- Use a graphical configuration tool.
- Edit the configuration file manually.
- Use SWAT, the SAMBA Web Administration tool, a utility that allows you to configure SAMBA using a Web browser.

Each of these methods has plusses and minuses. Manual editing has the steepest learning curve but provides the greatest level of flexibility. Graphical configuration tools are the simplest option but somewhat restrictive. SWAT provides ease of use and flexibility but can be difficult to get running because of the security risk it presents.

In the following sections, I first explain using a graphical utility (in this case, Fedora Core's `system-config-samba` tool) to set up a very basic SAMBA configuration. Next, I cover editing the SAMBA configuration file by hand. You will see that this method is not all that difficult and provides a great level of flexibility. Finally, I cover SWAT briefly.

SYSTEM-CONFIG-SAMBA

Fedora Core includes a utility called `system-config-samba` that makes it very easy to create simple SAMBA configurations. To access this utility, open the main menu and choose the menu path Applications → System Settings → Server Settings → Samba, or open a terminal window, and give the command `system-config-samba`. You are prompted for the superuser's password. Enter it, and click the OK button.

Note

Distributions differ with regard to whether they have this sort of graphical configuration tool. You may wish to take a close look at your distribution's documentation or Web site if you're not sure whether such a tool exists on your distribution.

The Samba Server Configuration window opens, as shown in Figure 18-1.

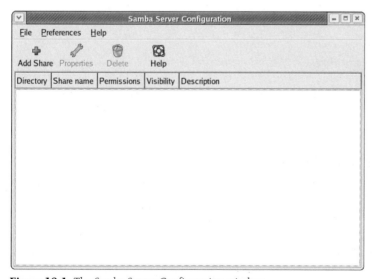

Figure 18-1: The Samba Server Configuration window.

The first step is to add the directory that you want to share. Assume that you have created a directory called /Samba that will serve as the file sharing directory for your organization. Click the Add button to open the Create Samba Share window, shown in Figure 18-2.

Figure 18-2: The Create Samba Share window.

In the Directory: field, enter the name of the directory that you wish to have shared (in this case, /Samba.) In the Share name: field, enter the name by which the shared directory will appear to the Windows clients (samba-share in the figure). In the Description: field, you can enter a brief description of the directory. This is optional, but it never hurts. In this case, the description is: A shared directory for demonstration.

Below those spaces are a couple of radio buttons under the heading Basic Permissions. Select Read-only if you do not want people to be able to change the contents of the directory, or Read/Write if you wish to allow changes. In the example, choose Read/Write because you want users to be able to put files into this directory.

Next, click the Access tab. You will see the access management properties, as shown in Figure 18-3.

Figure 18-3: The Create Samba Share window showing the Access tab.

In this tab, you can restrict access to only certain users, or you can allow access to everyone. As we have not yet discussed how to add users to the SAMBA system, choose Allow access to everyone and click OK. The share should now appear in the main pane of the Samba Server Configuration window.

Adding Users to SAMBA

An alternate method for providing access to SAMBA is to restrict access to certain directories to specific users. To do this, you must enable your users to have access to the SAMBA server. You need to do the following:

1. Make sure each user has an account on the machine hosting the SAMBA server.

2. Provide each user with a SAMBA password. You can do this using the smbpasswd command. At a terminal prompt, assume superuser privileges and type the command smbpasswd username, where username is the name of the user that you want to add. You are prompted for a password. Type in a password. You are asked to confirm it.

At this point, the user should be able to access the SAMBA server. Any share that has user-level security enabled will require the user to enter his or her password before accessing that share.

Users can change their SAMBA passwords by logging into the host machine and giving the smbpasswd command themselves. They are prompted for their old password and then asked to give and confirm a new password.

Before you can use the shared directory, you still need to configure a couple of general server options. These control the way the server behaves in general, as opposed to being specific to the share you just created (an important distinction if you've got more than one share).

From the Samba Server Configuration window, click the Preferences menu and select Server Settings. This opens the Server Settings window, shown in Figure 18-4.

Figure 18-4: The Server Settings window.

In the Workgroup: field, give your workgroup a name. In this example, call it test group. In the Description: field, give your workgroup a description, Samba Server in the example. (The description is optional.) Now click the Security tab. The Server Settings window now shows the Security tab, as displayed in Figure 18-5.

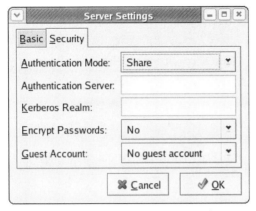

Figure 18-5: The Server Settings window showing the Security tab.

Make sure that Authentication Mode is set to Share, that Encrypt passwords is set to No, and that Guest Account is set to No guest account. (This will prevent people without an account on the system from accessing the share.) Click OK.

At this point, your SAMBA server is ready to use. Before you are able to see the share on the network, however, you need to start the server (or restart it if it's already running). To do this, select menu path Applications → System Settings → Server Settings → Services, or open a terminal window and give the command `system-config-services`. This opens the Service Configuration utility, shown in Figure 18-6.

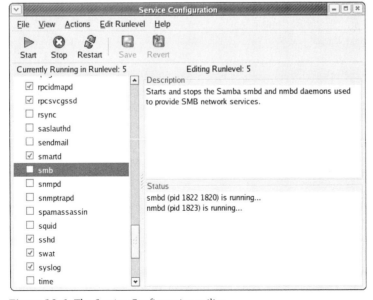

Figure 18-6: The Service Configuration utility.

In the left-hand panel, scroll down until you see smb and click to highlight it. In the bottom-right pane, you should see a message telling you whether the smb and nmbd services are running. If they're not running, click the Start button. If they are running, click the Restart button. A message should pop up telling you that the start or the restart has been successful. Click OK to dismiss this message. At this point, your SAMBA server should be running, and the share you created should be available for browsing.

Note

The preceding procedure will work on Fedora Core only. You'll need to check your system's documentation for the proper procedure for starting servers if you're using something else.

EDITING THE CONFIGURATION FILE BY HAND

Most people generally prefer not to edit configuration files by hand, but in the case of SAMBA, this may well be the best route to take. While not quite as simple as using a graphical tool, editing the configuration file by hand is not nearly as difficult as it is with other types of servers. This is because the designers of SAMBA went out of their way to create a configuration file syntax that is easy to read, and a set of configuration options that have logical, intuitive names. SAMBA comes with a very well written manual page just for the configuration file. (Give the command man smb.conf to see it.) Some distributions (notably Fedora Core) include a default configuration file with detailed comments to get you started.

The SAMBA configuration file is usually located at /etc/samba/smb.conf. If you want to edit the existing file, you can open it in a text editor. (Do this as the superuser if you want to be able to save your changes.) Alternatively, you can change the name of the existing file to something like /etc/samba/smb.conf-old, and create a new one.

Note

We haven't talked too much about text editors thus far, aside from mentioning them in Chapter 11. Text editors are somewhat like word processors in that they allow you to highlight text, cut-and-paste, and perform similar tasks, but unlike word processors, they don't format text. This is an important distinction because a word processor inserts formatting instructions in the file that determine the way the file displays, both on screen and on paper. A text editor does do this. So it's important that for editing configuration files, you use a text editor such as GEdit or KWrite, and *not* a word processor like OpenOffice.org Writer.

My favorite text editor is called NEdit. It ships on some distributions but not others. It is not tied to either the GNOME or KDE desktop but works equally well on both of them. If it's not already on your system, you can download it at www.nedit.org. It is not necessary that you use NEdit; any plain text editor will do. See Chapter 11 for information on some other text editors, such as Gedit or Kedit.

There are also editors that work only in text mode, such as vi and emacs. Using these requires you to learn a few commands and hotkey mappings. It's worth taking the time to learn to use one or more of these (if only because you never know when you might find yourself working on a machine without a GUI enabled), but a discussion of them is beyond the scope of this book.

In this example, you're going to move and rename the default configuration file and start a new one from scratch.

1. Open a terminal window and give the command `su -`. At the prompt, enter the superuser password.

2. Give the command `cd /etc/samba` to move from your current directory into SAMBA's configuration directory.

3. Next, run `mv smb.conf smb.conf-old` to change the name of the `smb.conf` file to `smb.conf-old`. Now you are ready to create a new `smb.conf` file.

4. Type `nedit smb.conf`. The NEdit editor opens, as shown in Figure 18-7.

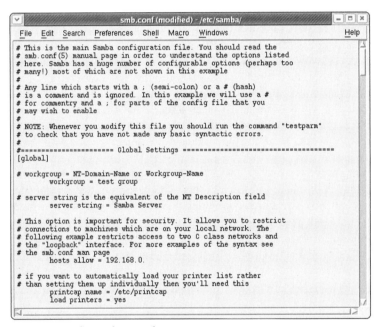

Figure 18-7: The NEdit text editor.

Note

Because both GUI tools and editing text by hand are covered in this chapter, I'd like to alert you to a potential problem. It is possible that in editing a text file by hand, you can accidentally do something that will confuse the GUI tool. This is not usually a catastrophic situation, but it can be confusing. Normally, the GUI tools are not nearly as advanced as SAMBA itself, so some configurations can be problematic.

You may want to try to avoid this problem by using the GUI tool to create your basic configuration, and then doing fine-tuning by hand.

Now you can create your configuration file. As you can see in Figure 18-7, the `smb.conf` file is organized into sections with each section denoted by a keyword in square brackets, such as `[global]`. A section continues until another bracketed keyword is reached. Within each section are a number of parameters that take the form

```
name = value
```

where `name` is the name of the parameter and `value` is the setting that you want that parameter to have. For example, if you want set a share's permission to read/write, you set the parameter in this way:

```
writable = yes
```

Global Settings

The first section in your configuration file should be the `[global]` section. In this section, you can define options that will be in effect for all shares being served by the SAMBA server. You can also define options that do not apply to any particular share but are relevant to the operation of the server itself. Here is a sample:

```
[global]
    workgroup =  test group
    security = share
    server string = Samba Server
```

The global section of this code defines three parameters, and they are exactly equal to the options you set using the Server Settings window in Fedora's `system-config-samba` utility. In fact, `system-config-samba` does nothing more than write these options into the `smb.conf` file. Note that the lines underneath the section keyword are indented. As with shell programming, this is done for readability. Visually scanning the file, it's easy to see where new sections begin.

Share Settings

Now that you have defined your global parameters, you can set up a share. The keyword for your share is the name that you want it to have; in this case, `samba-share`. Give this share all the attributes that you defined for it using `system-config-samba`:

```
[samba-share]
    comment = A shared directory for demonstration
    path = /Samba
    writable = yes
    guest ok = yes
```

And there it is. The `samba-share` section together with the `global` section is all you need to set the server up in this way. Save the file, making sure that it has the path name `/etc/samba/smb.conf`.

User-Based Authentication

Sometimes you want to restrict access to certain shares to a particular user or group of users. For example, suppose that you want to give each user access to his or her home directory. You would need to set up a share that looked like this:

```
[homes]
    comment = Home Directories
    browsable = no
    writeable = yes
    security = user
```

Note that you do not need to specify a path name for the home directories. The server can create these on the fly by using the information about each user's home directory in the /etc/passwd file. By specifying that security = user you ensure that each user can access his or her home directory only and no one else's.

All that remains now is to start (or restart) the server. In the previous section, you learned how to start the server using Fedora's system-config-services. Here, you see how to do it using text commands appropriate for a Knoppix system.

Note

The following procedure works on many distributions, not just Knoppix. The only stipulation is that different distributions will place the startup scripts in different locations. In general, if you can find a directory called init.d, that's where they'll be. If you do not find an init.d directory, odds are your distribution doesn't use this kind of startup procedure. In this case, you'll need to check your distribution's documentation to find out what kind of startup procedure it does use.

On Knoppix, open a terminal window, and use the su - command (and password) to assume superuser powers if you haven't done so already. If the server is not already running, give the following command:

```
/etc/init.d/samba start
```

If it is already running, type the following:

```
/etc/init.d/samba restart
```

If you don't know if it's running or not, run the following command to find out:

```
/etc/init.d/samba status
```

Tip

Instead of checking the status of the server every time you try to start it, you can always just start it using `/etc/init.d/samba restart`. If the server isn't already running, the part of that program that stops the server simply fails, and it skips straight to the part where it starts it again. This saves you the time of checking whether it's already running.

USING SWAT

SWAT (SAMBA Web Administration Tool) is a program that installs a small Web server on your system. Once installed, you can access that server and use it to configure your SAMBA server from a Web browser. The advantage of this is that you can configure your server from any machine; you don't have to be on the same machine upon which the server is running.

The disadvantage is that SWAT does create something of a security risk. It's not a severe thing—anytime you run a server on your system (including a SAMBA server), you create an opening that can be exploited by a hacker. This doesn't mean you shouldn't run SWAT, but it does mean that you'll need to jump through a few hoops to get it running. Here's a step-by-step rundown of what you need to do to get SWAT running:

1. Make sure SWAT is installed. As you did with the SAMBA package, you need to make sure that the SWAT package is installed. The SWAT package is sometimes designated `samba-swat`, and sometimes simply `swat`. Check to see if the package is installed, and, if not, install it. If your distribution comes with SAMBA, you probably already have SWAT on the installation medium along with SAMBA. If not, you can download it from `www.samba.org`.

   The usual locations for SWAT's files are `/usr/sbin/swat`, `/usr/share/swat`, or `/opt/swat`. If you don't have any of those files or directories, you probably don't have SWAT installed.

2. Make sure the service is registered. Assuming you're using a package manager to install SWAT, this will probably be done for you, but it's worth checking anyway. Give the command

   ```
   more /etc/services
   ```

   Use the space bar to scroll through the file. You should see a line that looks like this:

   ```
   swat            901/tcp                 # Samba Web Administration Tool
   ```

   If you scroll through the entire file and you are unable to find this line, open the `/etc/services` file in a text editor and add it to the end of the file. Then save the file and close the editor.

3. Configure `inet.d` or `xinet.d`. Depending on your distribution, you will have a program called either `inet.d` or `xinet.d`. These are *superservers* that exist to handle incoming connections to a number of relatively infrequently used services. `xinet.d` and `inet.d` do essentially the same thing, but `xinet.d` is newer and more configurable. The following instructions begin by describing the way to configure SWAT under `inet.d`, and then move on to the somewhat more complicated `xinet.d`.

   a. Given that Knoppix uses `inet.d`, I use it as the example for how to configure `inet.d`. First, open a terminal window and become the superuser (`su -`). Then, open the file `/etc/inetd.conf` in a text editor. Find a line that looks something like this:

   ```
   swat stream tcp nowait root /usr/sbin/swat -port 901
   ```

   If you don't see a line like this, add it, and then save the file. Restart `inet.d` by giving the following command:

   ```
   /etc/init.d/inetd restart
   ```

   b. For `xinet.d`, I use Fedora Core as an example. Under Fedora, open a terminal window and become root. Move to the directory `/etc/xinet.d`. In that directory, you should find a file called `swat`. Open that file in a text editor. You should see something that looks like this:

   ```
   service swat
   {
           port            = 901
           socket_type     = stream
           wait            = no
           only_from       = 127.0.0.1
           user            = root
           server          = /usr/sbin/swat
           log_on_failure  += USERID
           disable         = yes
   }
   ```

   Where it says `disable = yes` change the `yes` to `no`. Also, comment out (that is, put a hash mark in front of) the line that says `only from = 127.0.0.1`. Your finished file should look like this:

   ```
   service swat
   {
           port            = 901
           socket_type     = stream
           wait            = no
   #       only_from       = 127.0.0.1
           user            = root
           server          = /usr/sbin/swat
           log_on_failure  += USERID
   ```

```
        disable        = no
}
```

Now, restart the `xinet.d` server by typing **/etc/rc.d/init.d/xinetd restart**. You should now be ready to use SWAT.

Note

You should not comment out the `only_from` line if you want to restrict access to SWAT. Leaving the value set to `127.0.0.1` allows it to be used only from the machine that it's running on. Alternatively, you could change the value to the IP address for another machine if you want to allow access from that machine only.

After you have the entire configuration completed, you're ready to start using SWAT. Open a Web browser (see Chapter 12), and in the location field, type **localhost:901**. You should see the main SWAT page, shown in Figure 18-8 in the Mozilla Firefox browser.

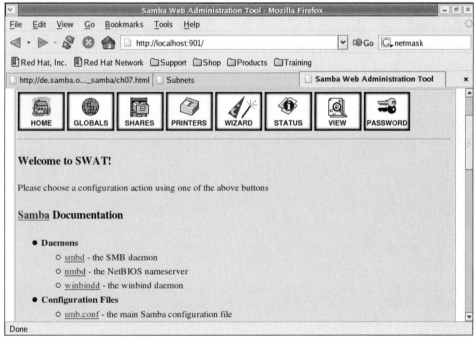

Figure 18-8: The main SWAT page.

The main SWAT page lists several documentation options. You can look at the manual pages for any number of SAMBA-related programs, or you can look at some terrific SAMBA resources by clicking on any of the links under the Books heading. (Scroll down to the end of the page to see the links.)

Note

One of the nice features of SWAT is the fact that the documentation to which it's linked is always up-to-date. SWAT takes its documentation directly from the manual pages, which are part of the SAMBA package. When you upgrade your SAMBA packages, you automatically upgrade the manual pages, and the documentation linked on the main SWAT page is automatically upgraded as well.

When you're ready to configure your server, use the buttons along the top of the page. Click the Globals button to configure global parameters as shown in Figure 18-9.

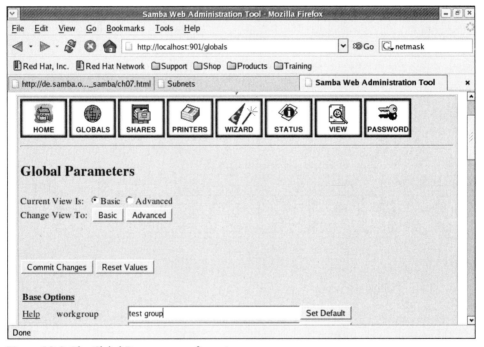

Figure 18-9: The Global Parameters configuration page.

Unlike `system-config-samba` and similar tools, SWAT gives you the opportunity to configure just about every option that exists. You don't have to configure all of these — the most common ones are at the top. Note that next to every option is a Help link. If you are unsure what a particular option does, click the link to see the section of the `smb.conf` manual page where that option is described.

When you have finished configuring global options, click the Shares button to configure your shared directories. The Shares Parameters page, shown in Figure 18-10, appears.

To create a new share, enter the name you want to give the share in the Create Share field and click the button. This expands the view to show several options you can set for the share as shown in Figure 18-11. Alternatively, you can select an existing share from the Choose Share drop-down list.

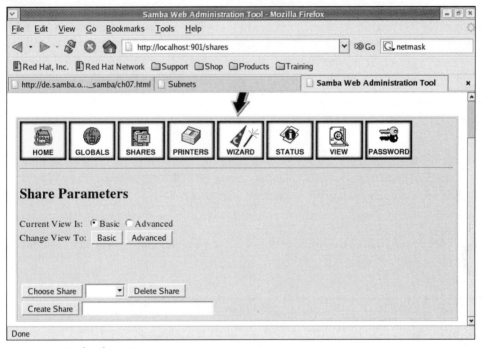

Figure 18-10: The Shares Parameters page.

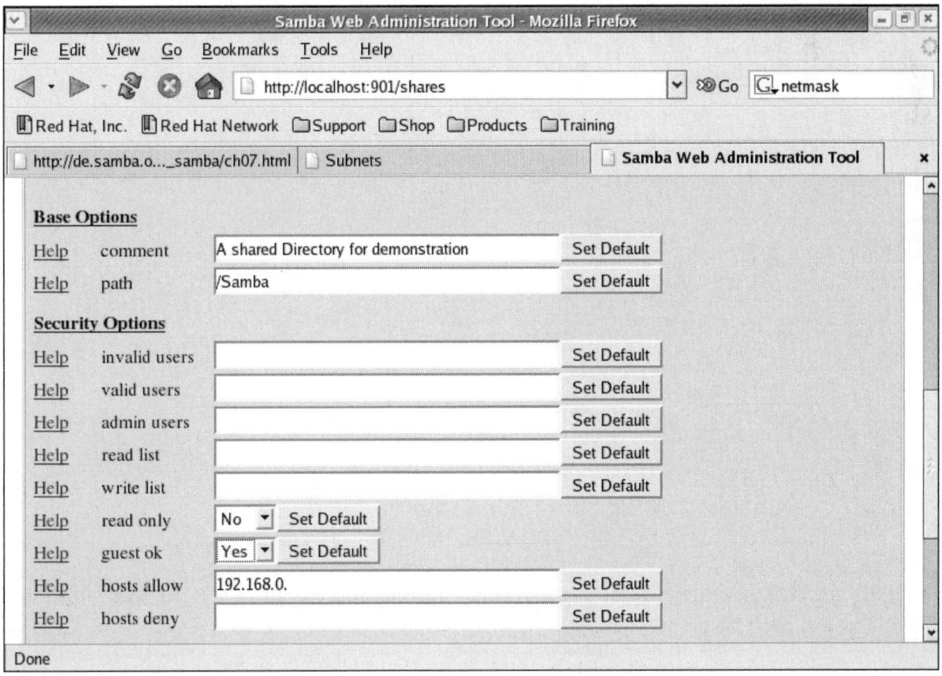

Figure 18-11: Share creation options.

From this window, you can set options for newly created shares or change settings for existing shares. In Figure 18-11, you can see that the options for `samba-share` have already been populated. Under Base Option, the comment reads `A shared Directory for demonstration`, and the path is identified as `/Samba`. To complete the configuration, scroll down to Security Options and change the read only option to `no` and the guest ok option to `yes`. Now you have configured your share, and you're ready to save your changes. Click the Commit Changes button to save your changes.

Caution

When you use SWAT to configure your SAMBA server, it creates a new configuration file every time you save your changes. That means that if you had configured anything by hand, or left any comments in your old file, they are now lost. Make sure you take this into account when using SWAT.

Next, you need to restart the server. Click the Status button at the top of the screen to go to the Server Status page, shown in Figure 18-12.

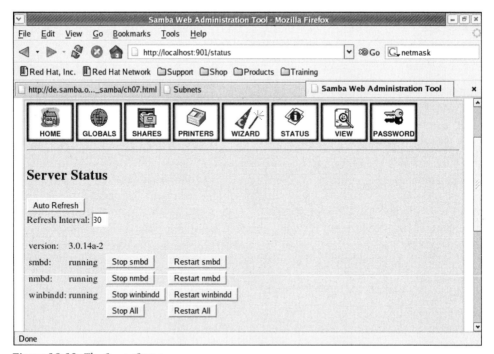

Figure 18-12: The Server Status page.

Click the buttons marked Restart smbd and Restart nmbd. At this point, your SAMBA shares should be available for browsing.

Setting up the Windows clients

In theory, setting up SAMBA clients on Windows should be easy. In practice, it can require some fiddling. As you might expect, Microsoft is less than enthused about the fact that a free software package provides the same functionality as its expensive server software, and it seems as though every version of Windows contains some feature that, while not outright breaking compatibility with SAMBA, can make it difficult to configure.

With that in mind, this section takes you through the process of setting up a SAMBA client on Windows XP Home Edition. The process for setting up a client on other versions of Windows should be similar, but you may have to do a little digging to find out the exact procedure.

Note

If you run into problems, you might want to have a look at any of a number of SAMBA resources on the World Wide Web. The place to start is www.samba.org. The documentation at that site gives you lots of information, including troubleshooting tips for common problems.

1. Open the Start menu and click My Network Places. This opens the Windows Explorer to the My Network Places page, as shown in Figure 18-13. You may see your share already displayed. If this is the case, you're done. Simply click on your share, and an Explorer window opens showing the contents of the share.

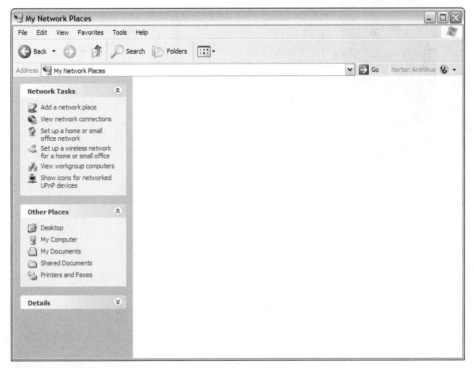

Figure 18-13: Windows Explorer showing My Network Places.

2. If you do not see your share displayed, click the link marked Add a network place in the left-hand pane. This opens the Add Network Place wizard, shown in Figure 18-14.

   Read the text on the wizard's first page and click Next to continue.

3. On the next page (Figure 18-15), select Choose another network location and click Next.

4. The next page asks you, "What is the address of this network place?" (see Figure 18-16). In the field labeled Internet or network address, type *****Server***\samba-share** (replacing *Server* with the name of the machine on which SAMBA is running. You can also use the IP number of this machine, \\192.168.0.1\samba-share.) Click Next to continue.

5. On the next screen, you are asked, "What do you want to name this place?" Enter a name and click Next.

6. Read the information on the final page. If you want Windows Explorer to open with the network location displayed in the Address bar, as shown in Figure 18-17, leave the check in the checkbox. If not, click to remove it. Click Finish.

You are now ready to use your SAMBA share.

Figure 18-14: The Add Network Place wizard.

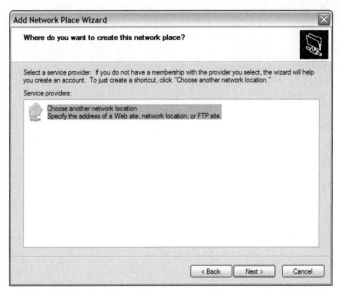

Figure 18-15: Where do you want to create this network place?

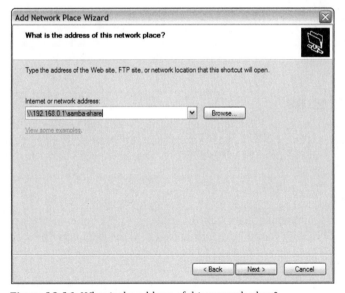

Figure 18-16: What is the address of this network place?

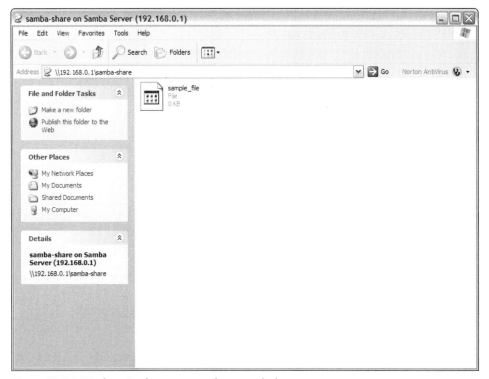

Figure 18-17: Windows Explorer, open to the network share.

Setting up Linux clients

The primary purpose of SAMBA is Linux-to-Windows file sharing. While the first choice for Linux-to-Linux file sharing would probably be NFS (see the related section later in the chapter), it is also possible for Linux machines to make use of Samba shares. There are two ways to do this: via a file manager or by using text commands.

USING A FILE MANAGER

The easiest way of accessing SAMBA shares on a Linux machine is to use a file manager that has a built-in SAMBA client. Both GNOME's Nautilus file manager and KDE's Konqueror have the ability to access SAMBA shares.

Konqueror

If you're using Knoppix, or any other distribution with a KDE desktop, you can access SAMBA shares using the Konqueror file manager. Simply open Konqueror, and under the Go menu, select Network Folders. A list of available network folders is shown in the browser window. Click the icon marked Samba shares to see a list of available SAMBA shares, as shown in Figure 18-18.

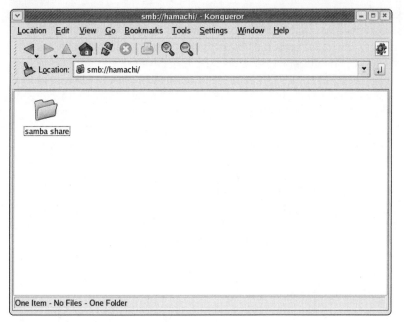

Figure 18-18: Use Konqueror to show SAMBA shares.

Nautilus

Using Nautilus is similar but requires a slightly different approach. Open Nautilus, and in the location bar, type **smb:/**. You now see a list of available SAMBA shares, as in Figure 18-19.

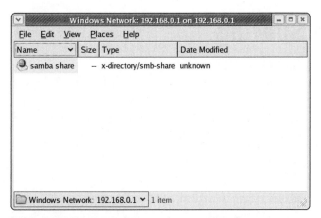

Figure 18-19: SAMBA shares as shown in Nautilus.

USING TEXT COMMANDS

Linux just wouldn't be Linux if there weren't a way to do the job with text commands. In this case, the command you need to use is smbmount, and it takes the name of a server and share as a source and a *mount point* as a destination. A mount point is simply an empty directory. So, for example, let's say your mount point is /mnt/Samba. If you don't have this, you can create it by giving the command mkdir /mnt/Samba. You should also give read and write permission on this directory to everyone with the command chmod a+rw /mnt/Samba. Now, you can mount a SAMBA share like this:

```
smbmount //Server/samba-share /mnt/Samba
```

Again, replace Server with the name of the machine on which you are running the SAMBA server. (You could also use an IP number for the server name as in smbmount //192.168.0.43/samba-share /mnt/Samba.) Note that both server and share names are case sensitive. Note also the double slash preceding the name of the server. After you have the share mounted, you can simply move into the directory /mnt/Samba and access the files as if they were located on the local machine's hard drive.

Setting up Macintosh clients

Although most *PC Magazine* readers are probably Windows users, it's possible that you might have a network with several different kinds of machines, including Macintosh.

Like Nautilus and Konqueror, the Macintosh file manager — Finder — has built-in support for the SMB protocol. To access a SAMBA share from a Macintosh, open Finder, click on the Go menu, and select Connect to Server. The Connect to Server window opens. In the server address field, type **smb://*server name/share name***. So, to access the share in our example, type smb://Server/samba-share.

Linux-to-Linux File Sharing

While it is perfectly possible to share files among Linux machines using SAMBA (and indeed, there's no real reason not to), there is another method available as well. This method is called NFS, the Network File Service. There is no real reason to prefer NFS to SAMBA for Linux-to-Linux file sharing, except that almost all Linux systems should be configured to use NFS out of the box. In other words, it's fairly rare that you should have to install any NFS software. Also, NFS is a standard on many other types of Unix systems, so it is particularly well suited to run in a mixed-Unix environment.

Setting up an NFS server

NFS is a function of the Linux kernel, so you don't need to install client or server software. You may, however, want to check to make sure that you have a package called nfs-utils. If you don't have it, it should be on your installation media or available for download from your distribution's Web site. Install the package using whichever package management system comes with your distribution.

GRAPHICAL METHOD

Some distributions, such as Fedora Core, come with graphical NFS configuration programs. (Knoppix does not, so if you're using Knoppix, you'll have to use the text-mode method described in the following section.) The Fedora Core configuration program is called `system-config-nfs` and can be started by giving that command in a terminal window or by using the menu path Applications → System Settings → Server Settings → NFS. When you start `system-config-nfs`, you are prompted for the superuser password.

After you give the password, the NFS Server Configuration window opens as shown in Figure 18-20.

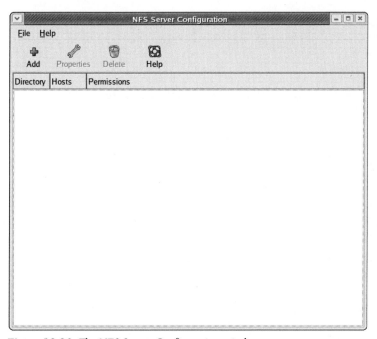

Figure 18-20: The NFS Server Configuration window.

Notice that this looks almost exactly the same as the corresponding window in `system-config-samba`, and indeed it functions in a very similar manner. To add a directory to be shared (assuming that you've created a directory called `/nfs` to be exported), click the Add button to open the Add NFS Share window shown in Figure 18-21.

Type **/nfs** in the Directory: field; in the Host(s): field, you can add a list of client machines that will be allowed to access this share. There is also a pair of radio buttons that allow you to designate the share as Read-only or Read/Write. These options have the same function as they do in SAMBA. Add the relevant information and click OK. The new share should appear in the main NFS Server Configuration window.

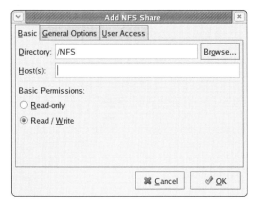

Figure 18-21: The Add NFS Share window.

You'll need to start or restart the NFS server for the new configuration to take effect. You can do this by using `system-config-services`, as you did for SAMBA (look for the service called `nfs`), or by opening a terminal window and giving the command (as the superuser):

```
/etc/rc.d/init.d/nfs restart
```

At this point you should be able to access the share from the remote machine.

Caution

As noted before, this command works only if your startup scripts are located in the `/etc/rc.d/init.d` directory. If they're located elsewhere, you'll need to change the command's path to reflect that.

TEXT MODE METHOD

Like SAMBA, the NFS server can also be configured via text mode. You do this by editing the `/etc/exports` file. Open that file in a text editor, and add the following line. (You can put it anywhere; I usually put such lines at the end of the file.)

```
/nfs                    192.168.0.12(rw)
```

Here, `/nfs` is the directory you want to export, `192.168.0.12` is the machine that will be allowed to access the share and `(rw)` stands for read/write, which is the type of access you want to allow to the share. (Read-only would be designated `(ro)`.) Save the file, and restart the NFS server as you did in the previous section. You should now be able to access the share from the remote machine.

If you want to enable more than one machine to access a particular directory, you can list each machine separately, like so:

```
/nfs                192.168.0.12(rw) 192.168.0.14(rw)
```

Or you can specify a range of machines, like this:

```
/nfs                192.168.0.0/255.255.255.0(rw)
```

The second method allows access from any machine with an IP number between 192.168.0.0 and 192.168.0.127. (The second part of that address is a *netmask*, which modifies the address to the left of the slash. For more information about netmasks, see `www.johnscloset.net/primer/subnet.html`.)

Setting up NFS clients

There are two ways to access NFS shares from a client machine. The first way accesses the share temporarily. That is, the share is available until it is removed from the client or until the client machine is turned off. If, after that, you want to access the share again, you will need to go through the procedure again. The second way causes the client to access the server every time the machine is turned on.

TEMPORARY ACCESS

Shares can be accessed temporarily using the `mount` command. To do this, you need to have a mount point (an empty directory) and you need to know the IP number of the server machine. So first, create a mount point; for example:

```
mkdir /mnt/nfs
```

(You need to do this as root.) Also, make sure that read/write permission is enabled for everyone:

```
chmod a+rw /mnt/nfs
```

Now that you have a mount point, you can mount the remote directory on the local file system, like so:

```
mount 192.168.0.1:/nfs /mnt/nfs
```

If, on the client machine, you move into the `/mnt/nfs` directory, you can now see the contents of the `/nfs` directory on the server machine. The contents of the server's exported directory behave exactly as if they were on the client machine's local drive.

PERMANENT ACCESS

If you wish to have the contents of a remote directory available every time you boot the client machine, you can configure the client machine to mount the remote directory automatically. You do this by editing the `/etc/fstab` file on the client machine.

Caution

Editing the `/etc/fstab` file on the client machine, while not dangerous in itself, can lead to a problem: If the server machine is not available for any reason — for example, if it is down, or if it is off the network — it can cause the client machine to hang during boot-up. This is not a fatal problem, as the procedure will eventually time out, but it can slow down the client machine's boot-up process significantly.

Open `/etc/fstab` in a text editor. You should see something that looks more or less like this:

```
# This file is edited by fstab-sync - see 'man fstab-sync' for details
/dev/VolGroup00/LogVol00 /                ext3    defaults        1 1
LABEL=/boot              /boot            ext3    defaults        1 2
none                     /dev/pts         devpts  gid=5,mode=620  0 0
none                     /dev/shm         tmpfs   defaults        0 0
none                     /proc            proc    defaults        0 0
none                     /sys             sysfs   defaults        0 0
```

Each line of the `/etc/fstab` file represents part of the file system that is running on the machine. You may have more or fewer entries than you see here, but they will all be in this general format. To this file, add the line (again, anywhere in the file):

```
192.168.0.1:/nfs         /mnt/nfs         nfs     rw              0 0
```

The first entry is the name (or IP number) of the server, and the path to the exported directory. The second entry is the mount point. The third is the file system type (in this case `nfs`), and the fourth is any options that you want to pass to the mount program (in this case `rw` for read/write). The final two entries are file system options, which for an NFS file system should be 0 and 0.

Save the file, and give the command

```
mount -a
```

This remounts all of the file systems listed in `/etc/fstab`, including the NFS system you just added. At this point you should be able to access the NFS share just as you did in the previous section.

Summary

Linux can share files between Linux, Windows, and Macintosh using SAMBA, or between Linux and other Linux or Unix machines using NFS. A Linux machine running SAMBA and NFS can make a good, low-cost file server for a small- to medium-sized network.

Chapter 19

Adjusting Your Internet Settings

All modern Unix and Unix-like systems are designed to support networking out of the box. Linux networking revolves around Transmission Control Protocol/Internet Protocol (TCP/IP) networking, which, as the name implies, is the core type of networking used on the Internet. Most aspects of your system's networking configuration are set as part of the installation process for your Linux distribution, from detecting the type of Ethernet card that is present in your machine to configuring that card's network interface so that it works correctly on your local area network (LAN) or through your connection to the Internet via an Internet service provider (ISP).

Things always change in the computer world, which is especially true in the area of networking. You may switch ISPs, buy a new Ethernet card for your machine, want to integrate your system into a home or business LAN environment with a gateway to the Internet, or do other changes that will require modifying your system's networking configuration. For example, a common task when moving a machine from an ISP-based connection to a SOHO (small office, home office) LAN is reconfiguring it so that it uses a static IP address rather than getting its IP address via DHCP. Luckily, modifying the network configuration of a Linux machine is extremely easy. Chapter 7 discussed initial networking configuration. This chapter gives you the more detailed information that you need to understand how networking is configured on Linux systems and explains the networking configuration files that are used by every Linux distribution. Although different Linux distributions each provide their own graphical tools for configuring networking, all of these tools maintain and modify the same underlying text-format configuration files.

This chapter focuses on Linux networking using an Ethernet card and only touches upon using TCP/IP over a traditional telephone modem. Chapter 7 discussed configuring Point to Point Protocol (PPP) or Point to Point Protocol over Ethernet (PPPoE) connections to the Internet. This chapter focuses on reconfiguring existing Ethernet connections regardless of how they have been established.

Overview of the Linux TCP/IP System

Like support for any hardware device, the lowest-level support for networking in your Linux system is the device driver for your Ethernet card. This device driver must either be compiled into your Linux distribution's kernel or available as a loadable kernel module when you boot your system. The device driver knows how to send and receive packets using a transport-layer networking protocol such as TCP/IP. TCP/IP is just one of many networking protocols that can be used to move packets over Ethernet networks, but it is also the most important when using a wide area network (WAN) such as the Internet. TCP/IP is the transport layer for most of the higher-level networking protocols that are used directly by applications. Some common application-level networking protocols are the Server Message Block (SMB) and Common Internet File Services (CIFS) protocols used by Microsoft Windows systems and the HTTP protocol that forms the foundation of the Internet's best-known application, the World Wide Web.

TCP controls communication over the physical network, while IP controls higher-level issues such as *routing,* which is the term for forwarding network information from one network to another if the recipient is not on the same network segment as the one on which a network communication originates. For convenience' sake, I won't differentiate between TCP and IP throughout the rest of this chapter since their capabilities are generally thought of as a single unit today. This chapter also focuses on configuring interfaces for IP version 4 (IPv4), which is the most common version of the IP protocol used today. Most Linux systems also support IP version 6 (IPv6), which uses longer hexadecimal addresses to support a much larger set of Internet addresses. Nonetheless, almost all Internet configuration today is done via IPv4. (And you therefore don't have to learn hexadecimal notation — yet.)

TCP/IP hosts uniquely identify themselves through 32-bit numbers known as *IP addresses,* which are split up into four 8-bit numbers called *octets.* TCP/IP hosts therefore have address such as 192.168.6.64, often referred to as dotted-quad notation, because each of the four octets of the IP address is separated from the next by a period. Dotted-quad notation also uses decimal equivalents of the octal numbers for the convenience of those of us who don't think in octal.

IP addresses on the Internet are assigned to companies, government entities, and universities by a central authority, the Network Information Center (NIC). IP addresses are conceptually divided into a network number, contained in the leading octets, and a host number, contained in the remainder. The NIC hands out network numbers, in which you can then assign and use your own host numbers.

Network host number are divided into several common classes:

- **Class A networks** are the networks 1.0.0.0 through 127.0.0.0, where the network number is expressed in the first octet. Because only the first 24 bits are used for the network number, the rest can be used as host addresses, which enables Class A network providers to define approximately 1.6 million hosts. All of the 126 Class A network addresses have already been assigned by the NIC.

- **Class B networks** are the networks from 128.0.0.0 through 191.255.0.0, where the network number is expressed in the first two octets. There can therefore be up to 16,320 Class B networks, each with 65,024 hosts. Most of the Class B network addresses have already been assigned by the NIC.

- **Class C networks** are the networks from 192.0.0.0 through 223.255.255.0, where the network number is expressed in the first three octets. There can therefore be nearly two million networks, each of which can have up to 254 hosts. Most businesses, universities, and ISPs use Class C network addresses.

- **Class D, E, and F networks** fall into the range from 224.0.0.0 through 254.0.0.0, and are either experimental or are unused. These terms are therefore rarely used.

The final component of an IP address is a *netmask,* which is a 32-bit (4-octet) number that is used as a mask (through a logical OR operation) with your host's IP address to more finely divide the IP address into network and host parts. The zeroes in a netmask identify the host portion. For example, the standard netmask on most home or small business networks is 255.255.255.0, which means that 254 hosts are available because the host portion of the address will always be expressed in the last octet.

If you're sufficiently detail-oriented to have checked my math, you'll note that the quantities of hosts in the previous list and paragraph don't strictly add up. This is because host numbers that contain octets that include the value 0 or 255 are reserved for special purposes. An address where all of host part bits are zero refers to the network itself, while one where the host octet is 255 is known as a *broadcast address.* Broadcast addresses enable simultaneous communications to all hosts on a network segment.

Two network addresses on each host have special meaning to that host. The IP address 0.0.0.0 is known as the *default route;* this is the default address to which packets not intended for a host on the local network segment are sent for forwarding purposes. In reality, modern TCP/IP systems use another host, known as the *default gateway,* for forwarding packets to hosts that they can't directly contact on their network segment. The IP address 127.0.0.0 is known as the *loopback address,* which provides an internal mechanism for TCP/IP networking. The address 127.0.0.1 is usually assigned to the *loopback interface,* which enables each host to communicate with itself over the network without actually sending packets externally through an Ethernet interface.

IP addresses are logical entities, assigned to machines by system administrators. Each Ethernet card also has a unique physical address that uniquely identifies it in the known universe. These physical addresses, known as Media Access Control (MAC) addresses, are mapped to IP addresses using protocols known as Address Resolution Protocol (ARP) and Reverse Address Resolution Protocol (RARP). However, even IP addresses are inconvenient to remember; surely, eBay's network traffic numbers would suffer if everyone had to remember that www.ebay.com was 66.135.192.123.

Special Address Spaces for Private Networks

The TCP/IP addressing scheme also includes two ranges of IP addresses that are known as nonroutable IP addresses. These are the address spaces 192.168.0.0/16 and 10.0.0.0/8. All private networks without a connection to the Internet are free to use addresses in these ranges (basically 192.16.8.*.* and 10.0.0.*). TCP/IP communications from machines that use addresses in these ranges cannot be routed over the Internet. Using these special, nonroutable IP addresses makes it possible for businesses and SOHO networks to use valid IP addresses, without just using addresses at random that are actually officially in use on the Internet.

At this point, if your home, business, or academic network uses addresses in these families but still has Internet connectivity, you're probably wondering what the heck I'm talking about. Don't worry, we're both right — networks that use nonroutable IP addresses typically send packets bound for the Internet through a gateway system that knows how to map internal addresses to specially formed externally visible addresses using something called *Native Address Translation.* The upshot of this is that hosts on the Internet, and thus outside the gateway, think that your packets are coming from its valid Internet address, while the gateway keeps track of which internal host sent which packets and correctly forwards the packets to your internal host and IP address. Very cool indeed.

Name resolution is the technical term for the process of figuring out the human-readable name associated with a specific host and can be done in different ways on Linux systems. Many Linux hosts use a text file, /etc/hosts, to track IP addresses on small, local networks, but this quickly becomes impractical for identifying the IP addresses with hosts on medium-size networks and is out of the question on large networks such as the Internet. Almost all Linux systems therefore use a mechanism called the *domain name service* (DNS) to contact hosts known as *name servers* (or *DNS servers*).The name servers maintain a database of mappings between host names and IP addresses and know how to contact other domain name servers in the event that they can't identify the IP address for some specific host.

As you can see in the rest of this chapter, Linux provides some very simple, easy-to-use mechanisms for specifying your system's TCP/IP configuration and related information.

Networking from an Administrator's Perspective

As discussed in the previous section, the combination of physical MAC addresses, IP addresses, and DNS provides a powerful, flexible mechanism for identifying and contacting hosts on large networks such as the Internet. The key administrative aspects of configuring Linux networking consist of setting the Ethernet information for a specific host, identifying networking resources such as your system's default gateway and DNS servers, and controlling how your Linux system tries to look up host names and map them to IP addresses. Luckily, all Linux systems use the same underlying commands to specify this information, regardless of which distribution you've installed. These commands are automatically executed for you when you boot a Linux system, using network configuration information that is stored in a variety of text files on your Linux system.

Most of the network system administration tasks on Linux systems consist of correctly setting the values in these configuration files, which you can do using a text editor. Different Linux distributions store this information in different places. For example, systems running the Red Hat Enterprise Linux, Fedora Core, and SUSE Linux distributions systems store network interface configuration information in text files located under the directory /etc/sysconfig, but the specific files that are used differ between SUSE and the other distributions. The Ubuntu and Debian Linux distributions store their basic network configuration information in files in the directory /etc/network, the most important of which is /etc/network/interface. As you see later in this chapter, many Linux distributions also provide graphical tools to simplify setting, maintaining, and updating this information. This is not only convenient for the new system administrator or someone used to using graphical tools for system configuration, but also it conveniently hides the internal details of the underlying files used. Once you settle on a specific Linux distribution, you'll want to become one with the files that it uses for network configuration, but the casual or multidistribution Linux user can save a lot of time and trouble by simply using graphical tools for Linux network configuration and administration.

More general network configuration information, such as the addresses of DNS name servers and the sequence in which your system looks in different locations for host-to-IP address mappings, is specified in the same text-format configuration files on all Linux systems. The files that contain critical pieces of this information are the following:

■ **/etc/nsswitch.conf** defines the sequence in which your Linux system should consult various resources to obtain different types of system information, including how to map host names to IP addresses. See the next section for more information about the contents and organization of this file.

■ **/etc/resolv.conf** defines the name servers that your Linux system should use to map host names to IP addresses and the default network domain that your system should use for hosts that are specified by short names only (for example, ubuntu as opposed to ubuntu. vonhagen.org). See the section on this file later in this chapter for more information about its format and available keywords.

The next two sections provide more detail about each of these standard Linux files and their organization.

Lookup order in /etc/nsswitch.conf

The file /etc/nsswitch.conf is a text file that defines the order in which your system should look for various system-level information. The name of this file stands for *name service switch,* where *name service* is the general term for any identifier that is important to the system, whether it is a username, group name, host name, network name, and so on. A sample /etc/nsswitch.conf file from a SUSE Linux system is shown following:

```
#
# An example Name Service Switch config file..
#

passwd: compat
group:  compat

hosts:          files lwres dns
networks:       files dns

services:       files
protocols:      files
rpc:            files
ethers:         files
netmasks:       files
netgroup:       files
publickey:      files

bootparams:     files
automount:      files nis
aliases:        files
```

Lines in this file that begin with a hash mark (#) are comments that are ignored when your Linux system parses this file. Blank lines are also ignored.

For networking configuration, the most critical entry in this file is the `hosts` entry. The entries following the `hosts` keyword and a semicolon is the list of available services that should be consulted, in order, when trying to resolve a host name. These entries are the following:

▪ **files:** This keyword refers to the file `/etc/hosts`, which is a text file that usually contains information about the system you're using but can also define all of the host name to IP address mappings for small networks that don't need to run a local DNS server. A sample section of this file that defines the IP address for the fully qualified host `ubuntu.vonhagen.org` with the short name `ubuntu` is the following:

```
192.168.6.23              ubuntu.vonhagen.org           ubunut
```

▪ he `/etc/hosts` file on Linux systems serves the same function as the `\winnt\system32\drivers\etc\HOSTS` file in later versions of Microsoft Windows and is therefore similar to the `\winnt\system32\drivers\etc\LMHOSTS` file, which maps IP addresses to NetBIOS names.

▪ **lwres:** This keyword refers to lightweight directory access protocol (LDAP) servers that are available on your network.

▪ **dns:** This keyword refers to the DNS servers that are specified in the `/etc/resolv.conf` file, which is discussed in the next section.

Depending on how your Linux system creates this file during installation, you may want to check this file to make sure that it identifies the right resources in the right order. A common problem in this file is that it may not include references to network services such as DNS, which means that your system will be able to map names to IP addresses only for those hosts that are listed in your system's `/etc/hosts` file.

Like most programs and configuration files in Linux, online help on the contents and format of this file is available using the Linux `man` command: `man nsswitch.conf`.

Name resolution in /etc/resolv.conf

The size of most networks today makes it impractical to maintain text files that define the mapping of IP addresses to host names in the `/etc/hosts` file. This is especially true in the case of the Internet, where you can't easily determine the IP address for hosts that are not under your control. To eliminate this problem, the domain name service was introduced in the early 1980s. DNS is a hierarchical collection of systems that run a DNS server that can be queried for the IP address that corresponds to a given host name. This query is known as a *name lookup*. The hierarchical nature of DNS means that if your system contacts a DNS server that doesn't know the IP address for a specified host name, that DNS server knows how to contact higher-level, more authoritative DNS servers that either have the information that you're looking for or know how to contact others that do. The highest-level DNS servers for the Internet are known as the *root name servers*, because they are at the top, or root, of the DNS lookup hierarchy.

A sample /etc/resolv.conf file from one of my systems is shown following:

```
domain vonhagen.org
nameserver 207.44.142.94
nameserver 204.127.202.4
nameserver 216.148.237.68
nameserver 207.44.212.82
```

The first entry in this file uses the domain keyword to specify the default domain to use when looking up short host names, such as win2k, ubuntu, myserver, and so on. This entry prevents you from always having to specify the name of your local network. In this case, my default domain is vonhagen.org, which means that if I try to contact a host named myserver, the DNS system first attempts to locate the IP address for that name, and then automatically looks for the IP address for the host myserver.vonhagen.org.

The remaining entries in this file identify the IP addresses of different name servers that your system should contact when trying to map host names to IP addresses. These name servers are queried in order, and are identified by their IP address because your Linux system would otherwise have to try to use DNS to map names to IP addresses, which would present an interesting bootstrapping problem when trying to find the IP address of the first name server in this file.

Like most programs and configuration files in Linux, online help on the contents and format of this file is available using the Linux man command: man resolv.conf.

Using Graphical Network Managers

As mentioned previously, almost all Linux distributions today provide graphical tools for network configuration or reconfiguration. Fedora Core and Red Hat Enterprise Linux systems include the system-config-network application shown in Figure 19-1. Graphical network configuration tools are important to Linux users and system administrators because they hide distribution-specific aspects of network configuration, such as the specific text files that hold basic network configuration information and where they are located. This is especially important to new Linux users because each distribution uses different files, settings in those files, and so on. Trying to remember where each and every distribution stores network configuration information can be a headache; using graphical network administration and management tools removes this pain.

All graphical network configuration tools enable you to store the key information for network configuration that were discussed in the previous section:

- IP address

- Netmask

- Default gateway (sometime also referred to as routing)

Figure 19-1 shows the initial screen of the graphical system-config-network tool used in the Red Hat Enterprise Linux and Fedora Core distributions.

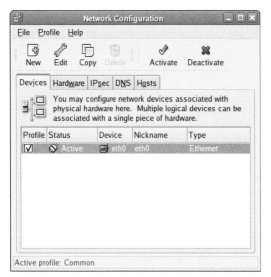

Figure 19-1: The system-config-network tool used by Fedora Core and Red Hat Enterprise Linux.

Selecting the Ethernet interface that you want to configure and clicking the Edit button displays the screen shown in Figure 19-2, where you can select between DHCP and static IP configuration and set the mandatory values for statically configuring an Ethernet interface.

Figure 19-2: Configuring a selected interface in the system-config-network tool.

Figure 19-3 shows the graphical network configuration tool that is provided by Novell's SUSE Linux. SUSE provides a single integrated suite of administrative tools known as YaST2 (Yet another System Tool), which provides separate modules for configuring system hardware, software, networking, installing and removing software, and so on. The screen shown in Figure 19-3 is the screen displayed after executing the command `yast2 lan` (for *local area network* configuration).

In SUSE's YaST2 tool, the default gateway information is provided on another screen and is referred to as Routing because the default gateway identifies the IP address through which any non-local network traffic should be directed. Figure 19-4 shows the YaST2 panel displayed when you click the Routing button shown in Figure 19-3. As you can see from this figure, SUSE's tool also enables you to do truly detailed network configuration, such as manually adding routing information to your SUSE system's routing table. This is something that you rarely (if ever) have to do, but it's nice to know that this capability is available in an easy-to-use graphical tool should you ever need it.

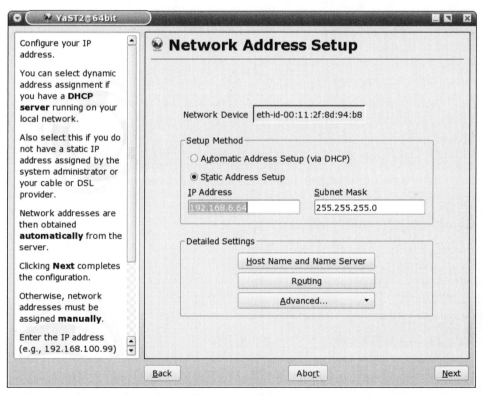

Figure 19-3: The network interface configuration module in SUSE's YaST2 administration tool.

Figure 19-5 shows the graphical network configuration tool provided by Ubuntu Linux, a relatively new but extremely popular Linux distribution based on Debian Linux and commanding a huge, helpful community of users.

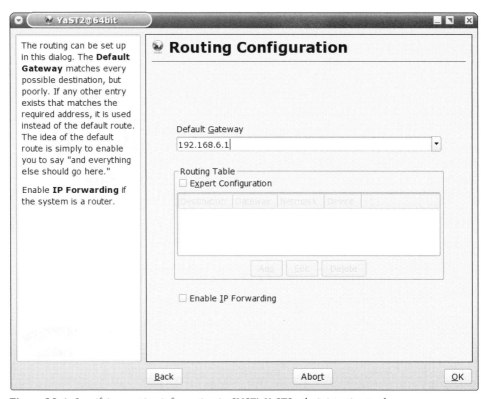

The routing can be set up in this dialog. The **Default Gateway** matches every possible destination, but poorly. If any other entry exists that matches the required address, it is used instead of the default route. The idea of the default route is simply to enable you to say "and everything else should go here."

Enable **IP Forwarding** if the system is a router.

Routing Configuration

Default Gateway

192.168.6.1

Routing Table
☐ Expert Configuration

Destination	Gateway	Netmask	Device

Add   Edit   Delete

☐ Enable IP Forwarding

Back   Abort   OK

Figure 19-4: Specifying routing information in SUSE's YaST2 administration tool.

Figure 19-5: Ubuntu's Network settings tool.

Given the popularity of networking nowadays, it's not unusual for computer systems to contain multiple Ethernet interfaces. After selecting the Ethernet interface that you want to configure and clicking the Properties button, Ubuntu's Network settings tool enables you to set the familiar values for that network interface, as shown in Figure 19-6.

Figure 19-6: Configuring a selected Ethernet interface in Ubuntu's Network settings tool.

Most Linux distributions provide their own graphical tools for network configuration, and some distributions, like Red Hat Enterprise Linux and Fedora Core, share the same tools. Moreover, every graphical Linux distribution provides graphical configuration tools. Manually configuring or updating an Ethernet interface on a Linux system is just as easy as it is on a Microsoft Windows or Apple Mac OS X system.

Configuring Network Settings from the Command Line

The previous section focused on the graphical tools that different Linux distributions provide in order to simplify network configuration. As mentioned in the beginning of this chapter, many Linux distributions store their network configuration information in different text files depending on how that distribution's startup sequence is implemented. However, regardless of the location in which this configuration information is stored, the underlying command-line commands that the system uses to apply this information are the same on every Linux distribution. If you want to preserve any manual changes that you've made across reboots of your system, you'll need to determine the names and locations of the files in which your distribution stores its network configuration information. The distribution-specific configuration files on popular Linux distributions are the following:

- **Debian/Ubuntu:** `/etc/network/interfaces` for interface-specific settings; `/etc/network/options` for general network configuration option settings

- **Fedora Core/Mandriva/Red Hat Enterprise Linux:** `/etc/sysconfig/network` for general networking settings; `/etc/sysconfig/network-scripts/ifcfg-eth0` for eth0; `/etc/wlan/wlan.conf` and `/etc/wlan/wlancfg-SSID` for wireless network card configuration

- **Gentoo:** `/etc/conf.d/net` for basic network card configuration for gateway and host with DHCP or static IP address; `/etc/conf.d/wireless` for wireless network card configuration

- **Novell Linux Desktop/SUSE:** `/etc/sysconfig/routes` for basic routing settings; `/etc/sysconfig/ifcfg-eth-id-??:MAC` for each interface

  (Novell Linux Desktop/SUSE interface configuration should really be done through YaST, as the latter file is confusing to name correctly.)

Knowing how to do network configuration from the command line is more than a quick way to demonstrate your Linux expertise; it also provides some advantages. Executing commands from the command line is much faster than going through a graphical user interface, and, because the underlying network configuration commands are the same on every Linux distribution, your knowledge is completely portable even when you switch Linux distributions, experiment with others, or are asked by a friend to help them straighten out networking on their system. You, too, can be a Linux wizard!

The core commands for networking configuration from the Linux command line are the `ifconfig` and `route` commands, which are explained in the next two sections.

Using the ifconfig command

The `ifconfig` (*interface configuration*) command is a key Linux administration command with its roots in the Unix command with the same name. The `ifconfig` command enables you to query and configure the state of all of the Ethernet interfaces on your system. A command with a similar name, `ipconfig`, is even provided on Windows systems as a command-line tool for network interface examination and configuration (though its syntax is, of course, different).

The most common use of the `ifconfig` command is to quickly query the state of one or all of the IP interfaces on your system. To get information about the current configuration and state of an Ethernet interface, execute the command `ifconfig interface-name`, where `interface-name` is the short name of the Ethernet interface that you want information about. The following example shows how to use the `ifconfig eth0` command to get information about the primary Ethernet interface on most Linux systems:

```
$ ifconfig eth0
eth0      Link encap:Ethernet  HWaddr 00:11:2F:8D:94:B8
          inet addr:192.168.6.64  Bcast:192.168.6.255  Mask:255.255.255.0
          inet6 addr: fe80::211:2fff:fe8d:94b8/64 Scope:Link
          UP BROADCAST RUNNING MULTICAST  MTU:1500  Metric:1
          RX packets:60606330 errors:0 dropped:0 overruns:0 frame:0
```

```
TX packets:85300243 errors:0 dropped:0 overruns:0 carrier:0
collisions:0 txqueuelen:1000
RX bytes:4194689406 (4000.3 Mb)  TX bytes:2156037797 (2056.1 Mb)
Interrupt:193 Memory:f7c00000-0
```

From this (somewhat verbose) output, you can see that Ethernet interface eth0 has the hardware (MAC) address 00:11:2F:8D:94:B8, has the IP address 192.168.6.64, that its netmask 255.255.255.0 is active (UP), and that it has successfully received (RX) and transmitted (TX) over fifty million packets successfully. At least I'm getting my money's worth out of my ISP!

Note

For information about the other fields in the output of the ifconfig command, see the online reference information for this command, which is available by executing the man ifconfig command from a Linux shell or terminal session.

To set information for an Ethernet interface you must do the following: You must execute the command ifconfig as root or via the sudo command. You must specify the short name of the Ethernet interface that you want to configure, the IP address that you want to associate with it, and the netmask keyword for this interface's IP address. You must state that you want to make the interface active (UP), as shown in the following example:

```
# ifconfig eth0 192.168.6.64 netmask 255.255.255.0 up
```

Like many Linux commands and general business activities, the absence of complaint indicates success. If you don't see an error message, the command has executed correctly, and your Ethernet interface is configured as requested.

Using the route command

The route command enables you to examine and modify the kernel's IP routing table, as shown in the following example:

```
$ route
Kernel IP routing table
Destination     Gateway         Genmask         Flags Metric Ref    Use Iface
192.168.6.0     *               255.255.255.0   U         0   0
0 eth0
link-local      *               255.255.0.0           U        0        0
0 eth0
loopback        *               255.0.0.0             U        0        0
0 lo
default         192.168.6.1     0.0.0.0               UG      0       0
 eth0
```

The most significant entries in the routing table are the entries for local network traffic and the entry for your system's default gateway, as identified in the `Destination` column in the output of the `route` command. The routing for network traffic to your local network is identified by an entry with the same first three octets as your local network, but with a zero in the fourth octet. In the example above, the entry for local network routing (`192.168.6.0`) says that the kernel routes all traffic to the local network through the system's `eth0` interface. Similarly, any traffic to hosts that are not on the local network segment, identified as `default` routing, is sent to the `Gateway` system `192.168.6.1` through the same Ethernet interface, `eth0`. A Linux system's default gateway is always identified by the presence of the `G` entry in the `Flags` column for that entry.

You will rarely need to change the system's routing table because this is configured automatically for you when your system boots using the information in your system's network configuration files. However, if you modify your system's IP address while the system is running or your local system administrator changes the configuration of your network, you may need to update the routing table. Typically, you would do this by using the system's graphical network configuration tools to modify your default settings and then reboot your system, but you can also do this by executing the `route del` command to delete an existing routing table entry and then using the `route add` command to add a new entry to the kernel routing table. You must execute these commands as the root user or via the `sudo` command because you are actually modifying data that is stored in the running Linux kernel. This is not something that an unprivileged user should be able to do!

For example, to change my system's routing table so that default traffic is now routed through the local IP address `192.168.6.66`, I would execute the following commands:

```
# route del default
# route add default gw 192.168.6.66
```

The first command deletes the current default route, and the second command sets the new default gateway to the IP address `192.168.6.66`. As mentioned previously, this is something that you would rarely, if ever, need to do, but it's nice to know that your Linux system provides the power to make these system-level changes quickly, by executing a few simple commands.

Note

If you change IP addresses on one of your systems and your network (or computer system) implements a firewall based on IP addresses, you may need to modify the configuration of your firewall (or at least restart it) to ensure that external network communication is working correctly. While this is especially true if you move systems from one network to another, it can still be significant when simply assigning a new IP address on the same network segment

Summary

Linux systems often have a bad rep as far as system administration and configuration go, especially in the area of network configuration. The people who propagate these fictions are people who haven't seen or used a Linux system recently. Today's Linux distributions provide graphical network configuration tools that are every bit the equal of the graphical configuration utilities provided on more common computer operating systems such as Microsoft Windows or Apple's Mac OS X.

Interestingly enough, both Windows and OS X also provide command-line configuration tools for network interfaces and routing — but few people know about or use them. The high quality and ease of use provided by the graphical network configuration tools in today's Linux distributions are rapidly helping to eclipse the use of the command-line tools and continue to make it easier than ever to use a Linux system.

Chapter 20

Linux Security Solutions

Although Linux is developed around an ideal of sharing and trust, the world is not always that kind. In this chapter you take a look at the various types of threats to your identity, data, and property and then review some practical steps you can take to neutralize them. The chapter includes extensive coverage of GNU Privacy Guard, an application that provides industrial-strength encryption for data. Finally, I cover some resources for learning more about security issues.

Note

Hacker or cracker? In the Linux community the title hacker is a mark of respect. A *hacker* is a person of great skill and arcane knowledge who can bend computers to his mighty will and make them do clever things undreamt of by their designers. In mainstream culture, a hacker is an evil villain who uses his technical prowess to steal or vandalize things. The real hackers are rather annoyed by this misuse of a noble word and have suggested using *cracker* to describe a malicious person who breaks into computers. But alas, the mainstream definition has become too firmly entrenched, so I use hacker to describe a bad guy in the rest of this chapter, albeit with a sigh and a wistful glance towards the true meaning of the word.

Security Threats

Many nasty things can happen to your system. You can categorize these into five broad areas:

- **Programming errors:** Programmers sometimes make mistakes that can be exploited by hackers. A common example of this is called a buffer overflow. Though buffer overflows can occur in programs written in other languages too, they are usually caused by a deficiency in C, which is the most popular language for coding Linux applications. A C program accepting input has to create a buffer of a fixed length to hold it. If the programmer does not carefully check the length of the input, it can overflow into other parts of memory, corrupting them. A hacker who knew a program was vulnerable could create special input guaranteed to overflow and containing code that bypasses system checks and does something malicious.

Viruses, worms, and trojans: The average Windows user is sadly all too familiar with what is collectively known as *malware* — harmful and unwanted programs that insert themselves into your system and range from the merely annoying to downright destructive. Is this really a problem for Linux users? Linux advocates say it isn't, but security experts don't rule out the possibility of Linux malware. Undoubtedly the bad guys will try harder to target Linux as it becomes more popular with the mainstream, but the chances of their succeeding are unlikely. The Linux permissions model means that programs cannot run unless they have been made executable first. Also, because running software under the `root` account is strongly discouraged, malware that somehow manages to get executed could at the most destroy one user's data, not the whole system. (Admittedly, that could still be quite a bad problem if the data is not backed up.)

Eavesdropping: Because most Internet protocols use plain text it is possible for someone who has access to the wires or routers that form your physical Internet connection to capture data as it whizzes past. If he can recover passwords or other sensitive information, it could spell disaster. The situation has become even worse with the popularity of wireless networks. Now you don't even need to do a wiretap to invade someone's bandwidth; an antenna and some simple software will do.

Spam: Unsolicited e-mail or spam is not so much a threat as an annoyance, but it is a relevant topic when discussing security. The task of using e-mail can be quite unpleasant if you have to wade through piles of junk to get to relevant messages. E-mail can also be used as a vehicle for malware.

Spammers have automated programs that trawl through the Internet looking for e-mail addresses to harvest. Other spammers pay good money to buy addresses that are known to belong to working accounts.

Another danger from spammers is on systems that have badly configured mail server software installed. Such servers can be hijacked and used to send out spam, possibly leading to the termination of your Internet service, the blacklisting of your mail server by other mail server administrators, and losses to your reputation because it will look like the spam came from you.

Other people: The most common security threats come not from strangers but from people you know. They may not intend to be malicious but could be dangerous anyway. A user might want to delete some of his files but accidentally delete some of yours instead. A bored system administrator might decide to while away the boring hours of the night shift by reading your e-mail. (This is considered highly unethical by professional system administrators.) Or your teenager could decide to use your account to do a little online shopping.

Social engineering is the age-old confidence trick where some smooth talker gets a gullible person to give him something valuable he shouldn't have, only instead of money or jewels, it's passwords or corporate secrets that he is after. All the security measures in the world mean nothing if you just allow a hacker to walk in through the front door.

Security Best Practices

Paranoid yet? Luckily, you can defend yourself against or at least mitigate the threats mentioned here. In this section, I go over some of the steps you should take.

Secure physical access to the system

Your efforts at security can easily be bypassed if a miscreant can reboot the system and start it up again from a Knoppix live CD. If your computer has a BIOS password option, use it. Configure the boot loader (see Chapter 4) to ask for a password. Keep the system in a locked room or at least out of the path of the public.

Use a firewall

Your first line of defense against attacks coming from across the network should be a *firewall*, a program that filters incoming network traffic. If you have a broadband connection to the Internet (cable modem or DSL) or a wireless router, the chances are you already have a hardware firewall. If you don't, no need to worry because Linux has powerful built-in firewall capabilities. (Setting up a Linux firewall is a must if you have a laptop you take out on the road.)

You are asked if you want to set up a firewall during the installation of most Linux distributions. Figure 20-1 shows an example from Fedora Core 4.

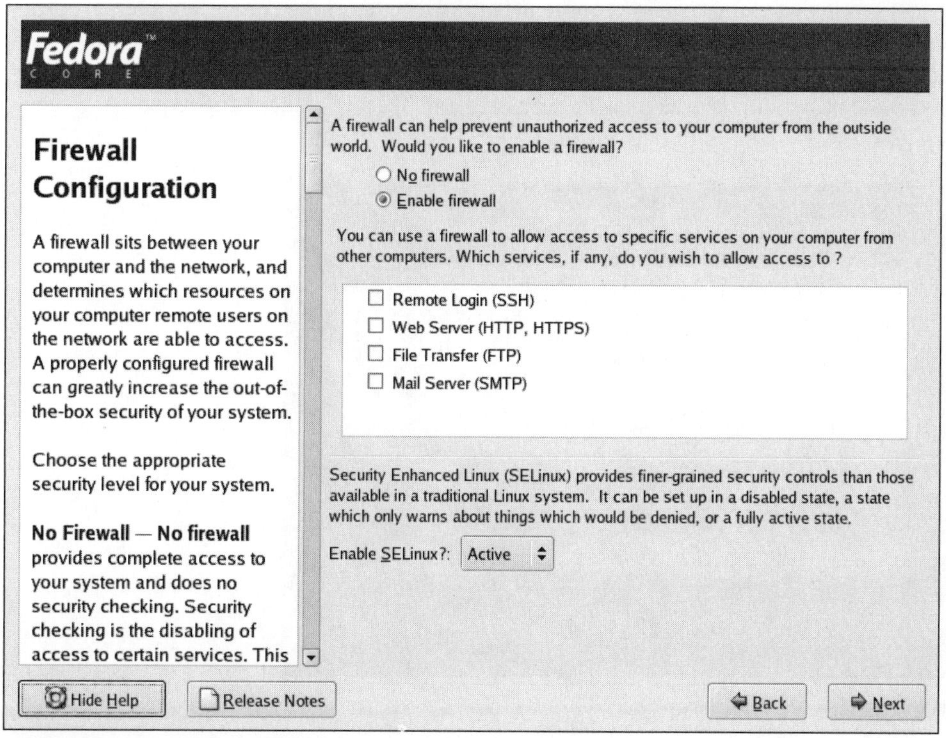

Figure 20-1: Firewall configuration dialog.

It's pretty straightforward. Just select Enable firewall and you're done. You can initiate network connections from your system to the outside world, but all incoming connections will be blocked. However, if your computer is running some kind of server software, it means that access to your server will be blocked too. So, the dialog allows you to make holes in the firewall for specific services. If you are running a mail, FTP, or Web server, check the appropriate box. I also recommend that everyone who needs to access their computer remotely check the box for Remote Login (SSH), for reasons explained later in this chapter.

The Enable SELinux option is very interesting but not yet widely used. Security Enhanced Linux (SELinux) is a new feature in Linux developed by the top-secret spies of the National Security Agency (NSA); it has the potential to revolutionize the Linux security architecture. Instead of one omnipotent `root` account with the power to access everything, power is shared between *roles* with sharply defined abilities. It's still quite new and not that widely used except in Fedora, which has championed it from the beginning. I would advise new users to enable the feature and then forget about it for the time being. Fedora does a good job of hiding all the details of SELinux behind the scenes in most simple cases.

If you didn't set up the firewall during installation or you want to go back and change something, you can run the `system-config-securitylevel` program. It comes in two flavors, a text mode and a graphical version. Figure 20-2 shows the text version.

Pressing the Customize button takes you to the screen shown in Figure 20-3.

This screen gives you the rest of the options from the installer and a few more besides. The first option is the entry for Trusted Devices. I have only one network interface in my PC, called `eth0`, but if there had been more, there would be checkboxes for each of them. Typically, a machine with multiple interfaces is one that connects two or more networks together; for example, an internal corporate network and the public Internet. By designating an interface as *trusted,* you effectively turn off the firewall for it. In this way you can still keep the firewall for the big, bad outside world and designate the corporate-facing interface as trusted, bypassing any filtering of incoming requests.

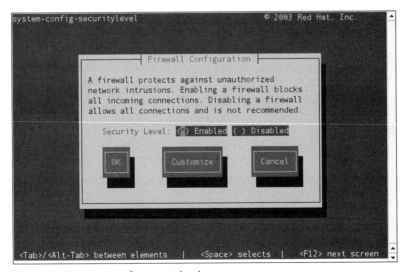

Figure 20-2: system-config-securitylevel.

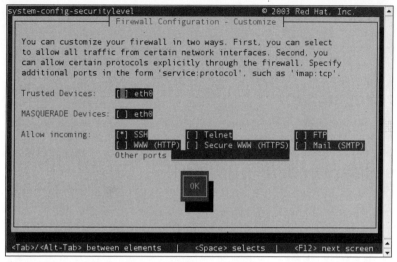

Figure 20-3: system-config-securitylevel customization.

The next option is for IP masquerading, and, like the trusted interface option, it can be applied on an interface-by-interface basis. This disguises the origin of a network packet passing through so it looks like it is coming from the masqueraded interface, not its real origin. This is typically used in scenarios where you have many computers sharing one IP address. You can give each one a local nonroutable IP address (as explained in Chapter 7) and have them all look to the outside world as if they had the real IP address.

The next few options are for making holes in the firewall for various services. Telnet is offered as a choice. Never select it. You always want to use SSH instead. WWW and secure WWW are made separate choices, but other than that, the options are the same as with the default installation.

Last, there is an entry called Other Ports that enables you to allow custom services through the firewall. As the instructions say, you specify them in the form `service:protocol`.

Note

How do you know what the name and protocol for a service are? See the discussion of the `/etc/services` file in the "Uninstall services you don't need" section of this chapter for details.

Back up regularly

Chapter 14 discusses backups in detail. Apart from the obvious advantages of having an extra copy of your data available if something goes wrong, having backups is good idea from a security point of view because if you suspect your system has been tampered with, you can compare it to a backup to check whether anything has changed.

Remember to make sure the place your backup media is stored is also physically secured.

Don't use the superuser account

It's been said elsewhere in this book, but it bears repeating: Don't use the `root` account for anything more than essential system administration tasks. Have mail for root forwarded to an ordinary user account and read it and do other everyday tasks from there.

Don't make files executable

Don't change the permissions on unknown files to make them executable unless you know exactly what they do. Never, under any circumstances, make such files `setuid` or `setgid`. (See Chapter 13.)

Use permissions and ownership

Make full use of Linux's permissions and ownership system. This stops other users from being able to read (or delete) your files. For every task that requires special handling, create a separate user account and make sure any automated scripts or executables it uses run as that user.

Log out or use a screensaver

A simple but effective technique for maintaining security is to log out when you are finished. If you can't or you keep forgetting, the next best thing is a screensaver that locks the screen and reenables it only after you reenter your password.

Use SSH rather than Telnet for remote access

Telnet is a program that lets you log in to another computer and work on it remotely in text mode. Telnet is one of the oldest network applications; it's actually even older than the Internet. However, it has the fatal flaw that it transmits and receives everything in plain text. As I mention earlier in this chapter, this leaves the door open for eavesdroppers. Luckily, there is another program, Secure Shell (SSH) that does the same thing but encrypts communications. Fedora uses an open source implementation of SSH called openssh. It is split into two RPM packages for flexibility in installation: `openssh-clients`, which you need to access other computers, and `openssh-server`, if you want other people to be able to access yours. (In that case, remember to allow incoming SSH to pass through your firewall.)

You can improve security with SSH by doing away with passwords altogether. Instead SSH uses cryptographic keys to determine that you are who you say you are. Start by changing to the `.ssh` subdirectory of your home directory and running the `ssh-keygen` program to create a key:

```
$ cd ~/.ssh
$ ssh-keygen -t dsa -f id_dsa
```

When prompted by `ssh-keygen` to enter a password, just press Enter. What the program is doing is creating two files encrypted with the DSA cipher. (Other ciphers are available, but this is the recommended choice.) The `id_dsa` is the private key, which you keep secret on your computer. The other, `id_dsa.pub`, is the public key. The public key can be placed on a remote computer you wish to access. Make a directory called .ssh in your home directory on the remote server if it doesn't exist already. Copy id_dsa.pub into a file called authorized_keys2 in that directory. (The 2 signifies it is the location for DSA keys. The authorized_keys file is used to store keys using other ciphers.) The authorized keys2 file can store multiple public keys if you want access from several different machines.

```
$ cd ~/.ssh
$ scp your.local.pc:~/.ssh/id_dsa.pub .
$ cat id_dsa.pub >> authorized_keys2
```

Make sure the permissions on the .ssh directory and authorized_keys2 keys are tight so they cannot be tampered with, and delete the id_dsa.pub file now that you don't need it anymore.

```
$ chmod 700 ~/.ssh
$ chmod 640 ~/.ssh/authorized_keys2
$ rm ~/.ssh/id_dsa.pub
```

Now back to your local computer. When you make an SSH connection to the remote computer, the public and private keys are compared, and if they match, you are logged in. Once you have SSH set up correctly, you should never use Telnet again.

Prefer encrypted versions of other protocols

Secure protocols typically use either Secure Sockets Layer (SSL) or Transport Layer Security (TLS). They require the use of a digital certificate, which is a special file digitally signed by some trustworthy organization (called a certification authority) and which establishes your server's identity.

You can act as your own certification authority with scripts included in the openssl package. The trouble with such self-signed certificates is that most software will raise a red flag and ask the user if he really wants to trust it before continuing. Smarter programs will ask only once, but some will ask with every connection. If that's tolerable for you, self-signed certificates are an option. Otherwise, you can buy a commercial certificate from vendors such as Verisign (www.verisign.com/).

Nowadays, most plain text Internet protocols also have versions that use encryption, and you should use them whenever possible.

- openssh comes with programs called scp and sftp, which can replace FTP.

- All the common mail servers support SMTP over SSL/TLS (smtps). (Note you still need to allow plain SMTP access in order to receive mail from the vast majority of servers that don't speak smtps.)

- Most IMAP servers support IMAP over SSL/TLS (imaps).

- Apache and other Web servers support HTTP over SSL/TLS (https.) Using https is a must if you want to do e-commerce.

Cross-Reference

For a good introduction to the theory and practice of public key cryptography, see the article on the subject in the online encyclopedia Wikipedia (`http://en.wikipedia.org/wiki/Public_key_cryptography`). A tutorial with a focus on secure messaging can be found at `www.opengroup.org/messaging/G260/pki_tutorial.htm`. Another good tutorial from Verisign, a leading vendor of digital certificates, is at `www.verisign.com.au/repository/tutorial/digital/intro1.shtml`.

Prefer open source software

The cure for buffer overflows and other programming errors is for programs to be written perfectly — which is easier said than done. Open source software has an important advantage over proprietary software in this regard. Because the source code of a typical Linux program is available for all to see, many more programmers are looking at it, and this increases the chance of a programming error being noticed. Having noticed such errors, the open source community doesn't have to wait for a vendor to create a fix. They are free to create a fix themselves and distribute it to anyone who wants it. Therefore, even if open source software doesn't start out perfect, it tends to improve greatly over time.

So, if you have a choice between installing proprietary software or its open source equivalent, pick the latter.

Install from source

Given the choice between an application that is distributed in binary format (even though open source) and as source code — particularly when the application comes from some unfamiliar place — people who are serious about security prefer source code. This way they can check to make sure it doesn't contain any hidden surprises. This is more practical for users who have experience in programming, which unfortunately excludes most of the public. However, once you become familiar with Linux and are ready for a new challenge, learning how to compile and install programs from source is a useful skill to acquire.

Keep up with patches and upgrades from your distribution

The developers of each Linux distribution regularly update software included in the distribution as security problems are discovered. After installation, your first task should be to install all the security updates that have accumulated since your distribution was released. After that, you should check regularly for new updates. The default setup of the GNOME desktop in Fedora includes an applet that notifies you if new updates are available. Chapter 15 explains how to install these updates using the `rpm` and `up2date` commands.

Fedora also has a read-only mailing list for announcements of security updates and other useful news called `fedora-announce-list`, which is an important resource for the system administrator. You can subscribe to it at `www.redhat.com/mailman/listinfo/fedora-announce-list`. This is what a typical security advisory looks like:

```
From: "Dave Jones" <davej@redhat.com>
```

```
To: fedora-announce-list@redhat.com
Subject: [SECURITY] Fedora Core 4 Update: kernel-2.6.13-1.1532_FC4
```

The subject contains the tag [SECURITY] if it is a security advisory, so you can use that tag to filter it to higher priority in your e-mail. Following the tag is the version of Fedora the update applies to and the name of the package.

Here follows a unique reference for the update:

```
Date: Thu, 20 Oct 2005 14:09:15 -0400


------------------------------------------------------------------

Fedora Update Notification
FEDORA-2005-1013
```

Use this in any discussion about the update.

The first part of the advisory gives a quick abstract of the package:

```
2005-10-20
------------------------------------------------------------------


Product      : Fedora Core 4
Name         : kernel
Version      : 2.6.13
Release      : 1.1532_FC4
Summary      : The Linux kernel (the core of the Linux operating system)
Description :
The kernel package contains the Linux kernel (vmlinuz), the core of any
Linux operating system.  The kernel handles the basic functions
of the operating system:  memory allocation, process allocation, device
input and output, etc.


------------------------------------------------------------------
```

The main part of the advisory is a changelog for the package so you know which problems have been fixed in this update:

```
* Wed Oct 19 2005 Dave Jones <davej@redhat com> [2.6.13-1.1532_FC4]
- Fix CAN-2005-2973 (ipv6 infinite loop)
- Disable ACPI burst again, it's still problematic.
- Update to the final upstream variant of the IDE/SATA fix.

* Sun Oct 16 2005 Dave Jones <davej@redhat com> [2.6.13-1.1531_FC4]
- Stop IDE claiming legacy ports before libata in combined mode.

* Sun Oct 16 2005 Dave Jones <davej@redhat com> [2.6.13-1.1530_FC4]
```

```
  - Enable ACPI EC burst.
  - Reenable change of timesource default.

* Tue Oct 11 2005 Dave Jones <davej@redhat com> [2.6.13-1.1529_FC4]
- 2.6.13.4

* Thu Oct  6 2005 Dave Jones <davej@redhat com>
- Fix information leak in orinoco driver.

* Wed Oct  5 2005 Dave Jones <davej@redhat com>
- Further fixing to the 8139too suspend/resume problem.

* Mon Oct  3 2005 Dave Jones <davej redhat com> [2.6.13-1.1528_FC4]
- 2.6.13.3

* Sun Oct  2 2005 Dave Jones <davej@redhat com> [2.6.13-1.1527_FC4]
- Disable debug messages in w83781d sensor driver. (#169695)
- Re-add a bunch of patches that got accidentally dropped in last
update.
  - Fix suspend/resume with 8139too
  - Fix usbhid/wireless security lock clash (#147479)
  - Missing check condition in ide scsi (#160868)
  - Fix nosense error with transcend usb keys (#162559)
  - Fix sk98lin vpd problem. (#136158)
- Fix IDE floppy eject. (#158548)

* Fri Sep 30 2005 Dave Jones <davej@redhat com>
- irda-driver smsc-ircc2 needs pnp-functionality. (#153970)
- Reenable /proc/acpi/sleep (#169650)
- Silence some selinux messages. (#167852)
```

The numbers in parentheses, like #169695, are tracking numbers in Fedora's bug tracking system, Bugzilla. You can access Bugzilla at `https://bugzilla.redhat.com/bugzilla/index.cgi`.

References like `CAN-2005-2973` are candidates for inclusion in the Common Vulnerabilities and Exposures (CVE) list. Like the `FEDORA-2005-1013` number, this reference number is a way of standardizing references to security issues. The difference is that CVEs are cross-distribution, indeed cross–operating system, and they are assigned per problem rather than per package. The CVE list is managed by the Common Vulnerabilities and Exposures Project (`www.cve.mitre.org/`) sponsored by the U.S. government's Department of Homeland Security. A very recent change was made to the system. Previously `CAN` was used as the prefix for suspected problems still under investigation and `CVE` for confirmed problems. As of October 19, 2005, `CVE` is used as the prefix for both types of advisory.

The Web site for the CVE list describes it as a *dictionary of vulnerabilities*, not a database. A related government program, the National Vulnerability Database (`http://nvd.nist.gov/`), provides a more convenient interface to CVE and other public security vulnerability resources.

```
---------------------------------------------------------------------
This update can be downloaded from:
   http://download.fedora.redhat.com/pub/fedora/linux/core/updates/4/


0f7703b95fb10eea8ba98fe867b82420   SRPMS/kernel-2.6.13-1.1532_FC4.src.rpm
7e3ad0a0e7a6e37cbae3776000e11c33   ppc/kernel-2.6.13-1.1532_FC4.ppc.rpm
3f2a8e75dac0cec3c90b034d7383611c   ppc/kernel-devel-2.6.13-1.1532_FC4.ppc.rpm
d19ec852ccbc3690abf31d9c9c6a9760   ppc/kernel-smp-2.6.13-1.1532_FC4.ppc.rpm
062795f1071ac14c3be8550a8dea7da1   ppc/kernel-smp-devel-2.6.13-1.1532_FC4.ppc.rpm
155ef19342f4e6a2f7101571d94a806b   ppc/debug/kernel-debuginfo-2.6.13-
1.1532_FC4.ppc.rpm
7a6512ba50c89027f29f9ee6287b0c52   ppc/kernel-2.6.13-1.1532_FC4.ppc64.rpm
de5f9dbd2f92c109e6716f0be46ee927   ppc/kernel-devel-2.6.13-1.1532_FC4.ppc64.rpm
927afe801c27c63b978b56301874741e   x86_64/kernel-2.6.13-1.1532_FC4.x86_64.rpm
39e31c3cd1e3d1fc0ac5d28883b4bc08   x86_64/kernel-devel-2.6.13-
1.1532_FC4.x86_64.rpm
7fb1e1c29c22272094f69f91698b3445   x86_64/kernel-smp-2.6.13-1.1532_FC4.x86_64.rpm
5f6ba16565169dd9c20273a0ce834b1b   x86_64/kernel-smp-devel-2.6.13-
1.1532_FC4.x86_64.rpm
14c9b85f3373eb754d2611a450eff2ef   x86_64/debug/kernel-debuginfo-2.6.13-
1.1532_FC4.x86_64.rpm
cfe12770e33239b793e4546f773d1c0a   x86_64/kernel-doc-2.6.13-1.1532_FC4.noarch.rpm
e69850944046a4d0e3ebca7e9e5733ad   i386/kernel-2.6.13-1.1532_FC4.i586.rpm
e1bf283bb61abfbf567ea9580020cda5   i386/kernel-devel-2.6.13-1.1532_FC4.i586.rpm
e1e6f867ff5f53b084c00cb5bc4bcba0   i386/debug/kernel-debuginfo-2.6.13-
1.1532_FC4.i586.rpm
02b9690c11f38be3b2b524c22d975812   i386/kernel-2.6.13-1.1532_FC4.i686.rpm
2da650f41f0f5cfa360a447f8d81f676   i386/kernel-devel-2.6.13-1.1532_FC4.i686.rpm
756af7f9309326f6ee1535feb9a67ff2   i386/kernel-smp-2.6.13-1.1532_FC4.i686.rpm
4a3027b0eb9aa06447d64f12c63af92b   i386/kernel-smp-devel-2.6.13-
1.1532_FC4.i686.rpm
5bbf11f714cda26731276905919e9d95   i386/kernel-xen0-2.6.13-1.1532_FC4.i686.rpm
d69f77d7176ba9d8f8d4950bcf1160df   i386/kernel-xen0-devel-2.6.13-
1.1532_FC4.i686.rpm
ac59450e8d94759a27c3e3b4a3ee5284   i386/kernel-xenU-2.6.13-1.1532_FC4.i686.rpm
73ed6e93745c5a45133e00de78606a53   i386/kernel-xenU-devel-2.6.13-
1.1532_FC4.i686.rpm
835e768c70b2469e828a2086cdca588b   i386/debug/kernel-debuginfo-2.6.13-
1.1532_FC4.i686.rpm
cfe12770e33239b793e4546f773d1c0a   i386/kernel-doc-2.6.13-1.1532_FC4.noarch.rpm


This update can also be installed with the Update Agent; you can
launch the Update Agent with the 'up2date' command.
---------------------------------------------------------------------
```

The rest of the advisory consists of file names for the updated packages along with md5sums, which allow you to check whether the package has been tampered with. This is detailed in the next section of this chapter.

In the information arms race between hackers and users, using tools such as vendor security lists, bugtracking systems, CVE, and NVD is vital for making sure you stay ahead of the game.

Check for tampering with checksums

How do you know the software you downloaded is actually what the author uploaded? FTP sites and Web servers can be hacked and their contents replaced by seemingly legitimate copies that contain viruses or trojans. Luckily, mathematics can come to the rescue. There are certain mathematical algorithms that can be applied to each byte of a file to create a checksum — a long number that creates a unique signature for the file. If even one byte of the file is changed, the checksum changes to an entirely different number. By publishing the checksum for the correct file in some secure location, a vendor can give users a way to verify the integrity of their downloads.

A popular algorithm for checksums is called MD5. When applied to a file, it produces a 128-bit checksum (usually displayed as 32 hexadecimal digits for brevity) that is often referred to as an *md5sum*. You can check md5sums on the command line with a program also called `md5sum`. Assume you downloaded the updated kernel `kernel-2.6.13-1.1532_FC4.i586.rpm` mentioned in the previous section and you want to check its md5sum. You would do this:

```
$ md5sum kernel-2.6.13-1.1532_FC4.i586.rpm
e69850944046a4d0e3ebca7e9e5733ad  kernel-2.6.13-1.1532_FC4.i586.rpm
```

As you can see from the advisory, this is indeed the correct md5sum so you can trust that the file has not been tampered with.

There is another checksum algorithm called SHA1, which is in use though it is not as popular as MD5. A command-line program called `sha1sum` lets you verify SHA1 checksums in the same way as `md5sum`.

Check for tampering with rpm

You can also use `rpm` to verify the integrity of an installed file with the `-V` (*verify*) option. Say you want to verify `/bin/cat`:

```
$ rpm -Vf /bin/cat
$
```

Well, that wasn't very informative was it? Due to what I consider a bad design decision by the developers of `rpm`, a file that passes all verification tests doesn't give any output. Had this file actually been changed (I edited the `/bin/cat` binary myself) you would have got output like this:

```
$ rpm -Vf /bin/cat
S.5....T. /bin/cat
```

This time there is feedback showing which tests have failed. The possible values here are:

S = The size of the file has changed.

M = The file's permissions have changed.

5 = The md5sum has changed. Unfortunately, while rpm stores md5sums and can check them, it doesn't have an option to display it. Another bad design decision!

L = The file is a symlink, which has changed to point to a different file. This test will fail even if the symlink is deleted and recreated pointing to the same file.

D = The file represents a device, and its device number has changed. This could mean it is now pointing to a different piece of hardware with potentially disastrous consequences.

U = The file's user ownership has changed. Be very suspicious if this was a setuid program.

G = The file's group ownership has changed. Again, be very suspicious if this was a setgid program.

C = The file's creation time has changed. This means either that the file didn't exist before and has been created or that the original file was deleted and a new one created with the same name.

T = The file's modification time has changed.

Failure in some of these tests does not necessarily mean you've been hacked. Configuration files such as /etc/passwd are almost certain to have changed. rpm -V puts a c before the name of a file it considers to be a configuration file. It is possible for other files to fail a test for innocuous reasons too, so don't blindly trust the results of this command. Rather, use it as a basis for identifying files that need to be investigated in more detail.

You can verify all the files on your computer with the -a option. This is likely to be a huge list, so you will want to save the results into a file to read at your leisure.

```
$ rpm -Va > files_on_my_system.txt
```

Actually, the list won't include quite *all* the files on your system. rpm -Va excludes the following:

- Files that were not installed using the rpm package manager or front ends to it like yum or up2date, including files installed by third-party packages and files you installed yourself

- Files that were autogenerated by the package when it was installed

- Files created by the package after installation

  (For instance, if you install a word processor, the documents you write with it are not recorded in rpm -V's database.)

rpm -v is not perfect, but it can be a useful audit tool; so, I recommend you use it.

Uninstall services you don't need

In order to attack your system there has to be some kind of entry point a hacker can exploit. Your firewall will do a good job of blocking any attempts at intrusion, but it may not be foolproof. If there is nothing there, however, for a hacker to actually hack, you can guarantee no intrusion will occur. So, it is a good idea to deactivate any outside-connecting service you aren't using.

How do you know what's actually listening on your computer? The `netstat` command, as its name suggests, gives you information about the status of the Linux kernel's networking features. Before proceeding, you might want to reread the overview of the networking system in Chapter 7 as you will be using some of the concepts introduced there. When you are ready, type this command:

```
$ netstat -l-A inet -v
```

The `-l` option to `netstat` says display information for only those programs listening for connections. `-A inet` means list all the programs using the Internet low-level networking protocols, Transmission Control Protocol (TCP), User Datagram Protocol (UDP), and raw sockets. This is the output from my computer; yours will probably be a little different.

```
Active Internet connections (only servers)
Proto Recv-Q Send-Q Local Address           Foreign Address         State
tcp        0      0 *:sunrpc                *:*                     LISTEN
tcp        0      0 localhost.localdomain:ipp   *:*                 LISTEN
tcp        0      0 localhost.localdomain:5335  *:*                 LISTEN
tcp        0      0 localhost.localdomain:smtp  *:*                 LISTEN
udp        0      0 *:32768                 *:*
udp        0      0 *:bootpc                *:*
udp        0      0 *:1000                  *:*
udp        0      0 *:5353                  *:*
udp        0      0 *:sunrpc                *:*
udp        0      0 *:ipp                   *:*
```

For each server capable of connecting, `netstat` displays some information. The only column you are really interested in is the Local Address. It consists of a host name or asterisk and a port number separated by a colon. If the server is listening on only one interface, the host name of that interface is given. If it listens on all available interfaces, an asterisk is displayed. The port number is the TCP or UDP port the server is listening to. Many protocols use a standard (*well-known*) port and a list of well-known ports is kept in the `/etc/services` file. If the port is well known, its name or number is given in the `netstat` output. You can use this information to determine which programs are responsible for listening on a particular port.

The first service on the list is `sunrpc`, which a search of `/etc/services` reveals is also known as the `portmapper`. It is used as part of applications such as Network File System (NFS). If you are not using NFS or similar services, this would be a good candidate to uninstall. Which package do you need to uninstall? You can use `yum` to search through package descriptions for the word `portmapper`:

```
yum search portmapper
Searching Packages:
Setting up repositories
Reading repository metadata in from local files


portmap.i386                        4.0-65                    base
Matched from:
portmapper
The portmapper program is a security tool which prevents theft of NIS
(YP), NFS and other sensitive information via the portmapper.  A
portmapper manages RPC connections, which are used by protocols like
NFS and NIS.


The portmap package should be installed on any machine which acts as a
server for protocols using RPC.
```

Now you know it is the portmap package you need to uninstall.

The next service is the Internet Printing Protocol (IPP). It is listening on the loopback or local-host interface only, which is sensible because you don't want random people on the Internet to be able to print to your printer. This one can stay as it is.

The next one also listens on localhost, but port 5335 is not listed in /etc/services. You can still find out which service it is with the lsof command. lsof stands for *list open files*. Given a file (remember, Linux tries to make all system resources, even TCP/IP ports, look like files), lsof will tell you which program has it open. For a port, you have to use the -i option to lsof and run it as root:

```
# lsof -i tcp:5335
COMMAND    PID    USER    FD    TYPE DEVICE SIZE NODE NAME
mDNSRespo 2023 nobody     7u    IPv4   5198       TCP
localhost.localdomain:5335 (LISTEN)
```

Unfortunately, the name of the program has been cut off. No worries, the locate command can tell you what the full name is likely to be:

```
$ locate mDNSRespo
/var/run/mDNSResponder.pid
/var/lock/subsys/mDNSResponder
/usr/share/man/man8/mDNSResponder.8.gz
/usr/lib/libmDNSResponder.so.0.0.0
/usr/lib/libmDNSResponder.so.0
/usr/bin/mDNSResponder
/etc/howl/mDNSResponder.conf
```

```
/etc/rc.d/rc0.d/K66mDNSResponder
/etc/rc.d/rc3.d/S34mDNSResponder
/etc/rc.d/rc1.d/K66mDNSResponder
/etc/rc.d/rc4.d/S34mDNSResponder
/etc/rc.d/rc6.d/K66mDNSResponder
/etc/rc.d/init.d/mDNSResponder
/etc/rc.d/rc2.d/K66mDNSResponder
/etc/rc.d/rc5.d/S34mDNSResponder
```

Hmm, lots of choices. Based on what you have learned about the Linux file system structure, you probably guessed /usr/bin/mDNSResponder is the right file. And if you read the program's man page, you can learn what it does and decide if you want to keep it. If you do want to remove it, once again you have to know which package it belongs to. Armed with a file name, you can use rpm's -qf option to determine the package name:

```
$ rpm -qf /usr/bin/mDNSResponder
howl-0.9.8-3
```

If you search for a file that was not installed via rpm, rpm -qf will give you a result like this:

```
rpm -qf /etc/resolv.conf
file /etc/resolv.conf is not owned by any package
```

In that case you would have to use one of the other methods described in this section to determine where it came from.

Deactivate services you don't need but don't want to uninstall

Sometimes you don't want to uninstall a service altogether but just stop it from running. For instance, you might have started configuring it but want to wait till you've learned more before finally making it live. You can control how a service starts up with the system-config-services command. You saw in Chapter 18 that services are started up by scripts in /etc/init.d, which are symlinked into directories called /etc/rc0.d through /etc/rc6.d and which define runlevels. So switching to runlevel 5 for instance, runs all the /etc/init.d scripts that have the appropriate symlinks in /etc/rc5.d. system-config-services manages adding and removing these symlinks for you. system-config-services can be found under Desktop → System Settings → Server Settings in the GNOME menus. Figure 20-4 shows you what it looks like.

You can adjust whether a service is started either in one particular runlevel or in all runlevels (in practice this is only 3, 4, and 5) and do one-time only starts, stops, or restarts of services in the current runlevel.

Figure 20-4: system-config-services.

Deactivate inetd services you don't need

Some services need to be used only occasionally; Linux runs them from a special program called `inetd`. Fedora uses an implementation of `inetd` called `xinetd` (which confusingly has nothing to do with the X window system). You can use `system-config-services` to manage them as well.

Uninstall any other software you don't need

It's not just Internet services; desktop software can also be exploited, though admittedly this is probably harder to do. Still, why give hackers the opportunity? If you didn't make a custom package selection when you installed Fedora, you inevitably ended up with some packages you don't need. Find them and remove them.

Install a spam filter

The e-mail clients discussed in Chapter 9 contain sophisticated tools for filtering out spam. If your organization has many users, it may be preferable to install antispam filters on the mail server itself. A popular open source spam filter is Spamassassin. Installing Spamassassin to work with the Postfix mail server is covered in Chapter 22.

Hide your e-mail address

A good way to avoid spam is to minimize the exposure your address receives. If you are running a mail server of your own, you can create an unlimited supply of throwaway e-mail addresses to use for joining mailing lists, registering for Web sites, and so on. Then you can reserve your main address for giving out to the people you actually want receive mail from. You can also obfuscate your address when it appears in a public place like a Web page, for example, by displaying the @ sign as the word "at". Even a simple trick like this can throw off many spam harvesters. Another trick is to have your e-mail address embedded as an image instead of plain text. Bear in mind that making spammers jump through hoops to get your address also means making legitimate users jump through hoops to get your address. Some may decide it is not worth the effort to contact you if you make it too difficult.

Encrypt your files and protect your identity with GnuPG

Even though it is important to protect your operating system, if worst comes to worst and your computer is hacked, your OS can be reinstalled. Your personal data on the other hand is unique and priceless. To protect your data as it sits on your disk, use public key encryption.

Your identity is also valuable. If a hacker managed to break into your computer and steal information that can be used to impersonate you, all kinds of havoc could result. Public key encryption can also be used to create digital signatures to authenticate your identity online. The next part of this chapter explains how to create digital signatures and encrypt files and data with a public key encryption program called GnuPG.

Trust but verify, or it's not paranoia if they're really out to get you

It's not good enough to set up some security barricades and then just sit back thinking you are safe. You have to make security an ongoing process in order for it to be effective. You also cannot rely merely on technology. Some of the biggest hacks have been caused by the naiveté or greed of people. Be suspicious if you get an e-mail saying you will get a large amount of money if only you'll verify your identity by giving your bank account number. If someone claiming to be from your ISP asks for your password to do some "account maintenance," get a contact number and call the head office to determine if he or she is telling the truth. There are many scenarios con men can come up with to swindle you. Assume nothing, trust your common sense when something seems fishy, educate yourself about common types of scams, and dole out the least personal information necessary. Then you will be safest from online fraud.

Using GnuPG

You came across one use of public key encryption earlier in this chapter in the section about SSH. `id_dsa` and `id_dsa.pub` are the two halves of the cryptographic key SSH create in order to establish the identity of your user account. There is a program called GNU Privacy Guard (GnuPG) that uses the same principles to implement public key encryption. It may be open source and free of charge, but GnuPG provides cryptographic power that's based on the research of the world's top researchers. To follow along with the examples in the next few pages, install the `gnupg` package if it isn't already present.

Creating a key

The actual name of the GnuPG program is `gpg`. It has many options to perform all the tasks needed to decrypt and encrypt. The first step in using GnuPG is to create a public and private key pair. This is done using gpg's `-gen-key` option:

```
$ gpg -gen-key
This program comes with ABSOLUTELY NO WARRANTY.
This is free software, and you are welcome to redistribute it
under certain conditions. See the file COPYING for details.

gpg: directory `/home/jaldhar/.gnupg' created
gpg: new configuration file `/home/jaldhar/.gnupg/gpg.conf' created
gpg: WARNING: options in `/home/jaldhar/.gnupg/gpg.conf' are not yet
active during this run
gpg: keyring `/home/jaldhar/.gnupg/secring.gpg' created
gpg: keyring `/home/jaldhar/.gnupg/pubring.gpg' created
Please select what kind of key you want:
```

GnuPG starts by creating a .gnupg directory in your home directory and populating it with some files. The `gnupg.conf` file contains various options for `gpg`, some of which you will be changing later. The `pubring.gpg` file contains your public key and `secring.gpg` contains your secret key. The public key is the part that gets sent around to other people. The secret key should under no circumstances be revealed to anyone. GnuPG then asks some questions:

```
   (1) DSA and Elgamal (default)
   (2) DSA (sign only)
   (5) RSA (sign only)
Your selection?
```

The first question is about which cryptographic cipher to employ. In most cases, you will want to accept the default choice, 1.

The next question asks you how long you wanted the generated key to be:

```
DSA keypair will have 1024 bits.
ELG-E keys may be between 1024 and 4096 bits long.
What keysize do you want? (2048)
```

For every bit extra in length, the key becomes exponentially harder to break so it would seem that picking the largest possible size is always the best choice, but the flip-side is that longer keys take longer to encrypt and decrypt and use more processor power to do so. The suggested default, 2048, is a good compromise.

Added security can be obtained in certain situations by having a key automatically become invalid after some time. The next question asks if you want to set an expiration date on your key. Unless you have some special scenario in mind, you should choose 0 to make the key valid indefinitely. You are asked to confirm your choice.

```
Requested keysize is 2048 bits
Please specify how long the key should be valid.
         0 = key does not expire
      <n>  = key expires in n days
      <n>w = key expires in n weeks
      <n>m = key expires in n months
      <n>y = key expires in n years
Key is valid for? (0)
Key does not expire at all
Is this correct? (y/N) y
```

The next step is to enter your name, email address and an optional comment to create the key's user ID. You should use the most commonly used variant of your name and your primary email address here:

```
You need a user ID to identify your key; the software constructs the
user ID
from the Real Name, Comment and Email Address in this form:
    "Heinrich Heine (Der Dichter) <heinrichh@duesseldorf.de>"

Real name: Linus Torvalds
Email address: linus@example.com
Comment: Linux inc.
You selected this USER-ID:
    "Linus Torvalds (Linux inc.) <linus@example.com>"

Change (N)ame, (C)omment, (E)mail or (O)kay/(Q)uit? o
```

You are asked to enter the passphrase twice to ensure it's spelled correctly:

```
You need a Passphrase to protect your secret key.

Enter passphrase:
Repeat passphrase:
```

A passphrase, as the name suggests, is like a password but can (and should) be a whole phrase. In fact, the longer it is, the better, though you can run into the same problems as with a long or hard to remember password: It can be too hard to remember. If you forget the passphrase, there is no way to recover it and the key will become unusable. So choose carefully here.

```
We need to generate a lot of random bytes. It is a good idea to perform
some other action (type on the keyboard, move the mouse, utilize the
disks) during the prime generation; this gives the random number
generator a better chance to gain enough entropy.
```

The mathematical algorithms used to create the key depend heavily on random numbers. The problem is: How do you get truly random numbers from a decidedly nonrandom machine? The only really unpredictable element is you, the user. By just doing things like typing or moving the mouse around, you increase the randomness of the numbers your computer generates. Generating the key can take some time especially if you specified a long key length.

Eventually the key is created. GnuPG presents some information about the newly created key:

```
gpg: key 0ACC9546 marked as ultimately trusted
public and secret key created and signed.

gpg: checking the trustdb
gpg: 3 marginal(s) needed, 1 complete(s) needed, PGP trust model
gpg: depth: 0  valid:   2  signed:   0  trust: 0-, 0q, 0n, 0m, 0f, 2u
pub   1024D/0ACC9546 2005-10-20
      Key fingerprint = FF81 7890 87FA 2A2F 7466  2A1B 8E29 33AD 0ACC 9546
uid                  Linus Torvalds (Linux inc.) <linus@example.com>
sub   2048g/9202C034 2005-10-20
```

The *fingerprint* is the actual binary code contained within the key. Just as your fingerprints are unique to you, the key's fingerprint uniquely identifies it. It is usually shown as a sequence of hexadecimal digits. For short, you can use the last eight hexadecimal digits of the fingerprint to refer to the key.

The web of trust

The other information contained in the GnuPG output concerns how trustworthy the key is. A big problem with public key encryption is how to know if the key is actually associated with the person it says it is. It's as if you're hiring a new employee — they can give you an impressive resume, but do you really know whether they've done all the things they say they have? You have to contact the references listed on the resume to see if they will vouch for the accuracy of the statements made by the candidate and whether they think he is trustworthy.

In the same manner, if you have contacted me and trust my integrity, and if I have met Linus Torvalds and verified that key 0ACC9546 does belong to him, you can also trust that key 0ACC9546 belongs to him. GnuPG has the ability to add signatures to a key and display them. So you can list the signatures of a key and see who considers it trustworthy. In turn, you can sign the keys of other people and the trust that has been placed in your key will carry over to them. This is called the *web of trust* and it extends across the entire world.

The GnuPG web of trust and public key encryption in general depends on private keys being kept absolutely secret.

- Do not keep your private key on a computer that is connected to the Internet. If the computer gets hacked your private key might get stolen.

- Do not keep your private key on a computer where you don't know or can't trust the system administrator. The superuser has the power to override file permissions, snoop through memory, or watch keyboard activity, any of which could be used to steal your key.

▪ Do not use your private key over an unsecured protocol such as Telnet. The possibility of eavesdropping has already been mentioned for such protocols. You should use SSH and other encrypted protocols instead.

A good solution for keeping your private key safe yet accessible is to store it on a CD-ROM or one of the cheap, tiny USB flash drives that are now available. Then you can carry it around, use it as needed, and then put it away in a safe place somewhere.

Revoking a key

In the event of your private key being compromised, don't feel ashamed. The responsible thing to do is to immediately publicize this fact as far and wide as possible so other people know not to trust it. You should also do this if the key is no longer in use. How will they know it is really you announcing the invalidity of your key and not a thief instead? When you create a key you should also immediately create what is known as a revocation certificate using GnuPGs' -gen-revoke option:

```
$ gpg -o revoked.key -gen-revoke 0ACC9546

sec  1024D/0ACC9546 2005-10-20 Linus Torvalds (Linux inc.) <linus@example.com>

Create a revocation certificate for this key? (y/N) y
Please select the reason for the revocation:
  0 = No reason specified
  1 = Key has been compromised
  2 = Key is superseded
  3 = Key is no longer used
  Q = Cancel
(Probably you want to select 1 here)
Your decision? 1
Enter an optional description; end it with an empty line:
> Got Hacked.
>
Reason for revocation: Key has been compromised
Got Hacked.
Is this okay? (y/N) y
```

You should provide the security community with some information about why you are revoking this key.

Of course, you need to specify the passphrase or anyone would be able to create a revocation certificate for your key:

```
You need a passphrase to unlock the secret key for
user: "Linus Torvalds (Linux inc.) <linus@example.com>"
1024-bit DSA key, ID 0ACC9546, created 2005-10-20

Enter passphrase:
```

GnuPG creates the revocation certificate in the file `revoked.key.` and gives you some advice about what to do with it:

```
ASCII armored output forced.
Revocation certificate created.

Please move it to a medium which you can hide away; if Mallory gets
access to this certificate he can use it to make your key unusable.
It is smart to print this certificate and store it away, just in case
your media become unreadable. But have some caution:  The print system of
your machine might store the data and make it available to others!
```

`Mallory` is a stock name for a malicious hacker that security researchers use in examples. If your name is Mallory don't take it personally!

Uploading and downloading keys

Where do other people find your public key? There are repositories of public keys on the World Wide Web called keyservers. Revocation certificates should also be uploaded to them. GnuPG allows you to upload your key to the keyservers and download other people's keys from them. You upload your key with the `-send-keys` option:

```
$ gpg -send-keys 0ACC9546
```

Similarly, you download other peoples keys into your keyring with the `-recv-keys` option:

```
$ gpg -recv-keys 0f0f0f0f
```

In both cases, you use the short form of the key's fingerprint to identify it.

You can also export a public key into ASCII text so that, for example, you can mail it to someone, with the aptly named `-export` option:

```
$ gpg -export -armor 0ACC9546 > mykey.txt
```

And you can import a key into your keyring with—you guessed it—the `-import` option. Specifying `-armor` to either `-import` or `-export` informs GnuPG that the key is in ASCII not binary format:

```
$ gpg -import -armor < hiskey.txt
```

All these operations work on revocation certificates as well as public keys.

Digital signatures and encryption

Once you have got a person's public key, either from a file or a keyserver, you can begin using it to verify messages or other files he has signed, as follows:

```
$ gpg -verify somedata.file
gpg: Signature made Tue 25 Oct 2005 01:12:11 AM EST using DSA key ID 0ACC9546
gpg: Good signature from "Linus Torvalds (Linux inc.) <linus@example.com>"
gpg: WARNING: This key is not certified with a trusted signature!
gpg:           There is no indication that the signature belongs to the owner.
Primary key fingerprint: FF81 7890 87FA 2A2F 7466  2A1B 8E29 33AD 0ACC 9546
```

As well as telling you whether the signature is valid or not, GnuPG also gives you some information about how trustworthy it is.

If your correspondent has encrypted the file instead of just signing it, you can decrypt it with the -decrypt option. The -o option specifies the output file:

```
$ gpg -o decrypted.data -decrypt encrypted.data
```

And you can sign or encrypt data for him:

```
$ gpg -sign some.data
You need a passphrase to unlock the secret key for
user: "Linus Torvalds (Linux inc.) <linus@example.com>"
2048-bit DSA key, ID 0ACC9546, created 2005-10-20

Enter passphrase:
```

This compresses the data as it signs it so the file becomes unreadable. If you have an ASCII file to sign and you want it to remain that way, use the -clearsign option instead. Use the -encrypt option to encrypt data.

Signing keys

A common feature at Linux events is a *keysigning party* where many people gather to verify and sign each other's GnuPG keys, thereby further strengthening the web of trust. The web of trust can work only if people are very careful about whose keys they sign. So, never sign a key for someone you have not met face to face. When meeting for the purpose of keysigning, always ask to see a drivers license or similar official photo ID and a hard copy of the key's fingerprint. If anything about the situation seems dubious, don't sign or your own reputation might suffer. If you do think the key is trustworthy, you can sign it with the -edit-key option.

```
gpg --edit-key 0f0f0f0f
gpg (GnuPG) 1.4.1; Copyright (C) 2005 Free Software Foundation, Inc.
This program comes with ABSOLUTELY NO WARRANTY.
This is free software, and you are welcome to redistribute it
under certain conditions. See the file COPYING for details.


pub  1024D/0F0F0F0F  created: 2005-10-20  expires: never      usage: CSA
                     trust: unknown       validity: unknown
```

```
sub  1024g/F0F0F0F0  created: 3005-10-20  expires: never       usage: E
[ unknown] (1). A.N. Other (Examples-R-Us) <another@example.com>


Command> sign


pub  1024D/0F0F0F0F  created: 2005-10-20  expires: never       usage: CSA
                     trust: unknown       validity: unknown
 Primary key fingerprint: 48DF D000 3BE7 1FF8 D9C1  5832 DA46 0E47 0F0F 0F0F


     A.N. Other (Examples-R-Us) <another@example.com>


Are you sure that you want to sign this key with your
key "Linus Torvalds (Linux inc.) <linus@example.com>" (0ACC9546)


Really sign? (y/N) y
You need a passphrase to unlock the secret key for
user: "Linus Torvalds (Linux inc.) <linus@example.com>"
1024-bit DSA key, ID 0ACC9546, created 2005-10-20


Enter passphrase:
Command> quit
```

Some people prefer to take the signed key and upload it directly to the keyservers with the -send-keys option while others export it with -export and send it to the signee so he can upload it at his leisure.

GnuPG has even more features than the ones shown here. These are just the most commonly used ones. For more information about this program, visit the GnuPG Web site at www.gnupg.org/.

Learning More About Security

Depressingly, hackers continue to think of new ways to harm you. Here are some resources that will help you keep up-to-date with the latest issues you need to be aware of to keep safe.

- The Forum on Risks to the Public in Computers and Related Systems (http://catless.ncl.ac.uk/Risks) discusses topics related to security and other problems that occur in computers and other automated systems.

- Security expert Bruce Schneier has a monthly newsletter about security issues that you can subscribe to at www.schneier.com/crypto-gram.html. It is readable by the layman, entertaining, and provides a lot of insight into the security questions of the day.

- An article from the Wikipedia online encyclopedia (http://en.wikipedia.org/wiki/Alice_and_Bob) explains Mallory and other stock names used in discussing security. Wikipedia also has good articles on subjects such as encryption or buffer overflows.

- Security Focus (`www.securityfocus.net/`) is a Web site that contains news and opinions on security issues. The site also hosts BugTraq, a mailing list that is frequently the first place new exploits are announced.

- LinuxSecurity.com (`www.linuxsecurity.com/`) is also a gathering point for security information, but it has a stricter focus on Linux than the other Web sites mentioned.

Most hackers aren't actually that smart. They are only *script kiddies* who know how to perform exploits by rote but rely more on the negligence of their targets rather than any kind of deep knowledge of how computers work. They are easily confounded by administrators who keep up with what's going on in the security world by using resources and practices like those discussed in this chapter.

Summary

Your system is susceptible to many of threats, bet there are effective countermeasures you can take against them. Especially if you come from a Windows background, the whole subject may seem quite daunting. You may wonder if Linux is worth the bother if you have to put this much effort into securing it. Such a view, however, is based on false premises. It's actually even harder to keep Windows secure, as the many stories in the news about viruses and spyware remind us. It just may not seem harder because security information is often obscured or suppressed in the Microsoft world. The Linux traditions of openness, sound technology before profits, and peer review will serve you much better in the long run.

Part V

Server Solutions

Chapter 21

Web Server Solutions

Ⓞne function in which Linux excels is that of an easy-to-use, low-cost Web server. In addition to having an inexpensive (or free), server-oriented operating system that runs on off-the-shelf hardware, you also have at your disposal the most popular and, in my opinion, best Web server software that exists: Apache. Apache is free software (although some vendors do offer modified Apache servers for a price) and has been used in just about any capacity you can imagine for a Web server.

This chapter covers the basics of getting an Apache server up and running. Like many servers, Apache is configured mainly via the editing of text files. So fire up your favorite text editor, and let's get started.

Note

Some Linux distributions ship with graphical Apache configuration tools. On the whole, if you're serious about using Apache, understanding the text files and how to edit them is probably the best way to keep a handle on what you're doing. Nevertheless, if you're interested in trying one of these tools out, consult your distribution's documentation.

Getting and Installing Apache

Most major distributions have jumped at the chance to include the extremely popular free software package, Apache. Odds are, whichever distribution you're using, Apache is on it. You should be able to install it from your installation media in the same way that you'd install any other software package. In fact, there's a good possibility that Apache is already on your system. If your package management system supports querying, you can check that way, or you can search for a file named httpd. httpd, which is often located in the /usr/bin directory, in the main Apache executable file. If you find that file, Apache is likely already installed.

If Apache is on neither your system nor your installation medium, you can download it from http://httpd.apache.org/download.cgi. The downloads at this site are all in the form of source code. Instructions on compiling Apache from source code are included with the package, and

Chapter 15 provides a general overview of the process. In the unlikely event that your distribution's installation CDs do not include an Apache package, you may be able to find one at either the distribution's or Apache's Web site.

Configuring Apache

After you have Apache installed, you'll need to do some basic configuration to get it running. Before you dive right into editing your configuration files, though, you'll need to have some information handy, so find out the following and write it down:

- Your domain name (in this case `example.com`.)

- The full machine name (host name) of the Web server machine (`www.example.com`)

- The full machine names of other machines on the network (`comp1.example.com`, `comp2.example.com`, etc.)

- The IP numbers of your domain and of all the machines on the network (192.168.0.1, 192.168.0.2, etc.)

Once you've got that information, you can start editing the configuration files.

Note

A *domain name* is a name like `example.com`—a standard Internet address. In order for these names to work on Apache (or in general, for that matter), you can't just make them up. Domain names must be registered through one of the agencies that are licensed to perform this service. You can find a domain name registrar by consulting the list at `www.icann.org/registrars/accredited-list.html`.

By default, Apache puts its configuration files in places that certain distributions don't like. When the distributors build the packages, they sometimes change the locations of these files. The upshot of this is that your distribution may have its configuration files in a nonstandard location. (This is complicated by the fact that the default locations were changed in the transition from Apache 1.3 to Apache 2.0 and further by the fact that different naming schemes are used for different Unix variants.)

The upshot is that you're going to need to find these configuration files on your machine. The most likely places for them to be are `/etc/httpd`, `/etc/apache`, `/usr/local/apache`, or `/usr/local/apache/conf`.

Note

Fedora Core uses `/etc/httpd`, while Knoppix uses `/etc/apache`.

Once you've found the directory where the configuration files are kept, you can access the configuration files. The file you are primarily interested in is the one designated `httpd.conf`. Open this file in a text editor and look at it. There are a lot of comments in this file, and you can learn a lot about how to configure Apache just by reading them.

The general format of the configuration file works this way: The file contains directives that may apply to the server as a whole or which may be limited to one or more virtual domains. *Virtual domains* are a way of using a single server to serve content for more than one domain name at a time. As noted previously, these domain names must be registered. You can find more information about hosting virtual domains on an Apache server at `www.onlamp.com/pub/a/apache/2003/07/24/vhosts.html`.

Tip

If you just want to test Apache and not actually set up a domain, you can identify its server by IP number instead of by domain name. A URL such as http://192.168.0.111 is perfectly valid.

Configuration directives

The default configuration file included with Apache contains most of the directives that you need to get a server set up, along with some reasonable default values for certain parameters. The rest of this chapter looks at certain sections of the file that you will either definitely need to change (or complete), or that you might need to make a decision about.

Tip

Before you start editing the main configuration file, make a backup. You can do this very simply by giving the command `cp httpd.conf httpd.conf.backup`. This way, if you make a mistake and can't figure out how to undo it, you can simply delete the file and use the backup to create a new default file. (If that happens, be sure to make a *new* backup before editing the original backup.)

SERVERROOT

The `ServerRoot` directive defines the place where Apache looks for its configuration files. The relevant section of the `httpd.conf` file looks like this:

```
# ServerRoot: The top of the directory tree under which the server's
# configuration, error, and log files are kept.
#
# NOTE!  If you intend to place this on an NFS (or otherwise network)
# mounted filesystem then please read the LockFile documentation
# (available at <URL:http://httpd.apache.org/docs
# 2.0/mod/mpm_common.html#lockfile>);
```

```
# you will save yourself a lot of trouble.
#
# Do NOT add a slash at the end of the directory path.
#
ServerRoot "/etc/httpd"
```

By default, the ServerRoot directive should be set to a directory such as /etc/httpd, /etc/apache, or wherever you found the configuration file that you're working on. Unless you have a compelling reason to do so, you should probably leave this directive alone.

Note

As with shell programs, lines preceded by a hash mark sign (#) are comments. The server ignores these. If you see a directive line commented out, such as

```
#ServerRoot
```

and you need to set this directive, remember to remove the hash mark so that the server will recognize the directive.

LISTEN

The Listen directive allows you to bind Apache to a particular network address or port. By default, Apache listens on port 80, but many people bind it to nonstandard ports when testing new Web sites. (Port 8080 is common for this purpose.) The relevant section looks like this:

```
# Listen: Allows you to bind Apache to specific IP addresses and/or
# ports, in addition to the default. See also the <VirtualHost>
# directive.
#
# Change this to Listen on specific IP addresses as shown below to
# prevent Apache from glomming onto all bound IP addresses (0.0.0.0)
#
#Listen 12.34.56.78:80
Listen 192.168.0.1:80
```

To bind to a nonstandard port, simply change the value to something else. Remember to change it back to port 80 when you're ready to take your site live, as people will not know to use the non-standard port when looking for your site. Check your /etc/services file to make sure that you're not using a port that's already in use.

Tip

When using a nonstandard port for testing, you need to include the port number in the site's URL when open-ing the site in a browser. For example, if you're working on the site mydomain.com and using port 8080 for testing, you'd enter the URL as http://mydomain.com:8080 in your browser's location bar. If you leave off the :8080 suffix, the browser sends its request to port 80.

USER AND GROUP

The User and Group directives are used to specify under which user and group IDs Apache will run. This is an important security consideration because if a hacker were to gain control of the Apache program, it might be possible to do damage were Apache to run under a privileged ID. Typically, Apache will run as apache or httpd. You will probably not want to change this unless you have a good reason.

```
# If you wish httpd to run as a different user or group, you must run
# httpd as root initially and it will switch.
#
# User/Group: The name (or #number) of the user/group to run httpd as.
#  . On SCO (ODT 3) use "User nouser" and "Group nogroup".
#  . On HPUX you may not be able to use shared memory as nobody, and the
#    suggested workaround is to create a user www and use that user.
#  NOTE that some kernels refuse to setgid(Group) or semctl(IPC_SET)
#  when the value of (unsigned)Group is above 60000;
#  don't use Group #-1 on these systems!
#
User apache
Group apache
```

SERVERADMIN

The ServerAdmin directive specifies the e-mail address of the server's administrator. You should change this directive to contain your e-mail address. This address appears on pages that the server generates, such as error messages.

```
# ServerAdmin: Your address, where problems with the server should be
# e-mailed.  This address appears on some server-generated pages, such
# as error documents.  e.g. admin@your-domain.com
#
# ServerAdmin root@localhost
ServerAdmin webmaster@example.com
```

SERVERNAME

The ServerName directive sets the domain name for the server. Despite the fact that this can be set automatically, it's a good idea to set it manually here, as well. If you don't have a registered domain name for your site, use the machine's IP number here. You're also setting the port here, so make sure this agrees with the port number you set in the Listen directive.

```
# ServerName gives the name and port that the server uses to identify itself.
# This can often be determined automatically, but we recommend you specify
# it explicitly to prevent problems during startup.
#
# If this is not set to valid DNS name for your host, server-generated
# redirections will not work.  See also the UseCanonicalName directive.
#
# If your host doesn't have a registered DNS name, enter its IP address here.
# You will have to access it by its address anyway, and this will make
# redirections work in a sensible way.
#
#ServerName new.host.name:80
ServerName www.example.com:80
```

DOCUMENTROOT

The DocumentRoot is a very important directive. DocumentRoot specifies where you will put your HTML documents so that they can be served to browsers that will connect to the server. The directory specified in this directive should have been created when you installed the Apache package. You can change this directory if you want to, but unless the specific location of your HTML files is important to you, it's probably best to leave it where it is. When you create your HTML files, you should place them in this directory. You can create subdirectories within this directory, and you should be able to access those as well.

For example, if your DocumentRoot is set to /var/www/html, and you have created the file /var/www/html/example.html, you should be able to access that page as http://mydomain. com/example.html. If you create the subdirectory subdir and move example.html into that directory, you should be able to access it as http://mydomain.com/subdir/example.html.

```
# DocumentRoot: The directory out of which you will serve your
# documents. By default, all requests are taken from this directory, but
# symbolic links and aliases may be used to point to other locations.
#
DocumentRoot "/var/www/html"
```

Note

Any other directory referred to in this file is interpreted as being relative to the document root. In other words, if you refer to a directory elsewhere, say /subdir, it will be interpreted as /var/www/html/subdir.

<DIRECTORY>

At this point, we move into a slightly different section of the `httpd.conf` file. Here we can define rules for specific directories. For example, say that you have created `/var/www/html/subdir`, and you want to define specific directives for that subdirectory specifically. You would do so in this format:

```
<Directory /subdir>
    Options FollowSymLinks
    AllowOverride None
</Directory>
```

Here we have the word `Directory` contained within angle brackets, followed by a directory name. This is paired with a corresponding directive: `</Directory>`. Between these two directives are a number of other directives. The `<Directory>` and `</Directory>` directives act here like HTML tags, defining attributes for the material contained between them. In this case, the tags restrict the scope of the action of the enclosed directives. In other words, instead of acting on the server as a whole, these directives apply only to the directory specified in the first `<Directory>` tag (`/subdir` in this case).

The following section of the `httpd.conf` file sets out certain options that apply to the `DocumentRoot` directory and all of its subdirectories:

```
# This should be changed to whatever you set DocumentRoot to.
#
<Directory "/var/www/html">

#
# Possible values for the Options directive are "None", "All",
# or any combination of:
#    Indexes Includes FollowSymLinks SymLinksifOwnerMatch ExecCGI MultiViews
#
# Note that "MultiViews" must be named *explicitly* --- "Options All"
# doesn't give it to you.
#
# The Options directive is both complicated and important.  Please see
# http://httpd.apache.org/docs-2.0/mod/core.html#options
# for more information.
#
    Options Indexes FollowSymLinks

#
# AllowOverride controls what directives may be placed in .htaccess files.
# It can be "All", "None", or any combination of the keywords:
#    Options FileInfo AuthConfig Limit
#
    AllowOverride None

#
```

```
# Controls who can get stuff from this server.
#
    Order allow,deny
    Allow from all

</Directory>
```

Note

Most Apache installations are configured for basic use right out of the box. If you want to understand the specifics of the options and directives listed in this section, consult the documentation at www.apache.org.

DIRECTORYINDEX

The DirectoryIndex directive defines the name of the default file in any given directory. For example, if you send your browser to www.mydomain.com without any file specified, you will get the index file for the document root directory. With this directive, you can define several alternative names, and Apache will search for a file by that name, in order. For example, if you give the filenames index.html and index.htm, Apache searches first for index.html and then for index.htm.

```
# DirectoryIndex: sets the file that Apache will serve if a directory
# is requested.
#
# The index.html.var file (a type-map) is used to deliver content-
# negotiated documents.  The MultiViews Option can be used for the
# same purpose, but it is much slower.
#
DirectoryIndex index.html index.html.var
```

A sample configuration

In this section, you set up a sample configuration for a very basic Web server. Please keep in mind that every site's needs are different, but a configuration similar to the one given here will at least serve to demonstrate how to get a simple server up and running. Here are some very basic assumptions before starting:

- You do not have a registered domain name. You are setting up a server for testing purposes, and will refer to it by IP number. (You will change this assumption later so that you can see how to use a domain name in your configuration.)

- The IP number of your server machine is 192.168.0.1.

- You are using Knoppix. (We look at the defaults for some directives on Knoppix, but you will not change them.)

Here is the process, step by step, of getting Apache up and running:

1. Locate the configuration file. On Knoppix, the main Apache configuration file is located at `/etc/apache/httpd.conf`.

2. Make a backup copy of the configuration file. Remember that on Knoppix you must use `sudo` if you want to do anything with superuser privileges, so in order to make a copy of the configuration file, you must give the following command:

   ```
   sudo cp /etc/apache/httpd.conf /etc/apache/httpd.conf .backup
   ```

3. Open the file in a text editor. In this example we use KWrite as our text editor. From a terminal, give the command

   ```
   sudo kwrite /etc/apache/httpd.conf
   ```

   (In this case, it's better to give the `kwrite` command from a terminal window instead of starting it from the main menu because you want to run KWrite as the superuser. This allows you to save the changes you make in the configuration file, which is owned by `root`.)

   You should see the file open in the KWrite window, as shown in Figure 21-1.

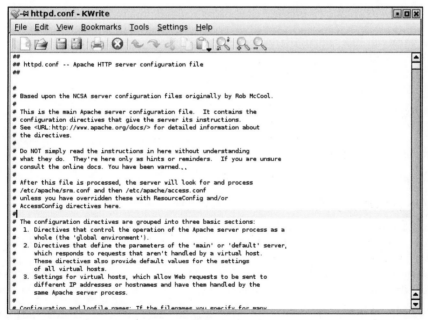

Figure 21-1: KWrite, showing the httpd.conf file.

4. Make your edits. Now you can make a few changes to your configuration file. Here are the directives you want to look at. (Scroll through the file until you find them; they're not all together like this in the actual file.) Each directive is listed at least twice: first with the default value(s) given in the file and second with the value that I recommend you give it. The default values are commented out (that is, preceded by hash marks), and the recommended value stands alone.

```
# Listen 3000
# Listen 12.34.56.78:80
Listen 192.168.0.1:80

# Port 80
Port 80     # Leave as is

# User www-data
# Group www.data
User www-data        # Leave as is
Group www-data       # Leave as is

# ServerAdmin  webmaster@Knoppix
ServerAdmin <Your email here>

# ServerName localhost
ServerName 192.168.0.1

# DocumentRoot /var/www
DocumentRoot /var/www   # Leave as is
```

Now save the file, and exit the editor.

5. Create a quick index file. Go to the directory /var/www and edit the file index.html. In that file, type the following:

```
<H1>Welcome to Apache</H1>
```

Save the file, and make it readable to all (chmod a+r index.html).

6. Start the server. Give the following command:

```
/etc/init.d/apache start
```

Remember, this command might be different if you're using a distribution other than Knoppix. The Apache server should now be running and ready to serve your Web page.

7. Try it out. At this point, open a Web browser (Konqueror or Firefox), and in the location bar type **http://192.168.0.10**. You should see the line that you typed in Step 5 displayed in bold text as in Figure 21-2.

At this point, you're ready to make further edits to your Web page and develop your content.

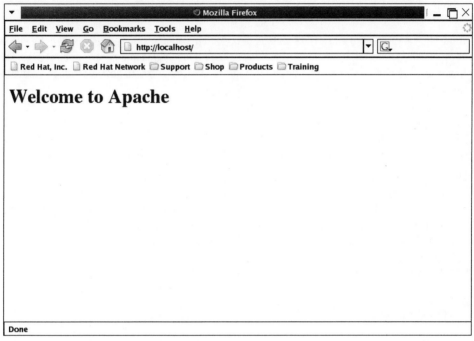

Figure 21-2: A very basic Web page.

If You Have a Domain Name

In this example, I have been going on the assumption that you don't have a registered domain name. You don't need a domain name to set up and test a server, but without one, you will not be able to make your Web pages available to the public. Earlier in this chapter, I refer you to a Web page that contains a list of agencies licensed to register domain names to the public. Registration is fairly inexpensive; so, if you feel that you'd like to take the plunge and register a name, there's really no reason not to.

One thing you should be aware of when you do register a name is that you're going to need access to a domain name service (DNS) server. A DNS server translates your domain name into an IP number so that when people type `yourdomain.com` into their Web browser, they'll be directed to the proper location on the Internet to find your Apache server. It is possible to run a DNS server yourself, although it is somewhat complicated, and beyond the scope of this book. It is also possible to find DNS services on the Internet for a price. This price is usually fairly inexpensive, and some services have easy-to-use Web interfaces that allow you to be quickly up and running. There are even free services, but they are not usually as responsive or easy to use as the pay services. In any event, you can find these by typing **DNS service** into your favorite search engine.

Continued

If You Have a Domain Name *(Continued)*

Once you've got a name and a DNS service to go with it, you can set up your server to be available to the public. This is fairly simple and involves changing the values of a couple of directives. For this example, assume that you've registered the name mydomain.com. To get your Apache server to answer to that name, set the following directive:

```
ServerName mydomain.com
```

and restart your server. Once the DNS service kicks in (and this could take as long as a couple of days), the public should be able to access your site from the outside world.

Remember that you need a static IP address (one that doesn't change). A lot of broadband and DSL services provides you with a dynamic address, which may work for a while, but when your IP address changes, the DNS no longer points your domain to the proper address. It is possible to work around this — some DNS services offer a service that can be periodically updated via a program that you run on your machine — but these workarounds are probably not the best solution if you need reliable access to your server from the Internet.

Tuning Apache's Performance

Web server performance can be a big deal. You can run a Web server on your desktop workstation that may be more than adequate for experimentation or even for serving the needs of a small department; but once you start serving many clients, you're likely to find that all that traffic can easily grind your server to a halt.

There are lots of ways to set up servers for maximum performance. These include setting up dedicated servers (machines that do nothing but serve Web pages), distributed servers (machines that direct other machines to serve content), and so forth, but one of the most basic things you can do is to set some parameters on your Apache configuration to best suit the type of traffic you anticipate.

This section is intended to be a very brief introduction to Apache performance tuning. It is by no means an exhaustive treatise on the subject, but this should be enough to at least get you thinking about the kinds of things you need to consider.

Apache's performance tuning controls take the form of directives in the httpd.conf file. Remember that you'll need to restart the server each time you change values in the file. You may need to experiment with different values before you find the ones that work best for you.

- **Timeout:** The Timeout directive controls how long the server waits before sending a timeout message. The timeout message is the message that is sent when there's a problem connecting to the server. You may have seen this sort of message when you've tried to connect to a site that isn't available. The Timeout directive's value is the number of seconds that the server will wait.

  ```
  # Timeout: The number of seconds before receives and sends time out.
  #
  Timeout 120
  ```

- **KeepAlive:** The `KeepAlive` directive controls whether to allow persistent connections. A persistent connection means that a browser can make more than one page request per connection. Setting `KeepAlive` to on can speed things up for users, but it also means that they may be connected to your server for longer than they would be otherwise.

```
# KeepAlive: Whether or not to allow persistent connections (more
# than one request per connection). Set to "Off" to deactivate.
#
KeepAlive Off
```

- **MaxKeepAliveRequests:** The `MaxKeepAliveRequests` directive controls the number of requests a persistent connection can make before the client is required to reconnect. Practically speaking, this means that the higher the number, the longer clients will be connected before the server kicks them off.

```
# MaxKeepAliveRequests: The maximum number of requests to allow
# during a persistent connection. Set to 0 to allow an unlimited
# amount.
# We recommend you leave this number high, for maximum performance.
#
MaxKeepAliveRequests 100
```

- **KeepAliveTimeout:** The `KeepAliveTimeout` directive determines how long (in seconds) the server waits for the next request from a persistent connection before deciding that it isn't persistent anymore.

```
# KeepAliveTimeout: Number of seconds to wait for the next request
# from the same client on the same connection.
#
KeepAliveTimeout 15
```

- **Prefork MPM:** Prefork MPM isn't a directive but rather an Apache module. We haven't discussed Apache's modules, but in a nutshell, the Prefork MPM module determines how many Apache processes can be running at the same time and how they will handle multiple incoming connections. (Apache can create duplicates of itself — a process known as *forking* — in response to incoming connections.)

The directives enclosed within the Prefork MPM code block each have their own role to play in determining how the server handles incoming load:

- **MinSpareServers:** The minimum number of idle processes that will wait for incoming requests

- **MaxSpareServer:** The maximum number of idle processes that can exist before Apache starts shutting down idle processes

- **StartServers:** The number of idle copies of Apache that will be start when the main server is started

- **MaxClients:** The total number of Apache processes that can be running at any given time

- **MaxRequestsPerChild:** The number of requests that any one process can serve before exiting

```
# prefork MPM
# StartServers: number of server processes to start
# MinSpareServers: minimum number of server processes which are kept
# spare
# MaxSpareServers: maximum number of server processes which are kept
# spare
# ServerLimit: maximum value for MaxClients for the lifetime of the
# server
# MaxClients: maximum number of server processes allowed to start
# MaxRequestsPerChild: maximum number of requests a server process
# serves
<IfModule prefork.c>
StartServers        8
MinSpareServers     5
MaxSpareServers    20
ServerLimit       256
MaxClients        256
MaxRequestsPerChild  4000
</IfModule>
```

Summary

Apache is the most popular Web server software in existence. It is free software and is bundled with most major Linux distributions. Apache is a powerful and flexible server package and can be quite complicated to configure; however, it is possible to get a basic configuration up and running without too much trouble.

Chapter 22

Mail Server Solutions

Having seen the way Linux can operate as a Web server or as a file server, it probably comes as no surprise that Linux also makes an excellent mail server. However, unlike Web and file servers, mail servers come with added levels of complexity. While getting a basic mail server up and running is not too difficult, the consequences of misconfiguration can be considerable. People from the outside world may find that their mail to you cannot be delivered, and people within your organization may find themselves effectively cut off from important communications.

This should not necessarily deter you. The benefits of running your own mail server can be quite rewarding. In particular, you can control how spam is handled and provide alternate means of access, such as Web-based mail programs, to your users' mail.

The granddaddy of Unix mail servers is a program called Sendmail. I don't cover Sendmail in this chapter for one compelling reason: It is an unbelievable nightmare to configure. In fact, Sendmail configuration is so complicated and unintuitive that it's not often done by hand. Sendmail is usually configured by using the macro program M4. M4 allows the administrator to set configuration options, and then the program itself creates the configuration file.

While this is an interesting exercise, and can certainly teach one a great deal about some of the more arcane aspects of Linux administration, it's not ideal for the beginner, nor for someone who wants to get a mail server running with a minimum of fuss.

This chapter focuses on the far more intuitive Postfix. Postfix is a slightly less flexible program than Sendmail, but it performs the basic functions of a mail server well and is much easier to configure. I also cover the Dovecot POP/IMAP server and give you brief introductions to the Web mail program SquirrelMail and the junk-mail filtering program SpamAssassin.

How Electronic Mail Works

Before getting into the specifics of setting up a mail server, it's worthwhile to understand some of the general concepts involved. E-mail is a little more complicated than other sorts of Internet communications. Rather than a single server, there are three types of servers that all work together to get mail where it needs to go. The three types of servers are *mail submission agents* (MSAs), *mail transport agents* (MTAs), and mail delivery agents (MDAs). In practice, the MSA and MTA functions are handled by the same program, but they are two distinct functions and should be thought of as such. MDA programs are generally separate.

When you send an e-mail, your mail program — the client — connects to an SMTP server (an MSA). This server takes your mail and connects to an MTA at the destination site. The MTA checks to make sure that the e-mail is in a valid format and that the intended recipient exists. If this is indeed the case, the MTA accepts the message and delivers it into a *mailbox,* which is a specially designated file or directory. When the recipient is ready to read the message, her e-mail program — another client — connects to the MDA and asks if there's any new mail. The MDA reads the mailbox and delivers any new mail to the client. Figure 22-1 shows how the system works.

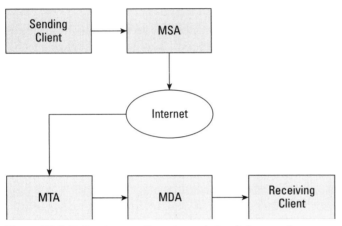

Figure 22-1: Delivering e-mail requires a chain of clients and servers.

In order to have a working e-mail system, you must install and configure an SMTP server/MTA, and an MDA.

MDAs generally come in the form of POP and IMAP servers. POP stands for Post Office Protocol, and the POP servers that you will see most often are, in fact, POP3 servers. POP3 is the third revision of the POP protocol. IMAP stands for Internet Message Access Protocol and is newer than the POP protocol. Most decent MDAs support both POP and IMAP protocols, although some can be configured to use one but not the other. The type of mail clients you're using determines the protocol that you must use. The MDA covered in this chapter, Dovecot, supports both protocols; if you have any question as to which you should use, you can always configure it to use both.

As a matter of general procedure, the best way to deal with the multiple servers required for a functioning e-mail system is to take it one step at a time. That is, get one thing working before you move on to the next. This is the approach for the remainder of this chapter: You install and configure one component, test it in order to make sure it's working, and then move on to the next.

Note

Even more than with a Web server, setting up a mail server requires a domain name. While it is technically possible to send mail to an IP number, it's not an especially useful thing to do. You'll need to have DNS service set up as well, with a mail exchange (MX) record pointing to the IP number of the machine upon which you will install your mail server. Your DNS service can help you to set up the appropriate MX record. (See Chapter 21 for details about how to register a domain name and find a DNS service.)

For the remainder of this chapter, I assume that you have a domain name (the example in the chapter is example.com) with an appropriate MX record.

Installing and Configuring Postfix

The example in this chapter involves setting up a mail server on Fedora Core. Setting up a mail server on Knoppix is not really practical for two reasons: Knoppix's slowness can lead to difficulty in delivering mail, and installing Postfix on a live CD-based machine will simply lead to the server being lost any time the machine is rebooted. (This is true of any server running on a live CD, by the way. Even something as simple as a Samba or Apache server will be lost upon reboot. It is possible to save a configuration from Knoppix or to customize the installation and burn a new CD, but if your intent is to run persistent servers, you're probably better off dedicating a machine to Linux, doing a traditional installation, and running them on that.)

Step 1: Install the software

As with any server, the first step is to acquire and install the software. Unlike Apache or Samba, Postfix is not a default application for Fedora Core, so it is unlikely that it was installed when you set up your system. It is, however, included with the distribution, so you should be able to find the Postfix RPM package on your installation CDs. (Links to packages for other distributions can be found at www.postfix.org/packages.html.)

However, if you prefer, you can also download it from any of the Fedora Core mirrors listed at http://fedora.redhat.com/download/mirrors.html. Once you've got the package, install it as described in Chapter 15. In this case, you can do it with the command:

```
rpm -ivh postfix-2.1.5-2.2.i386.rpm
```

(Note that the version number may be different depending on whichever version of Postfix is current when you do this.) Once you've got the package installed, you are ready to configure your software.

Step 2: Configure Postfix

As with Apache, you configure Postfix by making changes to the default configuration file that is supplied with the package.

Open a terminal window, assume superuser powers (su -), and move to the /etc/postfix directory (cd /etc/postfix). The central Postfix configuration file is called main.cf. As with Apache, you should make a backup copy of this file, so give the command

```
cp main.cf main.cf.backup
```

This way, if you find that you have misconfigured Postfix, and you can't figure out what you did wrong, you can simply delete your configuration file and start over from scratch with the default.

Next, use your favorite text editor to open the main.cf file; for the example, I use gedit (shown in Figure 22-2), launched with the command gedit main.cf. (Using a text command to launch gedit in this case allows the file to be open with superuser privileges. If you launch gedit from the main menu, you do so with your regular user privileges.)

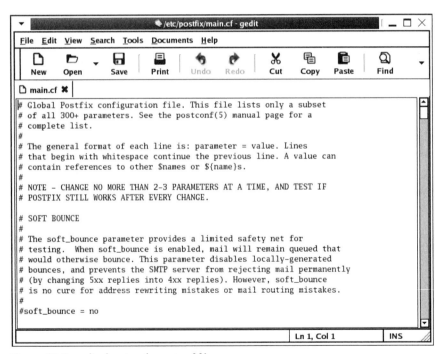

Figure 22-2: gedit showing the main.cf file.

Take a few minutes to read over the file. There are plenty of comments to give you an idea of what the various parameters do. Most of the parameters in the file have reasonable default values, but some will need to be changed to values specific to your system. Some parameters have several values specified, with all but one commented out. To use a commented-out value, simply remove the hash mark at the beginning of the line, and place a new hash mark at the beginning of the default value that you want to remove.

Tip

It's always a good idea to comment out values that you don't want and add new ones rather than to delete lines. That way, you can see what an old value was. If your new value doesn't work, it's a simple matter to go back to the old value. Also, make sure you leave comments of your own if you're making a complicated configuration change. This will help you to retrace your footsteps later, should the need arise.

Let's look at a few specific parameters and make any changes that need to be made. For this example, suppose that you've registered the domain name example.com, and you're setting this machine up to be the main mail server for that domain. You have decided to name this machine mail.example.com, and you have an MX record in your DNS server that points the hostname mail.example.com to the machine's IP address, 192.168.0.111

Note

The IP address 192.168.0.111 will not work if you want a mail server to be accessible from the Internet. Any IP addresses that begin with 192.168. are reserved for private, internal networks, meaning that anyone can use them and that they will never be registered to any one specific network. You must use an IP address that can be attached to a machine on the Internet. You should have gotten this IP number from your Internet service provider or system administrator.

MYHOSTNAME

The myhostname parameter does exactly what you'd imagine from its name: it sets the machine name (hostname) to which Postfix will answer. You must set this to the name of your machine, in this case mail.example.com. Look for this section in the main.cf file:

```
# INTERNET HOST AND DOMAIN NAMES
#
# The myhostname parameter specifies the internet hostname of this
# mail system. The default is to use the fully-qualified domain name
# from gethostname(). $myhostname is used as a default value for many
# other configuration parameters.
#
#myhostname = host.domain.tld
```

Comment out the last line, or leave it commented out if it already is, and add the line

```
Myhostname = mail.example.com
```

MYDOMAIN

The mydomain parameter is similar but without the hostname component. This parameter controls the domain name for which Postfix will accept mail. The relevant section of the main.cf file should look like this:

```
# The mydomain parameter specifies the local internet domain name.
# The default is to use $myhostname minus the first component.
# $mydomain is used as a default value for many other configuration
# parameters.
#
mydomain = example.com
```

MYORIGIN

The myorigin parameter relates to how Postfix acts in its role as an SMTP server, that is, how it acts when sending mail to other sites. It is sometimes but not always the case that you will use a different server to send mail than to receive it. For example, many Internet service providers require that you use their SMTP server to handle outgoing mail and will block mail coming out of individual machines on their networks. This is because spammers often use poorly configured mail servers to relay their mail. If you attempt to use Postfix to send mail and find that it isn't getting out, this may be the problem. In any case, myorigin assumes that you *can* send mail from your local machines. If you can't, there's no harm in configuring it anyway.

myorigin tells Postfix the format to use when it tells remote mail servers where the current message is coming from. Normally, the value of this parameter will be the same as the value of either the myhostname or mydomain parameter and can be set in this fashion:

```
# SENDING MAIL
#
# The myorigin parameter specifies the domain that locally-posted
# mail appears to come from. The default is to append $myhostname,
# which is fine for small sites. If you run a domain with multiple
# machines, you should (1) change this to $mydomain and (2) set up
# a domain-wide alias database that aliases each user to
# user@that.users.mailhost.
#
# For the sake of consistency between sender and recipient addresses,
# myorigin also specifies the default domain name that is appended
# to recipient addresses that have no @domain part.
#
#myorigin = $myhostname
myorigin = $mydomain
```

As in shell programming (see Chapter 11), you can use the value of a previously set variable by prepending a dollar sign to it. In the example, `myorigin` is set to the value of `mydomain`, that is, to `example.com`. When Postfix connects to remote mail servers, the remote server now sees addresses from your site as taking the form of `user@example.com`.

INET_INTERFACES

The `inet_interfaces` parameter controls the network interface to which remote mail servers are allowed to connect. (See Chapters 7 and 19 for discussion of network interfaces.) If your machine has more than one network interface, this parameter allows you to select which one you want to use for incoming mail. You are not restricted to only one, however.

```
# RECEIVING MAIL

# The inet_interfaces parameter specifies the network interface
# addresses that this mail system receives mail on. By default,
# the software claims all active interfaces on the machine. The
# parameter also controls delivery of mail to user@[ip.address].
#
# See also the proxy_interfaces parameter, for network addresses that
# are forwarded to us via a proxy or network address translator.
#
# Note: you need to stop/start Postfix when this parameter changes.
#
inet_interfaces = all
#inet_interfaces = $myhostname
#inet_interfaces = $myhostname, localhost
#inet_interfaces = localhost
```

Note here that the default value for this parameter is `all`, which allows incoming mail to connect to any interface. If your machine has one interface only, you can leave it configured like this. If you have more than one interface, leaving `inet_interfaces` set to `all` may present a security risk, so you might want to narrow it. If you prefer, you can leave it set to `all` while getting your server set up. Once you've established that it's working, you can narrow this parameter; however, as the comments note, you will need to restart the server if you do.

MYDESTINATION

The `mydestination` parameter controls the domain(s) for which Postfix accepts mail for final delivery. This configuration, the default for Fedora Core, should work:

```
# The mydestination parameter specifies the list of domains that this
# machine considers itself the final destination for.
#
# These domains are routed to the delivery agent specified with the
# local_transport parameter setting. By default, that is the UNIX
# compatible delivery agent that lookups all recipients in /etc/passwd
```

```
# and /etc/aliases or their equivalent.
#
# The default is $myhostname + localhost.$mydomain. On a mail domain
# gateway, you should also include $mydomain.
#
# Do not specify the names of virtual domains - those domains are
# specified elsewhere (see VIRTUAL_README).
#
# Do not specify the names of domains that this machine is backup MX
# host for. Specify those names via the relay_domains settings for
# the SMTP server, or use permit_mx_backup if you are lazy (see
# STANDARD_CONFIGURATION_README).
#
# The local machine is always the final destination for mail addressed
# to user@[the.net.work.address] of an interface that the mail system
# receives mail on (see the inet_interfaces parameter).
#
# Specify a list of host or domain names, /file/name or type:table
# patterns, separated by commas and/or whitespace. A /file/name
# pattern is replaced by its contents; a type:table is matched when
# a name matches a lookup key (the right-hand side is ignored).
# Continue long lines by starting the next line with whitespace.
#
# See also below, section "REJECTING MAIL FOR UNKNOWN LOCAL USERS".
#
mydestination = $myhostname, localhost.$mydomain, localhost, $mydomain
#mydestination = $myhostname, localhost.$mydomain, localhost, $mydomain
#mydestination = $myhostname, localhost.$mydomain, localhost, $mydomain,
#    mail.$mydomain, www.$mydomain, ftp.$mydomain
```

At this point, you should be ready to test your configuration. Save your file and exit the editor.

Step 3: Turn off Sendmail and turn on Postfix

On a default installation of Fedora Core, it's fairly likely that Sendmail was installed, and was started when you booted your machine, so in order to test Postfix you need to turn Sendmail off. From your superuser's shell prompt, give the command

```
/etc/rc.d/init.d/sendmail stop
```

If Sendmail is installed and running, this will stop it. If not, you'll see an error message. Now give the command

```
/etc/rc.d/init.d/postfix start
```

You should see a message telling you that Postfix has been started.

Note

This is a one-time change, and if you were to reboot the computer at this point, you would start Sendmail rather than Postfix. Making the change permanent is explained later in the chapter.

Step 4: Test Postfix

Now that Postfix is running, you need to test it to make sure that it can both receive and send mail (taking into account the above note about sending mail).

To test that Postfix can receive mail, return to your terminal window and give the command:

```
telnet 127.0.0.1 25
```

This opens a Telnet session to port 25, which should be answered by Postfix. (Telnet is a program that allows for interactive logins to a remote machine.) By connecting to 127.0.0.1, you connect to the machine you're already on. You should get a greeting that looks like this:

```
Trying 127.0.0.1...
Connected to localhost.localdomain (127.0.0.1).
Escape character is '^]'.
220 mail.example.com ESMTP Postfix
```

At this point, you are connected. You can now engage in a dialog with the server. An example of such a dialogue is reproduced below. The boldfaced lines are what you would type, and the regular face lines are what Postfix would say back to you. (Don't forget: Replace mail.example.com and user@example.com with your machine name and e-mail address.)

```
telnet 127.0.0.1 25
Trying 127.0.0.1...
Connected to localhost.localdomain (127.0.0.1).
Escape character is '^]'.
220 mail.example.com ESMTP Postfix
helo me
250 mail.example.com
mail from: user@example.com
250 Ok
rcpt to: user@example.com
250 Ok
data
354 End data with <CR><LF>.<CR><LF>
This is a test of the Postfix mail server.
250 Ok: queued as 67DB75F7
```

```
·  quit
   221 Bye
   Connection closed by foreign host.
```

At this point, you should have sent yourself an e-mail containing the sentence "This is a text of the Postfix mail server." At a (nonsuperuser) shell prompt, give the command `mail`, and you should be able to see that message. (You can't use a regular e-mail program at this point because you have not configured your POP or IMAP server.) Exit mail by typing **q**.

To test outgoing mail, the easiest thing to do is to simply send an e-mail to a remote address. If you have a remote e-mail address, such as a Google Mail, Yahoo! Mail, or other type of account, or even a home or business account that is on a different network than the one you're using for this server, send a message to that account. If, for example, you have the address `user@gmail.com`, open a text editor and create this file:

```
From: user@example.com
To: user@gmail.com

This is a test of outgoing mail.
```

Save the file, and give it the name `mailtest.txt`. Now give the command

```
cat mailtest.txt | mail user@gmail.com
```

When you check the Google Mail account, you should see the message there. (Be aware that it could take some time for the message to show up.)

If you can both send and receive mail using Postfix (or just send if your ISP restricts outgoing mail), Postfix is configured, and you can now move on to setting up your POP/IMAP server.

The Dovecot Mail Delivery Agent

There are a number of mail delivery agents (MDAs), and they all do more or less the same thing: They allow mail clients to connect to the server and download mail. None of them is terribly difficult to set up and run, so the one you choose is really up to you. This chapter focuses on the Dovecot server because it is fairly representative and very straightforward.

Note

You don't need to use an MDA if you're reading your mail on the same machine that your MTA is running. The MTA puts the incoming mail into a mailbox directory, and most Linux mail clients can read mail directly from these directories. However, if you want to read mail from another machine, you definitely need an MDA. Since they're fairly easy to set up anyway, you might as well do it. That way, you'll be prepared if your mail server moves beyond the realm of experiment.

Step 1: Install Dovecot

Dovecot is included with the Fedora Core distribution; so, before you do anything else, check to see if it's already installed. Run the command

```
rpm -qiv dovecot
```

If Dovecot is already installed, you should see this:

```
Name        : dovecot               Relocations: (not relocatable)
Version     : 0.99.11                    Vendor: Red Hat, Inc.
Release     : 1.FC3.4                Build Date: Thu 21 Oct 2004 12:34:42
PM EDT
Install Date: Mon 09 May 2005 01:04:42 PM EDT    Build Host:
tweety.build.redhat.com
Group       : System Environment/Daemons    Source RPM: dovecot-0.99.11-
1.FC3.4.src.rpm
Size        : 1434685                   License: LGPL
Signature   : DSA/SHA1, Thu 21 Oct 2004 01:09:33 PM EDT, Key ID b44269d04f2a6fd2
Packager    : Red Hat, Inc. <http://bugzilla.redhat.com/bugzilla>
URL         : http://dovecot.procontrol.fi/
Summary     : Dovecot Secure imap server
Description :
Dovecot is an IMAP server for Linux/UNIX-like systems, written with security
primarily in mind.  It also contains a small POP3 server.  It supports mail
in either of maildir or mbox formats.
```

If Dovecot is not installed, you'll need to install the package. You should be able to find it on your installation CD, or if you prefer you can download it. You should be able to find it at the same site from which you might have downloaded Postfix.

If you're not using Fedora Core, you can find links to packages at www.dovecot.org/download.html.

Step 2: Configure Dovecot

As the superuser, open the file /etc/dovecot.conf in your favorite text editor, as shown in Figure 22-3.

There are really only a couple of parameters you need to check here. Scroll down until you find a section that looks like this:

```
# Protocols we want to be serving:
#  imap imaps pop3 pop3s
protocols = imap imaps pop3
```

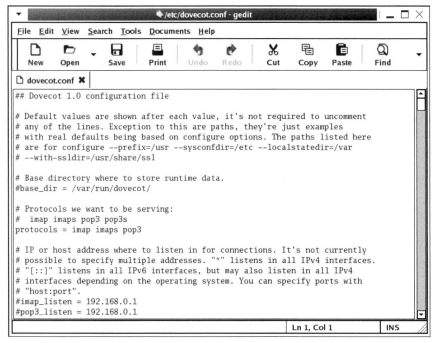

Figure 22-3: gedit showing the /etc/dovecot.conf file.

Make sure that the value of this parameter includes all of the following: imap, imaps, and pop3. Next, scroll down a little further and look for something like this:

```
# IP or host address where to listen in for connections. It's not currently
# possible to specify multiple addresses. "*" listens in all IPv4 interfaces.
# "[::]" listens in all IPv6 interfaces, but may also listen in all IPv4
# interfaces depending on the operating system. You can specify ports with
# "host:port".
imap_listen = *
pop3_listen = *
```

If your machine has more than one network interface, set both of these parameters to the IP number of the interface upon which you want clients to connect. If you want to allow clients to connect on all interfaces or if you only have one interface, you can set the value of these parameters to *, which designates *any interface.*

Save the file and exit the editor.

Note

The `/etc/dovecot.conf` file has many more parameters. Most of these are security oriented; if you intend to run a server that people can connect to from the Internet, it's a good idea to learn how to configure these, inasmuch as the configuration as described in this chapter will leave your server completely unsecured. I strongly recommend that you take some time and learn about Dovecot's security options. You can find full documentation on all of Dovecot's configuration parameters at `http://wiki.dovecot.org/`.

Step 3: Start and test the server

As with any other server, you need to start it before you can connect to it. For this, you can either use `system-config-services` or simply give the command

```
/etc/rc.d/init.d/dovecot start
```

Assuming there are no problems, you should now be able to connect to the server and download mail. You can test that Dovecot is accepting connections by logging in via the Telnet program, as you did for the Postfix server. First, exit the superuser account — you need to do this as a regular user.

Second, give the following command:

```
telnet 127.0.0.1 110
```

You should get the following in response:

```
Trying 127.0.0.1...
Connected to localhost.localdomain (127.0.0.1).
Escape character is '^]'.
+OK dovecot ready.
```

At this point, you can enter into a dialogue with the server. Below is a sample dialogue. As with Postfix, your entries are shown in bold:

```
telnet localhost 110
Trying 127.0.0.1...
Connected to localhost.localdomain (127.0.0.1).
Escape character is '^]'.
+OK dovecot ready.
user <your username>
+OK
pass <your password>
+OK Logged in.
```

```
list
+OK 3 messages:
1 959
2 11366
3 47602
.
stat
+OK 344 2368530
quit
+OK Logging out.
```

In this instance, there were three messages. It's possible that you might have no messages or many more. It all depends on how many e-mail messages Postfix has delivered into your mailbox. For this test, however, we're not concerned with how many messages you have but rather simply the fact that you can talk to the server. Notice that all of the server's responses begin with +ok. This is the server's way of telling you that there are no problems.

Step 4: Configure Postfix and Dovecot to start at boot

Now that both Postfix and Dovecot are up and running, you should configure them to start at boot time, so that any time you reboot the machine, they will start automatically. This saves you the trouble of having to start them by hand and the many headaches that can come from forgetting to do that.

Give the command `system-config-services`, or choose the menu path Desktop → System Settings → Server Settings. You are prompted for the superuser password. Once you give it, you should see the Service Configuration window as shown in Figure 22-4.

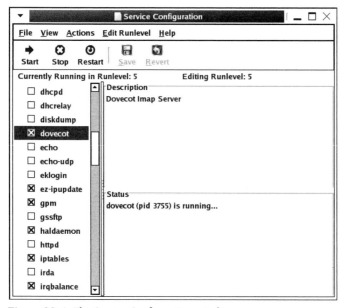

Figure 22-4: The Service Configuration window.

Configuring Mail Clients

We discussed the configuration of e-mail clients such as Evolution and Thunderbird in Chapter 12. Configuring mail clients for your newly configured mail server is more or less the same. Every person who is receiving mail at your server needs to have an account on the server machine. (If you don't want them logging into the machine for general use, you can change their default shell to `/bin/false`.)

When you configure the mail clients for use with the new server, you must enter the name or IP number of your server as the POP or IMAP server (that is, the incoming mail server), and you must also enter it as the name of the outgoing mail server, if your Internet connection allows you to send mail directly from your machine. Otherwise, you must enter the name of your Internet service provider's SMTP server. The figure shows KMail being configured to receive incoming mail from `mail.example.com`.

KMail configuration for your new server.

If you have configured Dovecot according to the instructions in this chapter, you can specify either POP3 or IMAP as your mail protocol. Dovecot handles both. If you have a compelling reason to choose one over the other, you can configure Dovecot to use that protocol only. In that case, you need to make sure that any mail client you use is configured to use that protocol.

Notice that in the left-hand column some of the services have check marks next to them. These are the services that are configured to start upon system boot. Find the entries for Dovecot and Postfix (the services are listed in alphabetical order), and make sure they have check marks. Then, click on the File menu and select Save Changes. You can then exit the Service Configuration program.

At this point, you are done. You have successfully configured a basic e-mail server, and you are ready to accept incoming mail and deliver it to clients.

Note

The `system-config-services` program is specific to Fedora Core (and other Red Hat products), and also depends on your running a GUI on your server machine. If you are using Fedora Core, but you wish to accomplish the same task from a shell prompt, give this command:

```
chkconfig --add dovecot
```

If you are not using Fedora Core, the process may be a bit trickier. You will need to consult your system's documentation and find out the procedure for starting services at boot time. Some distributions may have a graphical tool for this. Such tools are often referred to as *runlevel editors* or *service configuration tools*. If your system has no such tool, you should be able to find information about the startup scripts that control it. You may need to edit one of these files and insert a line directing it to start the service.

Serving Mail via the Web

What do you do when you're away from your home or your office and you need to get your e-mail? You can take your laptop with you if you have one and hope to find an Internet connection somewhere, but that's not always practical. And if you have configured Dovecot to refuse connections from outside your local network (a reasonable security precaution), you won't be able to get your mail that way, anyway.

A practical solution to this dilemma is Web mail. Web mail programs are e-mail programs built for the Web. Simply log into your Web mail server from any Web browser, and you can get your mail.

SquirrelMail is such a program and is bundled with Fedora Core; so, you can install it from your installation media or from one of the Fedora mirror sites (or from `www.squirrelmail.org` for non-Fedora distributions).

To run SquirrelMail, you need to have a working installation of Apache. See Chapter 21 for an overview of how to get Apache up and running. You also need to have Dovecot configured to use the IMAP protocol.

If you install SquirrelMail from an RPM on Fedora Core, the RPM installation program takes care of much of the configuration for you. You will notice that there is a new file in the `/etc/httpd/conf.d` directory called `squirrelmail.conf`. This is an addendum to the Apache configuration file. (By default, Apache is configured to read all the files in the `/etc/httpd/conf.d` directory and treat their contents as if they were part of Apache's main configuration file.) You will also find a new directory called `/etc/squirrelmail`. This is where the SquirrelMail configuration files live.

Open the file `/etc/squirrelmail/config.php` in a text editor, as shown in Figure 22-5.

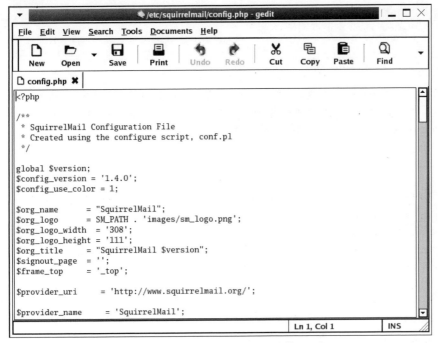

Figure 22-5: gedit showing the SquirrelMail configuration file.

You're not going to do any configuration here, but take a look at the format of the file. This file is written in a programming language called PHP. PHP is a language used for Web programming, so it's no surprise that it should be used for SquirrelMail. PHP's syntax is fairly easy to navigate, and any parameters that you might want to change are generally given as variable values. It is possible, however, to run SquirrelMail out of the box on Fedora Core, and that's what we're going to do.

Open a Web browser, and in the location bar type `http://example.com/webmail` (replace `example.com` with the name of your domain.) You should see the SquirrelMail login screen as shown in Figure 22-6.

Enter your username and password, and you are taken to your SquirrelMail inbox, as shown in Figure 22-7.

At this point, you can use SquirrelMail just as you would any other e-mail program. There are links to various default folders and links that allow you to set up new folders, to create and edit an address book, to compose new mail, and so on.

SquirrelMail can be customized, but it takes some knowledge of HTML, Style Sheets, and PHP to do it effectively. If you are interested in reading more, there's plenty of documentation and links at `www.squirrelmail.org`.

Figure 22-6: Logging into SquirrelMail.

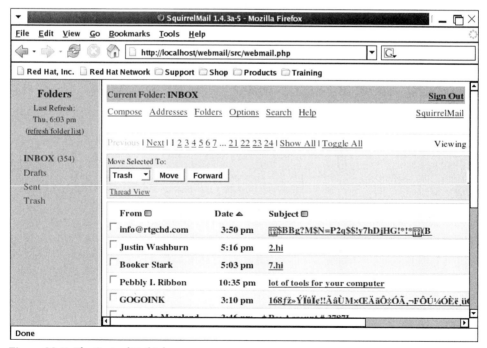

Figure 22-7: The SquirrelMail inbox.

Dealing with Spam

Everyone hates spam, and with good reason. Unsolicited commercial e-mail wastes the recipient's time and network bandwidth. It is also a delivery vehicle for viruses, worms, adware, spyware, and all sorts of malicious programs. Add to that content that is often fraudulent or obscene, and it should be clear to everyone that spam is just plain no good. ISPs and mail administrators spend a good amount of time fighting spam, and they mostly do a good job of it. Nevertheless, a user can still get dozens, if not hundreds, of spam e-mails every day. Fighting spam is, at best, an inexact science.

Still, there are steps you can take to reduce the amount of spam coming into your e-mail system. First, you can use the spam-filtering functions of your e-mail client, as explained in Chapter 12. Beyond that, the most basic way of dealing with spam is to install and use a program called SpamAssassin. Part of the Apache project, SpamAssassin is free software and is bundled with Fedora Core. Check to see if SpamAssassin is installed (`rpm -qiv spamassassin` on Fedora Core; `locate spamassassin` on other platforms) and if it's not, install it.

Next you must configure Postfix to use SpamAssassin to scan incoming mail. Become the superuser, and open the file `/etc/postfix/master.cf` in a text editor, as shown in Figure 22-8.

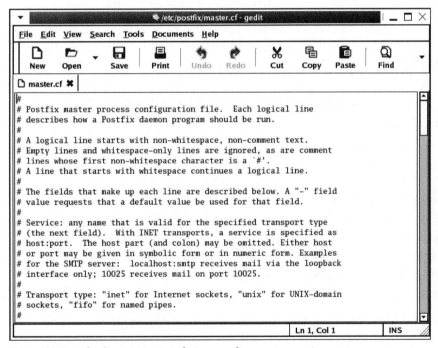

Figure 22-8: gedit showing /etc/postfix/master.cf.

Find the line that looks like this:

```
smtp    inet  n    -    n    -    -    smtpd
```

And change it to look like this:

```
smtp    inet  n   -   n   -   -    smtpd -o content_filter=spamassassin
```

Now, scroll to the end and add this line:

```
spamassassin unix  -   n   n   -   -   pipe
    user=nobody argv=/usr/bin/spamc -f -e /usr/sbin/sendmail -oi -f
    ${sender} ${recipient}
```

You must make sure that the above is all on one line, or else you must start the subsequent lines with whitespace in order for Postfix to be able to read the line correctly. Save your change and exit the file.

Note

The example configuration uses the command /usr/sbin/sendmail. This is because the Sendmail MTA was the only one available for Unix for many years. For this reason, the sendmail command was integrated intensively into Unix systems. Consequently, the command is still there but is often an alias for one or more other commands.

After you've done these things, restart Postfix. SpamAssassin should now be checking your mail. SpamAssassin adds the text [SPAM] to anything it thinks is spam. You can check for flagged spam in your inbox visually. Many e-mail programs allow you to set up rules that automatically move your flagged messages to another directory. I recommend using the visual method until you are sure that SpamAssassin is flagging mail correctly.

Note

Fighting spam is an inexact science. SpamAssassin is popular enough that many spammers will test their methods against it. For this reason, running SpamAssassin as-is with no additional configuration may not provide a lot of protection. You may wish to consider an add-on program such as Maia Mailguard (www.renaissoft.com/maia/). Such programs require a certain investment in terms of time spent learning to use them, but you may find the resources saved to be well worth it.

Summary

Running an electronic mail server is a fairly complex task. Whether you're just trying to set up a simple server or you're serving mail for an entire domain, you'll need to consider many components for a working mail system. Using Postfix and Dovecot, you can set up a relatively simple system. This will provide you with a platform for further development and experimentation. Should you decide to get a bit more ambitious, you can think about trying a Web mail solution like SquirrelMail or combating spam with SpamAssassin. Although administering an e-mail server can be a complex task, time spent learning the craft — whether by reading the documentation for your software or by simply rolling up your sleeves and diving into it — will be rewarded down the road in a smoothly running, mostly spam-free e-mail system.

Chapter 23

Proxy Server Solutions

As it does with mail and the World Wide Web, Linux makes an excellent proxy server solution. Running a proxy server can speed up your network's Web browsing and network communications in general, as well as allow you to exercise control over what comes into your network.

A proxy server stands between your local network and the outside world. When a machine on a proxied network requests something, a Web page, for example, from the Internet, it connects to the proxy server, rather than connecting directly to the remote Web server. The proxy server then connects to the remote server, fetches the page, and passes it back to the local client.

At this point, the astute reader may be wondering how can adding a middleman, as it were, to the process *speed up* connections? The answer lies in the process of *caching*. When a proxy fetches a page, it keeps a copy of that page in its cache for some period of time. If the page is requested again, it serves the page from its cache without having to make a second connection. In this way, frequently accessed pages are served without the time and bandwidth overhead of an Internet connection.

Moreover, a proxy allows the network administrator to inspect what goes in and out of the network from a central location and to place restrictions on what may go in and out. These restrictions can be based on network addresses (domain names or IP numbers) or on content. Many workplaces, for example, use proxy servers to prevent employees from accessing pornographic or frivolous Web sites. In more extreme cases, a proxy server can be used to *white list* remote sites. In other words, machines on the local network would not be able to access anything except for those sites that are explicitly allowed by the proxy.

Types of Proxy Servers

There are basically two ways of setting up a proxy server in Linux. One method is to use Linux's native network management capabilities to create a firewall that allows or disallows connections based on the rules that you supply. The advantage of this type of setup is that it takes advantage of capabilities that already exist in the Linux kernel. Being kernel functions, moreover, these operations are executed very quickly and efficiently.

A Word about Hardware

At least some of the performance you can expect to get out of Squid depends on your hardware configuration. Squid's caching functions rely on memory (RAM) and hard disk space. The more memory you can devote to Squid, the faster it runs. Likewise, the faster your hard drive, the better Squid runs.

How big a system do you need? There are no hard-and-fast rules. To a great extent it's going to depend on how much traffic your server is going to see. This depends on factors such as the number of users you have, how much they use the Internet, whether they tend to go to the same sites over and over again, or go to different sites all the time, and so forth. The more traffic, obviously, the greater the hardware requirements. As of 1998 (the date from which this section of Squid's documentation originates), the Squid developers were recommending a system with at least 512MB of memory and five 9GB SCSI hard drives (presumably for use as a single RAID array). I suspect that this sort of setup was meant to serve an active network and is therefore probably overkill for a more modest network.

However, at this writing (late 2005), memory and disk space are both relatively cheap. If you decide that running Squid is for you and you want to dedicate a machine to it, I recommend that you buy as much memory as you can afford.

Memory is probably the single most important hardware feature in determining Squid's speed. Squid caches frequently accessed items in memory in order to serve them faster. The more memory you can devote to Squid, the more items it can cache there and the faster it will run.

When Squid's cache exceeds the size of its memory allotment, it moves things into hard disk storage. It is at this point that hard drive performance becomes a factor. For practical purposes, a good solid hard drive with plenty of storage should be fine.

Of course, if your purpose in the short term is simply to experiment, don't buy anything. You can get Squid up and running on a minimal setup, and as long as you don't place too much of a load on it, you should be able to use it without any problems.

There are, however, several downsides to this type of setup:

- The kernel's network filtering functions are not very easy to use. These functions use commands that are quite complicated in their operations and are not designed to be used by beginners.

- You do not get the advantage of caching. A kernel-style proxy can give you good management and logging, but it does not cache Web objects, and you would not reap the speed advantages of caching.

- You would have to write the entire firewall yourself.

For these reasons, I do not recommend and do not cover this type of proxy solution. Instead, this chapter focuses on something more accessible to the novice administrator: a software-based proxy server.

A software-based server will lose a bit of the speed advantage over a kernel-based one because its operations take place in application space rather than in kernel space, but, on decent hardware, the difference is not great and is largely compensated for by the speed advantage of caching.

The most popular proxy server available for Linux is called Squid. Squid is free software and is bundled with many popular Linux distributions, including Fedora Core and Knoppix. In this chapter, I focus on running Squid on Fedora Core. Because Squid requires fast access to memory and hard drive space, it's not particularly well suited to running on a live CD-based distribution. This is not to say it can't be done, but there are distinct performance advantages to be had by running it on a fully installed distribution. In any case, beyond installation and some minor details, the process of setting up and running Squid should be more or less identical on any distribution.

Installing and Configuring Squid

If you've read the previous two chapters, you know the drill by now: Download and install the software if necessary, configure the server, start the server, and configure the clients. Squid is bundled with both Fedora Core and Knoppix and should also be included with most other major distributions. Before you do anything else, check to see if Squid is already installed on your system. The main executable file is usually found at /usr/sbin/squid. If Squid is not installed, you'll need to install it.

You should be able to find the Squid package on your installation medium. If you would prefer to download it, I recommend that you download the package *only* from your distribution's Web site or FTP server. Because of the central role that Squid plays in managing network connections, you don't want to use a package from a source that you don't know and trust. Indeed, if you have the slightest doubt about a package's origins, you shouldn't use it. For the most secure installation possible, you should download the source code from the Squid Web site (www.squid-cache.org) and compile it yourself (see the related sidebar).

Once you've got the software installed, you need to edit the configuration file. In this case, the file is located at /etc/squid/squid.conf.default. Copy this file to /etc/squid/squid.conf by giving the command cp /etc/squid/squid.conf.default /etc/squid/squid.conf. Then open /etc/squid/squid.conf in your favorite text editor, as shown in Figure 23-1.

The default version of the squid.conf file is very well commented, so it's fairly easy to find your way around. The values given for the parameters are all of the default values that are hard coded into Squid. They are all commented out. You need to uncomment a parameter only if you want to change it. (There are a few exceptions to this in places where the Squid developers feel strongly that you should use a particular setting. For basic Squid installations, it's probably best to leave these uncommented lines as they are.)

Rolling Your Own

Many experienced system administrators prefer to compile their software packages from source code rather than using the precompiled binary packages that are available. In some cases, it's a matter of old-school pride rather than practical considerations, but, in other cases, there may be solid reasons for doing so. One of the most compelling reasons is that of security. Anytime you install a binary package, you're placing your trust in the person or organization that issued the package. You have no way of knowing whether the packager has inserted any malicious code into the package.

I talked about compiling from source code in Chapter 15, but it's worth taking a moment to revisit the subject with specific attention to Squid. Compiling from source code is not difficult, but it does require attention to some details not required when installing binary packages. As mentioned in Chapter 15, you must have a complier (usually `gcc`) installed on your system along with all of the libraries that Squid needs to use at compile time. This is generally not a problem unless you've done a minimal installation of your distribution. On Fedora Core, for example, you may wish to run `system-config-packages` and make sure that you've got the `development` package group installed.

Once you've done this, you can download the source code package from `www.squid-cache.org`. As of this writing, the latest stable version of the source code comes in a package called `squid-2.5.STABLE10.tar.gz`. The `.tar.gz` suffix indicates that it is a compressed archive file. Before you can compile it, you need to unpack the archive. First, give the `su -` command to assume superuser privileges, and then move the archive file into a usable directory, such as `/tmp`. At this point, you can unpack the archive with the command

```
tar xvfz squid-2.5.STABLE10.tar.gz
```

When the tar program has finished its operation, you should have a new directory called `/tmp/squid-2.5.STABLE10`. Move into this directory. There you will find files named `INSTALL` and `README`. Read these files.

At this point, you may have some choices to make. If you want to do a regular default installation of Squid, execute the following steps. If you want to customize your Squid installation, go to `www.squid-cache.org` and read the page `www.squid-cache.org/Doc/FAQ/FAQ-2.html`. This page explains the compile-time configuration options.

For a default installation, give these commands:

```
./configure --prefix=/usr/local/squid
make all
make install
```

At this point, the Squid executable has been created and all of the auxiliary files have been placed where they should be. Note, however, that the main configuration file will be located in `/usr/local/squid/sbin/squid/` rather than in `/etc/squid/`.

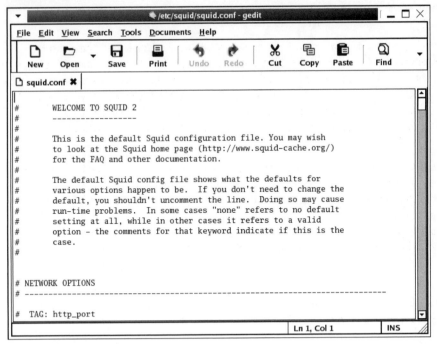

Figure 23-1: gedit showing /etc/squid/squid.conf.

You will probably want to customize at least a few settings, though. Scroll down the file until you find this section:

```
# OPTIONS WHICH AFFECT THE CACHE SIZE
# --------------------------------------------------------------------------

#TAG: cache_mem      (bytes)
#  NOTE: THIS PARAMETER DOES NOT SPECIFY THE MAXIMUM PROCESS SIZE.
#  IT ONLY PLACES A LIMIT ON HOW MUCH ADDITIONAL MEMORY SQUID WILL
#  USE AS A MEMORY CACHE OF OBJECTS. SQUID USES MEMORY FOR OTHER
#  THINGS AS WELL. SEE THE SQUID FAQ SECTION 8 FOR DETAILS.
#
#  'cache_mem' specifies the ideal amount of memory to be used
#  for:
#  * In-Transit objects
#  * Hot Objects
#  * Negative-Cached objects
#
#  Data for these objects are stored in 4 KB blocks.  This
#  parameter specifies the ideal upper limit on the total size of
```

```
#   4 KB blocks allocated.  In-Transit objects take the highest
#   priority.
#
#   In-transit objects have priority over the others.  When
#   additional space is needed for incoming data, negative-cached
#   and hot objects will be released.  In other words, the
#   negative-cached and hot objects will fill up any unused space
#   not needed for in-transit objects.
#
#   If circumstances require, this limit will be exceeded.
#   Specifically, if your incoming request rate requires more than
#   'cache_mem' of memory to hold in-transit objects, Squid will
#   exceed this limit to satisfy the new requests.  When the load
#   decreases, blocks will be freed until the high-water mark is
#   reached.  Thereafter, blocks will be used to store hot
#   objects.
#
#Default:
# cache_mem 8 MB
```

As the comments state, the `cache_mem` parameter is used to specify how big the memory (RAM) cache will be. The default value is 8MB, but if you have a machine with a substantial amount of RAM, you may want to increase this. For example, suppose that you have a machine with 512MB of memory, and you want to devote 256MB to Squid's cache. You can do so by changing the last line of the above section to this:

```
cache_mem 256 MB
```

Note that I have removed the hash mark from the beginning of the line. As the comments say, this parameter affects *only* the amount of memory used for the cache. Squid uses memory for other things as well, so be sure to take this into account when deciding how much memory you want to devote to the cache.

A note on terms here: You will notice that the comments refer to "in-transit" objects, "hot" objects, and "negative-cached" objects. It's worthwhile to know what these are. *In-transit* objects are objects that are actively being accessed by clients. As such they're the most important types of objects. They need to be moved quickly and efficiently and, therefore, they are the ones with the highest priority when it comes to being kept in memory. *Hot* objects are those that are frequently accessed. Keeping hot objects in memory provides a performance advantage in that these objects do not have to be fetched from remote sites every time they're accessed. *Negative-cached* objects are things like the error codes one gets when trying to access a nonexistent Web page. Squid stores these so that external requests are not made for inaccessible objects.

When the memory cache gets full, Squid begins to store objects on the machine's hard drive. Squid uses some complex logic to determine which objects are moved to the disk and which remain in memory, and there are a few parameters that bear on what happens here. In all likelihood, you shouldn't need to change these settings, but you should at least be aware of them:

```
#TAG: cache_swap_low(percent, 0-100)
#TAG: cache_swap_high       (percent, 0-100)
#
#The low- and high-water marks for cache object replacement.
#Replacement begins when the swap (disk) usage is above the
#low-water mark and attempts to maintain utilization near the
#low-water mark.  As swap utilization gets close to high-water
#mark object eviction becomes more aggressive.  If utilization is
#close to the low-water mark less replacement is done each time.
#
#Defaults are 90% and 95%. If you have a large cache, 5% could be
#hundreds of MB. If this is the case you may wish to set these
#numbers closer together.
#
#Default:
# cache_swap_low 90
# cache_swap_high 95


#TAG: maximum_object_size    (bytes)
#Objects larger than this size will NOT be saved on disk.  The
#value is specified in kilobytes, and the default is 4MB.  If
#you wish to get a high BYTES hit ratio, you should probably
#increase this (one 32 MB object hit counts for 3200 10KB
#hits).  If you wish to increase speed more than your want to
#save bandwidth you should leave this low.
#
#NOTE: if using the LFUDA replacement policy you should increase
#this value to maximize the byte hit rate improvement of LFUDA!
#See replacement_policy below for a discussion of this policy.
#
#Default:
# maximum_object_size 4096 KB


#TAG: minimum_object_size    (bytes)
#Objects smaller than this size will NOT be saved on disk.  The
#value is specified in kilobytes, and the default is 0 KB, which
#means there is no minimum.
#
#Default:
# minimum_object_size 0 KB


#TAG: maximum_object_size_in_memory (bytes)
#  Objects greater than this size will not be attempted to kept in
#  the memory cache. This should be set high enough to keep objects
#  accessed frequently in memory to improve performance whilst low
```

```
#  enough to keep larger objects from hoarding cache_mem .
#
#Default:
# maximum_object_size_in_memory 8 KB
```

These parameters detail the relationship between what's in memory and what's in the disk cache. You may want to adjust these parameters depending on the amount of memory and disk space you have available. Excessive swapping between the memory and disk caches slows down performance quite a bit, so it's important to allocate enough memory to keep swapping to a minimum. Likewise, you'll want to keep your disk allowances set so that objects can be moved in and out as needed. In general, you can start with the defaults and tune them as the need arises.

One other option that you may want to customize is the cache_dir option. This option defines the directory that Squid uses when it moves memory objects onto the hard drive. The default value for this option is /var/spool/squid, which is a reasonably good value. If you're looking to do a more heavy-duty installation, you may wish to create a hard drive partition that will house only the Squid cache file. You can name this directory anything you want, as long as you remember to set the cache_dir parameter's value to the name of that directory. Other options must be set along with the name of the directory; here is the relevant section of the configuration file:

```
#TAG: cache_dir
#Usage:
#
#cache_dir Type Directory-Name Fs-specific-data [options]
#
#You can specify multiple cache_dir lines to spread the
#cache among different disk partitions.
#
#Type specifies the kind of storage system to use. Only "ufs"
#is built by default. To enable any of the other storage systems
#see the --enable-storeio configure option.
#
#'Directory' is a top-level directory where cache swap
#files will be stored.  If you want to use an entire disk
#for caching, this can be the mount-point directory.
#The directory must exist and be writable by the Squid
#process.  Squid will NOT create this directory for you.
#
#The ufs store type:
#
#"ufs" is the old well-known Squid storage format that has always
#been there.
#
#cache_dir ufs Directory-Name Mbytes L1 L2 [options]
#
#'Mbytes' is the amount of disk space (MB) to use under this
```

```
#directory.  The default is 100 MB.  Change this to suit your
#configuration.  Do NOT put the size of your disk drive here.
#Instead, if you want Squid to use the entire disk drive,
#subtract 20% and use that value.
#
#'Level-1' is the number of first-level subdirectories which
#will be created under the 'Directory'.  The default is 16.
#
#'Level-2' is the number of second-level subdirectories which
#will be created under each first-level directory.  The default
#is 256.
#
#The aufs store type:
#
#"aufs" uses the same storage format as "ufs", utilizing
#POSIX-threads to avoid blocking the main Squid process on
#disk-I/O. This was formerly known in Squid as async-io.
#
#cache_dir aufs Directory-Name Mbytes L1 L2 [options]
#
#see argument descriptions under ufs above
#
#The diskd store type:
#
#"diskd" uses the same storage format as "ufs", utilizing a
#separate process to avoid blocking the main Squid process on
#disk-I/O.
#
#cache_dir diskd Directory-Name Mbytes L1 L2 [options] [Q1=n] [Q2=n]
#
#see argument descriptions under ufs above
#
#Q1 specifies the number of unacknowledged I/O requests when Squid
#stops opening new files. If this many messages are in the queues,
#Squid won't open new files. Default is 64
#
#Q2 specifies the number of unacknowledged messages when Squid
#starts blocking.  If this many messages are in the queues,
#Squid blocks until it receives some replies. Default is 72
#
#When Q1 < Q2 (the default), the cache directory is optimized
#for lower response time at the expense of a decrease in hit
#ratio.  If Q1 > Q2, the cache directory is optimized for
#higher hit ratio at the expense of an increase in response
#time.
```

```
#
#The coss store type:
#
#block-size=n defines the "block size" for COSS cache_dir's.
#Squid uses file numbers as block numbers.  Since file numbers
#are limited to 24 bits, the block size determines the maximum
#size of the COSS partition.  The default is 512 bytes, which
#leads to a maximum cache_dir size of 512<<24, or 8 GB.  Note
#you should not change the coss block size after Squid
#has written some objects to the cache_dir.
#
#Common options:
#
#read-only, this cache_dir is read only.
#
#max-size=n, refers to the max object size this storedir supports.
#It is used to initially choose the storedir to dump the object.
#Note: To make optimal use of the max-size limits you should order
#the cache_dir lines with the smallest max-size value first and the
#ones with no max-size specification last.
#
#Note that for coss, max-size must be less than COSS_MEMBUF_SZ
#(hard coded at 1 MB).
#
#Default:
#cache_dir ufs /var/spool/squid 100 16 256
```

Here, /var/spool/squid is the top level of the directories that Squid creates for its disk cache. If you change the name of the directory in this parameter, it creates them elsewhere. If, for example, you installed your Linux system with the /var directory on its own disk partition, you might not have enough disk space left on that partition to put your Squid cache there as well. In such a case, you might want to put it elsewhere. If you were planning to dedicate an entire machine to use as a Squid server, you might want to create a partition just for Squid to use.

The other parameters that can be given to the cache_dir variable control the number and sizes of files that are created under the top-level directory and the file system type. Tinkering with these variables affects performance in ways that are touched upon in the preceding comments. More information on performance-tuning Squid can be found at http://squid.visolve.com/squid/index.htm.

It is, of course, possible to run Squid with all of its values set to the default (that is, without doing anything at all to the configuration file), and this is fine for a very small-scale installation.

Now that you have Squid configured, you can start the server. As usual, you do this using the command

```
/etc/rc.d/init.d/squid start
```

Configuring Squid to start at boot

Now that Squid is running, you should configure it to start at boot time, so that any time you reboot the machine it will start automatically.

Give the command `system-config-services` or choose Desktop → System Settings → Server Settings. You are prompted for the superuser password. Once you give it, you should see the Service Configuration window.

Notice that in the left-hand column, some of the services have check marks next to them. These are the services that are configured to start upon system boot. Find the entry for Squid (the services are listed in alphabetical order) and make sure they have check marks. Then click on the File menu and select Save Changes. You can then exit the Service Configuration program.

At this point, you are done. Squid is configured and running. Next, you can configure your clients to use the proxy for their Internet connections.

Note

The `system-config-services` program is specific to Fedora Core (and other Red Hat products) and also depends on your running a GUI on your server machine. If you are using Fedora Core, but you wish to accomplish the same task from a shell prompt, give this command:

```
chkconfig --add squid
```

If you are not using Fedora Core, the process may be a bit trickier. You will need to consult your system's documentation and find out the procedure for starting services at boot time. Some distributions may have a graphical tool for this. Such tools are often referred to as *runlevel editors* or *service configuration tools*. If your system has no such tool, you should be able to find information about the startup scripts that control it. You may need to edit one of these files and insert a line directing it to start the service.

Configuring Squid Clients

Now that you have your proxy server configured, you need to configure your client machines to use it. There are two different ways to do this, and they are somewhat dependent on the operating system. The easiest way to do this is by configuring your Web browser to use the proxy server. This is relatively simple, but the drawback to this approach is that if you're using a program other than your Web browser (an FTP client program, say), the proxy will not be used. The other way is to configure your proxy in the general network parameters. In this section, I cover configuring Web browsers, as well as general network configuration for Windows, Linux, and Macintosh clients.

Configuring a Web browser

Configuring a Web browser is done from within the browser itself, so the method used is dependent on the browser in question. The following sections show the configuration for Mozilla Firefox and Internet Explorer.

MOZILLA FIREFOX

Under the main menu, select Preferences. When the Preferences window appears, select the icon marked General. In the bottom portion of the screen, under the Connection section, click the Connection Settings button. The Configure Proxies to Access the Internet window appears, as shown in Figure 23-2:

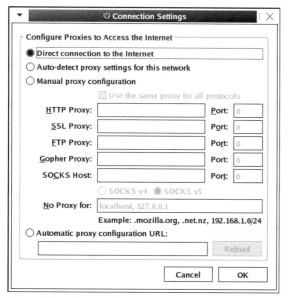

Figure 23-2: The Configure Proxies to Access the Internet dialog.

Check the Manual Proxy Configuration button, and then enter the IP number of the proxy server machine and port in the space provided. (By default, the port number is 3128, but you can configure this using the `http_port` parameter in the `squid.conf` file.) Next, click OK to return to the main Preferences window, and click OK again.

INTERNET EXPLORER

Configuring Internet Explorer to use a proxy server is not nearly as straightforward as one might expect. The option to use a proxy server is in a somewhat obscure location.

From the main Explorer window, select the Tools → Internet Options from the dropdown menu. The main Internet Options window appears. Select the Connections tab and click the LAN Settings button. The Local Area Network (LAN) Settings window opens, as shown in Figure 23-3:

Figure 23-3: The LAN Settings window.

In the lower pane, labeled Proxy server, click the checkbox beside Use a proxy server for your LAN. Enter the IP number and port number in the fields provided. (Again, 3128 is the appropriate port unless you configured Squid differently.)

If you want to specify different addresses or ports for different services, click the Advanced button. This opens the Proxy Settings window, where you can configure proxy settings on a service-by-service basis. When you are done, click OK.

Configuring general network settings

If you need proxies for connections other than a Web browser, you need to configure your network settings to send other types of connections to the proxy server. This procedure is slightly different depending on whether your client machines are Windows, Linux, or Macintosh machines.

WINDOWS

To configure a Windows client machine, from the Start menu, select Control panel → Network and Internet Connections → Internet Options. The Internet Properties window opens. Select the Connections tab and then click the LAN Settings button. The Local Area Network (LAN) Settings window opens, as shown in Figure 23-3. Follow the instructions provided in the previous section to enter the IP and port numbers.

LINUX

Configuring the use of proxies under Linux is somewhat dependent on the distribution being used. Under Fedora Core, it is fairly easy to configure a proxy. From the desktop menu, select Preferences → Network Proxy, and the Network Proxy Configuration window opens, as shown in Figure 23-4.

Click the radio button labeled Manual proxy configuration and enter the IP number and port of the proxy server for each service you wish to have proxied.

Knoppix has no general proxy configuration-setting tool. On Knoppix, your best bet is to set your proxy configuration in your browser, as discussed above.

For any other Linux distribution, consult the distribution's documentation.

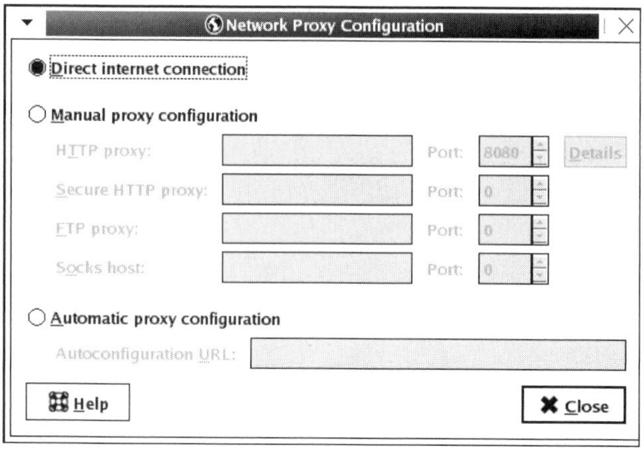

Figure 23-4: Network Proxy Configuration.

MACINTOSH

From the Dock, click the System Preferences icon (the light switch with the Apple symbol). The System Preferences window opens. Under Internet and Network, click the Network icon. Just above the lower pane, click the Proxies button. This shows the proxy selection options.

In the left-hand pane, highlight the service for which you want to configure a proxy. Then, to the left, enter the IP number and port number of the proxy server. Back in the left-hand pane, click the checkbox next to the service to indicate that the proxy server should be used. When you have finished click Apply Now.

Access Control with Squid

At this point, we're going to turn the discussion of proxies back to the server. The configuration that you've developed above is a cache, but it does not use Squid to control access to remote sites. This section shows you how to configure access control lists.

Many system administrators like to use proxies to control what clients can and cannot access in the outside world. Whether this is for general security, productivity enhancement, protection from liability, or other purposes, you may sometimes want to be able to control what comes into your local network. Squid can be configured as this type of proxy using a tool called an *access control list,* or ACL. A full discussion of ACLs is not possible here; here are the basics.

Suppose that some of the people in your organization are spending too much time playing fantasy football online. You would therefore like to block access to any Web site with the word "football" or the word "sports" in the URL. To do this, add the following lines to your /etc/squid/squid.conf file:

```
acl Football1 url_regex football
acl Sports1 url_regex sports
http_access deny Football1
```

```
http_access deny Sports1
http_access allow all
```

The first line creates an ACL called `Football1` that consists of any URL that contains the regular expression `football`.

Note

A *regular expression* (sometimes referred to as a *regex*) is a construct used to match textual elements. Different systems and programming languages implement regular expressions differently, but the idea is that you can create a regular expression that might match one or more pieces of actual text. For example, suppose that, in our regular expression system, we use the period character (.) to stand for any single letter. We could then create the regular expression `c.t`, which would match the words "cat," "cut," "cot," or any other combination of three characters that begins with *c* and ends with *t*.

In the football example, the regular expression is `football`, which matches only the word "football," but will match it in any context. For example, it would match the URLs `www.football.com`, `www.fantasy football.com`, `http://worldwidefootball.com`, or any other URL containing the world "football." Writing regular expressions can be something of an art form in itself, and indeed, there are entire books devoted to the subject. For the purposes of this discussion, however, it is sufficient to use whole words, keeping in mind that they will be matched in any context.

The second line does the same thing, only using the word "sports." The third and fourth lines direct the Squid proxy to deny HTTP (Web) access to any site using a URL that contains the regular expressions found in the ACL `Football1` or `Sports1`. The final line tells the server to allow access to all other URLs.

A more thoroughgoing discussion of access control lists can be found at `www.squid-cache .org/Doc/FAQ/FAQ-10.html`.

Summary

The Squid proxy server can be used to cache objects for more-efficient use or to control access to remote sites. Installation and configuration is fairly straightforward, and clients can be configured on any major platform. By caching frequently used objects in memory, Squid can substantially reduce the amount of network bandwidth that would otherwise be used in accessing remote sites. In addition, Squid gives administrators a significant amount of control over what users can and cannot access and provides detailed log files, which can be used to analyze network traffic patterns.

PC Magazine®
Linux® Solutions

Index

Symbols

* (asterisk), 291
- (dash character), 221
\$ (dollar sign), 68, 164
= (equals operator), 177
! (exclamation point), 175
> (greater than character), 171–172
(hash mark), 68, 164, 175, 252
. (period character), 415
| (pipe character), 173

A

AbiWord word processing application, 11
access control lists (ACLs), 414–415
account setup
    GAIM messenger program, 200–201
    instant messaging, 199
    Thunderbird e-mail program, 195
accounts. *See also* group accounts
    deleting, 66
    `/etc/passwd` file, 58–59
    GUIs (graphical user interfaces), 209
    KUser User Manager program, 213–214
    new account creation, 65, 211–214
    passwords, 64, 69–72
    permissions, setting up, 218–222
    private, 65
    root, 63
    superuser, 63, 207–208, 342
    switching between, 68
    system, 214
    `system-config-users` program, 64
    UID (user ID), 58
    user name information, 67
ACLs (access control lists), 414–415
active windows, 124

adapters, hardware issues, 28–29
address book options, Evolution e-mail program, 194
address contacts, Evolution e-mail program, 192
Address Resolution Protocol (ARP), 323
addresses, IP
    broadcast, 323
    classes, 322
    default route, 323
    dial-up Internet connections, 86–87
    loopback addresses, 323
    MAC (Media Access Control), 323
    name resolution, 324, 326–327
    native address translation, 323
    netmasks, 323
    number assignment, 76–77
    octets, 322
    subnet, 76
    unique, 76
`Address:0` boot prompt option, 42
`adduser` command, 211–212
Adobe Acrobat plug-in, 139
Advanced category, Firefox Web browser, 187
Advanced Packaging Tool. *See* APT
antispam features, 196–197, 353
AOL Instant Messenger (AIM) service, 199
Apache software package
    configuration, 366–367, 372–374
    directories, 371–372
    `DirectoryIndex` directive, 372
    `DocumentRoot` directive, 370
    `Group` directive, 369
    installation, 365–366
    `KeepAlive` directive, 377

continued

419

continued

GNU General Public License

Version 2, June 1991

Copyright © 1989, 1991 Free Software Foundation, Inc.

59 Temple Place—Suite 330, Boston, MA 02111-1307, USA

Preamble

The licenses for most software are designed to take away your freedom to share and change it. By contrast, the GNU General Public License is intended to guarantee your freedom to share and change free software—to make sure the software is free for all its users. This General Public License applies to most of the Free Software Foundation's software and to any other program whose authors commit to using it. (Some other Free Software Foundation software is covered by the GNU Library General Public License instead.) You can apply it to your programs, too.

When we speak of free software, we are referring to freedom, not price. Our General Public Licenses are designed to make sure that you have the freedom to distribute copies of free software (and charge for this service if you wish), that you receive source code or can get it if you want it, that you can change the software or use pieces of it in new free programs; and that you know you can do these things.

To protect your rights, we need to make restrictions that forbid anyone to deny you these rights or to ask you to surrender the rights. These restrictions translate to certain responsibilities for you if you distribute copies of the software, or if you modify it.

For example, if you distribute copies of such a program, whether gratis or for a fee, you must give the recipients all the rights that you have. You must make sure that they, too, receive or can get the source code. And you must show them these terms so they know their rights.

We protect your rights with two steps: (1) copyright the software, and (2) offer you this license which gives you legal permission to copy, distribute and/or modify the software.

Also, for each author's protection and ours, we want to make certain that everyone understands that there is no warranty for this free software. If the software is modified by someone else and passed on, we want its recipients to know that what they have is not the original, so that any problems introduced by others will not reflect on the original authors' reputations.

Finally, any free program is threatened constantly by software patents. We wish to avoid the danger that redistributors of a free program will individually obtain patent licenses, in effect making the program proprietary. To prevent this, we have made it clear that any patent must be licensed for everyone's free use or not licensed at all.

The precise terms and conditions for copying, distribution and modification follow.

Terms and Conditions for Copying, Distribution and Modification

0. This License applies to any program or other work which contains a notice placed by the copyright holder saying it may be distributed under the terms of this General Public License. The "Program", below, refers to any such program or work, and a "work based on the Program" means either the Program or any derivative work under copyright law: that is to say, a work containing the Program or a portion of it, either verbatim or with modifications and/or translated into another language. (Hereinafter, translation is included without limitation in the term "modification".) Each licensee is addressed as "you".

   Activities other than copying, distribution and modification are not covered by this License; they are outside its scope. The act of running the Program is not restricted, and the output from the Program is covered only if its contents constitute a work based on the Program (independent of having been made by running the Program). Whether that is true depends on what the Program does.

1. You may copy and distribute verbatim copies of the Program's source code as you receive it, in any medium, provided that you conspicuously and appropriately publish on each copy an appropriate copyright notice and disclaimer of warranty; keep intact all the notices that refer to this License and to the absence of any warranty; and give any other recipients of the Program a copy of this License along with the Program.

   You may charge a fee for the physical act of transferring a copy, and you may at your option offer warranty protection in exchange for a fee.

2. You may modify your copy or copies of the Program or any portion of it, thus forming a work based on the Program, and copy and distribute such modifications or work under the terms of Section 1 above, provided that you also meet all of these conditions:

   a) You must cause the modified files to carry prominent notices stating that you changed the files and the date of any change.

   b) You must cause any work that you distribute or publish, that in whole or in part contains or is derived from the Program or any part thereof, to be licensed as a whole at no charge to all third parties under the terms of this License.

   c) If the modified program normally reads commands interactively when run, you must cause it, when started running for such interactive use in the most ordinary way, to print or display an announcement including an appropriate copyright notice and a notice that there is no warranty (or else, saying that you provide a warranty) and that users may redistribute the program under these conditions, and telling the user how to view a copy of this License. (Exception: if the Program itself is interactive but does not normally print such an announcement, your work based on the Program is not required to print an announcement.)

   These requirements apply to the modified work as a whole. If identifiable sections of that work are not derived from the Program, and can be reasonably considered independent and separate works in themselves, then this License, and its terms, do not apply to those sections when you distribute them as separate works. But when you distribute the same sections as part of a whole which is a work based on the Program, the distribution of the whole must be on the terms of this License, whose permissions for other licensees extend to the entire whole, and thus to each and every part regardless of who wrote it.

Thus, it is not the intent of this section to claim rights or contest your rights to work written entirely by you; rather, the intent is to exercise the right to control the distribution of derivative or collective works based on the Program.

In addition, mere aggregation of another work not based on the Program with the Program (or with a work based on the Program) on a volume of a storage or distribution medium does not bring the other work under the scope of this License.

3. You may copy and distribute the Program (or a work based on it, under Section 2) in object code or executable form under the terms of Sections 1 and 2 above provided that you also do one of the following:

a) Accompany it with the complete corresponding machine-readable source code, which must be distributed under the terms of Sections 1 and 2 above on a medium customarily used for software interchange; or,

b) Accompany it with a written offer, valid for at least three years, to give any third party, for a charge no more than your cost of physically performing source distribution, a complete machine-readable copy of the corresponding source code, to be distributed under the terms of Sections 1 and 2 above on a medium customarily used for software interchange; or,

c) Accompany it with the information you received as to the offer to distribute corresponding source code. (This alternative is allowed only for noncommercial distribution and only if you received the program in object code or executable form with such an offer, in accord with Subsection b above.)

The source code for a work means the preferred form of the work for making modifications to it. For an executable work, complete source code means all the source code for all modules it contains, plus any associated interface definition files, plus the scripts used to control compilation and installation of the executable. However, as a special exception, the source code distributed need not include anything that is normally distributed (in either source or binary form) with the major components (compiler, kernel, and so on) of the operating system on which the executable runs, unless that component itself accompanies the executable.

If distribution of executable or object code is made by offering access to copy from a designated place, then offering equivalent access to copy the source code from the same place counts as distribution of the source code, even though third parties are not compelled to copy the source along with the object code.

4. You may not copy, modify, sublicense, or distribute the Program except as expressly provided under this License. Any attempt otherwise to copy, modify, sublicense or distribute the Program is void, and will automatically terminate your rights under this License.

However, parties who have received copies, or rights, from you under this License will not have their licenses terminated so long as such parties remain in full compliance.

5. You are not required to accept this License, since you have not signed it. However, nothing else grants you permission to modify or distribute the Program or its derivative works. These actions are prohibited by law if you do not accept this License. Therefore, by modifying or distributing the Program (or any work based on the Program), you indicate your acceptance of this License to do so, and all its terms and conditions for copying, distributing or modifying the Program or works based on it.

6. Each time you redistribute the Program (or any work based on the Program), the recipient automatically receives a license from the original licensor to copy, distribute or modify the Program subject to these terms and conditions. You may not impose any further restrictions on the recipients' exercise of the rights granted herein. You are not responsible for enforcing compliance by third parties to this License.

7. If, as a consequence of a court judgment or allegation of patent infringement or for any other reason (not limited to patent issues), conditions are imposed on you (whether by court order, agreement or otherwise) that contradict the conditions of this License, they do not excuse you from the conditions of this License. If you cannot distribute so as to satisfy simultaneously your obligations under this License and any other pertinent obligations, then as a consequence you may not distribute the Program at all. For example, if a patent license would not permit royalty-free redistribution of the Program by all those who receive copies directly or indirectly through you, then the only way you could satisfy both it and this License would be to refrain entirely from distribution of the Program.

If any portion of this section is held invalid or unenforceable under any particular circumstance, the balance of the section is intended to apply and the section as a whole is intended to apply in other circumstances.

It is not the purpose of this section to induce you to infringe any patents or other property right claims or to contest validity of any such claims; this section has the sole purpose of protecting the integrity of the free software distribution system, which is implemented by public license practices. Many people have made generous contributions to the wide range of software distributed through that system in reliance on consistent application of that system; it is up to the author/donor to decide if he or she is willing to distribute software through any other system and a licensee cannot impose that choice.

This section is intended to make thoroughly clear what is believed to be a consequence of the rest of this License.

8. If the distribution and/or use of the Program is restricted in certain countries either by patents or by copyrighted interfaces, the original copyright holder who places the Program under this License may add an explicit geographical distribution limitation excluding those countries, so that distribution is permitted only in or among countries not thus excluded. In such case, this License incorporates the limitation as if written in the body of this License.

9. The Free Software Foundation may publish revised and/or new versions of the General Public License from time to time. Such new versions will be similar in spirit to the present version, but may differ in detail to address new problems or concerns.

   Each version is given a distinguishing version number. If the Program specifies a version number of this License which applies to it and "any later version", you have the option of following the terms and conditions either of that version or of any later version published by the Free Software Foundation. If the Program does not specify a version number of this License, you may choose any version ever published by the Free Software Foundation.

10. If you wish to incorporate parts of the Program into other free programs whose distribution conditions are different, write to the author to ask for permission. For software which is copyrighted by the Free Software Foundation, write to the Free Software Foundation; we sometimes make exceptions for this. Our decision will be guided by the two goals of preserving the free status of all derivatives of our free software and of promoting the sharing and reuse of software generally.

NO WARRANTY

11. BECAUSE THE PROGRAM IS LICENSED FREE OF CHARGE, THERE IS NO WARRANTY FOR THE PROGRAM, TO THE EXTENT PERMITTED BY APPLICABLE LAW. EXCEPT WHEN OTHERWISE STATED IN WRITING THE COPYRIGHT HOLDERS AND/OR OTHER PARTIES PROVIDE THE PROGRAM "AS IS" WITHOUT WARRANTY OF ANY KIND, EITHER EXPRESSED OR IMPLIED, INCLUDING, BUT NOT LIMITED TO, THE IMPLIED WARRANTIES OF MERCHANTABILITY AND FITNESS FOR A PARTICULAR PURPOSE. THE ENTIRE RISK AS TO THE QUALITY AND PERFORMANCE OF THE PROGRAM IS WITH YOU. SHOULD THE PROGRAM PROVE DEFECTIVE, YOU ASSUME THE COST OF ALL NECESSARY SERVICING, REPAIR OR CORRECTION.

12. IN NO EVENT UNLESS REQUIRED BY APPLICABLE LAW OR AGREED TO IN WRITING WILL ANY COPYRIGHT HOLDER, OR ANY OTHER PARTY WHO MAY MODIFY AND/OR REDISTRIBUTE THE PROGRAM AS PERMITTED ABOVE, BE LIABLE TO YOU FOR DAMAGES, INCLUDING ANY GENERAL, SPECIAL, INCIDENTAL OR CONSEQUENTIAL DAMAGES ARISING OUT OF THE USE OR INABILITY TO USE THE PROGRAM (INCLUDING BUT NOT LIMITED TO LOSS OF DATA OR DATA BEING RENDERED INACCURATE OR LOSSES SUSTAINED BY YOU OR THIRD PARTIES OR A FAILURE OF THE PROGRAM TO OPERATE WITH ANY OTHER PROGRAMS), EVEN IF SUCH HOLDER OR OTHER PARTY HAS BEEN ADVISED OF THE POSSIBILITY OF SUCH DAMAGES.

END OF TERMS AND CONDITIONS